Literary visions of
multicultural Ireland

MANCHESTER
1824
Manchester University Press

For Pablo Manuel

Literary visions of multicultural Ireland

The immigrant in contemporary Irish literature

Edited by Pilar Villar-Argáiz

Manchester University Press

Published by Manchester University Press
Altrincham Street, Manchester M1 7JA, UK
www.manchesteruniversitypress.co.uk

British Library Cataloguing-in-Publication Data is available

Library of Congress Cataloging-in-Publication Data is available

ISBN 978 0 7190 9732 4 paperback

First published by Manchester University Press in hardback 2014

This paperback edition first published 2015

Printed by Lightning Source

Contents

List of contributors

Charles I. Armstrong is Professor of British Literature at the University of Agder in Norway. He is the current President of the Nordic Irish Studies Network and a visiting scholar at Wolfson College, University of Cambridge. Armstrong specialises in Irish Studies, poetry from Romanticism to the present, W.B. Yeats, and Northern Irish poetry. He has published *Figures of Memory: Poetry, Space and the Past* (2009) and *Romantic Organicism: from Idealist Origins to Ambivalent Afterlife* (2003), in addition to being a co-editor of *Crisis and Contemporary Poetry* (2011) and *Dislocating Postcolonial: Travel, History and the Ironies of Narrative* (2006). His essays and reviews have been published in a wide number of essay collections, in addition to journals such as *Literature and Religion*, *Coleridge Bulletin*, *Scandinavian Studies*, and *Prosopopeia*.

Wanda Balzano is the Director of Women's and Gender Studies at Wake Forest University, USA. Balzano's research focuses on Irish Studies, feminist critical theory, gender and religion in Irish literature and film, representations of women in comparative literature, and cross-cultural intersections of women's writing with the classics, philosophy, and religion. Her critical essay on Abigail Child was recently published in the *Millennium Film Journal*. An essay on Beckett and social justice is forthcoming in a book of essays on *Waiting for Godot*. With Anne Mulhall and Moynagh Sullivan she edited *Irish Postmodernisms and Popular Culture* (2007). She also co-edited with Moynagh Sullivan the special issue of *The Irish Review* on Irish feminism (2006). In 1999, she edited the Special Irish Issue of *Ex Libris* on *Irish Contexts* (1999). Several of her reviews have appeared in *The Irish Literary Supplement* and the *Irish University Review*.

David Clark was born in Edinburgh, Scotland, and is Senior Lecturer in English Studies at the University of A Coruña, Spain. He has held executive positions in both national and international Associations for Irish Studies and has published widely on contemporary Irish and Scottish writing. He co-edited the volume of essays *As Nove Ondas* (2003) and is co-author, with Antonio de Toro, of the book *British and Irish Writers in the Spanish Periodical Press* (2007). His most recent publications are *In the Wake of the Tiger: Irish Studies in the Twenty-First*

Century (2010) and *To Banish Ghost and Goblin: New Essays on Irish Culture* (2010).

Margarita Estévez-Saá is Senior Lecturer in English and American Literature at the University of Santiago de Compostela, Spain. She is the author of *El proble-ma de la caracterización en la obra de James Joyce (2002)*, co-author with Anne Mac Carthy of *The Anatomy of Bernard MacLaverty's Triumph over Frontiers (2002)*, and has co-edited, among others, the volumes *Silverpowdered Olivetrees: Reading Joyce in Spain (2003)*, *Nuevas perspectivas críticas en la literatura ir-landesa (2004)*, *Reading Joyce from the Peripheries* (2006), and *New Insights on Irish Literature* (2006). She is Secretary of The Spanish James Joyce Society and co-editor of the scholarly journal *Papers on Joyce*. She has published essays on Joyce, Muriel Spark, Doris Lessing, P.D. James, Janet Frame, modern and post-colonial literature, contemporary Irish literature, critical theory, and feminist criticism.

Anne Fogarty is Professor of James Joyce Studies at University College Dublin, Ireland, Director of the James Joyce Research Centre, and Head of the School of English, Drama, and Film, University College Dublin. She was President of the International James Joyce Foundation 2008–2012. She has been Director of the Dublin James Joyce Summer School since 1997 and was Associate Director of the Yeats Summer School from 1995–1997. She was editor of the *Irish University Review* 2002–2009 and is founder and co-editor with Luca Crispi of the *Dublin James Joyce Journal*, established in 2008. Fogarty has edited special issues of the *Irish University Review* on Spenser and Ireland, Lady Gregory, Eiléan Ní Chuilleanáin, and Benedict Kiely, and has published widely on aspects of con-temporary Irish fiction and poetry. She is currently completing a study of the historical and political dimensions of *Ulysses*, entitled *James Joyce and Cultural Memory: Reading History in* Ulysses.

Jason King lectures in English at the University of Limerick, Ireland. He was also an Assistant Professor in English and Canadian Irish Studies at Concordia University, USA; a visiting professor at the Université de Montréal, Canada; and a lecturer in English at the National University of Ireland, Maynooth. His pub-lications include a special issue of *The Irish Review* on 'Memoir, memory, and migration in Irish culture' (2012), *Ireland and the Americas: Culture, Politics, History* (2008), a special issue of the *Canadian Journal of Irish Studies* on 'Irish-Canadian connections' (2005), as well as numerous articles and chapters about Irish diasporic writing in journals and edited collections on both sides of the Atlantic.

Carmen Zamorano Llena is Associate Professor in English at Dalarna University, Sweden, and Assistant Editor of *Nordic Irish Studies*. She was also a lecturer in

English at the University of Lleida, Spain (1999–2008). Zamorano Llena has published on contemporary Irish and British poetry and fiction, focusing on analysis of feminism, representations of postnational identity, globalisation, migration, and ageing. She is the co-editor of *Representations of Irish Identity: A Postnationalist Approach* (2010), *Urban and Rural Landscapes in Modern Ireland* (2012), and *Transcultural Identities in Contemporary Literature* (forthcoming). In 2011 she was awarded a three-year research grant by the Swedish Research Council (Vetenskapsrådet) to develop her research project entitled 'Globalisation, migration and communal narratives of belonging: changing national narratives in contemporary Irish and British fiction'.

Charlotte McIvor is Lecturer in English (Drama, Theatre, and Performance Studies) at the National University of Ireland, Ireland. She received her Ph.D. in Performance Studies from the University of California, Berkeley, in 2011 with a designated emphasis on gender, women, and sexuality. McIvor has also taught at California College of the Arts and Santa Clara University, USA. Her essays have appeared or are forthcoming in *Irish University Review*, *Modern Drama*, *Public* and *InVisible Culture: An Electronic Journal for Visual Culture* and edited collections including *Crossroads: Performance Studies and Irish Culture* (2009) and *Deviant Acts: Essays on Queer Performance* (2009). She is currently working on a forthcoming book *The New Interculturalism: Race, Gender, Immigration and Performance in Post-Celtic Tiger Ireland*, which argues that theatre and performance are at the centre of conceptualising interculturalism as social policy and aspiration in contemporary Ireland.

Paula Murphy is a lecturer in the Department of English in Mater Dei Institute of Education, a College of Dublin City University, Ireland. She is the author of *The Shattered Mirror: Irish Literature and Film 1990–2005* (2008), the co-editor of *New Voices in Irish Literary Criticism* (2007), and the general editor of the online journal *REA: A Journal of Religion, Education and the Arts*. Murphy has published numerous articles and book chapters on contemporary Irish drama, fiction, and film in publications such as *The International Journal of Baudrillard Studies*, *Americana: The Journal of American Popular Culture*, *Irish Studies Review*, and *The Irish University Review*.

Katherine O'Donnell is Director of the Women's Studies Centre at the School of Social Justice, University College Dublin, Ireland. She has published widely in the area of gender and sexuality studies, and the intersection with Irish literary history. Other research interests include race science in Ireland, and feminist and postcolonial theory. She is co-editor of *Queer Masculinities 1550–1800* (2006), *Love, Sex, Intimacy and Friendship between Men* (2003), and *Palgrave Guide to Irish History* (2009). With Ernesto Vasquez del Aguila she is the founder managing editor of the journal *Gender, Sexuality and Feminism* published by Michigan University Press. Her academic prizes include the Peel Memorial Award, the University of California at Berkeley Chancellor's Prize for Prose, and the University College Dublin President's Teaching Award.

Katarzyna Poloczek works as a Senior Lecturer at the University of Lodz, Poland. In her doctoral dissertation, she has examined the works of Eavan Boland, Paula Meehan, and Nuala Ní Dhomhnaill. She has published many articles devoted to Irish Studies, mostly on contemporary Irish women's poetry. Her research also involves gender studies, contemporary culture, and literary theory. Together with Marta Goszczynska, she has co-edited the collections *Changing Ireland: Transformations and Transitions in Irish Literature and Culture* (2010), and *The Playful Air of (Light)ness in Irish Literature and Culture* (2011).

Maureen T. Reddy is Professor of English and Director of the Women's Studies program at Rhode Island College, USA. She has received numerous awards for excellence for her research on feminist studies, and on race and nation in Irish popular culture. She is the author of many books, including *Crossing the Colour Line: Race, Parenting and Culture* (1994), *Everyday Acts Against Racism* (1996), and *Traces, Codes, and Clues: Reading Race in Crime Fiction* (2002). She is the co-editor of other titles, including *Race in the College Classroom: Pedagogy and Politics* (2002), *Narrating Mothers: Theorizing Maternal Subjectivities* (1991), and *Mother Journeys: Feminists Write about Mothering* (1994).

Loredana Salis is a Research Associate in English Literature and a lecturer of English Language at the Department of Humanities, Università di Sassari, Italy. A former graduate from the University of Ulster, Ireland, she obtained there an MA in Irish Literature in English (2001) and a Ph.D. in Comparative Literatures with a thesis on the reworking of classical theatre in contemporary Irish drama (2005). While in Northern Ireland she worked as Research Associate in Literary Heritages and conducted research on the migrant communities of Ireland and their representations on the Irish stage, part of which has formed the basis for the volume *Stage Migrants*: *Representations of the Migrant Other in Modern Irish Drama* (2010). She has also published articles on the Irish Travellers, the Polish and Lithuanian communities in Northern Ireland, the Antigone myth in Italy, the contemporary appeal of Elizabeth Gaskell's novels, and patterns of pilgrimage in Ireland between tradition and globalisation.

Michaela Schrage-Früh is currently a lecturer at the University of Limerick, Ireland, where she teaches German in the School of Languages, Literature, Culture, and Communication. Her book *Emerging Identities: Myth, Nation and Gender in the Poetry of Eavan Boland, Nuala Ní Dhomhnaill and Medbh McGuckian* was published in 2004. She has published widely on contemporary

Irish, Scottish, and English poetry, fiction, and drama. Her most recent contributions include essays for the special issue on Paula Meehan in *An Sionnach* (2009) and the essay collection *The Poetry of Medbh McGuckian: the Interior of Words* (2010). She is currently completing her book-length study entitled *Dreaming Fictions, Writing Dreams*, which explores interrelations between dreaming and English literature from an interdisciplinary perspective.

Amanda Tucker is an Assistant Professor of English at the University of Wisconsin-Platteville, USA, where she teaches Irish, Postcolonial, and British literatures. Her research focuses on transnational and globalisation studies. She has published extensively on this topic and her articles have appeared in *New Hibernia Review*, *Irish University Review*, and the *Irish Literary Supplement*. Currently she is working on a book-length project on Irish literature, diaspora, and globalisation, tentatively titled *Irish Writing and the Transnational Imaginary, 1900–2007*.

Pilar Villar-Argáiz is a Senior Lecturer of English in the Department of English and German Philology at the University of Granada, Spain, where she obtained a European Doctorate in Irish Literature. She is the author of the books *Eavan Boland's Evolution as an Irish Woman Poet: An Outsider within an Outsider's Culture* (2007) and *The Poetry of Eavan Boland: A Postcolonial Reading* (2008). She has published extensively on contemporary Irish poetry and fiction, and the theoretical background and application of feminism and postcolonialism to the study of Irish literature. Her edited collections include *Literature and Theatre in Crosscultural Encounters* (2006). Her research has been published in numerous journals of her field, including *New Hibernia Review*, *Irish University Review*, *Contemporary Women's Writing (Oxford Journal)*, *Estudios Irlandeses*, and *Études Irlandaises*.

Eva Roa White is Associate Professor of English at Indiana University Kokomo, USA. She was born in Spain, raised in Switzerland, and has lived in several countries, including Saudi Arabia. Her research focuses on transnational literature and Immigration Studies. She has authored *A Case Study of Ireland and Galicia's Parallel Paths to Nationhood* (2004) and published articles about identity migration and hyphenated cultural and national identities in Irish, Galician, and South Asian Studies, which have appeared in *New Hibernia Review*, *South Asian Review* and in the essay collections *In the Wake of the Tiger: Irish Studies in the Twenty-First Century* and *(M)Othering the Nation: Constructing and Resisting Regional and National Allegories Through the Maternal Body*. Excerpts from her memoir in progress, *The Immigrants' Daughter: Back to Galicia*, have been published in *Transnational Literature*, *Natural Bridge*, *disClosure*, and *Marco Polo*. She is presently at work on a new book, *Hybrid Selves, Grafted Identities: The Immigrant Other*.

Foreword:
the worlding of Irish writing

Declan Kiberd

There has been much talk in recent years of the worlding of Irish writing, in line with the proclamation of Ireland's as one of the most globalised economies in Europe. But it's not at all clear just how worlded Irish writing now is. Certainly, more writers are living abroad and writing about overseas life than were doing so in, say, 1990. The decade which followed that year was one in which Irishness became sexy, as people used Celtic pubs, the memoirs of Frank McCourt or the spectacle of Riverdance to connect with their inner Paddy.

That was, of course, a mixed blessing, for it was more often the simplified forms of identity that passed through the filters of the international circuits. Global capital might be breaking up rural communities but its sponsors in their leisure time still wanted to read about local colour; and so McCourt's thematic – that Ireland was as desperately interesting and as interestingly desperate as ever – fell on receptive ears. The more inflected rural depictions of John McGahern didn't sell anything like as many copies. Whereas McCourt felt able to heighten colours to a point of caricature, scaling things up to make them interesting, McGahern took the view that Irish life was inherently so extreme that the artist had to scale things down to make them credible. His US publishers have shown a consequent nervousness about how to market his books. His last great work of fiction *That They May Face the Rising Sun* had its title altered to *By the Lake*, lest American readers might think that it was a tour guide to Japan.

All of which might recall for us something that W.B. Yeats wrote in 1900: 'Every Irish writer is faced with a choice – either to express Ireland or to exploit her'. Yeats saw that choice as one made between using native material for the condescending amusement of a largely overseas audience addicted to comedy and bucklepping[1] on one hand or the more arduous task of expressing a people to themselves with all the ensuing dangers of theatre riots and outright censorship.

The decade prior to Yeats's declaration had seen, if anything, too much world-ing of Irish writing. Bernard Shaw was fast becoming the most famous writer in the world but at the price (he said himself) of being 'a faithful servant of the English people'. And before Shaw's rise, there had been Oscar Wilde. In Yeats's mind, both men, for all their genius, were reduced too often to the status of mere performers. They wished to be artists, keeping one eye resolutely on their subjects, but felt compelled to keep the other eye on their audience. Like the black man in American cities, both men got fed up of the feeling of being perpetually 'on'; and then Wilde, anyway, was put off. For Yeats, the only realistic answer was to bring it all back home: to found a theatre and publishing company in Dublin, as part of a programme to gather a national audience.

Yeats had his wish: but if you are uncharitable enough to measure the time which this leader of the national revival spent at various locations, you find that he spent more months and years out of Ireland than in. Shaw had, after all, said that as long as Ireland produced men with sense enough to leave her, she did not exist in vain.

Once the censorship system of the new State took away from many writers the slim chance they had of earning a living as full-time authors among their own people, there was a new choice – either to become a teacher or get out. Anyone who wonders why so many stories and novels of the mid-twentieth century are set in schools should take due account of that. For those who left, Frank O'Connor spoke most eloquently when he said that he liked to return to Ireland every year or so just to remind himself what a terrible place it was.

When I began reading novels in the 1960s, I noticed a strange thing. Despite Yeats's best efforts, there were few native publishing houses, other than those devoted to coteries of poets; and the work of all the leading Irish prose writers was displayed in Hannas, Hodges Figgis or Eason's bookshops in alphabetical order alongside that of overseas authors: O'Brien alongside O'Hara, McLaverty close to Mailer. Even though the first chair of Anglo-Irish Literature was founded at University College Dublin in 1964, the booksellers of Dublin did not seem to regard Irish writing in English as a distinct category. Perhaps they feared offending those lingering purists who asserted that the national mind was available only in the Irish language.

By the 1970s and 1980s all this had changed. It was as if, by some distant fiat of the aggiornamento, Pope John XXIII had licensed not only street-dancing at the Fleadh Cheoil but also the separate cataloguing of Irish writing in the nation's bookshops. Some of the cooler, more hip young people didn't completely warm to this. They wanted an international style; they despised the Abbey Theatre's annual revival of a Synge or O'Casey play for the busloads of tourists; they wanted to be counted one with Borges, Broch and Benjamin, not David, Mangan, Ferguson. This was eventually reflected in a very animated debate between the two great Johns of the Irish novel, Banville and McGahern. 'I want to open a window on Europe', said Banville, who had written a superb trilogy about Copernicus, Kepler and Newton. 'Yes', replied a sardonic McGahern, 'and I suppose you think that I am forever trying to slam it shut'.

The irony, so many years after that exchange, is that we can now see Banville's novels about the collapse of late-medieval Europe into conflict between Catholicism and Protestantism as a none-too-covert rendition of the overwhelming nature of the clash in Northern Ireland and, indeed, of the less dramatic battle to secure for scientific subjects a more central place in the syllabus of schools in the south. I once asked Banville how he could so unerringly recreate the ways in which a world of alchemists and spells in central Europe made way for that of modern science. He laughed and said 'That was easy. I grew up in Wexford in the 1950s'. The other irony, to which McGahern was in his sardonic way drawing attention even at the time of their exchange was that, despite his near-constant focus on the people of North Leitrim, he had in his art assimilated at a very deep level the techniques and themes of Flaubert, Proust, Tolstoy, and Saint-Beuve.

By the onset of full-throttle globalisation in the 1990s, these sub-divisions in Irish writing had become all too predictable. Even as young people from Poland, France, Nigeria, and China flowed into Dublin, Irish authors began to make a point of setting some of their novels in New York, Berlin or Central America. Yet each of them, once featured in the *New York Times* or *London Review of Books*, seemed to get renationalised as fast as any bank. Colm Tóibín became forever, lest we forget, 'the Irish novelist Colm Toibin', just as in the *Times of London* in the 1930s readers were informed of the peregrinations around Rocquebrun of 'the Irish poet W.B. Yeats'. When you consider that one of Tóibín's more successful campaigns in his native country was to have the playing of the national anthem abolished in the Abbey Theatre, you have to admit that there is something plaintive about his fate.

The Ireland that emerged in the later 1990s was in many ways a multicultural place. Even the lowly *Evening Herald* issued every Tuesday afternoon a Polish supplement; evangelical churches for Nigerians opened their doors across the inner suburbs of Dublin; the country came to a regular standstill celebrating the Chinese New Year; and a grand-daughter of one of the Vietnamese 'boat people' took first place in Irish in the country's Leaving Certificate examination. You might, therefore, expect the emergence of new and complex forms of narrative to capture these hybridities and complications. There have been some, well documented in the following pages; and other, less obvious explorations in poems by Seamus Heaney, Medbh McGuckian, and in work by Irish-language poets, who by very definition start as multicultural. Such inflections are found most effectively of all, perhaps, in a play like *Dancing at Lughnasa* by Brian Friel:

by presenting two plots unfolding at different speeds, this brilliantly solves the technical problem of how to render the phenomenon known as 'uneven development'. This play also registers the impact of 'liberation theology' and of the missionary experience on parish life in Ireland.

But in the novel, the form in which one would expect to find the subtlest exploration of the Irish encounter with the Other, there has been far less than in earlier generations (though honourable mention must be made of work by Joseph O'Connor, Hugo Hamilton, and some others discussed in this volume). Most of the younger novelists, however, have (for perhaps shrewdly judged technical reasons) abandoned the attempt to describe a whole society (despite that society being rather small) and prefer to focus on this or that sub-group – a graduating class from a college, the workers in a restaurant, the members of a musical group, and so on. One of the best of the novelists, Keith Ridgway, summed up the problem in calling one of his books *The Parts*. It is as if authors now write novels about those 'submerged population groups' which Frank O'Connor once thought better-suited to the short story, about the denizens of Dalkey or Coolock or a midlands town. Within Dublin, nobody seems to want to write a 'Wandering Rocks' panoptic narrative, still less one in the style of James Plunkett's *Strumpet City*.

Even more remarkable is the fact that those few authors intrepid enough to dramatise the encounter with immigrants present those immigrants almost invariably as 'new Irish' and almost never for what they are and for what they bring in themselves. Great play is made of Poles or Nigerians who can use a little Hiberno-English. While the State proudly issues citizenship papers, the writers often bring their subjects on an arduous set of seminars in Irish Studies, explaining this or that tradition to polite, accepting receivers. One might wonder for exactly whose benefit these seminars are conducted – for publishers in London or New York still in search of that damned elusive Irishness; or for the authors themselves, who grew up in a revisionist system which took so much of the national narrative away that they must now seize gratefully on the latest incomer as a pretext for teaching themselves what they should know anyway, their own traditions? Some of those authors who helped to junk many national traditions are the very ones now employing novelistic narrative in order to teach them to newcomers. It is as if the contemporary, cutting-edge novel has one primary use for the foreigners: to make them more Irish than the Irish themselves. A new updated Statutes of Kilkenny cannot be far off.

In her book *Strangers to Ourselves*, Julia Kristeva says that we encounter the stranger in others in order to uncover the hidden, untransacted parts of ourselves. She observes that in countries such as France, which receive many immigrants, the right-wing parties are forever fretting about the national culture, the one which ideally (in their minds) the incomers will embrace, whereas the left-wing attends more to the culture which the newcomers bring with them. Modernity works best when both cultures receive equal attention from all parties and there is a hope of a consequent newness through fusion. Something like that happened in cuisine, music, and literature during the earlier years of the Celtic Tiger up to the year 2002. Many incomers displayed a thoughtful interest in Irish traditions still very new to them, but they also carried their own past with pride and with the hope of using elements of it to connect with Ireland. One of the incomers in those years, Zeljka Doljanin, has observed that after 2002 there was less fusion and less thoughtfulness. As the country fell in thrall to a mindless consumerism, many incomers showed little interest either in the lore of their own ancestors or in that of Ireland. Like some of the Irish, some of the newcomers lost the run of themselves too.

Dr Doljanin has made, however, an even more radical analysis in her doctoral dissertation. The years of transition were also those in which a distinctive Irish currency (many notes featuring writers and intellectuals) was replaced by the euro banknotes, featuring bridges and buildings in the style of the Lubjanka. The loss of a sure sense of identity among Irish people (related to the decline of history as a secondary school subject) made it more difficult for them to deal confidently with the Other, at just that phase in history when there were more Others than ever. Dr Doljanin's study notes the consequent and strangely introverted spasms of those recent novels which often seem to deal with incomers like herself but almost always treating such persons as mere backdrop.

She wanted to write a thesis on the Other in contemporary Irish writing, but found herself driven back to a consideration of the classical rather than contemporary authors. If you want accounts of negotiations with the Other, you have only to read *Gulliver's Travels*, *Castle Rackrent* (which anticipates Joyce in considering the treatment of Jews in Ireland), *Ulysses*, Beckett's writings and, indeed, those of McGahern. These authors all came out of a monocultural Ireland yet somehow – perhaps even because of this – they managed to explore alterity. Perhaps one could guess at what has happened in the years between their time and ours. A few years ago, while reading the closing episodes of *Ulysses* with students in Dublin, I casually asked them if a thirty-eight year-old man of vaguely eastern aspect met them in the Temple Bar at one in the morning and invited any of them back to his kitchen, would they go? 'Not on your life' was the universal answer. That is our loss and theirs. Cities, as Richard Sennett has said, were once places in which the uses of disorder allowed people to dice with their own strangeness. Now there are only suburbs and shopping malls, designed to protect most people from the sort of chance encounters which are the life-blood of all narrative.

Shortly before he died in 2006, I asked McGahern whether he thought Zeljka Doljanin's thesis was true. He thought it was and told a story to explain how a traditional Ireland that seemed monocultural could nonetheless produce many people able to imagine all sorts of persons quite unlike themselves. 'When I grew up in Leitrim in the 1940s', he said, 'if you got up on a bicycle and travelled ten miles, you were already in a foreign country. The people's way of walking as well as talking, of holding their heads and moving their bodies – it was all so different from what you knew'. A bike-ride, he sardonically added, was not just the prelude to a sexual opportunity in that society: it was also a rehearsal for the emigration which would be the lot of so many. It is an oft-forgotten fact that between 1921 and 1985 one in every two persons born in the Irish State had to leave it. Long before Tiger Ireland, they were 'worlded', whether they chose to be or not.

Declan Kiberd
Donald and Marilyn Keough Professor of Irish Studies
University of Notre Dame, USA

Notes

1   Bucklepping was defined by Patrick Kavanagh as an act of stage-Irish gymnastics whereby a man walking along will suddenly jump into mid-air, crack both his heels against his buttocks and then proceed to walk on. Kavanagh described the spending of millions of pounds on RTÉ television's budget as 'the national bucklep'.

Acknowledgements

There are a number of people whose names do not appear in the following pages but who have been essential in the completion of this book. First, thanks to Encarni and Leanne, for blessing me daily with your wise advice and warm friendship. Other colleagues and friends who have supported my research in numerous, unconditional ways and who I would like to acknowledge here are Inés Praga Terente, Jody Allen-Randolph, Eibhear Walshe, Marie Noland, Anthony Haughey, and Graeme Porte. My heartfelt gratitude as well to a series of admired Irish writers who have participated in the book in various ways: Eavan Boland, Mary O'Donnell, Theo Dorgan, Paula Meehan, and Michael O'Loughlin. Above all, thanks to all the contributors of the volume; without their diligence and expertise, this project would not have been possible.

Acknowledgements are due to the following editors for granting permission to reproduce these extracts:

Excerpts from 'Site for Sale', from *Landing Places. Immigrant Poets in Ireland* by Eva Bourke and Borbála Faragó. Copyright © 2010 by Kinga Olszewska. Used by permission of Dedalus (www.dedaluspress.com).

Excerpts from 'Bread', from *New and Selected Poems* by Pat Boran. Copyright © 2007 by Pat Boran. Used by permission of Dedalus (www.dedaluspress.com).

Excerpts from 'Les Français Sont Arrivés, Die Deutschen Auch', 'Explorer' from *The Ark Builders* by Mary O'Donnell. Copyright © 2009 by Mary O'Donnell. Used by permission of Arc Publications.

Excerpts from 'Alex in the Garden', from *The Place of Miracles: New and Selected Poems* by Mary O'Donnell. Copyright © 2006 by Mary O'Donnell. Used by permission of New Island.

Excerpts from 'A Latvian Poet Writes an Ode to Capitalism', 'A Latvian Poet Spends Xmas in Foley Street', 'The Cormorant', 'A Latvian Poet Reads Yeats's *A Vision* in the Oliver St John Gogarty', from *In This Life* by Michael O'Loughlin. Copyright © 2011 by Michael O'Loughlin. Used by permission of New Island.

Excerpts from 'On the 7 am Luas to Tallaght', from *Night and Day: Twenty Four Hours in the Life of Dublin City* by Dermot Bolger. Copyright © 2008 by Dermot Bolger. Used by permission of New Island.

Excerpts from 'Travel Light', from *External Affairs: New Poems by Dermot Bolger* by Dermot Bolger. Copyright © 2008 by Dermot Bolger. Used by permission of New Island.

Excerpts from 'Reflections', from *Night and Day: Twenty Four Hours in the Life of Dublin City* by Dermot Bolger. Copyright © 2008 by Betty Keogh. Used by permission of New Island.

Excerpts from 'Warriors', from *Night and Day: Twenty Four Hours in the Life of Dublin City* by Dermot Bolger. Copyright © 2008 by Eileen Casey. Used by permission of New Island.

Excerpts from 'Nigerian Lady on Tallaght High Street', from *Night and Day: Twenty Four Hours in the Life of Dublin City* by Dermot Bolger. Copyright © 2008 by Siobhan Daffy. Used by permission of New Island.

Excerpts from 'I am a Nigerian from West Africa', from *Night and Day: Twenty Four Hours in the Life of Dublin City* by Dermot Bolger. Copyright © 2008 by Adenice Adedoyin. Used by permission of New Island.

Excerpts from 'Word', from *The Full Indian Rope Trick* by Colette Bryce. Copyright © 2005 by Colette Bryce. Used by permission of Picador, Pan Macmillan, London.

Excerpts from 'In the Name of God and of the Dead Generations', from *Asylum Road* by Mary O'Malley. Copyright © 2001 by Mary O'Malley. Used by permission of Salmon.

Excerpts from 'Dublinia', from *A Perfect V* by Mary O'Malley. Copyright © 2006 by Mary O'Malley. Used by permission of Carcanet Press Limited, UK.

Excerpts from 'Tourism', from *Between Here and There* by Sinéad Morrissey. Copyright © 2002 by Sinéad Morrissey. Used by permission of Carcanet Press Limited, UK.

Excerpts from 'Fever', 'Drum', 'Journey', 'Survivor', 'An Fear Marbh: Homage to the Dingle-Man', 'Warrior', 'Inlets', from *'Survivor' – Representations of the 'New Irish:' Dúchas Dóchasach* by Michael Hayes and Jean 'Ryan' Hakizimana. Copyright © 2007 by Michael Hayes. Used by permission of Cambridge Scholars Publishing.

Excerpts from 'The Vibrator', from *Profit and Loss* by Leontia Flynn. Copyright © 2011 by Leontia Flynn. Published by Jonathan Cape. Used by permission of the Random House Group Limited.

Excerpts from '57% Irish', from *The Deportees and Other Stories* by Roddy Doyle. Copyright © 2007 by Roddy Doyle. Published by Jonathan Cape. Used by permission of the Random House Group Limited.

In covering copyright expenses, the editor would like to acknowledge the support of the Spanish Ministry of Science and Innovation through the research projects Community and Immunity in Contemporary Fiction in English (grant reference FF12009–13244); and The Construction of Otherness in the Public Domain: A Critical Study of the Case of Ireland (grant reference FFI2011–25453). Special thanks are due to their respective main researchers: Julián Jiménez Hefferman and Encarnación Hidalgo Tenorio.

Pilar Villar-Argáiz

1

Introduction: the immigrant in contemporary Irish literature

Pilar Villar-Argáiz

Celtic Tiger Ireland and inward migration

When Ireland became part of the European Union in 1973, the country entered a new phase of rapid social, political, and economic transformation. This radical change was perceived at all levels of Irish life. Ireland's gradual transformation from a predominantly agricultural economy to a hi-tech multinational one was simultaneously accompanied by other influential events such as the rise and success of the women's movement, the shrinking influence of the Catholic Church, and noteworthy political achievements in the North such as the 1998 Good Friday Agreement. New descriptions were needed for identifying this fresh and almost unrecognisable Ireland which was emerging. In 1994, the economist Kevin Gardiner coined the now ubiquitous term 'Celtic Tiger', referring to the unprecedented financial boom of the country. During this Celtic Tiger period, which lasted approximately from the early 1990s to the first years of the twenty-first century, Ireland was often depicted as the most globalised country in the world.[1]

One of the immediate consequences of the economic success of the country was the reversal of emigration, from outward to inward migration. For the first time in history, Ireland became a destination not only for tourists and students, but also for EU nationals, asylum-seekers, political refugees, and the so-called economic migrants. The growth of these diasporic communities, especially in the years 1997–2001, profoundly altered the ethnic landscape of Irish society. As Titley, Kerr, and King O'Rían (2010: 22) explain, statistics show that nearly 250,000 people migrated to Ireland in the period between 1995–2000. As a result, it was stipulated in 2007 that one person in ten was born outside the Republic (2007 census of the Central Statistics Office). With the arrival of immigrants, mainly from Eastern Europe, China, and Africa,[2] D.P. Moran's exclusivist equation of 'Irish Irish' with Gaelic and (white) Catholics has been consistently challenged and proved to be untenable. This increasingly multicultural composition of Irish society is perceived in one of the most explicit exhibitions of national pride, St Patrick's Day Parade. In recent years, this has displayed 'new [multiethnic] forms of Irish identity' (Salis, 2010: 33–4). Indeed, in the 2012 St Patrick's Day Greetings from the President of Ireland, Michael D. Higgins, to Irish people around the world, there is praise for 'the inclusive and generous spirit of St Patrick', which inspires this national celebration to 'accommodate all ages, all communities and all ethnicities'. The 'global Irish family' that is addressed in Higgins' speech not only encompasses the Irish diasporic community abroad, but also a more ethnically diverse community within the borders of the Republic, also composed of people not necessarily 'Irish' by birth.[3]

The profound impact that migration has had on the island has been examined from various perspectives.[4] Barret, Bergin, and Duffy (2006), for instance, have analysed its effects on the economy of the country; and Crowley, Gilmartin, and Kitchin (2006) its consequences for legislation on Irish citizenship. The increasing cultural and racial diversity of Irish society and the subsequent anxiety over traditional notions of Irish identity led to the publication in 2001 of *Multi-Culturalism: The View from the Two Irelands*, a brief book featuring essays by two of the island's most prominent cultural critics, Edna Longley and Declan Kiberd, and a preface by the then President Mary McAleese. Other works which have recognised the impact of the immigrant experience in Ireland are the special issue of the journal *Translocations, Irish Immigration, Race and Social Transformation* (Fanning and Munck, 2007), and Bryan Fanning's 2007 collection of essays, both gathering multidisciplinary studies on the migration debate.[5] Most research, however, has been conducted in the area of racism and xenophobia and the controversial impact of migration at the social and political levels. These have been extensively studied by Bryan Fanning (2002), Ronit Lentin (2001a; 2001b; 2002; 2008), Robbie McVeigh, who co-edited two volumes with Lentin in 2002 and 2006,[6] and more recently by Gerardine Meaney (2010), whose monograph *Gender, Ireland, and Cultural Change* offers an illuminating analysis of the consequences of the racialisation of Irish national identity in contemporary representations of immigrant women and their children. The edited volume *Facing the Other: Interdisciplinary Studies on Race, Gender, and Social Justice in Ireland* (Faragó and Sullivan, 2008) also constitutes an important contribution, as it examines the contemporary intercultural and interethnic tensions in Ireland from a broad range of perspectives, including the artistic and sociological. Indeed, the present collection is appearing at a time of heightened interest in the cultural and literary contexts of Irish migration, as evidenced by the recent special issues of *The Irish Review* (King and O'Toole, 2012) and *Éire Ireland* (Mac Éinrí and O'Toole, 2012).

The cultural effects of migration

Inward migration has had inevitable consequences for the literature which has been produced in Ireland from the beginning of the Celtic Tiger period onwards. Although in contrast to Britain, the literary world in Ireland is still overwhelmingly 'white', this is undoubtedly changing as large-scale immigration has altered the ethnic composition of Irish society. One of the earliest examples of literature produced by the so-called 'new Irish' is provided by the immigrant writer Cauvery Madhavan, whose first novel *Paddy Indian* (2001) signalled 'the arrival of the new minorities to the Irish literary scene' (Zamorano Llena, 2011: 97). Madhavan's work was later followed by the intercultural narratives of Iranian-born Marsha Mehran and by the weekly newspaper *Metro Éireann*, which regularly publishes stories centred on race issues.[7] The work of the 'new Irish' has had a particular impact on the theatrical arena. Ursula Rani Sarma and Bisi Adigun are two of the most representative playwrights belonging to this first literary generation of immigrants in Ireland. In particular, Adigun is well known for his rewriting in 2007 of Synge's *The Playboy of the Western World*, a play co-written with Roddy Doyle which features a Nigerian Christy Mahon. Other theatrical multiethnic projects include the Dublin-based African theatre company, Arambe Productions, and 'The Tower of Babel', initiated by the Calypso theatre company. Both are successful attempts by immigrant artists and journalists to foster, in Reddy's words (2007: 16), 'an integrationist, celebrate-difference racial discourse' in Ireland, one which accommodates the culture of the newly arrived communities.[8]

The effects of Ireland's multiethnic reality are also observed in the multiplicity of literary texts by Irish writers, both male and female, which engage simultaneously with issues of nationhood and ethnicity. Ever since Donal O'Kelly's production for the Abbey Theatre in 1994, *Asylum! Asylum!*, there has been a profusion of literary productions by Irish artists exploring the presence of the migrant Other in Irish culture and social life. One of the first Irish-born writers to delve into the changing racial landscape of the country was Hugo Hamilton, whose groundbreaking memoir, *The Speckled People* (2003), anticipated the now increasing literary concern with 'outsiders coming from other cultures to blend with the existent culture and change it' (interview with Allen-Randolph, 2010: 19). Hamilton's work has been followed by others such as Roddy Doyle, one of the most prolific writers on multicultural Ireland. For Doyle, his recent work has been informed by the attempt 'to embrace the new changes in Ireland creatively, rather than see them as statistics' (148). Ireland's multiethnic reality is also palpable in the work of other prominent writers such as Dermot Bolger, Colum McCann, Kate O'Riordan, Emer Martin, and Éilís Ní Dhuibhne, among others.

It is important to bear in mind, however, that not all Irish artists have responded so openly and rapidly to Ireland's new multiethnic landscape. To start with, there are writers who are not interested in recording this social aspect of the country. Others find this experience too new, and like Sebastian Barry in *The Pride of Parnell Street* (2008), experiment with new themes briefly, only to leave them aside for later. It seems that Ireland's economic and demographic changes have occurred too quickly for writers to reflect them adeptly. It is precisely this aspect that is alluded to by Kiberd in his 2003 essay 'The Celtic Tiger: a cultural history', reprinted in *The Irish Writer and the World* (2005: 269–88). Kiberd illustrates the inability of artists to capture accurately Ireland's shifting reality by means of the metaphor of a moving object whose velocity cannot be ably reflected in a photograph: 'The pace of change may be just too fast for most, for it is never easy to take a clear photograph of a moving object, especially when you are up close to it. Nothing, after all, is more difficult to realise than the present – we are always at its mercy more than we are its masters' (276). This might explain the gestation, throughout the 1990s, of three successful literary works – Frank McCourt's *Angela's Ashes*, John McGahern's *Amongst Women*, and Brian Friel's *Dancing at Lughnasa* – which were set in the past, rather than in the context of prosperous Celtic Tiger Ireland. According to Kiberd (281), these works conceal a form of 'masked modernity'. While the impression is that they are obsessed by history, they are actually using the past to achieve a better understanding of the present. Kiberd articulates this cultural contradiction – which he describes as 'the strange blend of backwardness and forwardness' – as follows:

> The country has gone through in the past century and a half the sort and scale of changes which took four or five hundred years in other parts of Europe. No wonder that people have looked in the rear-view mirror and felt a kind of motion-sickness, or have sought to conceal the underlying modernity of their lives by giving them the surface appearance of the ancient. (280)

In any case, not all literary works during the Celtic Tiger period nostalgically retreated to the past. Keith Ridgway's novel *The Parts* (2003), for instance, accurately reflects Ireland's rapid changes. Nevertheless, as Kiberd contends, its very title indicates that a 'complete' assessment of Ireland's present condition is impossible, as this will always be inevitably incomplete and partial (277). The implication of Kiberd's argument on the literary works produced in the last decade of the twentieth and the beginning of the twenty-first centuries is that Irish writers need to acquire the perspective afforded by time, as the reality of multicultural Ireland is too recent to be completely understood. Indeed, the example of other countries (particularly former empires such as Spain, France or England) shows that the impact and effect of immigration on the cultural sphere of a nation is a slow and, at times, troubled process, particularly with respect to the incorporation of ethnic Others in the mainstream literary sphere.

Ten years have now passed since Kiberd's claim in 2003 that '[t]here is no major celebration or corrosive criticism of [Ireland's profound social change] in good novels, plays or poetry' (2005: 276), and his assertion is being challenged by the publication of numerous works which have brought centre-stage the existence of migrant communities in Ireland, a presence rarely perceived before in Irish literature. Some iconic examples include in short fiction Roddy Doyle's *The Deportees* (2008), in the theatrical arena Dermot Bolger's *The Ballymun Trilogy* (2010) and, in the literary field of poetry, Michael O'Loughlin's *In This Life* (2011). In this sense, the silence that Kiberd diagnosed over the decade of the 1990s on a whole range of issues seems to be overcome; we now begin to perceive, over the past few years, a gradual moving away from themes of the past to Ireland's multicultural reality in the twenty-first century. It is precisely this emerging multiethnic character of Irish literature that is addressed by this collection of essays.

In spite of the fact that Ireland is now effectively what could be called a multicultural society, multiculturalism is still an issue which requires analysis at an artistic and literary level in the specific context of Irish studies. As explained above, the last decade has witnessed a proliferation of studies on race and multiculturalism in Ireland. However, there is insufficient research on the literary representations of the so-called 'ethnic Otherness' that prevail in a society where everything that distances itself from the white Irish majority is secluded to the margins, particularly immigrants and Travellers.[9] This collection of essays tries to fill this research lacuna, by assessing the cultural effects of inward migration in relation to contemporary Irish literature.

In particular, the book examines literary representations of the exchanges between the Irish host and its foreign 'guests', which have become common aspects of everyday life in twenty-first-century Ireland. Key areas of discussion are: What does it mean to be 'multicultural', and what are the implications of this condition for contemporary Irish writers? How has literature in Ireland responded to inward migration? Have Irish writers reflected in their work (either explicitly or implicitly) the new influx of immigration? If so, are elements of Irish traditional culture and community maintained or transformed? In other words, does contemporary Irish literature confirm ethnonational boundaries by drawing upon cultural difference? Or does it dissolve all forms of local specificities by celebrating hybridity and cross-fertilisation within the geographical space of Ireland? What is the social and political efficacy of these intercultural artistic visions?

While these issues have received sustained academic attention in literary contexts with longer traditions of migration, they have yet to be extensively addressed in Ireland today. One of the first commentators to analyse the profound effects that globalisation was having on Irish culture was the journalist Fintan O'Toole, in his incisive and provocative collection of essays *The Ex-Isle of Erin* (1997) and its analysis of work by Dermot Bolger, Michael O'Loughlin, and Paul Durcan. However, it was not until a decade later that the impact of inward migration upon Irish literature was explicitly discussed in scattered academic studies, mostly articles and essays. Some of these pioneering studies include Jason King's groundbreaking essays on Irish multiculturalism and drama (2005a; 2005b; 2008), Maureen Reddy's incisive examination of Roddy Doyle's short fiction (2007), Loredana Salis's illustrative analysis of Irish theatrical representations of the migrant Other (2010), and Amanda Tucker's (2010) and Carmen Zamorano Llena's (2010; 2011) eloquent discussions of the multicultural agenda of contemporary Irish novelists and poets.[10] All in all, Irish multiculturalism has not been analysed as exhaustively as is needed; the assessment of the immigrant experience in the work of Irish writers is something which has not been comprehensively addressed, in spite of the profusion of novels, short stories, poems, and plays about the Irish encounter with Otherness.[11] Hence the relevance of this collection, which aims, among other things, to enrich the hermeneutical debate revolving around the concept of multiculturalism in present-day Ireland.

Models of interculturalism in Ireland

Multiculturalism is certainly a contested concept in recent political, cultural, and literary discourses, and it is sometimes used imprecisely and contradictorily, together with other slippery terms such as 'interculturalism', 'diversity', and 'integration'. Generally speaking, it could be claimed that 'multiculturalism' refers to the cultural and ethnic diversity present in most societies (Hall, 2000: 209–10; Watson, 2000: 106–7). Some critics have established a distinction between this term, describing a factual and static diversity, and 'interculturalism', which denotes the actual interaction between coexisting cultures (Bernasconi, 1998; De Lucas, 1994). In this collection of essays, both terms are used (i.e. 'multiculturalism' and 'interculturalism') in order to refer to contemporary literary works which reflect this diversity or advocate, in a more or less explicit way, the acceptance of and interaction with ethnic and cultural difference in Ireland.

Since the beginning of the twenty-first century, debates on Irish multiculturalism have usually been articulated in terms of an opposing dialectics. As has been meticulously shown, there are two competing views on how Ireland has responded to the unprecedented arrival of contemporary migrants (King, 2005b: 50; Tucker, 2010: 107–8). One of these responses is that developed by cultural theorist Declan Kiberd in his 2001 essay 'Strangers in their own country: Multiculturalism in Ireland', reprinted in *The Irish Writer and the World* (2005: 303–20). Kiberd claims that – due to its former historical experience of emigration – Ireland is naturally receptive to its new multicultural reality and that, in the words of former Minister of Integration Conor Lenihan, 'there's an emotional sense of understanding about what immigrants are going through' (quoted in Deparle, 2008). As traditionally diasporic people, the Irish know how to relate to immigrants coming to their country now, as they have also experienced the realities of displacement, rootlessness, and racist discrimination abroad: 'If the migrant is a sign of the modern, then the Irish were modern earlier than most peoples, enduring the fate of uprooting, of learning a new language, of leaving a neolithic civilisation and settling in modern conurbations' (Kiberd, 2005: 317).[12] Furthermore, Kiberd maintains that Ireland has always been a multiethnic society and this allows the country to be more 'eclectic, open, assimilative' (312).[13]

This 'liberal model of interculturalism' in Ireland, as King calls it (2005b: 50), is challenged by another trend which maintains the existence of hostility, xenophobia, and fear in Irish responses to the diasporic communities. As has been variously theorised in recent years, the processes of globalisation are both inclusionary and exclusionary: even though this new global area fosters intercultural and interethnic exchanges of all kinds, it also projects an intense sense of immunisation. These two views of globalisation as enabling and utterly restrictive have been exposed by Zygmunt Bauman in his analysis of unstable global societies 'in liquid modern times' (2007: 96). According to this critic, globalisation triggers not only a potential hybridisation of communities, but also what he calls 'global fear', that is, fear of a menacing, unknown Other which drives people to adopt radical defensive attitudes and reproduce 'protective' prejudices (97).[14] This rise in racism can be partly explained by the shattering of national identities, which in turn increases the level of anxiety and cultural instability. In the particular context of Ireland, this would explain the re-emergence of a new type of conservative nationalism, what Gerard Delanty (1996) identifies as a 'nationalism of resistance', in which 'nationality is coming increasingly to be defined in opposition to immigrants'.[15]

For those critics who oppose Kiberd's 'liberal' model of Irish multiculturalism, this new 'nationalism of resistance' identified by Delanty was reflected in the controversial 2004 Citizenship Referendum. According to this Referendum, children who are born to non-Irish parents are not entitled to the same rights as those born to Irish parents: rather than being considered Irish citizens, they are classified as 'Irish-born children' (IBCs). Consequently, the Referendum is viewed by some in Ireland as a racist attempt to reinforce at a legal and institutional level monocultural, rather than multicultural, notions of Irishness.[16] This viewpoint is defended by Ronit Lentin, whose research on immigration in Ireland is intrinsically determined by her background as an Israeli Jew. Lentin talks about the white 'racialisation' of the Irish and the revival of exclusivist notions of Irish identity with the Citizenship Referendum (2001a; 2002).[17] A similar argument is put forward by journalist Fintan O'Toole, who, together with Lentin, frequently writes columns for the now iconic Irish multicultural newspaper *Metro Éireann*. In *The Ex-Isle of Erin*, when addressing the question of Irish tolerance for other cultures, O'Toole maintains that even during the extreme circumstances of the Holocaust of the Second World War, the Irish showed 'great reluctance' to accept the immigration of Jewish refugees. As a consequence, he concludes, we could talk historically about two different Irelands:

> A pre-modern one contained on the island itself which assumed that the natural state of a culture was one of monolithic purity, and a post-modern one outside the island, able to cope with the global intermingling of race, ethnicity and religion. These two Irelands do not succeed each other in a logical chronological order. The more open precedes the less open. (O'Toole, 1997: 131)

In line with Lentin and O'Toole, sociologist Bryan Fanning claims that Ireland is not as 'inclusionary' as recent media and political discourses would want us to believe (2002: 185). According to Fanning, the Republic exhibits what he calls a 'weak multiculturalism' where the 'image of diversity proliferates, but where the aim is to manage diversity rather than contest inequalities' (179). A similar viewpoint is held by Kuhling and Keohane in their 2007 study *Cosmopolitanism Ireland: Globalization and Quality of Life*. As these authors maintain, various models of multiculturalism can be adopted at the political and social levels. First of all, we can speak of 'an older model of assimilation, whereby the minority group adopts the culture and values of the majority (67)'.[18] This model, now outdated, has been generally replaced by 'a newer, more interactive model', in which both the minority and the majority groups absorb some elements of the other culture and values. Finally, we can also talk about 'the model of cultural pluralism', according to which the minority and majority groups 'maintain their own culture and values, distinct from each other' (*ibid.*). According to these sociologists, the Irish State has usually adopted an assimilationist approach and not one based on cultural pluralism, leaving untouched the 'native' monocultural hegemonic structure and maintaining the structural inequalities experienced by the minority group of immigrants (*ibid.*). As a result, 'Ireland has a multicultural economy, but not a multicultural society' (*ibid.*), or as they further contend, 'contemporary Ireland is anti-cosmopolitan' (153).

The multicultural stance of Irish writers

There are, therefore, more who argue against Kiberd's 'liberal' model of Irish multiculturalism than are in favour of it. The lack of consensus, together with the disparity between these two competing models, might stem from the contradictory positions that the Irish State has adopted since the early 1990s on immigration: on the one hand, implementing exclusionary and restrictive immigration policies while at the same time encouraging equality and diversity through movements such as the KNOW Racism campaign (Kuhling and Keohane, 2007: 60). But, what about contemporary Irish writers? Are they similarly contradictory? Or do they exhibit a more unconditionally receptive attitude towards the presence of migrants in the country?

This collection of essays takes up this heated debate in Irish Studies by considering, in King's words, 'whether Irish culture is inherently hospitable or insular in relation to cultural difference, intrinsically racialised or receptive to external cultural influence' (2005b: 57). Of course, not all writers in Ireland are interested in reflecting the new ethnic diversity of the island in their work. Furthermore, in line with Kiberd's argument, we could claim that some artists need the perspective afforded by time in order to chart more accurately the social changes produced in twenty-first-century Ireland. In any case, there is also a significant corpus of Irish authors who address the impact of inward migration, although their degree of explicitness varies. While this theme is incipient for many writers, there are others who have engaged more extensively with these social and cultural changes, by openly acknowledging over the years the presence of non-Irish outsiders and the need to negotiate with other foreign cultures, languages, and religious practices. These literary texts on multicultural, interethnic encounters also disclose other butterfly effects of globalisation. There is an increasing interest on the side of many contemporary Irish writers to reveal what Carmen Zamorano Llena (2011: 85) identifies as 'the dark underbelly of the Celtic Tiger', that is to say, the negative effects of globalisation in the Irish context: the consequences of capitalist frenzy (i.e. environmental destruction or conspicuous consumerism), political corruption, and the rise of racism and xenophobia in some cases. The tone and style adopted in these intercultural artistic visions also varies. Some writers adopt a humorous and compassionate stance on the matter (Hugo Hamilton, for instance), while others are more openly incisive, political, and hence polemical (such as Roddy Doyle).

Most theorists of multiculturalism agree on the fact that for a genuinely pluralist society to flourish, one should not seek the assimilation of the Other, but rather the uncritical acceptance of racial and ethnic differences and the recognition that different cultures can interact, enriching one another. This belief is also shared by those writers who have talked about Ireland's current multiethnicity in interviews or for whom the theme of inward migration is a pressing issue in their work. The interviews with artists and writers gathered in Jody Allen-Randolph's *Close to the Next Moment* (2010) are especially illustrative in this respect. Hugo Hamilton, for instance, claims that one of his 'hopes is that the immigrants coming into Ireland will transform the country in a truly positive way', and he continues: 'We need these people from elsewhere, not just to clean our homes, but also to understand the world on a much more profound and multi-layered level' (Allen-Randolph, 2010: 23). Novelist Colm Tóibín has also talked about 'the real addition these new nationalities and cultures have made to Ireland' and he therefore defends 'an open [although 'unsustainable'] door policy' (175). Similarly, Irish-language poet Cathal Ó Searcaigh views the contact with immigrants and outsiders from other cultures as potentially productive:

> Personally I'm delighted by this rainbow river of culture that is sweeping through our lives here in Ireland now. We never before experienced such creeds, such languages, such colours in our midst. It's healthy to open up to the uniqueness and the strangeness of these cultures. We will be enriched by their differences, their diversity, their ethnic perspectives. (220)

Another literary voice who has expressed a similar view in relation to Ireland's present multiethnic reality is poet Paula Meehan. As Meehan has claimed:

> The future of Irish poetry can only be enriched beyond measure by the gradual working into it of the many traditions entering the island with the newcomers. Both poetry in English and in Irish will be enriched but there will also be, already is, intense interaction with the new languages coming onto the island. … Not only will the rivers of language flowing in with the newcomers but their formal traditions in song, prayer, chant, their oral and their literary traditions both, will become new resources for the island's next generation of poets. (Villar-Argáiz, 2010)

Meehan's perception of the contemporary poetic panorama in twenty-first-century Ireland is also shared by Eavan Boland. In an interview, Boland asserts that immigrant events have altered 'the perception of cultural norms in Ireland' in a similar way to the sudden upsurge of women's writing in the 1980s (Villar-Argáiz, 2012: 119). As she puts it: 'When I was younger Irish literature seemed to be drawn on a paradigm which was male and traditional. Women's poetry altered that and required the literature to make a new space, not without considerable resistance. Now immigrant voices require another new space' (*ibid.*). In any case, Boland also believes that literature is not necessarily responsible for representing social transformation, as she claims when asked about the role of poets in relation to immigration:

> I don't think writing has a place in achieving an 'integrated, multicultural Ireland'. That's not its purpose. It shouldn't have a cultural agenda of this kind. It's a very

over-designed role for it. On the contrary, Irish writing will move forward, as it always has, through the voices of individual writers – some of whom may have no social commitment of any kind. The purpose is good writing; the role is no more and no less than that. (*Ibid.*)

Boland's comment serves as a reminder of the existence of contemporary Irish writers upon whom immigration has not exerted any impact whatsoever, and the fact that, for some artists, literature should stand outside an explicit ideological (or political) stance of social denunciation.

The aesthetic openness to cultural diversity and the alertness to the voices of the marginalised mentioned above are observed in the literature produced by the Irish writers discussed in these chapters. What binds all these literary voices together is the *recognition* of the co-presence in Ireland of people from different ethnonational backgrounds. As Ben Pitcher claims in *The Politics of Multiculturalism*, acknowledging the 'facticity of difference' is the starting point for any examination of 'an already existing socio-political reality of which cultural difference has become a defining feature' (2009: 2). Pitcher continues,

the existence of cultural difference – whether understood in terms of race, ethnicity or religion – has become fully acknowledged as a constitutive part of the societies within which we live today. In this most basic of senses, and irrespective of the extent to which it is tolerated, celebrated or condemned, multiculturalism describes the widespread recognition that we can no longer be in any doubt as to whether or not cultural difference is there to stay. (*Ibid.*; quoted in Titley, Kerr, and King O'Rían, 2010: 21)

This politics of *recognition* defines the multicultural stance of the Irish writers under examination. As Charles Taylor argues in his influential *The Politics of Recognition* (1994), the demand for recognition is a basic human need, as it leads to the construction of meaningful selfhood. In other words, the construction of a healthy identity depends on being recognised as peculiar and equal in dignity. Generally speaking, it is this 'politics of equal recognition' of the distinctiveness of the migrant Other that is put into practice in the literary works analysed in this collection.

This 'politics of recognition' advocated by Charles Taylor in his study of multiculturalism has been sharply challenged in the Irish context by sociologist Ronit Lentin. As Lentin claims, Irish multiculturalism has often been 'anchored in a liberal politics of recognition of difference', which does 'not depart from western cultural imperialism' and is 'therefore inadequate in terms of deconstructing inter-ethnic power relations' (2001a). In other words, such a multicultural approach runs the risk of creating separatist ethnic groupings, leaving the structures of power intact while fixing the boundaries between the majority and the minority and maintaining ethnically homogeneous notions of Irishness. As

Lentin continues, 'instead of a "politics of recognition" of new ethnic minorities, integrating them to an unquestioned existing Irish society, a "politics of inter-rogation" of the Irish "we" is required'. This 'politics of interrogation' implies problematising Irishness itself, by not simply embracing difference, but also by challenging 'the notion of Ireland as a monoculture' (*ibid.*).[19]

Although the literary approach of contemporary Irish writers towards themes like immigration is multiple and varied, a common trend can be identi-fied. Most of the artists discussed in the following chapters tend simultaneously to combine their *recognition* of alterity and difference with Lentin's politics of *interrogation*, because of their constant urge to reassess insular and monocul-tural conceptions of Irishness. Regardless of the level of explicitness with which they address the presence of migrant communities in Ireland, what is clear is that these writers believe that it is no longer credible to adhere to a monolithic, monoethnic Irish identity. In this sense, they tend to defend a more inclusive form of 'civic nationalism', a notion radically opposed to 'ethnocentric national-ism', as Richard Kearney explains in *Postnationalist Ireland*: 'Civic nationalism conceives of the nation as including all of its citizens – regardless of blood, creed or colour. Ethnocentric nationalism believes, by contrast, that what holds a community together is not common rights of citizenship (or humanity) but common ethnicity (or race)' (1997: 57).[20]

Apart from this dual process of *recognition* and *interrogation*, some of these Irish writers also celebrate cultural difference by highlighting the positive ben-efits of migration on Ireland and engaging in a process of fruitful *interaction*. As seen above, this stance is best described in terms of the concept of 'inter-culturalism'. Although both terms – 'multiculturalism' and 'interculturalism' – have often been used interchangeably, and in inconsistent and contradictory ways, they should not be confused. Unlike 'multiculturalism', which simply sig-nals the recognition of difference and alterity, 'interculturalism' points towards a more dynamic inter-relationship with the Other. As Titley, Kerr, and King O'Rían (2010: 38) put it, 'interculturalism' is generally conceived as 'a way of encouraging dialogue, curiosity and integration between cultures', while 'mul-ticulturalism' can eventually lead 'towards separatism and parallel cultural existences'. As stated in the previous section, both terms – 'multiculturalism' and 'interculturalism' – will be employed in the collection, in order to signify the various stances adopted by the Irish writers, in their recognition, celebration of and/or interaction with difference.[21]

Nonetheless, these literary acts of *recognition*, *interrogation*, and *interaction* seem to fail at times. Not all the writers discussed in the following pages chal-lenge with the same efficiency the (now discredited) multicultural politics of assimilation or the strict separation between immigrants and the Irish majority. As Declan Kiberd suggests in the Preface to this collection, some artists run the risk of uncritically absorbing the migrant minority to the ways of the main-stream culture, by presenting 'immigrants almost invariably as "new Irish" and almost never for what they are and for what they bring in themselves'. Indeed, a common critique in some of the contributions here is that some Irish writers tend to distort the real experiences of immigration, by favouring the white native perspective, or by using the immigrant as a subsidiary figure, appearing merely in the backdrop. As Amanda Tucker shows in her contribution, the work of Claire Keegan and Roddy Doyle displays a limited vision of multiculturalism, by failing to record the real difficulties and anxieties inherent in Ireland's response to its new multiethnic reality. A similar view is hinted at in Armstrong's and Schrage-Früh's respective contributions on contemporary Irish poetry. Their analyses of poems by Seamus Heaney, Derek Mahon, Eileen Casey, and Siobhan Daffy, among others, display these authors' disinterest in the private stories and motivations of foreigners, as the concern generally lies with what the encoun-ter with Otherness reveals about Irish identity itself. For his part, David Clark discloses the tendency in Irish crime fiction to homogenise immigrants as in-nocent victims of unscrupulous Irish people, echoing the denunciation made by Bisi Adigun in 2007, who claimed to be 'tired of seeing black characters' mainly as 'prostitutes, slaves, servants or mentally unstable' (Mac Cormaic, 2007).

In spite of such drawbacks, contemporary Irish literature cannot be blamed nowadays for ignoring the perspective of immigrants. Some outstanding exam-ples analysed in this study – most notably Dermot Bolger, Michael O'Loughlin, and Hugo Hamilton – openly take some risks in their explicit, conscious adop-tion of the immigrant voice, placing immigrants at the centre of their work as protagonists. Of course, such ventriloquism is not unproblematic, as it raises inevitable issues concerning entitlement, simplification, and misrepresentation (problems which are eased in the case of Hamilton, as a 'new Irish' writer of hybrid German-Irish identity).

The political praxis of art

In his 1997 study *Postnationalist Ireland*, Richard Kearney defends the essential role of the arts when exerting political praxis, by asserting the formative role of narratives – what Kearney calls the 'political imaginary' – in the socio-political development of the nation-state (1997: 189). This social and political compo-nent of art underlies the work of many of the Irish writers discussed here. As Charlotte McIvor shows in her contribution, the work of some white Irish-born playwrights since the mid-1990s is closely related to a wider political activism on immigration policies and other diverse movements including anti-poverty initiatives and community development.

Indeed, implicit in this collection is the premise that literature can implement change, that it can transform, in a positive way, conventional world-views.[22] That is why the poems, plays, short stories, and novels are analysed here as powerful sites of agency, as politically and culturally relevant texts within their socio-historical context. In different degrees, these texts seem to advocate a rethinking of other, less restrictive, understandings of Irish belonging and citizenship. In other words, they point to a utopian future in which Ireland, rephrasing Hickman, is no longer considered 'as a nation that … *includes* Others', but as 'a nation *of* Others' (original emphasis; 2007: 23). In this country of the future, ethnicity would no longer become such a contested issue, as Nigerian-born writer Adigun envisages when commenting on the current state of Irish theatre:

> In recent years, a number of productions have tried to depict the fact that Ireland is no longer a monocultural society – albeit usually through the introduction of a character who is an asylum seeker or a refugee. I have yet to see an Irish theatre production where a black actor comes on stage to play a role that has no relevance to his/her skin. (Adigun, 2004: 31; quoted in Lanters, 2005: 35)

The literary works examined in this collection are, therefore, timely artistic statements in a country in which, as we have seen, some recent laws aimed at restraining the flow of inward immigration appear to some as revealing a subtle form of racism. Most of these texts imagine some form of multicultural conviviality which is utterly lacking in Irish social life. As Jason King claims, Irish drama enables a yet-to-be observed pluralism in the Republic. The ideal of interculturalism expressed in multiethnic projects such as 'The Tower of Babel' or in plays such as *Parable of the Plums* was clearly at odds with the actual life experiences of the immigrant actors, who were later incarcerated in Dublin airports and received several threats of deportation (King, 2005b: 46–55). A similar argument is endorsed by Loredana Salis, who points out that 'the worrying truth about the state of Irish arts and artists [is] that to this day they are expected to do what politics and the State fail to do, and in this specific case [their need is] to find a solution to the contentious issues of migration and social integration' (2010: 37). It will be interesting to see whether this social integration advocated by the arts will eventually lead to the affirmation and acceptance of differences in real Irish life.

Overview

This collection analyses the impact of Ireland's multiethnic reality on the poetry, drama, and fiction produced by contemporary Irish writers. The literary texts under examination cover a period of time from the decade immediately before the beginning of the so-called Celtic Tiger period to 2012, a year marked by the economic crisis that has swept Ireland and other European countries. This fluctuating period in Ireland's history is observed through the eyes and thoughts of Irish-born writers who come to terms with their country's increasing multi-ethnicity. In this sense, the main emphasis of the collection lies on these writers' perceptions of inward migration and their view of the current state of affairs in the new multicultural Ireland. Of course, immigrant writers are also offering their own perspectives on the matter, and their views are indeed acknowledged in many chapters. Nevertheless, the viewpoint of the incoming migrant, although present in most contributions, is not the scope of this collection and another full-length study might usefully be dedicated to the many interesting and highly successful literary works which are currently been published by the so-called 'new Irish'.

A book of this nature is likely to raise some critical controversy, given the many risks involved in looking at the immigrant solely from the 'native' perspective: the reinforcement of a them/us binary, the dangers of essentialising, stereotyping, and exoticising those Others (in a similar way to what the Irish have historically experienced), the political advisability of speaking on behalf of the minority, and a potentially dangerous disregard for the voice of the immigrant. However, this one-dimensional nature of the volume is academically necessary for a number of reasons. For the first time, there is enough material to produce a book of such a nature, given the profusion in the last decades of literary works by Irish-born writers dealing with immigrant characters. This one-sided perspective gives homogeneity to the collected essays and follows the lead of the numerous monographs, published in the field of postcolonial studies, which adopt a similar one-dimensional approach in their exclusive concern with the perspective provided by the British Empire (Edward Said's *Orientalism* being one of the most prominent examples). A collection of essays mixing the natives' and the immigrants' perspectives would divert attention from some of the issues which inevitably arise in the act of writing from the point of view of the centre rather than the periphery. By focusing solely on the perspective provided by Irish-born writers, the essays answer (in different and thus enriching ways) questions such as these: When talking about the Other, can the Irish writer avoid the reinforcement of binaries? Are Irish writers entitled to speak on behalf of the minority? How can they overcome the pitfalls involved in such an act? Is it necessary for them to give up their privilege as 'natives', as writers belonging to the mainstream culture? Can the voice of the subaltern truly emerge in this kind of literature? In this sense, a genuinely comprehensive coverage of subject matter can be achieved by focusing on how the literary discourse of the privileged majority deals with the minority. Undoubtedly, this book will prompt a wealth of material in the near future, of studies which will either extend the analysis of some of these topics or apply a similar approach to the study of other authors in Ireland.[23] Furthermore, the issues explored here are relevant not only to the contemporary context of Ireland, but also to any other society that hosts immigrants and is subsequently composed of a large number of 'non-nationals', a term that is largely avoided here, given its controversial connotations.[24]

The earliest text which is examined is Clare Boylan's novel *Black Baby* (1988) and, among the most recent literary works, we come across Éilís Ní Dhuibhne's collection of short fiction *The Shelter of Neighbours* (2012). Most of these texts explicitly address the theme of inward migration by narrating interethnic encounters between the Irish host and the foreign 'guest'. However, some other interracial and cross-cultural encounters beyond the geographical frontiers of Ireland are explored, as they are highly relevant to current debates around Irish multiculturalism and the present context of Ireland as a host country for contemporary migrants.

It is also important to stress that – while the term 'immigrant' is widely used throughout the book and this term might obscure the differences among the non-Irish-born citizens living in Ireland today – different types of migration and migrants are being considered. Political refugees, for instance, constitute the main characters of Emer Martin's novel *Baby Zero* and Michael Hayes's volume of poetry *'Survivor' – Representations of the 'New Irish': Dúchas Dóchasach*. The reality of these exiled Others radically differs from the experience of the more favoured immigrants recreated in the fiction of Mary Rose Callaghan or Elizabeth Wassell – who come to Ireland attracted by the cultural and social possibilities of the country – and also from the short-term visitors portrayed in the poetry of Derek Mahon and Sinéad Morrissey, among others.

The seventeen chapters have been grouped into four Parts with the aim of revealing connections and establishing a dialogue between them. Part I is suggestively entitled 'Irish multiculturalisms: obstacles and challenges'. Editing a collection on Irish writers' representations of non-Irish-born minorities inevitably raises troubling questions about authenticity, credibility, and (mis) representation. Are Irish writers the most appropriate spokespersons of new multicultural Ireland? Do they run the risk of homogenising difference by writing about the periphery from the vantage point of the centre? How should they represent Irish multiculturalism? Should they adopt an optimistic or rather a realistic approach? Which is the best way to address this issue? To whom are their works addressed? Chapters 2–5 attend to these and other related problems which unavoidably emerge in any analysis of contemporary Irish literature in the multicultural context of twenty-first-century Ireland. In her detailed assessment of the presence of white Irish-born playwrights in the development of community arts in Ireland, Charlotte McIvor suggests the problematics involved in negotiating the authors' whiteness in relation to the minority communities in Ireland. Irish-born playwrights such as Donal O'Kelly, Declan Gorman, and

Charlie O'Neill must confront the ethical question of how to speak convincingly on issues concerning migration and racism, as individuals belonging to the privileged 'white' and 'native' majority of Ireland. As McIvor implies, they manage to avoid the pitfalls involved in such a task by infusing their work with a political activism which is built on previous paradigms of social and community engagement. Furthermore, community arts work fosters genuine interculturality through the cooperation and interaction on stage of ethnically diverse individuals.

The second contribution by Amanda Tucker continues problematising Irish multiculturalism through its analysis of the contemporary fiction of Irish-born writers Roddy Doyle, Claire Keegan and Emma Donoghue, and immigrant author Cauvery Madhavan. Tucker maintains that there are two ways of representing multiculturalism in Ireland: as an 'obstacle' that can be easily overcome by the hospitality, friendliness, and goodwill of Irish people, or as 'a complicated and unresolved process', which leads to cultural anxiety and conflict. Whereas Doyle and Keegan adopt the first stance on the matter, by minimising the problems posed by Irish multiculturalism, Donoghue and Madhavan offer a more complex representation of cross-cultural encounters which better reflects the difficulties experienced by immigrants today. In this sense, for Tucker, the most contested issue in current multicultural representations is not who speaks and from which perspective, but rather how the interaction between the Irish and the immigrants is represented.

Chapter 4 by Pilar Villar-Argáiz also delves into the numerous, complex ways of representing multiculturalism in Ireland, this time from the perspective of Irish poets. Villar-Argáiz starts by briefly assessing the work of an immigrant poet from Poland, Kinga Olszewska, in order to consider it alongside recent poems by Colette Bryce, Mary O'Donnell, and Michael O'Loughlin. These writers are interested in deriding and/or debunking the ideal 'liberal' model of Irish multiculturalism, which often permeates literary and cultural texts in their uncritical celebration of a truly integrated and unconditionally hospitable Ireland. Bryce, for instance, discloses the patronising and xenophobic attitudes behind official discourses in Ireland, in a poem which suggestively recalls the 2004 Citizenship Referendum. Bryce's blatant critique of an ideal multicultural Ireland is also recorded by O'Donnell and O'Loughlin, who, in different ways, explore multiethnicity from the viewpoint of the centre and that of the periphery.

Chapter 5 by Margarita Estévez-Saá, which closes Part I, analyses the depiction of immigrants in Celtic Tiger and post-Celtic Tiger novels, revealing – like the previous chapters – the existence of diverse literary responses to multiethnicity in Ireland (hence the plural title of this section, 'Irish multiculturalisms'). Estévez-Saá identifies an evolution in the Irish novels published between 2000 and 2010. In those novels published in the initial years of the new millennium, such as those by Mary Rose Callaghan, Elizabeth Wassell, and Anne Haverty, immigrants appear in the background, as secondary characters coexisting – but not interacting actively – with the main Irish protagonists. It is not until a few years later, in the novels published by Chris Binchy, Peter Cunningham, and Hugo Hamilton, that immigrants acquire a voice of their own in the texts, and genuine interculturality between Irish-born and non-Irish-born characters is presented as a possibility.

Part II, 'Rethinking Ireland as a postnationalist community', gathers four contributions which explore, from diverse perspectives, how the experience of immigration has challenged traditional concepts of Irishness. The radical trans- formation of Ireland from a relatively homogeneous population to a much more ethnically, linguistically, and religiously diverse one has prompted writers to re-imagine what it means to be Irish. This imaginary reconstruction becomes even more difficult with the current dissolution of previous ideological and re- ligious certainties. As Fintan O'Toole (2010: 3) explains in *Enough is Enough*, 'the old landmarks have disappeared. The twin towers of southern Irish identity – Catholicism and Nationalism – [are] teetering.'

Bearing in mind this prevailing uncertainty surrounding traditional notions of Irishness, it is not surprising that one of the issues most debated nowadays in discussions on Irish multiculturalism is how to preserve local identities while at the same time fostering a genuine openness to Otherness and alterity. Academic attempts to maintain this interconnection between local traditions and external influences are usually articulated by means of the concept of 'post- nationalism'. In the Irish context, this term is largely associated with the work of Richard Kearney, in particular his 1997 study *Postnationalist Ireland: Politics, Culture, Philosophy*. Kearney finds a 'triple-layered identity' when talking about the Irish nationhood today: the State, the expatriate abroad, and the regional communities within, composed at times of ethnic minorities which he identi- fies throughout his work as 'subnational communities' or 'subnational identities' (1997: 38, 58, 99). In this sense, the Irish nation can no longer be defined around the concept of *ethnicity* or 'in terms of a racially homogeneous "people" which seeks out a state appropriate to its unique identity' (3). 'Rethinking Ireland', as Kearney (11) puts it, 'means thinking *otherwise*'; it 'requires us to think beyond our inherited models of sovereignty, nation-state and nationalism, in order to create new paradigms of political and cultural accommodation between all the citizens' of the island. This involves, inevitably, expanding previous restrictive notions of Irishness and including 'diverse groups from within the frontiers of the island' (38).

The postnationalism advanced by Richard Kearney, which has been brought into question by a number of commentators in the new millennium,[25] is relevant in discussions of the new hybrid configurations established by the transnational migratory movements of the globalised world. Drawing upon the work of Kearney and/or other cultural theorists and philosophers, the four chapters in this section analyse the various ways in which contemporary Irish writers 'rethink' Irishness by incorporating the reality of 'postnational' Others. In her overview of Roddy Doyle's fictional and theatrical contributions in Chapter 6, Eva Roa White demonstrates how Irishness is, in his work, redefined in order to include hyphenated, hybridised identities. In particular, Roa White explores the issue of citizenship in Doyle's short story '57% Irish', revealing the political and ideological nuances of a text which openly vindicates the integration of the 'new Irish' in Ireland's mainstream society.

This reconceptualisation of stable definitions of individual and collective identities is also examined in Carmen Zamorano Llena's critical assessment of Hugo Hamilton's two most recent novels, *Disguise* and *Hand in the Fire* in Chapter 7. Zamorano Llena starts by exposing the limits of the concept of the 'migrant nation' defended in the mid-1990s by Kearney and the then President Mary Robinson, as such a concept runs the risk of reinforcing an ethnocultural base to definitions of Irish national identity. Zamorano Llena shows how such a monological understanding of collective identity is debunked in Hamilton's writings, which openly exercise what Lentin (2001a) calls a 'politics of interrogation' of conventional definitions of Irishness.

Similarly, Chapter 8 in this section by Anne Fogarty explores reconfigurations of traditional national identities in the short fiction of Edna O'Brien, Colm Tóibín, Anne Enright, Colum McCann, Mary O'Donnell, and Éilís Ní Dhuibhne. Drawing on Paul Ricoeur's observations about selfhood and Otherness, Fogarty demonstrates that these writers frequently use the figure of the immigrant in order to scrutinise, in the postnational context of Ireland, the shattering of conventional notions about self, family, and community. As Fogarty shows, the immigrant never appears as an isolated motif in fictional portrayals of contemporary Ireland. Rather, the description of such a character tends to be linked with incisive explorations of contemporary Irishness.

Irish poetry is the focus of Chapter 9 by Katarzyna Poloczek which closes this section. Poloczek studies work by Sinéad Morrissey, Mary O'Malley, and Leontia Flynn, revealing how these female poets use their personal experiences of global mobility to achieve a better understanding of modern Irish multicultural society. In the latter part of her chapter, Poloczek analyses Michael Hayes's daring attempt to record the daily life of asylum-seekers in *'Survivor' – Representations of the 'New Irish'*, coauthored with the African artist Jean 'Ryan' Hakizimana. By placing his poems beside Hakizimana's paintings, Hayes opens up an intercultural dialogue between cultures and traditions which genuinely reflects the hybridisation and polyphony of Irish society nowadays.

Part III gathers a group of five essays and is entitled "'The return of the repressed': "performing" Irishness through intercultural encounters'. In the particular context of Ireland, some responses to the arrival of new migrants have been interpreted as a reflection of Ireland's traumatic past. Ronit Lentin (2002: 233), for instance, claims that the painful memory of emigration, a memory which is usually hidden and repressed, is reawakened in the everyday encounters between the Irish host and the incoming migrant. This traumatic past which comes to haunt the host, in a process Lentin describes as the 'return of the repressed', must be fully acknowledged in order to achieve a healthy relationship with external Others. In other words, the first basis for the existence of true multiculturalism lies in the ability to acquire a complete knowledge of the roots of one's identity by means of interrogating and carefully examining the past.

Some theorists in Irish academia have defended this need to look back at Irish historical memory in order to foster an integrated Ireland, a country genuinely welcoming to new influences. Luke Gibbons (2002: 105) claims that '[t]he ability to look outward, and particularly to identify with the plight of refugees and asylum-seekers, may be best served by reclaiming those lost narratives of the past which generate new solidarities in the present'. For Gibbons, the act of welcoming other cultural influences cannot be based on an act of historical amnesia. In other words, it is only when one acknowledges his/her past (a past at times filled with memories of poverty and deprivation) that a truthful relationship with the migrant can be established. Similarly, Declan Kiberd, in his now iconic essay 'Strangers in their own country', defends the need for a sophisticated knowledge of history in order to be open to the presence of Others: 'those who lack a sophisticated sense of their own origins are more likely to seek a simplified version of the past, in whose name to lash out at the "foreign"' (2005: 314).[26]

Such a historical remembrance is put into practice by some contemporary Irish writers, in their need to establish specific points of connection between the reality of the newcomers and previous Irish nationals emigrating from the homeland. In Chapter 10 Paula Murphy demonstrates in her examination of Dermot Bolger's *The Ballymun Trilogy* how present multiculturalism in Ireland can be efficiently described in literary terms through the perspective of the country's long history of emigration. In his play *The Townlands of Brazil*, Bolger expresses his sympathy for the foreigner through his insistence upon the commonality of experience with Ireland's diasporic history.

Bolger also underscores this connection in his poetry, as Michaela Schrage-Früh shows in Chapter 11 on transculturality and recent Irish poetry. In her exploration of the hitherto under-researched poetry of Bolger and the recent work produced by other poets such as Mary O'Malley, David Wheatley, and Pat Boran, Schrage-Früh analyses the ways in which the immigrant experience is interpreted through the lenses of Ireland's shared transcultural experiences of exile, homelessness, and homesickness. This contribution also focuses on lesser known literary voices such as Betty Keogh, Eileen Casey, Siobhan Daffy, and Adenice Adedoyin, whose poems explore, in various ways, Julia Kristeva's realisation that we are ultimately all 'strangers to ourselves'.

Jason King in Chapter 12 also examines the ways in which contemporary Irish writers, particularly Hugo Hamilton, deliberately recuperate migrant memory in their work in order to visualise cultural hybridity and difference as modes of self-acceptance. King sets Hamilton's work beside that of his modernist predecessor James Joyce (in particular, *A Portrait of the Artist as a Young Man* and *Ulysses*), in order to compare notions of exile, homesickness, and displacement. Contributions such as this remind us of the relevance of reinterpreting, in the present context of twenty-first-century Ireland, canonical texts in order to reveal more fully their multicultural meanings, something that Declan Kiberd has also done at various points in *The Irish Writer and the World* (2005: 20, 305–7).

Part III also examines, from diverse perspectives, how traditional Irish stereotypes are maintained and reworked in contemporary narratives. Irish sociologists Kuhling and Keohane (2007: 68) have explained the various ways in which the presence of immigrants reaffirms the image of 'native' Irishness. As they claim, rather than 'celebrating what [they] are bringing to us from their culture', the general tendency in Ireland nowadays is to view the migrant as an external force that reinforces and reaffirms, in a flattering and refreshed way, the traditional national identity:

> Immigrants, simply by their presence, affirm our way of life, remind us of who we are, of where we've come from, and give legitimacy to what we have now and where we imagine ourselves in the future – affluent and progressive, a global, even cosmopolitan society, but still a moral community, a people with roots, traditions and a coherent collective history. … We welcome the immigrant not for the gift he or she brings from their culture, but for the affirmation and confirmation of what we imagine that we have already, our identity. (Kuhling and Keohane, 2007: 68–9)

The final two chapters of Part III explore how stereotypical Irishness is deliberately enacted in the encounters between the host society and the foreign Other. The phrase in the subtitle 'performing Irishness' is used deliberately here, and it draws mainly from the concept of 'gender performativity' developed by Judith Butler in her seminal book *Gender Trouble* (1990). As Butler claims, gendered identities are not based on some authentic essence but are socially constructed. In other words, they are the dramatic effect of our performances and repeated ways of acting in our daily, social life. This idea of identity as a performance which is enacted is closely related to the arguments developed Chapters 13 and 14. In her analysis of Keith Ridgway's novel *The Parts*, Katherine O'Donnell examines the ways in which the specificity of 'Irishness' is conveyed in relation to black Otherness. In particular, O'Donnell studies in detail the intercultural encounters between the protagonist, a 'typical' Irish character, and his African neighbours, and concludes that the novel mimics, or *performs*, the historical Irish 'empathy' for black people.

Chapter 14 also reflects on the ways in which Irishness is enacted and conveyed in recent literary articulations of multiculturality. In his chapter on contemporary Irish poets Derek Mahon, Sinéad Morrissey, Mary O'Donnell, and Seamus Heaney, Charles I. Armstrong focuses on the ways in which clichéd versions of identity are projected in relation to tourism in Ireland. Their poems on tourism can be studied comparatively with other more explicit literary discussions of immigration, as they also reveal interesting cross-cultural views and prejudices in the encounter between the Irish host and the foreign Other. In fact, tourists also form part, together with immigrants, of the new 'ethnospace' which is Ireland now, following Arjun Appadurai's definition of the term (1996: 33).

This study of Irish multicultural representations would be incomplete without acknowledging the importance of gender difference in shaping the power structures implicit in Ireland's new migratory spaces. Part IV, 'Gender and the city' acknowledges these gendered dimensions of Irish multiculturality by including two chapters which specifically address the connections between ethnicity, race, and gender. Firstly, in Chapter 15 Maureen T. Reddy offers a feminist reading of anti-racism in her analysis of Clare Boylan's *Black Baby*, a novel which explores capitalism, patriarchy, and racism as interlocked systems of oppression. As Reddy convincingly demonstrates, Boylan's 1988 novel can be viewed as a precursor to current writing on race and ethnicity in twenty-first-century Ireland. *Black Baby*, this contributor argues, reconceptualised race in a pioneering way, by considering its constitutive role in any serious attempt to undo the colonisation of Irish women.

Indeed, the interconnections between gender and race become pressing issues in the Ireland of the new millennium. Gender played a crucial role in the 2004 Citizenship Referendum; pregnant foreign women (particularly Third World women) were considered a threat, as the predominant view was that they were having babies to obtain access to birthright citizenship.[27] The controversy surrounding migrant mothers constitutes one of the most important thematic threads in Emer Martin's 2007 novel *Baby Zero*. Chapter 16, Wanda Balzano's contribution, carefully studies this novel in order to examine the often invisible and neglected interrelations between gender difference and contemporary multiethnicity in Ireland. The transnational aspect of Martin's fiction is here brought to the surface as a helpful frame of critical analysis of the intersections between gender and race in both Western and non-Western countries.

Part IV also includes two chapters which touch upon the changing geographical spaces of the city triggered by the influx of immigration. These new spatial configurations can be explained by means of the concept 'ethnoscape', a neologism coined by Arjun Appadurai in order to talk about the slippery linkage between ethnicity and space. As Appadurai (1996: 33) claims, this term suggests 'the landscape of persons who constitute the shifting world in which we live including tourists, immigrants, refugees, exiles, guest workers, and other moving groups and individuals [that] appear to affect the politics of (and between) nations to a hitherto unprecedented degree'. Some contributions in the collection have already shed light on the reconfigurations of new ethno spaces in contemporary Irish literature. While Paula Murphy's analysis of Dermot Bolger's *The Ballymun Trilogy* focused on the accommodation and reception of migrant workers in Ballymun (one of the areas in Dublin of greatest socio-economic disadvantage), Katherine O'Donnell's study of Keith Ridgway's novel *The Parts* showed how the 'boom town' of Dublin is described as an uncanny 'third space'.

Chapters 17 and 18 continue exploring this theme. Loredana Salis examines Ireland's shifting urban space in her chapter on the impact that immigration has exerted on recent plays by Sebastian Barry, Paul Mercier, and Dermot Bolger. The capital city of Dublin is portrayed as a modern, rapidly evolving landscape, where the new realities of racism and xenophobia coexist, at times uneasily, with the new confident atmosphere brought by the Celtic Tiger economic boom.

Urban spaces also become the backdrop for the literary works discussed by David Clark in Chapter 18. In his detailed assessment of the Irish crime fiction of the last decade, Clark analyses the way in which the novels of John Brady, Gene Kerrigan, Ingrid Black, and Niamh O'Connor, among others, portray immigrants as victims of Irish people, who often exploit them in criminal activities such as the trafficking of narcotics, prostitution, and the illegal movement of other immigrants. These migrant characters usually inhabit the 'mean streets' of Dublin, Galway, Limerick, and Cork. This signals the recent interest of Irish crime writers in setting their plots in 'homegrown' locations, in contrast to previous novels which tended to fictionalise crime in non-Irish settings.

Afterword: Irish literature in a period of crisis

This collection therefore covers work produced not only in the particular historical context of the Celtic Tiger, when the unprecedented phenomenon of inward migration radically transformed the fabric of Irish society, but also in the initial years of the post-Celtic Tiger period. As we enter into the second decade of the new millennium, the social and economic panorama of Ireland has changed dramatically. In 2010, net outward emigration increased for the first time since

1995 as not only immigrants but Irish-born people began to leave (O'Toole, 2010: 5–6; Titley, Kerr, and King O'Rían, 2010: 173). In this context, the intense and often contested debates on migration that dominated the headlines of Irish newspapers and broadcast media have inevitably dissipated and the focus inevitably shifts away to other heated concerns of contemporary Ireland, particularly the dire economic recession of the country.

In this context of economic turbulence, we might wonder whether recession has affected the representation of interethnic encounters. In other words, are writers still concerned with cross-cultural exchanges and, if so, are these envisioned as spaces of collision and confrontation or are they visualised as fruitful, productive sites of transformation? As Ireland enters what Bryan Fanning (2009: 179) calls an 'uncertain phase of cultural-economic nation building', the prospect facing Irish literature now is similarly uncertain. As Fintan O'Toole (2010: 18) suggests in *Enough is Enough*, Ireland's identity is still to be reinvented, bearing in mind the collapse in economic confidence and the decline of the prestige and solidity offered by previous key elements of Irish national identity, particularly the Catholic Church and national parties such as Fianna Fáil. Furthermore, the visit in May 2011 of Britain's Queen Elizabeth II and US President Barack Obama will inevitably exert an impact on the Irish national psyche, and one which can only be assessed in years to come.

In this context, Irish writers will inevitably experience a phase of introspection, which will allow them to mediate upon the rapid changes that Ireland has experienced since the last decade of the twentieth century. The deeply entrenched social inequalities of post-Celtic Tiger Ireland will probably be a major concern in the literature of the country. In *Enough is Enough*, O'Toole (2010: 194) claims that Ireland's current period of economic crisis can also be conceived positively, as it fosters the potential opportunity for the country to 'emerge as a much more equal society'. As he further claims, '[o]ne of the things that has happened as a result of the collapse of the boomtime economy is that Irish people have become much more conscious of inequality … ; awareness of the disparities in the distribution of wealth has increased sharply in the aftermath of the crash' (194–5). This view is also shared by Ciarán Benson, in his keynote lecture 'A national identity in crisis? Reflections on Ireland 2000–2011' delivered at an international conference of Irish Studies.[28] Benson claims that this new phase of economic recession offers the possibility for the construction of a more positive Irish national identity, one constructed upon conviviality and a genuine interest in Others. This 'appreciation of the desirability of plurality' might be reflected in the literature of the country. After all, and as Benson contends, 'poets, artists, musicians, writers, filmmakers' are nowadays the only 'creators of Irish identity who are still credible'. It will be interesting to observe whether this new awareness of inequality that O'Toole and Benson diagnose in present-day Ireland is reflected in the literature of the country.[29]

Notes

1   Official reports elaborated by the Globalisation Index considered Ireland the most globalised country on earth on three consecutive occasions between 2001 and 2003 (Kearney, 2003: 67).

2   The two largest ethnic groups in Ireland are the Chinese and the Polish communities; the other migrants generally belong to Latvian, Lithuanian, and Nigerian backgrounds (Titley, Kerr, and King O'Rían, 2010: 56).

3   This letter was distributed by electronic mail on behalf of the Ambassador of Ireland in Spain, Justin Harman, to all members of the Spanish Association of Irish Studies (AEDEI).

4   For a comprehensive bibliography of research on immigration in Ireland, see Mac Éinrí and White (2008).

5   Some of the most interesting contributions in the 2007 special issue of *Translocations* include Mary Hickman's socio-economic discussion of the transformations of Irish society, Silvia Brandi's analysis of the implicit racism and the ideological manipulation of the texts in support of the 2004 Irish Citizenship Referendum, and Nicola Yau's exploration of identity among second-generation Chinese in Celtic Tiger Ireland. Bryan Fanning's 2007 edited collection, *Immigration and Social Change in the Republic of Ireland* deals with the subject of contemporary Irish immigration from the disciplines of psychology, geography, law, and social policy.

6   See also Fricker and Lentin's 2007 study on migration and global networks in Ireland. Studies such as these have originated in the context of the Institute for International Integration Studies (IIIS) at Trinity College Dublin, of which Ronit Lentin is a founding member.

7   *Metro Éireann* was founded by two Nigerian journalists living in Dublin, Abel Ugba and Chinedu Onyejelem. See the official website of the newspaper (www.metroeireann. com/) for an exhaustive account of the objectives of this journal as 'the primary source of news and information on Ireland's fast-growing immigrant and ethnic communities'.

8   Another illustrative example of this increasing concern with the literature produced by immigrant writers is the creation in 2008 of the Women Writers in the New Ireland Network (WWINI) at University College Dublin, which fosters dialogue between female writers from migrant communities. Networks such as this put into practice the advocacy of some Irish sociologists to promote creative encounters and interchanges among ethnic groups in Ireland (e.g. Kuhling and Keohane, 2007: 212).

9   Important research on the writing of Travellers and about Travellers in Ireland has been conducted by Paul Delaney (2008) and José Lanters (2008). Some contemporary discussions on inward migration in the Irish context tend to include in their analyses the figure of the Traveller. See, for instance, Ronit Lentin (2001a), Robbie McVeigh (2008: 19), John Rex (2008: 7), Loredana Salis (2010: 48), and, more obliquely, Suzanna Chan (2007: 36).

10 With respect to immigrant writing in Ireland, some iconic academic contributions include Faragó's study on immigrant female poets (2008), Bourke and Faragó's (2010)

comprehensive anthology on immigrant poetry, Altuna García de Salazar's article on Marsha Mehran (2010), McIvor's study on minority-ethnic playwrights (2011), the analysis on multicultural literature in Ireland provided by González Arias, Morales Ladrón, and Altuna García de Salazar (2010), and Feldman and Mulhall's incisive exploration of the work produced by the Women Writers in the New Ireland Network (2012). The theme of immigration in Ireland and the cultural production associated with this is closely related to the so-called fields of Irish Diaspora Studies and Irish Migration Studies. Important work on this area has been carried out by Liam Harte, Bronwen Walter, and Mary Hickman, among others. While Harte has extensively published on the literature of the Irish diaspora (see, for instance, Harte, 2009), others such as Walter and Hickman have studied the experiences of Irish immigrants abroad from a sociological perspective (see Walter, 2011; and Crowley, Hickman, and Mai, 2012).

11   Some monographs have recently been published on the topic of cross-cultural encounters. See, for instance, Friberg-Harnesk, Porter, and Wrethed's *Beyond Ireland* (2011). However, the emphasis is not laid on the current context of twenty-first century multi-ethnic Ireland. An important exception is Egger and McDonagh's edited collection *Polish-Irish Encounters in the Old and New Europe* (2011), which explores the social, economic, political, and cultural interactions between Ireland and Poland, both historically and in the present context of the new millennium. Indeed, there is an increasing interest, in both the public and academic arenas, in the examination of the exchanges between the Irish host and its foreign 'guests'. In the first years of the new millennium, various conferences have obliquely dealt with the topic of how Irish literature responds to the presence of non-Irish immigrants. In 2009, in the National University of Ireland, the American Society for Irish Studies hosted the conference 'New Irish, Old Irish'; one of the themes of the conference was to explore the dynamics of immigration and settlement and their implications for the construction of Irish identities. This conference was later followed by others such as 'Ireland: East and West' (University of Zagreb), and The Eight International Conference run by The European Federation of Associations and Centres of Irish Studies (EFACIS), 'Ireland: Arrivals and Departures' (University of Salford); both were celebrated in September 2011 and addressed issues concerning intercultural exchange and the immigrant experience.

12   Kiberd's analysis of multiculturalism in Ireland has been criticised by Gerardine Meaney, who points to the dangers of using 'a postcolonial understanding of Irish history' as an 'alibi ... to avoid responsibility for either the Irish past or present' (2010: xv–xvi, 15).

13   Similar arguments have been put forward, for instance, by the journalist Sally Richardson (2005). See also Micheál Mac Gréil's *Pluralism and Diversity in Ireland* (2011). This study, based on a national survey of attitudes and opinions in the Republic of Ireland in 2007–08, confirmed the existence of tolerance towards ethnically diverse groupings. One of the factors contributing to the reduction of social prejudice with respect to the decade of the 1980s was an increase in economic security as a result of the Celtic Tiger. It would be interesting to see whether the recessionary times have changed this behavioural pattern, giving way to suspicion and hostility towards migrant communities.

14   Other critics who have also identified the reappearance of racism and ethnic prejudices in globalised multicultural encounters are Hall (1997: 5–7), Weedon (2004: 21–2), and Sen (2007: xiii).

15   The difference between this new form of nationalism and nineteenth-century nationalism is that the former 'is not so much an expression of the desire for territorial

expansion or to recover the occupied national territory from the hands of the coloniser; this new nationalism is rather the expression of opposition to minorities existing within the territory of the state' (Delanty, 1999: 277; quoted in Zamorano Llena, 2010: 145).

16   For an incisive analysis of the discriminatory nature of this Referendum, see Silvia Brandi (2007).

17   For a historical survey of the problematic links between Irish nationalism and racism, see Steve Garner (2004). Garner's work set the stage for later examinations of Irish 'racial' consciousness and the politicised racialisation of Irish identities, such as those carried out by Suzanna Chan (2007) and Katherine O'Donnell (2007). See also John Brannigan's *Race in Modern Irish Literature and Culture* (2009), which demonstrates, through the analysis of mid-century Irish literary works, the importance of race in the construction of Modern Ireland. For a pioneering exploration of Irishness as a white construct, and its relationship with gender identities, see Gerardine Meaney (2010).

18   John Rex (2008: 1) explains as follows this 'assimilationist' response to the presence of immigrants, strongly supported in countries such as France: the 'emphasis is placed upon all individuals having equal rights through relatively easy access to citizenship, while the separate organisations and cultures of immigrant minorities are discouraged'.

19   A similar argument is put forward by sociologist Shalini Sinha, who claims that a truly 'multi-ethnic Ireland' cannot be achieved 'without re-examining the Irish national identity' (2008: 21).

20   In his essay 'Multiculturalism in Ireland', Declan Kiberd also defends the need to foster a sense of 'civic nationalism' (2005: 319). This distinction between 'ethnic national-ism' and 'civic nationalism' has been sharply criticised by Paul James, one of the most sceptical critics of postnationalism, on the grounds that '[i]n some hands it is turned into a blinkered politics extolling the virtues of the kind of nationalism that the writer happens to hold' (1999). Kearney's ambitious postnationalist attempt to imagine an in-clusive concept of Irishness beyond the limits of geographical and ethnic boundaries has been the source of some critical controversy (see n. 25).

21   In any case, the efficacy of the terms 'multicultural' and 'intercultural' is at times ques-tioned in some chapters. Michaela Schrage-Früh in Chapter 11, for instance, prefers to use as a counterpoint the concept of 'transculturality', in order to remind us of the inherently hybrid nature of all cultures.

22   Although literature can exert some significant effect, it is important to note that it does not have the public impact that media has. According to Kiberd, the Irish media has been fundamental in shaping public perceptions of the migrants (2005: 312). As he claims, some exaggerated and sensationalised reports have been complicit in processes of discrimination. Kiberd is not the only critic in Ireland to accuse the media of pro-moting 'a climate of scapegoating' that has fuelled cultural anxieties and racist incidents in Ireland. Others such as Breen and Devereux (2003: 87–90) claim that the broadcast media is responsible for constructing the image of the threatening immigrant, particu-larly in relation to refugees and asylum-seekers (quoted in Persson, 2011: 58). For a comprehensive examination of the power of the media and broadcasting in represent-ing cultural diversity in Ireland, see Titley, Kerr, and King O'Rían (2010).

23   Given the sudden emergence in contemporary Irish literature of numerous images of immigration, there are some authors who are not dealt with in this book for matters of space. These include, among others, women writers such as Rosemary Jenkinson, whose 2004 collection of short stories *Problems Nos. 53 & 54* positions immigration in the context of post-Troubles Northern Ireland, and Kate O'Riordan with her novel

Memory Stones (2003), which voices deep-rooted prejudices against Africans in the Republic of Ireland. Scattered references to immigrants can also be found in Sean O'Reilly's *The Swing of Things* (2005) and in some stories included in Michael Farrell's *Life in the Universe* (2009) and Roddy Doyle's *Bullfighting* (2011). See, for instance, Farrell's 'The Rift Valley' and Doyle's 'Recuperation'.

24 In recent years, the phrase 'non-national' has been the object of some criticism, as immigrants do have a nationality. From this perspective, it would be preferable to identify immigrants in Ireland as 'not Irish nationals', rather than 'non-nationals'.

25 As an advocator of postnationalism, Kearney has been widely accused by some sceptical critics of being unrealistic when pronouncing the demise of states, nations, and nationalism. For James, for instance, there is little empirical evidence that nationalism will be less influential in the future and he also attacks the generalised tendency among critics such as Kearney to consider postnationalism as a way out of the problems posed by official nationalism (James, 2002: 3–18; 2006: 304–5). Others believe that Kearney still depends on nationalism as a conceptual framework, despite his earnest attempt to reject the idea of the nation. Goodman (2002: 12), for instance, sees postnationalism as 'a form of civic patriotism that can look very nationalistic for those on the outside,' while Graham claims that Kearney's thinking 'refuses the ability to conceptually reject and comprehend the ideological constructions and restrictions of the nation, and hopes instead to be able to preserve and move beyond it simultaneously' (Graham, 2001: 98). Another detailed critique of Kearney's concept of postnationalism has been undertaken by Sarah Fulford, who criticises the 'utopian' elements of his thinking and accuses Kearney of failing to identify the connections of postnationalism with postmodernism and capitalism (Fulford, 2002: 210–14). For an interesting analysis of the limits of Irish postnationalist discourse in providing a sufficient framework for the changes in Irish society, see Olszewska (2008).

26 A similar argument is also put forward by Michael Cronin (2008: 3), who advocates a strong connection to the local (and hence, historical roots) in the globalising area. Cronin proposes the notion of 'denizen' (as opposed to the impersonal and detached concept of the 'global citizen'), in order to refer to 'a person who dwells in a particular place and who can move through and knowingly inhabit that place'. Accordingly, as Cronin states, 'what denizenship posits is a knowledge from within', by relating closely to 'place myths, stories, personal associations' (5).

27 For a thorough analysis of the gendered aspects of access to citizenship in Ireland, see Garner (2011). The position of migrant mothers as the reproducers of future generations of Irish citizens has been analysed in detail by Ronit Lentin (2001b).

28 Delivered on 26 May 2011 at The Tenth Anniversary of the AEDEI Conference (Spanish Association of Irish Studies), University of Oviedo, Spain. Quoted with the permission of Ciarán Benson.

29 Such is the view of President Michael D. Higgins, who in a number of public lectures has vehemently argued that Irish literature, art, drama, and song play a vital part in the renewal and regeneration of the Irish society, and in the construction of 'a better model of Irishness', one 'which is inclusive and fair to all' (2012a; 2012b).

References

Adigun, Bisi (2004). 'In living colour', *Irish Theatre Magazine* 4.19: 31.

Allen-Randolph, Jody (2010). *Close to the Next Moment: Interviews from a Changing Ireland.* Manchester: Carcanet.

Altuna García de Salazar, Asier (2010). 'Marsha Mehran and multiculturalism in Irish fiction', in David Clark and Rubén Jarazo Álvarez (eds), *To Banish Ghost and Goblin: New Essays on Irish Culture In the Wake of the Tiger: Irish Studies in the Twentieth-First Century.* Oleiros: Netbiblo, 181–90.

Appadurai, Arjun (1996). *Modernity at Large: Cultural Dimensions of Globalization.* Minneapolis: University of Minnesota Press.

Barrett, Alan, Adele Bergin, and David Duffy (2006). 'The Labour Market characteristics and Labour Market impacts of immigrants in Ireland', *Economic and Social Review* 37.1: 1–26.

Bauman, Zygmunt (2007) [2006]. *Liquid Fear.* Cambridge and Malden: Polity.

Bernasconi, Robert (1998). '"Stuck inside of mobile with the Memphis Blues again": Interculturalism and the conversation of races', in Cynthia Willett (ed.), *Theorising Multiculturalism. A Guide to the Current Debate.* London: Routledge, 276–98.

Bourke, Eva and Borbála Faragó (eds) (2010). *Landing Places: Immigrant Poets in Ireland.* Dublin: Dedalus.

Brandi, Silvia (2007). 'Unveiling the ideological construction of the 2004 Irish Citizenship Referendum: A critical discourse analytical approach', *Translocations. The Irish Migration, Race and Social Transformation Review* 2.1: 26–47.

Brannigan, John (2009). *Race in Modern Irish Literature and Culture.* Edinburgh: Edinburgh University Press.

Breen, Michael and Eoin Devereux (2003). 'Setting up margins: Public attitudes and media construction of poverty and exclusion in Ireland', *Nordic Irish Studies* 2.1: 75–93.

Butler, Judith (1990). *Gender Trouble: Feminism and the Subversion of Identity.* New York and London: Routledge.

Chan, Suzanna (2007). 'Marching, minstrelsy, masquerade: Parading white Loyalist masculinity as "Blackness"', in Wanda Balzano, Anne Mulhall, and Moynagh Sullivan (eds), *Irish Postmodernisms and Popular Culture.* New York: Palgrave Macmillan, 26–38.

Cronin, Michael (2008). 'Languages of globalisation', *Nordic Irish Studies* 7: 1–14.

Crowley, Helen, Mary Hickman, and Nick Mai (2012). *Migration and Social Cohesion in the UK.* Basingstoke: Palgrave Macmillan.

Crowley, Una, Mary Gilmartin, and Rob Kitchin (2006). 'Vote yes for common sense citizenship: Immigration and the paradoxes at the heart of Ireland's "Céad Míle Fáilte"', *NIRSA Working Paper* 30: n.p. www.eprints.nuim.ie/1541/. Accessed on 10 January 2009.

De Lucas, Javier (1994). '¿Elogio de Babel? Sobre las dificultades del derecho frente al proyecto intercultural', *Multiculturalismo & Diferencia. Anales de la Cátedra Francisco Suárez*, 31: 15–39.

Delaney, Paul (2008). 'A discourse on nomadism: Travellers and Irish writing', in Borbála Faragó and Moynagh Sullivan (eds), *Facing the Other: Interdisciplinary Studies on Race, Gender and Social Justice in Ireland.* Newcastle: Cambridge Scholars Publishing, 232–43.

Delanty, Gerard (1996). 'Beyond the nation-state: National identity and citizenship in a multicultural society – a response to Rex', *Sociological Research Online* 1.3: n.p.

—— (1999). 'Die transformation nationaler identität und die kulturelle ambivalenz Europäischer identität: Demokratische identifikation in einem postnationalen Europa', in Reinhold Viehoff and Rien T. Segers (eds), *Kultur, Identität, Europa : Über die Schwierigkeiten und Möglichkeiten einer Konstrktion*. Frankfurt: Suhrkamp, 267–88.

Deparle, Jason (2008). 'Born Irish, but with illegal parents', *New York Times*, 25 February.

Egger, Sabine and John McDonagh (eds) (2011). *Polish-Irish Encounters in the Old and New Europe*. Oxford, Bern, and New York: Peter Lang.

Fanning, Bryan (2002). *Racism and Social Change in the Republic of Ireland*. Manchester: Manchester University Press.

—— (2009). *New Guests of the Irish Nation*. Dublin: Irish Academic Press.

—— (ed.) (2007). *Immigration and Social Change in the Republic of Ireland*. Manchester: Manchester University Press.

Fanning, Bryan and Ronaldo Munck (eds) (2007). *Translocations. The Irish Migration, Race and Social Transformation Review* 2.1.

Faragó, Borbála (2008). '"I am the place in which things happen": Invisible immigrant women poets of Ireland', in Patricia Coughlan and Tina O'Toole (eds), *Irish Literature: Feminist Perspectives*. Dublin: Carysfort, 145–66.

Faragó, Borbála and Moynagh Sullivan (eds) (2008). *Facing the Other: Interdisciplinary Studies on Race, Gender, and Social Justice in Ireland*. Newcastle: Cambridge Scholars Publishing.

Feldman, Alice and Anne Mulhall (2012). 'Towing the line: Migrant women writers and the space of Irish writing', in Piaras Mac Éinrí and Tina O'Toole (eds), *Éire Ireland. Special Issue: New Approaches to Irish Migration* 47.1/2: 201–20.

Friberg-Harnesk, Hedda, Gerald Porter, and Joakim Wrethed (eds) (2011). *Beyond Ireland: Encounters Across Cultures*. Oxford, Bern, and New York: Peter Lang.

Fricker, Karen and Ronit Lentin (eds) (2007). *Performing Global Networks*. Cambridge: Cambridge Scholars Publishing.

Fulford, Sarah (2002). *Gendered Spaces in Contemporary Irish Poetry*. Oxford, Bern, and New York: Peter Lang.

Garner, Steve (2004). *Racism in the Irish Experience*. London: Pluto.

—— (2011). 'Babies, bodies and entitlement: Gendered aspects of access to citizenship in the Republic of Ireland,' *Parliamentary Affairs* 60.3: 437–51.

Gibbons, Luke (2002). 'The global cure? History, therapy and the Celtic Tiger', in Peadar Kirby, Luke Gibbons, and Michael Cronin (eds), *Reinventing Ireland: Culture, Society and the Global Economy*. London and Sterling: Pluto, 89–107.

González Arias, Luz Mar, Marisol Morales Ladrón, and Asier Altuna García de Salazar (2010). 'The new Irish: Towards a multicultural literature in Ireland?', in David Clark and Rubén Jarazo Álvarez (eds), *In the Wake of the Tiger: Irish Studies in the Twentieth-First Century*. Oleiros: Netbiblo, 157–82.

Goodman, James (2002). 'Nationalism and globalism: Social movement responses,' *The International Scope Review* 4.8: 1–17.

Graham, Colin (2001). *Deconstructing Ireland: Identity, Theory, Culture*. Edinburgh: Edinburgh University Press.

Hall, Stuart (1997) [1996]. 'Who needs identity?', in Stuart Hall and Paul du Gay (eds), *Questions of Cultural Identity*. London: Sage, 1–18.

—— (2000). 'Conclusion: The multi-cultural question', in Barnor Hesse (ed.), *Un/Settled Multiculturalism. Diasporas, Entanglements, Transruptions*. London: Zed Books, 209–41.

Harte, Liam (2009). *The Literature of the Irish in Britain: Autobiography and Memoir, 1725–2001*. Basingstoke: Palgrave Macmillan.

Hickman, Mary J. (2007). 'Immigration and monocultural (re)imaginings in Ireland and Britain', *Translocations. The Irish Migration, Race and Social Transformation Review* 2.1: 12–25.

Higgins, Michael D. (2012a). 'Why Ireland is succeeding', *Think Ireland Inc.*, 17 May: n.p. www.thinkirelandinc.com/why-ireland-is-succeeding/. Accessed on 30 May 2012.

—— (2012b). 'Remarks by President Michael D. Higgins at the presentation of the Irish PEN Award for Literature to Joseph O'Connor', *Irish Pen (An Association for Irish Writers)*, 14 February: n.p. www.irishpen.com. Accessed on 19 June 2012.

James, Paul (1999). 'Beyond a postnationalist imaginary: Grounding an alternative ethic', *Arena*: n.p. www.findarticles.com/p/articles/mi_7043/is_14/ai_n28759280/?tag=content;col1. Accessed on 30 April 2012.

—— (2002) 'Principles of solidarity: Beyond a postnational imaginary', in James Goodman (ed.), *Protest and Globalisation: Prospects for Transnational Solidarity*. Sydney: Pluto, 3–18.

—— (2006). *Globalism, Nationalism, Tribalism: Bringing Theory Back In*. London: Sage.

Kearney, A.T. (2003). 'Measuring globalization: Who's up, who's down?', *Foreign Policy*, 1 February, 60–72.

Kearney, Richard (1997). *Postnationalist Ireland: Politics, Culture, Philosophy*. London: Routledge.

Kiberd, Declan (2001). 'Strangers in their country: Multi-culturalism in Ireland', in Edna Longley and Declan Kiberd, *Multi-Culturalism: The View from the Two Irelands*. Cork: Cork University Press in association with The Centre for Cross Border Studies, Armagh, 45–74.

—— (2005). *The Irish Writer and the World*. Cambridge: Cambridge University Press.

King, Jason (2005a). 'Interculturalism and Irish theatre: The portrayal of immigrants on the Irish stage', *Irish Review* 33: 23–39.

—— (2005b). 'Black Saint Patrick: Irish interculturalism in theoretical perspective and theatre practice', in Ondrej Pilný and Clare Wallace (eds), *Global Ireland: Irish Literatures for the New Millennium*. Prague: Litteraria Pragensia, 45–57.

—— (2008). 'Porous nation: from Ireland's "haemorrhage" to immigrant inundation', in Ronit Lentin (ed.), *The Expanding Nation: Towards a Multi-Ethnic Ireland*. Vol. I. Dublin: MPhil in Ethnic and Racial Studies, Department of Sociology, Trinity College Dublin, 49–54.

King, Jason and Tina O'Toole (eds) (2012). *The Irish Review. Special Issue: Memoir, Memory and Migration in Irish Culture* 44.

Kuhling, Carmen and Kieran Keohane (2007). *Cosmopolitanism Ireland: Globalization and Quality of Life*. London: Pluto.

Lanters, José (2005). '"Cobwebs on your walls": The state of the debate about globalisation and Irish drama', in Ondrej Pilný and Clare Wallace (eds), *Global Ireland: Irish Literatures for the New Millennium*. Prague: Litteraria Pragensia, 33–44.

—— (2008). *The 'Tinkers' in Irish Literature*. Dublin: Irish Academic Press.

Lentin, Ronit (2001a). 'Responding to the racialisation of Irishness: Disavowed multiculturalism and its discontents', *Sociological Research Online* 5.4: n.p.

—— (2001b). 'Pregnant silence: (En)gendering Ireland's asylum space', *Patterns of Prejudice* 37.3: 301–22.

—— (2002). 'Anti-racist responses to the racialisation of Irishness: Disavowed multiculturalism and its discontents', in Ronit Lentin and Robbie McVeigh (eds), *Racism and Anti-Racism in Ireland*. Belfast: Beyond the Pale, 226–39.

—— (ed.) (2008). *The Expanding Nation: Towards a Multi-Ethnic Ireland*. Vol. I. Dublin: MPhil in Ethnic and Racial Studies, Department of Sociology, Trinity College Dublin.

Lentin, Ronit and Robbie McVeigh (eds) (2002). *Racism and Anti-Racism in Ireland*. Belfast: Beyond the Pale.

—— (2006). *After Optimism? Ireland, Racism and Globalisation*. Dublin: Metro Éireann.

Longley, Edna (2001). 'Multi-culturalism and Northern Ireland: Making differences fruitful', in Edna Longley and Declan Kiberd, *Multi-Culturalism: The View from the Two Irelands*. Cork: Cork University Press in association with The Centre for Cross Border Studies, Armagh, 1–44.

Mac Cormaic, Ruadhán (2007). 'Signs of new vitality in how film and drama treat immigrants', *Irish Times*, 23 May. www.irishtimes.com/focus/gageby/changingplaces/articles/230507_article.html. Accessed on 13 May 2011.

Mac Éinrí, Piaras and Tina O'Toole (eds) (2012). *Éire Ireland. Special Issue: New Approaches to Irish Migration* 47.1/2.

Mac Éinrí, Piaras and Allen White (2008). 'Immigration into the Republic of Ireland: A bibliography of recent research', *Irish Geography* 41.2: 151–79.

Mac Gréil, Micheál (2011). *Pluralism and Diversity in Ireland: Prejudice and Related Issues in Early Twentieth-Century Ireland*. Dublin: Columba.

McAleese, Mary (2001). 'Foreword', in Edna Longley and Declan Kiberd, *Multi-Culturalism: The View from the Two Irelands*. Cork: Cork University Press in association with The Centre for Cross Border Studies, Armagh, vii–ix.

McIvor, Charlotte (2011). 'Staging the "new Irish": Interculturalism and the future of the post-Celtic Tiger Irish theatre', *Modern Drama* 54.3: 310–32.

McVeigh, Robbie (2008). 'Is sectarianism racism? The implications of sectarian division for multiethnicity in Ireland', in Ronit Lentin (ed.), *The Expanding Nation: Towards a Multi-Ethnic Ireland*. Vol. I. Dublin: Trinity College Dublin, 16–20.

Meaney, Gerardine (2010). *Gender, Ireland, and Cultural Change: Race, Sex, and Nation*. Abingdon and New York: Routledge.

O'Donnell, Katherine (2007). 'St Patrick's Day expulsions: Race and homophobia in New York's parade', in Wanda Balzano, Anne Mulhall, and Moynagh Sullivan (eds), *Irish Postmodernisms and Popular Culture*. New York: Palgrave Macmillan, 128–40.

Olszewska, Kinga (2008). 'The limits of post-nationalism: The works of John Banville and Mary O'Malley', *Nordic Irish Studies* 7: 135–46.

O'Toole, Fintan (1997). *The Ex-Isle of Erin: Images of a Global Ireland*. Dublin: New Island.

—— (2010). *Enough is Enough: How to Build a New Republic*. London: Faber & Faber.

Persson, Ake (2011). 'Recalibrating the mind: Globalization, viticulture, wine-tasting and change in Kate O'Riordan's *The Memory Stones*', in Hedda Friberg-Harnesk, Gerald Porter, and Joakim Wrethed (eds), *Beyond Ireland: Encounters Across Cultures*. Oxford, Bern, and New York: Peter Lang, 53–84.

Pitcher, Ben (2009). *The Politics of Multiculturalism*. Basingstoke: Palgrave Macmillan.

Reddy, Maureen T. (2007). 'Reading and writing race in Ireland: Roddy Doyle and *Metro Éireann*', in Wanda Balzano, Anne Mulhall, and Moynagh Sullivan (eds), *Irish Postmodernisms and Popular Culture: The Politics of Multiculturalism*. New York: Palgrave Macmillan, 15–25.

Rex, John (2008). 'National and transnational migrant communities: A European problem', in Ronit Lentin (ed.), *The Expanding Nation: Towards a Multi-ethnic Ireland*. Vol. I. Dublin: MPhil in Ethnic and Racial Studies, Department of Sociology, Trinity College Dublin, 1–7.

Richardson, Sally (2005). 'Multiculturalism is nothing new', *The Irish Democrat*, 19 May.

Salis, Loredana (2010). *Stage Migrants: Representations of the Migrant Other in Modern Irish Drama*. Newcastle upon Tyne: Cambridge Scholars Publishing.

Sen, Amartya (2007) [2006]. *Identity and Violence: The Illusion of Destiny*. London: Penguin.

Sinha, Shalini (2008). 'The right to Irishness: Implications of ethnicity, nation and State towards a truly multi-ethnic Ireland', in Ronit Lentin (ed.), *The Expanding Nation: Towards a Multi-Ethnic Ireland*. Vol. I. Dublin: MPhil in Ethnic and Racial Studies, Department of Sociology, Trinity College Dublin, 21–5.

Taylor, Charles (1994). *The Politics of Recognition*, in David T. Goldberg (ed.), *Multiculturalism: A Critical Reader*. Oxford: Blackwell, 75–106.

Titley, Gavan, Aphra Kerr, and Rebecca King O'Rían (2010). *Broadcasting in the New Ireland: Mapping Cultural Diversity*. Maynooth: National University of Ireland.

Tucker, Amanda (2010). '"Our story is everywhere": Colum McCann and Irish multiculturalism', *Irish University Review* 40.2: 107–28.

Villar-Argáiz, Pilar (2010). Private correspondence with Paula Meehan, 28 May.

—— (2012). 'Poetry as a "humane enterprise": Interview with Eavan Boland on the occasion of the 50th anniversary of her literary career', *Estudios Irlandeses: Spanish Journal of Irish Studies* 7: 113–20.

Walter, Bronwen (2011). 'Whiteness and diasporic Irishness: Nation, gender and class', *Journal of Ethnic and Migration Studies* 37:9: 1295–312.

Watson, C.W. (2000). *Multiculturalism*. Buckingham: Open University Press.

Weedon, Chris (2004). *Identity and Culture: Narratives of Difference and Belonging*. Maidenhead: Open University Press.

Yau, Nicola (2007). 'Celtic Tiger, hidden dragon: Exploring identity among second generation Chinese in Ireland', *Translocations. The Irish Migration, Race and Social Transformation Review* 2.1: 48–69.

Zamorano Llena, Carmen (2010). 'Glocal identities in a postnationalist Ireland as reflected through contemporary Irish poetry', in Irene Gilsenan Nordin and Carmen Zamorano Llena (eds), *Redefinitions of Irish Identity: A Postnationalist Approach*. Oxford, Bern, and New York: Peter Lang, 141–58.

—— (2011). 'Multiculturalism and the Dark Underbelly of the Celtic Tiger: Redefinitions of Irishness in Contemporary Ireland', in Hedda Friberg-Harnesk, Gerald Porter, and Joakim Wrethed (eds), *Beyond Ireland: Encounters Across Cultures*. Oxford, Bern and New York: Peter Lang, 85–100.

PART I

Irish multiculturalisms: obstacles and challenges

2

White Irish-born male playwrights and the immigrant experience onstage

Charlotte McIvor

Donal O'Kelly's *Asylum! Asylum!* premiered in 1994 on the Abbey Theatre's Peacock stage and was the first play by an Irish-born playwright to directly address the issue of racism and immigration in Celtic Tiger Ireland. O'Kelly represented the vanguard of a group of white Irish-born male playwrights including Charlie O'Neill, Declan Gorman, Dermot Bolger, Roddy Doyle, Jim O'Hanlon, Paul Meade, and Paul Kennedy who would deal with these issues head-on in their work throughout the 1990s and 2000s. In the context of an Irish theatre scene criticised by Jason King and George Seremba among others for being largely silent about social change related to immigration (King, 2005: 121; 2007: 41–2), the work of these men is both extremely important and crucially limited. As Patrick Lonergan argues, 'it is important not to exaggerate the value of white middle-class writers producing plays for white middle-class audiences about the marginalization of Ireland's most recent immigrants' (2004: 150). Lonergan implies that the perspectives of white Irish-born authors on these issues ultimately matter less than possible contributions by new immigrant or minority authors. How then is whiteness and class negotiated in plays on immigration by white Irish-born playwrights? To whom are these works addressed? How is it in conversation with the work of minority theatre artists in Ireland such as Bisi Adigun, George Seremba, Ursula Rani Sarma, Kunle Animashaun, and others? Does this work have a political agenda and how does it build on previous movements for social change within the Irish theatre, particularly the emergence of community arts in the late 1970s?

This chapter examines the work of select white Irish-born male playwrights who have engaged explicitly and repeatedly with questions of immigration, race, and ethnicity in their work. It focuses on the work of Donal O'Kelly, Declan Gorman, and Charlie O'Neill due to their engagement with these themes in relationship to their participation in the Irish community arts movement. In analysing these three authors, it situates their careers as playwrights in terms of the community arts movement's commitment to more equal access to art making. Their work in community arts provides potential models and infra-structures for engaging immigrant and minority individuals in Ireland as the creators – as well as subjects – of new works about their experiences. Their work is then located in the context of other treatments of these themes by white Irish-born male playwrights. While O'Kelly, O'Neill, and Gorman remain the sole identified authors of many of the plays referenced here, their broader ongoing efforts in the Irish arts scene have been continually focused towards a democra-tisation of access to art making for both Irish-born and immigrant members of Irish society, regardless of race, ethnicity or class.

The origins of Irish community arts can be traced to the late 1970s (Fitzgerald, 2004: 1). This diverse area of practice, including theatre, music, dance, circus, street performance, and multidisciplinary fine and visual arts projects emerged out of the most violent period of the Troubles and a background of poverty, drug use, and social exclusion on the island of Ireland as a whole. The socially engaged field of community arts is a vital precursor to contemporary Irish the-atre focused on immigration and the lives of minority individuals. In a 2003 forum on the history of community arts, Mowbray Bates grouped those work-ing in community arts into several specific categories:

> People who would be looking to push the boundaries of art, liberating art from museums and theatre spaces. Then there would be the direction of political ac-tivism and community development, the use of art in a creative way to further political campaigns, specific single issues. And I suppose then there would be people who would want to look at democratizing culture. (Bates *et al.*, 2004: 11)

The introduction of the arts into neighbourhood and non-specialist settings aimed to revitalise areas, provide a setting for dialogue and interaction between communities in conflict (at this time, perceived as Catholics and Protestants primarily), give a voice to disenfranchised individuals in inner-city neigh-bourhoods struggling with drug abuse and poverty, increase access to and participation in the arts, and even provide training in some practical job skills.

In the context of the Dublin theatre scene, as well as other regional centres such as Waterford and Galway, the range of activity in community arts practice from the late 1970s onward was matched by experimentation with performance in the streets and fringe theatre spaces. This work involved artists such as Donal O'Kelly, Charlie O'Neill, Declan Gorman, Raymond Keane, Jim and Peter Sheridan, Thom 'The Dice Man' McGinty, Annie Kilmartin, Fiona Nolan, and many others who were also participants in the community arts and social pro-test movements at the time (Fitzgerald, 2004: 7–29; 215–44). As Charlie O'Neill explained in an interview, the artists' performance experiments took the form of comedy sketches, burlesque plays, cabarets, political demonstrations, and street performances; and addressed subjects such as nuclear proliferation, poverty, unemployment, and women's rights (McIvor, 2009b).

In 1993, Donal O'Kelly and Charlie O'Neill were among the founders of Calypso Productions, a company dedicated to producing 'new issue-based writing for theatre' and promoting 'an awareness of social issues through the production of highly creative, innovative and new work for theatre' (Calypso Productions, 1999; see section 'Objectives'). Calypso's focus immediately transcended the borders of the Irish nation, with early productions such as O'Kelly's *Trickledown Town* (1994), exploring 'the effects international debt and structural adjustment programmes have on Third World countries' (*ibid.*; see section 'Productions'). By 1997, three years after the premiere of O'Kelly's *Asylum! Asylum!* at the Peacock, Calypso started producing plays and performance events dramatising issues related to immigration and the particular challenges of asylum-seekers and refugees. Their first offering was *Féile Fáilte*, a parade performance spectacle described thus:

> A theatrical parade from Temple Bar to the garden of the Civic Offices at Wood Quay in Dublin. We aimed to draw attention to the plight of refugees and to celebrate diversity in Ireland. A larger-than-life sized puppet of the Celtic Tiger, designed and built by Theatre of Fire, conveyed the exclusive Ireland prospering at the expense of the less well-off and marginalised. At the Civic Offices a dramatic finale included music from different cultures, film, fire-sculptures and firework displays. (*Ibid.*)

This performance highlights the intersection of economic justice issues with concerns over the mistreatment of refugees in Ireland in Calypso's work. By linking the issue of economics to their critical treatment of the asylum process, Calypso suggests that a 'celebration of diversity' in Ireland could only be accomplished through a rigorous critique of the financial system that undergirds the social relations of individuals, such as between majority and minority members of Irish society. They also established working relationships with emerging minority theatre artists like Bisi Adigun, who would go on to found Ireland's first African-Irish theatre company, Arambe Productions, in 2004.

While initially focused on the professional production of plays, Calypso eventually also founded Tower of Babel, which was 'an intercultural youth theatre, drama and film project which focuse[d] on the personal and professional development of young people aged 14–21 years enabling them to contribute to the creative industry in Ireland, pass on their knowledge to younger members and become arts facilitators, actors, performers, or writers' (Calypso Productions, 2008). By focusing on the professionalisation of young people, Tower of Babel asserted that participants in the programme would develop transferable skills to go out and challenge representations of 'Irishness' by creating art from the perspective of their diverse backgrounds and experiences. Thus, Calypso's remit focused not only on producing plays about immigrant and minority communities but creating the conditions for the development of minority artists as creators in their own right. Furthermore, in addition to his work founding Calypso, and writing the landmark pieces *Hurl* (performed by Barabbas in 2003) and *Dodgems* (performed by Cois Céim Dance Theatre in 2007), Charlie O'Neill would go on to serve as a consultant for the Fatima Mansions urban regeneration project, focusing again particularly on the role of arts and culture as a tool for community empowerment and social change in this primarily class-based context.[1]

In 1997, Declan Gorman and Declan Mallon co-founded Drogheda-based Upstate Theatre Project. Throughout Upstate's history, Gorman and Mallon have divided their work between producing professional work and leading community drama projects centred around group devising of new plays. Upstate's location in Drogheda – adjacent to the border counties of Louth, Monaghan, and Cavan – led to consistent funding throughout the years from the EU Peace and Reconciliation Programme. Their early work thus frequently focused on the legacy of the Troubles and the particular politics of this border region.

In 2007 Upstate Theatre Project launched the Louth International Theatre Project, which aimed to offer 'legally resident migrants an opportunity to be involved in the planning and delivery of a community-based drama project' and '[p]rovide a platform for Irish citizens and new migrants to participate hands-on in an imaginative and creative arts process within their local area' (Hayes, 2008: 3). This project built on Upstate's 2002 collaboration with Droichead Youth Theatre and a group of youths seeking asylum in Ireland and housed at the nearby Mosney Accommodation Centre, which is run by the Department of Justice, Equality, and Law Reform. They also collaborated with Jane Spearman, who had been working at Mosney as artist in residence, and through this connection ultimately brought together fifteen young people from Mosney and another fifteen from the Droichead Youth Theatre (McIvor, 2009c).[2] This resulted in a full production of an original murder-mystery play, *Steps*, which featured an interracial expectant couple, Nigerian Joseph and Irish Mary, on the run after Mary embezzled money from her bank job. Declan Gorman describes the collaborators in this project as 'from the four continents, with us making up the fifth' and including Nigerian, South African, Congolese, South American, and Russian individuals among others (*ibid.*).

Gorman's *At Peace*, professionally produced by Upstate, would follow in 2007 and featured a cast of seven Irish, African, and Eastern European actors as his story's focus shifted to the lives of new immigrants living in a border town after the Good Friday Peace Agreement. This play marked a decisive transition in the company's work from a focus on the aftermath of the Troubles to a more exclusive spotlight on cultural diversity in Ireland today. *At Peace* was presented in three languages: English, Yoruban, and Latvian, made possible through Gorman's collaboration with Bisi Adigun and Elita Baltaiskalna on the translations. This is to date the only play featuring minority characters to be presented with such large sections of dialogue in languages other than English, albeit with subtitles. *At Peace* thus addressed Latvian- and Yoruban-speaking individuals of Latvian and Nigerian descent as audience members, and not just subjects of the work. These audience members who were able to follow either language as well as English were thus able to experience a fuller version of the play text in performance than even Gorman, the Irish-born, English-speaking playwright. That being said, the linguistic complexity of the text made it impossible for Upstate to cast from within Ireland or even Britain. As a touring report on *At Peace* states, 'as there are very few registered actors in these regions from Nigeria or Latvia (especially any who can speak their native dialect and English fluently) we had to do an extensive search of Latvia, Britain and Nigeria to cast the play' (Upstate Theatre Project, 2007: 6). These practical difficulties in casting *At Peace* demonstrated that transferring the stories of immigrant lives onto the stage may occasionally exceed the present resources of the Irish theatre community. The grassroots mobilisation possible through community arts outreach programmes like Louth International Theatre Project or Tower of Babel is therefore vital for reaching and training the minority theatre artists of the future.

Prior to Upstate's recent shift in focus, Calypso's work on immigration and cultural diversity in the late 1990s and the early to mid-2000s represented the epicentre of this work in the Irish theatre scene at large. Yet, by the early 2000s, more new plays on these themes had begun to appear, still authored predominantly by 'white middle-class' male 'authors producing plays for white middle-class audiences' (Lonergan, 2004: 150) and mounted by companies including Druid Theatre, Fishamble: The New Play Company, and Storytellers Theatre. According to Lonergan, several of these works borrow 'from the cinematic model of the (usually black) boyfriend who is brought home for dinner to prove to a conservative father-figure (or the audience?) that he is really "just like us"' (Lonergan, 2009: 13). Social acceptance or integration of minority characters within Irish society is thus coded as sexual or romantic integration. Plays in this subgenre include Roddy Doyle's *Guess Who's Coming for the Dinner* (performed by Calypso Productions in 2001), Ken Harmon's *Done Up Like A Kipper* (by the Abbey Theatre, 2002), Jim O'Hanlon's *Buddhist of Castleknock* (by Fishamble, 2002),[3] Doyle and Bisi Adigun's *The Playboy of the Western World: A New Version* (by Abbey Theatre, 2007 and 2008), and Paul Kennedy's *Put Out the Light* (by New Theatre, 2010). The African male protagonists featured at the centre of most of these particular works frequently play on stereotypes of black masculinity, particularly sexuality, as potentially violent and threatening to white males.

Outside of the romance genre, however, there exists a more varied representation of intersections between race, ethnicity, and class in the work of this particular cadre of white Irish-born male playwrights. Donal O'Kelly's *Asylum! Asylum!* critiqued racism in the Irish legal system vis-à-vis a featured romance between a Ugandan man and a white Irish-born woman, but moved beyond romance as the centre of the plot. Brian Singleton (2011: 142) elaborates that 'O'Kelly's rare use of a realist form forces Irish audiences to confront a reality and does not allow the porous nature of allegory to permit an escape route from the unpalatable truths of society'. O'Kelly himself endorses this approximation of his approach: 'I wanted *Asylum! Asylum!* on within the Abbey building because I thought this [the Irish increase in asylum-seekers and their treatment] was a national question … That was why it was written in quite a straight-forward manner' (McIvor, 2009a). Coupled with the presentation of the play itself, O'Kelly arranged with then Artistic Director Patrick Mason to have tables with representatives from Amnesty International and the Irish Refugee Council among others in the lobby of the theatre for every performance, a move he calls 'a first in the National Theatre, as far as I know' (*ibid.*). No other play regarding immigration and racism in Ireland with such a directly political objective or approach to audience engagement has been staged at the Abbey since.

In another thematic cluster, Donal O'Kelly's dance theatre-piece *Farawayan* (performed by Calypso Productions in 1998), Paul Meade's *Mushroom* (by Storytellers Theatre, 2007), Dermot Bolger's *The Townlands of Brazil* (by Axis Ballymun, 2006), and Upstate Theatre Project's community drama piece *Journey from Babel* (2009), all place Celtic Tiger immigration in the context of Irish histories of emigration and interactions with other immigrants over time within Ireland and beyond. Working with an interracial cast, including Arambe's Bisi Adigun, *Farawayan* was 'not specifically set in any one place' and 'this largely non-verbal piece echoed the situation for refugees and asylum seekers in Ireland in the 1990s and Ireland's experience of emigration over many years' (Irish Playography, 2012). Bolger's *The Townlands of Brazil* focused on the forced emigration of Eileen, a young, unmarried, pregnant Irish-born woman, to 1960s London from the area on which the Ballymun Tower Block would be built in 1963. This event is juxtaposed with the story of the relationship between Eileen's son, Matthew, and a young Polish worker named Monika, who picks mushrooms, in 2006. In *Farawayan* and *The Townlands of Brazil*, therefore, Irish emigration is an event of the past, while immigration features as the contemporary event. While immigration into Ireland indeed reached record levels in the 1990s and early 2000s, O'Kelly and Bolger's approach to divide this history into a simple past and present maintains the fiction that minorities did not exist in Ireland prior to the onset of the Celtic Tiger. Growing communities of non-Irish-born immigrants have certainly diversified the racial and ethnic profile of the Irish population, but they join pre-existing minority ethnic groups identified by Ronit Lentin (2002: 227) as 'Travellers, Jews, Black-Irish people' among others such as the Chinese, who have lived in Ireland in small numbers since the 1950s (Ireland Expo, 2010; see section 'Chinese Community in Ireland'). Apart from the hyper-visible itinerant indigenous Traveller community, these groups 'have been largely invisible in the Irish "imagined community"' (Lentin, 2002: 227). Therefore, Ronit Lentin and Robbie McVeigh (2002: 21) emphasise that indeed 'Ireland was never the monoculture it told itself it was'.

Irish emigrant histories have been consistently evoked as injunctions for the Irish-born majority to treat immigrants more graciously outside the theatre as well. In *Migration Nation,* the Irish government's first official policy document on integration, the former Minister for Integration Conor Lenihan argues that:

> In purely historical terms it is not an exaggeration to state that the Irish identity is as much a product of those who left our shores as those who stayed at home … As our President Mary McAleese has said:
> *'We have a recent memory of the loneliness, the sense of failure evoked by our inability to provide for our own people and the courage it took to start a new life far from home.'*
> This Ministerial Statement of Policy is predicated on the idea that Ireland has a unique moral, intellectual and practical capability to adapt to the experience of inward migration. (Original emphasis; Office of the Minister for Integration, 2008: 67)

Lenihan's claim on histories of Irish emigration as the direct inspiration for the Ministerial Statement of Policy on integration and diversity decisively links the history of Irish emigrants to recent immigrants in Ireland. This statement suggests that a refusal to recognise newcomers within Irish society would be a refusal to recognise the history of the Irish nation itself. The experience of past (and present) Irish emigrants therefore becomes projected onto contemporary immigrants. Yet, a view of immigrants as first and foremost a projection of past Irish selves sublimates the specificity of individuals' experiences and obscures histories of movement in and out of Ireland prior to the onset of the Celtic Tiger.

In contrast to O'Kelly and Bolger's more partial view of Irish history, Paul Meade's *Mushroom* and Upstate's *Journey from Babel* played with narrative form to tell the interlocking stories of multiple generations. This tactic emphasised the movement of emigrants and immigrants to Ireland in and out of the island well before the 1990s. Meade and Upstate challenged theories of sudden social change by taking a longer view of social diversity in Ireland and thus granting deeper ownership of 'Irishness' to minority individuals living in the Irish nation.

In Meade's *Mushroom*, Martin, the son of a Romanian mother and Irish father, returns to Bucharest to get to know his uncle, Radu, and learn about his past while the interrelationships between a group of Polish and Romanians living in County Monaghan working as mushroom pickers forms the other major sub-plot. The play was 'devised by the playwright, with director Liam Halligan and the cast of six – three Romanian, two Polish, one Irish' (Meany, 2007: 46). Meade also conducted field research with migrant groups in Monaghan (Keating, 2007: 12). Meade's field research and devising process are techniques common to community arts processes, and while he remains the sole named playwright, the traces of this process remain in the work. Declan Burke argued that Meade's focus on personal experiences prevented *Mushroom* from becoming a 'state-of-the-nation polemic' and touted this as a selling point of the production (Burke, 2007). Burke implies here that Meade separates the personal from the political (individual's stories v. the state of the nation) in *Mushroom* but the play in fact makes purposely clear their deep entanglement. The play's frequent narrator, Andrzej, a Polish worker in his forties, tells the audience that

> Everyone asks me, 'You come here to work? Things are not so good for you back home? Will you stay? Do you have family?' They look at me they see a Polishman. I look at them and I think, I have worked all over the world, I fixed roofs in Italy, I built saunas in Germany, I sold kebabs by the Black Sea, I saw the Pyramids, I spoke to the oracle at Delphi, I … and you say, 'Good man yourself'. What do you think I am doing here? A job? I can get a job anywhere. I came because … but they don't understand. I came … I came because of Newgrange. (Meade, 2007: 3–4)

Andrzej positions himself here as a free agent, but his travels are enabled by shifts in each nation's labour market. The questions from Irish-born residents mark their understanding of the shifting landscape for migrant workers in Celtic Tiger Ireland, but Andrzej's narration of his personal reasons for coming to Ireland asserts his own agency in constrained circumstances. Workplace rights and sexual exploitation by employers (even when consensual) surface as major themes throughout the play although they are expressed at the level of individual rather than collective struggle. *Mushroom* thus critiques the instability and exploitation of the Irish labour market for migrant workers through relating migrants' personal stories of love, loss, and new beginnings or temporary stop-overs in Ireland.

Upstate's *Journey from Babel* was an ambitious site-specific piece devised by Irish, French, German, Austrian, Mexican, English, and North American residents of Drogheda during 2008 and 2009 with the guidance of Declan Gorman and Declan Mallon.[4] *Journey from Babel* took on multiple themes: immigration, emigration, mounting unemployment as the Celtic Tiger wound down, the sex industry, labour issues, and discrimination against pregnant female immigrants in the lead-up to the Citizenship Referendum, among other issues. Like *Farawayan*, the focus of the piece was frequently transnational with references made to the New York Triangle Shirtwaist Factory Fire in 1909 that claimed the lives of 146 workers and the deaths of 23 Chinese cockle-shell pickers in Lancashire's Morecambe Bay (Louth International Theatre Project, 2009: 15–17). Yet, the long-standing ethnic diversity of Ireland and previous histories of inward migration were also referenced in a professor's address to his class:

> Around the start of the eighteenth century, a large number of continental refugees were settled in Ireland with official help … In 1685, the main body of Huguenot refugees began to arrive, mostly from the countryside around the city of La Rochelle. Large Huguenot settlements were established in Portarlington, Youghal, Cork, Dublin, Waterford and Lisburn … In the course of time, they became thoroughly absorbed into Irish society through intermarriage, and names such as Boucicault, Le Fanu and Trench are still familiar in Ireland today. (16)

By interweaving this historical background with contemporary vignettes featuring Irish-born and immigrant or minority characters, as well as characters from outside Ireland, *Journey from Babel* mapped a complex history of Ireland's relationship in and to the world. The deep historical specificity of passages like the one above ensured that comparisons between Ireland and elsewhere were specific instead of broad. This piece thus consistently avoided simple binaries of 'past v. present' or the positioning of individual characters as 'inside v. outside' of Irish culture.

Through projects like *Journey from Babel*, Upstate's use of theatre to facilitate interaction between members of diverse racial and ethnic backgrounds living in Drogheda goes beyond seeking to educate individual participants and audiences on matters of racism and/or diversity. They rather utilise community arts as a tool through which to activate individual voices vis-à-vis ensemble effort. In this way, Upstate's work focuses on not only incubating future theatre artists, regardless of racial or ethnic background, but actively challenging who can be seen as an (Irish) artist in the first place. Their most recent 'intercultural arts participation project' (Upstate Theatre Project, 2012a), *The Mango Tree*, focuses on feelings of disconnection and isolation shared amongst inhabitants of a small town, perhaps one like Drogheda itself. While an African setting is mentioned by one character during the play in a story about their life, racial and ethnic difference or discrimination is not explicitly addressed (Upstate Theatre Project, 2012b: 7). Upstate's concerted outreach to minority communities since 2002 identifies individuals among these groups as marginalised and thus in particular need of access to cultural resources. However, their process working with Irish-born and minority participants does not pigeonhole these mixed groups into only telling stories about race, ethnicity, racism or displacement.

Upstate's approach with the Louth International Theatre Project has been similar to the company's community drama work done through funding from the EU Peace and Reconciliation Programme. In this earlier work, the objective was not to directly confront 'difference' as a category of experience or dramatise the history of conflict between Catholics and Protestants but rather use the drama process as an opportunity to tell new stories with diverse participants. On this point, Gorman elaborates:

> Is it storytelling, or is it actually concentrating on the politics? It's a little bit of the politics, but it's mainly storytelling … [O]nce you get the people to come in the door, you know, they don't want to rehearse in the room what they were rehearsing outside of the room. They want to dream together, and imagine and make stories together. And the very fact that they're doing it together is a much greater guarantee that they are listening and learning about themselves and about the other cultures in the room. (McIvor, 2009c)

This approach makes theoretically possible the creation of characters who in Lonergan's words might happen to 'come from Poland, or Nigeria, or wherever it might be' as opposed to 'acting as an emblem that will remind audiences who … are presupposed to be white, wealthy and Irish-born' (Lonergan, 2009: 14).

Yet, pairing (white) Irish-born and minority participants in a devised theatre or community arts process does not ensure egalitarianism or mutual respect. Declan Gorman stages this risk in *At Peace*, which dramatises white Irish-born Mrs. Reilly's unintentionally ignorant treatment of Nigerian immigrant Ogunseyi, during a rehearsal for an intercultural group presentation in a local drum festival. Ogunseyi consents to performing an Egungun possession ritual dance for the group, an act he regards as a ritual and not merely a performance. After the conclusion of Ogunseyi's dance, Mrs. O'Reilly exclaims:

> Mrs. Reilly: Wonderful! (*To the woman beside her*) Lovely. I mean they're all so lovely … the Blacks, the way they can dance.
> *An embarrassing silence falls.*
> Ogunseyi: Mrs. Reilly. I am not … I cannot … I did not intend to perform the ritual for your amusement or the entertainment of the class, like some kind of circus monkey! The Egungun ritual is a Yoruba spiritual tradition to do with honouring the dead. I am sorry. I cannot continue this work.
>
> (Gorman, 2007: 32)

Mrs. O'Reilly's comment about the 'Blacks' and the 'lovely way they dance' disrespects Ogunseyi's presentation of the dance as a sacred ritual. She also evokes stereotypes concerning the dancing ability of individuals of African descent that recur in histories of American slavery and blackface minstrel performance in a transnational context.[5] Her assertion may be far from malicious but it does express an ignorance of the histories that presage this encounter between Ogunseyi and herself in the moment of performance and ritual incantation.

Gorman therefore draws attention to performance as a powerful and productive act capable not only of bringing this intercultural group of Irish-born, Latvian, Nigerian, and other participants in *At Peace* together, but also expressing their lived and material differences from one another. The delicacy and necessity of this negotiation at the level of the individual and beyond surfaces throughout the work of Gorman, O'Neill, and O'Kelly as they train their efforts on using theatre and performance to explore issues of immigration and cultural diversity. They work through not only the thematic focus of their own works but by also facilitating and supporting community arts projects with participants diversified by race, ethnicity, gender and/or class. As O'Neill remarked regarding the attempted intervention of himself, O'Kelly, and others, 'I think what didn't have its place before was stories about outsiders or stories about the clashes and the beautiful interactions that happened when things started to get mixed up' (McIvor, 2009b). The work of these three men does not ultimately seek to speak for an/Other but point towards theatre and performance as acts that demand diverse accounts, careful negotiation when 'things started to get mixed up', and the broadest possible opportunities for participation amongst Irish society at large.

Instead of waiting for the arrival of an unequivocally acclaimed minority Irish playwright (though there are many playwrights already to choose from including Ursula Rani Sarma and Bisi Adigun), it would perhaps be more useful to attend in more detail to the theatrical and performance archive of community arts work engaging racially and ethnically diverse individuals not only to analyse individual works (such as the early offerings of Tower of Babel or Upstate's community-devised pieces) but also to account for the methodology and processes used to create these works. Just as Gorman calls attention to the richness of Mrs. O'Reilly and Ogunseyi's encounter creating work together within the theatrical frame of *At Peace*, similarly Irish theatre and performance scholars must investigate theatrical processes involving minority, immigrant, and Irish-born participants, especially in the context of community arts. This will permit scholars to pay closer attention to the stories of 'ordinary' people, Irish-born or otherwise, as described in the moment of theatrical creation and intercultural negotiation. This approach might most decisively shift the conversation from representation *of* diversity to representation *through* diversity in the contemporary Irish arts.

Notes

1   In 1995, a group of residents in Fatima Mansions – a Dublin-area housing estate with high drug use and crime rates – formed Fatima Groups United and began planning to revitalise the area and address the roots of the social issues plaguing the community. This resulted in a rebuilding of the area as well as ongoing social programming including an extensive arts component. The perceived success of this project has led to several reports detailing its process. See Donohue and Dorman (2006) as well as O'Baoill (2011) for documentation of the arts-based plan for the area.
2   My gratitude to former Upstate Theatre Project Manager Paul Hayes for sharing this grant application and the touring report on *At Peace* with me in January 2009. I would also like to acknowledge Upstate Theatre Project's Declan Gorman and Declan Mallon and Storyteller Theatre's Liam Halligan, for sharing the other unpublished scripts cited in this chapter including *Mushroom*, *Journey from Babel*, and *The Mango Tree*.
3   However, in *Buddhist of Castleknock*, Rai – the romantic partner in question – is female and 'English, of African extraction' (O'Hanlon, 2007: 12).
4   I participated in this process from January to March and May to June in 2009 as a participant-observer.
5   See Sadiya Hartman's *Scenes of Subjection* (1997), which argues that performative spectacles including slave auctions and public dances were central sites of public consumption that legitimised the institution of slavery and lack of humanity of the enslaved in nineteenth-century America. Works including Eric Lott's *Love and Theft* (1995) and W.T. Lahmon's *Raising Cain* (2000) trace white appropriations of black performance from practices witnessed in the context of slavery for the popular genre of blackface minstrelsy, largely performed by white individuals in a transnational context.

References

Bates, Mowbray, Ollie Breslin and Annie Kilmartin *et al.* (2004). 'Historical Forum', in Sandy Fitzgerald (ed.), *An Outburst of Frankness: Community Arts in Ireland. A Reader*. Dublin: TASC (A Think Tank for Action on Social Change) at New Island, 7–25.

Burke, Declan (2007). '*Mushroom*', *Sunday Times*, 1 July. www.lexisnexis.com.sculib.scu.edu:80/hottopics/lnacademic/. Accessed on 29 November 2011.

Calypso Productions (1999). 'Objectives', 'Productions'. www.homepage.eircom.net/~calypso/about.html. Accessed on 6 December 2011.

—— (2008). 'Tower of Babel'. www.calypso.ie/education.html/. Accessed on 15 September 2008.

Donohue, Joe and Peter Dorman (2006). *Dream/Dare/Do: A Regeneration Learning Manual*. Dublin: Fatima Groups United.

Fitzgerald, Sandy (2004). *An Outburst of Frankness: Community Arts in Ireland. A Reader*, Dublin: TASC (A Think Tank for Action on Social Change) at New Island.

Gorman, Declan (2007). *At Peace*. Unpublished script.

Hartman, Sadiya (1997). *Scenes of Subjection: Terror, Slavery and Self-Making in Nineteenth-Century America*. Oxford: Oxford University Press.

Hayes, Paul (2008). *Upstate Theatre Project's Louth International Theatre Project: Office of the Minister of Integration, Application Form for Immigrant Integration Small Grant Scheme*. Unpublished report.

Ireland Expo (2010). 'Chinese Community in Ireland'. www.irelandexpo2010.com/the_ chinese_community_in_ireland. Accessed on 17 October 2010.

Irish Playography (Irish Theatre Institute) (2012). *Farawayan*. www.irishplayography.com/ play.aspx?playid=171. Accessed on 1 March 2012.

Keating, Sara (2007). 'The immigrants' inside story', *Irish Times*, 5 June: 12. www//0-www. lexisnexis.com.sculib.scu.edu:80/hottopics/lnacademic/. Accessed on 29 November 2011.

King, Jason (2005). 'Canadian, Irish and Ugandan Theatre links: An interview with George Seremba', *The Canadian Journal of Irish Studies* 31.1: 117–21.

—— (2007). 'Black St. Patrick revisited: Calypso's 'Tower of Babel' and culture Ireland as global networks', in Karen Fricker and Ronit Lentin (eds), *Performing Global Networks*. Cambridge: Cambridge Scholars Publishing, 38–51.

Lahmon, W.T. (2000). *Raising Cain: Blackface Performance from Jim Crow to Hip Hop*, Harvard: Harvard University Press.

Lentin, Ronit (2002). 'Anti-racist responses to the racialisation of Irishness: Disavowed multiculturalism and its discontents', in Ronit Lentin and Robbie McVeigh (eds), *Racism and Anti-Racism in Ireland*. Belfast: Beyond the Pale, 226–38.

Lentin, Ronit and Robbie McVeigh (eds) (2002). 'Situated racisms: A theoretical introduction', *Racism and Anti-Racism in Ireland*. Belfast: Beyond the Pale, 1–49.

Lonergan, Patrick (2004). 'Half-hearted: Irish theatre, 2003', *New Hibernia Review* 8.2: 142–51.

—— (2009). 'All we say is "life is crazy": Central and Eastern Europe and the Irish stage', in Mária Kurdi (ed.), *Literary and Cultural Relations: Ireland, Hungary and Central and Eastern Europe*. Dublin: Carysfort, 9–30.

Lott, Eric (1995). *Love and Theft: Blackface Minstrelsy and the American Working Class*. Oxford: Oxford University Press.

Louth International Theatre Project (2009). *Journey from Babel*. Unpublished script.

McIvor, Charlotte (2009a). 'Interview with Donal O'Kelly', 16 February. Unpublished.

—— (2009b). 'Interview with Charlie O'Neill', 23 February. Unpublished.

—— (2009c). 'Interview with Declan Gorman', 14 March. Unpublished.

Meade, Paul (2007). *Mushroom*. Unpublished script.

Meany, Helen (2007). 'Mushroom project', *Guardian*, 29 June. www//0-www.lexisnexis.com. sculib.scu.edu:80/hottopics/lnacademic/. Accessed on 29 November 2011.

O'Baoill, Niall (2011). *A Local Imagine Nation: A Local Arts Plan for Rialto 2012–2016*. Dublin: Fatima Groups United.

Office of the Minister for Integration (2008). *Migration Nation: Statement on Integration Strategy and Diversity Management*. Dublin: Office of the Minister for Integration.

O'Hanlon, Jim (2007). *The Buddhist of Castleknock*. Dublin: New Island.

Singleton, Brian (2011). *Masculinities and the Contemporary Irish Theatre*. Houndsmill, Basingstoke, Hampshire: Palgrave Macmillan.

Upstate Theatre Project (2007). *Report to the Touring Experiment*. Unpublished report.

—— (2012a). *The Mango Tree (documentary)*, Declan Mallon (dir.).

—— (2012b). *The Mango Tree*. Unpublished script.

3

Strangers in a strange land?: the new Irish multicultural fiction

Amanda Tucker

In his seminal essay 'Imaginary Homelands', Salman Rushdie describes how, at a conference on modern writing, novelists struggled to articulate the purpose of their artform. After these (unnamed) fiction writers outlined the need for 'new ways of describing the world', another participant suggested that this objective might be limited. Rushdie argues that description is in fact political and, moreover, that 'redescribing the world is the necessary first step in changing it' (Rushdie, 1991: 13). He is particularly interested in how fictional representations might lead to systemic change and sets creative perspectives against official, government-sanctioned points of view: 'at times when the State takes reality into its own hands, and sets about distorting it, altering the past to fit its present needs, then the making of the alternate realities of art … becomes politicized' (14). Rushdie's assertions are well-supported by Irish literary history. As has been extensively documented, Irish writers and artists during the last part of the nineteenth and early twentieth century worked against the time-worn, politicised descriptions of the Irish as childlike, uncivilised, and altogether unequal to the challenge of self-governance. Though writers like Yeats, Joyce, and O'Casey differed markedly in their portrayals of Ireland – what Rushdie calls imaginary homelands, 'Indias of the mind' – they all worked to dispel these popular characterisations of the Irish. By creating a national culture, those involved in the Irish Revival played a crucial role in establishing independence. As a result, few countries hold their literary figures in as high regard as Ireland does.

In the wake of independence, however, the Republic of Ireland rejected the notion of multiple Irelands and focused on a Gaelic Catholic monolith as the epicentre of Irish culture. In response, a wave of Irish writers left in protest of State censorship and oppression. Today, the distinctions between the State and the artist are not so dichotomised: while the Irish State still rigidly defines

Irishness, artists often unwittingly reinforce the message of Ireland's resistance to multiculturalism.[1] One pertinent example is the short film titled *The Richness of Change* (2008), a ten-minute documentary that was commissioned by the Immigrant Council of Ireland and created by the Forum on Migration and Communications (FOMACS). Dedicated to creating social change in Ireland, FOMACS has proven particularly adept at shifting perceptions of immigrants from an amorphous group to distinct individuals: for instance, the animated project *Abbi's Circle* focuses on the daily life and challenges of a school-aged African migrant. As a result, it forces viewers to think about how regulations and laws like the 2004 Citizenship Referendum negatively affect children.

The Richness of Change, one of the organisation's first major projects, does not offer the same challenge. Composed of ten one-minute snapshots, the film documents the lives of ten immigrants in Ireland, including Floyd Jackson, one of only two black migrants featured in the production. His vignette begins with upbeat, whimsical music that is soon joined by Jackson's narration about meeting his future Irish wife in South Africa. In reminiscing over first coming to Ireland, Jackson quickly passes over any Irish anti-immigration or racist sentiment: 'you got looks, you got comments but that's life isn't it?' (Murphy, 2008). Throughout the short video, Jackson remains happy and relaxed, acting as living proof that twenty-first-century Ireland has become a globalised, multicultural society. However, in scrutinising this optimistic version of Irish multiculturalism, we begin to notice how various devices in the documentary de-emphasise the difficulties in the Irish immigration experience and reinforce negative ideas about race and migration. As its title suggests, *The Richness of Change* concentrates on the economic contributions that migrants have in Ireland rather than the cultural changes that multiculturalism has engendered. Jackson is depicted primarily as a worker: he wears his Dublin Bus Inspector uniform, a large portion of vignette is shot in an empty city bus, and much of his interview focuses on his profession. Perhaps most problematically – at least for North American viewers like myself – Jackson is seated towards the back of the bus, a geopolitical position that is deeply unsettling in terms of race and racial privilege.[2] Emphasising this subtext of racial hierarchy are the collective careers of the ten migrants: both Jackson and the other black participant, Cynthia Dortie, work in blue-collar jobs, as opposed to several of the white, European workers interviewed.

This reading is offered not to denigrate FOMACS; the organisation is doing valuable and socially productive work. But even for artists and organisations with the best of intentions, it is hard to move away from long-held, globally circulated ideologies about race, migration, and national culture. Even more so, it is hard for the readers and viewers of these cultural productions to remove themselves from these ideologies: if, as Rushdie suggests, writing is a politicised act, then reading is as well. This essay offers politicised readings of recent Irish multicultural fiction. The aim is not to evaluate the progressiveness of Irish writers or to assign gold stars of equality to some writers and withhold them from others, but rather, to investigate how twenty-first-century fiction in Ireland represents Irish multiculturalism as a social and cultural phenomenon. I want to be careful to take into account *all* Irish writers – in other words, both those born in the country and those who arrived later – so that we can move beyond the legitimised readings of Irish multiculturalism to see the view from the back of the bus. The first section examines stories by Roddy Doyle and Claire Keegan that present multiculturalism as an obstacle that can be overcome by the goodwill of Irish people. In the second section, I turn to Emma Donoghue and Cauvery Madhavan, who depict Irish multiculturalism as a complicated and unresolved process. Although these latter works have not received as much critical attention, they provide greater insight into multicultural Ireland.

Problems and solutions: Roddy Doyle, Claire Keegan, and Irish multiculturalism

In his multi-part series on migration, Ruadhán Mac Cormaic (2007) quotes the founder of the Dublin-based African theatre company Arambe, Bisi Adigun, as remarking that 'most attempts to depict in art the experience of migration are at least mediated, if not entirely conceived, through Irish eyes'. Adigun is best known for the adaptation of *The Playboy of the Western World* (2007), which he wrote with Roddy Doyle; yet it is Doyle who has received more attention for his representations of twenty-first-century Irish immigration. Doyle's collection *The Deportees* (2007) is the most easily accessible and therefore most well-known literary text on Irish multiculturalism. The stories from *The Deportees* come from his monthly contributions to *Metro Éireann*, and they make clear that Doyle considers multiculturalism to be the responsibility of the Irish-born rather than a burden solely for the 'new Irish'. In an interview with Maureen T. Reddy, Doyle remarks that the impetus for these stories was that 'the word "problem" was being used about immigrants and I was upset about that' (Reddy, 2005: 382). In his foreword to *The Deportees*, Doyle relates urban legends circulating around Dublin that involved social welfare abuse, home-run brothels, and animal sacrifice and asserts that these stories are meant to counter these negative depictions (Doyle, 2007: xii). This goal is certainly laudable, but it has also proven to be immensely difficult. Rather than confronting the racial and ethnic stereotypes that these urban legends and their creators invoke, several stories work to alleviate the anxieties voiced by white Irish in the wake of their home country's multicultural makeover.[3]

In examining Doyle's stories, the Marxist explanation that the 'cultural power of novels' relies on their ability to 'offer imaginary solutions to intractable problems at the level of social realism' is particularly useful (Cohen, 2010: 78). Doyle's stories solve the 'problem' of a diverse Ireland by presenting an idealised, idyllic version of multiculturalism. Unlike the fiction discussed in the next section, his stories gloss over systemic problems by focusing on the individual. The collection's first story 'Guess Who's Coming for the Dinner?' affirms the popular and erroneous assumption that the innate hospitality and graciousness of the Irish character will smooth the path for cross-racial interaction. There is conflict, of course: the main character, Larry Linnane, must confront his own racism when his daughter brings home Ben, a Nigerian refugee, for dinner. But as Maureen Reddy points out, 'the story is reassuring', for Ben has no romantic intentions towards Larry's daughter (2005: 381). Thus the story ends happily: simply by having Ben over for dinner, Larry has passed his one-time, self-imposed test of racism.[4]

'The Deportees' also focuses on a white Irish consciousness rather than an immigrant perspective (Reddy, 2005: 384–5). The story serves as a sequel to Doyle's novel *The Commitments* (1987), and the popular character Jimmy Rabbitte returns to form a new Northern Dublin band that includes among its many members African and Traveller singers, a Nigerian djembe player, and a Romanian father and son duo. The central conflict of the story – an anonymous xenophobe who repeatedly calls on the phone – is told only from Jimmy's point of view, and his is the only emotional response readers hear. These calls are more than a nuisance for Jimmy; they symbolise for him the fact that 'evil [is] out there' (Doyle, 2007: 48). While Jimmy's response is affecting and genuine, it seems strange that the band members do not hear or have the chance to react to these phone calls. These characters remain mostly one-dimensional and even seem interchangeable: as Jimmy remarks, 'some of them will leave, the band or the country; others will join, and some will come back' (76). Consequently, it appears as if it is the band members' amalgamated cultural difference rather than their individual talents and personalities that matter. 'The Deportees' thus corresponds to what Paul Gilroy calls 'corporate multiculturalism', 'in which some degree of visible difference from an implicit white norm may be highly prized as a sign of timeliness, vitality, inclusivity, and global reach' (2000: 21). Yet as Gilroy argues, this veneer of cultural difference only serves to obscure racial, economic, and gender inequalities.

Doyle's contribution to Irish multiculturalism cannot be overlooked, but it has been over-privileged. The stories collected in *The Deportees* are enchanting and magical, for with few exceptions, they suggest how interaction between the Irish and the non-Irish born can be meaningful and affirming for both groups. They therefore offer encouragement to the Irish people, even those reluctant towards social multiculturalism. However, these tales do little in asking the readers to actively engage in the stories. Half the stories, like 'Guess Who's Coming for the Dinner?' and 'The Deportees', feature Irish-born protagonists, and therefore do not ask readers to see from a migrant perspective. But even those that *do* present the inner voices of the 'new Irish' often downplay the difficulties of the migrant experience in Ireland. The closing story, 'I Understand', for instance, involves an asylum-seeker plagued by low-level criminals who want him to traffic their illegal wares. By the end of the story, however, he has met an attractive Irish girl and the threat of his persecutors has simply dissipated. Most of the stories in *The Deportees* follow a similar structure, effectively solving the problem of Irish multiculturalism.

Repeatedly compared to Flannery O'Connor's and William Trevor's work, Claire Keegan's fiction focuses on life in rural Ireland, which has seen less of a de-mographic shift than the country's urban centres. Only one of her stories, the eponymous tale from *Walk the Blue Fields* (2007), focuses on Irish multicultur-alism. In the story, a County Wexford priest officiates at the wedding of a former lover. Feeling spiritually bankrupt after this difficult event, the priest walks around the countryside and goes to a local Chinese healer. His interaction with the healer precipitates an epiphany, and the priest leaves feeling spiritually reju-venated. Shortly after 'Walk the Blue Fields' came out, Ruadhán Mac Cormaic used the story to illustrate the shortcomings of Irish fiction in treating inward migration, asserting that the Chinese character is 'more of a presence rather than a participant' (2007). In contrast, Alfred Markey reads the story's presenta-tion of Irish immigration much more sympathetically. Tracing how the story fits into the collection's broader themes of home and homelessness, Markey argues that, despite its lack of dialogue, the story suggests a meeting of the minds be-tween the priest and the healer through 'metaphorical language', in particular, the symbolism of an alabaster bowl (2010: 101). Markey suggests that the priest and the healer's encounter is the first of many, for their exchange has allowed the priest to 'rework his spiritual parameters to anchor them firmly in the less politicized space of nature' (*ibid.*).

Though these readings contrast markedly, both appear valid interpretations of the story. Markey's insistence of the collection's intertextuality is an insightful, albeit charitable, interpretation of Keegan's major tropes and themes. Yet Mac Cormaic's criticism rings equally true, for 'Walk the Blue Fields' severely limits the Chinese healer's agency or individuality. Although Mac Cormaic reads the healer as a 'spiritual rival' to the priest, doing so actually over-emphasises the character's significance in the story (2007). This character does not even have a name: others in the story and the omnipotent narrator simply refer to him as the 'Chinaman', a term that is negatively racialised.[5] He expresses no thoughts, feelings or desires: he is simply a vessel – the empty alabaster bowl of the story – on which the priest and the reader alike can project their own image. Indeed, Keegan's depiction parallels the American film trope of 'the magic negro', in which a spiritual and solicitous minority character, devoid of any inner life himself, helps white characters with their problems (Bogle, 2001).

Both Keegan and Doyle depict a non-threatening, non-challenging multicultural Ireland that attempts to solve the challenges of diversity through Irish hospitality and good will. Arguably, Doyle's stories in particular are popular because they ease cultural anxieties surrounding recent inward migration and its perceived threat to national culture. The Irish characters accommodate the non-Irish-born, but only for a limited amount of time, and after providing a warm meal, a listening ear, or in the case of Keegan's priest, a pocketful of money, they resume their normal lives. Their friendliness and charity does not create a bridge across cultures; it signifies their true Irish spirit. The immigrant characters, on the other hand, are not linked to this tradition, and while they might stay in Ireland, they remain distant from 'authentic' Irish culture.

Cultural anxiety and ambiguity: the cross-racial, multicultural Irish romance

Some of the most interesting and significant Irish multicultural fiction has been overlooked because of its genre. In contrast to the easy resolution in Doyle's and Keegan's fiction, the 'middlebrow' novels of Emma Donoghue and Cauvery Madhavan recognise the anxieties and contradictions that characterise Ireland's response to its changing demography. In the same essay that denounces Irish fiction for its silence regarding Irish multiculturalism and immigration, Mac Cormaic reluctantly suggests that '[t]he one genre that has tried to engage with the fast-track shifts of the Celtic Tiger years is chick-lit, but its authors are concerned broadly with one clique and its narrow-gauge preoccupations' (2007). Like most critics, Mac Cormaic dismisses the significance of chick-lit, suggesting that it is impossible for this genre to tackle serious issues like multiculturalism. Indeed, he implicitly contrasts what he sees as chick-lit's limited readership of white women in their twenties and thirties – the 'clique' he refers to – with 'migrants [who] are invisible' (2007). But as Pamela Butler and Jigna Desai (2008) have argued, assuming that all chick-lit focuses primarily on a normative female experience – coded as white and heterosexual – ignores a multitude of interesting novels, among them Donoghue's *Landing* (2007) and Madhavan's *Paddy Indian* (2001).

Popular women's fiction often focuses on the personal growth of a female protagonist and therefore typically involves a successful romantic relationship. In *Landing* and *Paddy Indian*, these relationships involve Irish and non-Irish characters. Jason King has argued that contemporary Irish authors 'develop an interracial romantic plotline as a symbolic shorthand for the resolution of cultural conflict, but their achievement of romantic fulfilment is based less on the accommodation rather than the elision of cultural differences that they propose to reconcile' (2009: 160). King's focus on 'the elision of cultural differences' provides an insightful lens with which to view Doyle's and Keegan's fiction, for as suggested earlier, both these writers 'solve' the problems and difficulties in Irish multiculturalism. Donoghue's and Madhavan's cross-racial relationships, however, work slightly differently. Both *Landing* and *Paddy Indian* end on an ostensibly happy note – an ending won, as King asserts, by neglecting cultural difference. But these novels lack closure, and their unresolved issues and unanswered questions point to persistent cultural anxieties about Irish multiculturalism. Thus Donoghue and Madhavan move beyond individual stories of cross-cultural contact to indicate how the power dynamics involved with race, citizenship, and gender shape and at times control individual relationships.

Although both novels have received generally positive notices, most reviewers have overlooked their ambiguity. For instance, when *Paddy Indian* came out in 2001, *The Times* asserted that it was a 'delightful debut' with 'mouth-watering descriptions of Indian cooking' but did not consider it a serious treatment of cross-cultural relations (Kidd, 2001). And despite Emma Donoghue's increasingly prominent career, *Landing* has been dismissed as a light-hearted love story between two wildly different women.[6] For the most part, reviews like *The Times*'s follow a similar strategy to the fiction discussed earlier. By complimenting a cultural Other – for either its exotic food or its happy lesbianism – they can display a liberal, progressive mindset that embraces Gilroy's 'corporate multiculturalism' (2000: 21). They do not, however, meet Bryan Fanning's criteria for 'strong' multiculturalism, which involves commitment beyond enjoying a non-normative cultural production (2002: 181).

Paddy Indian eschews the convention of a female protagonist and centres around Padhman, a Tamil doctor who begins his medical residency in Dublin and falls in love with his professor's daughter. Wealthy and highly educated, Padhman occupies a higher social and economic position than his Irish girlfriend Aiofe. Nonetheless, racial anxieties emerge during their first date. Padhman is certain that everyone is watching them disapprovingly: 'he had seen that sort of thing on American documentaries … the white men who hated their own, the slags who went for the blacks. The camera would then cut to the white women slyly hinting about greater sexual satisfaction … Padhman was nearly convinced the camera was panning to him next' (Madhavan, 2001: 81). This anxiety suggests how the interactions between the Irish-born and immigrants depend upon the global circulation of racial stereotypes: in this case, despite occupying a more privileged position in the hospital, Padhman worries that the sexualised ideologies of Orientalism shape how Aoife views him.

Padhman and Aiofe's relationship progresses beyond these initial worries, but the pair faces another obstacle with their mothers' disapproval. Aoife's mother attempts to hide her censure by being 'superficial and polite – too polite', while Padhman's parents react more directly: 'one mention of an Irish girl and they had turned and walked away' (Madhavan, 2001: 133, 175). By portraying Aiofe as an unsuitable partner, Madhavan forces Irish readers to see themselves from an immigrant perspective and shows that concerns about racial and national instability do not belong solely to the Irish. Basic questions such as where Padhman and Aiofe will live become vexed precisely because neither India nor Ireland appear to provide a welcoming environment for the couple. Padhman wonders: 'would he bring her to Madras, where she would be a total misfit? Could he do that to her?'; at the same time, he chafes under the idea of 'remaining "that foreigner" for the rest of his life' (159). The novel never resolves these difficulties: in fact, Padhman seems to deliberately side-step them by proposing to Aoife, figuring that they will 'tackle all the awkward bits' later (152). Aoife seems to share his optimistic, albeit naive, point of view, and agrees to marry Padhman. Although they seem to genuinely love one another, their success as a couple is uncertain.

That love does not resolve the complications of daily life is supported by the cross-racial romances of Donoghue's *Landing*, which tells of the long-distance love affair between the metropolitan Indo-Irish flight attendant Silé O'Shaughnessy and small-town Canadian historian Jude Turner. Silé's mother Sunita, a flight attendant like her daughter, illustrates the consequence of Padhman's insistence that 'one of us will have to give up a lot – everything – to be with the other' (Madhavan, 2001: 163). After marrying an Irishman, Sunita left India and completely assimilated to Irish culture. Towards the end of the novel, Silé is forced to consider the possibility that her mother committed suicide. She then reinterprets the previously romantic tale of her mother giving up her home country for love: 'she must have felt bits of her starting to crumble off as soon as she landed. She settled in Da's family house … she turned Catholic, stopped speaking Malayalam, got a little less Indian every year. She must have felt she was *withering*' (original emphasis; Donoghue, 2007: 310). Sunita Pillay O'Shaughnessy's experience thus counters the optimistic cross-cultural romance in *Paddy Indian*.

Sunita's migration also offers a disturbing counterpoint to Silé's planned migration to Canada to live with Jude. The pair is a classic case of opposites attract: Silé has made her career travelling the world; Jude, on the other hand, has spent

her entire life in the fictional town of Ireland, Ontario. While technological in-
novations like e-mail, phone conversations, and inexpensive flights allow Silé
and Jude to sustain their 'time zone tango', they cannot solve the pair's essential
dilemma of living two different lives in opposite parts of the world (Donoghue,
2007: 76). Eventually Silé determines to live in Canada in order to be with Jude,
but after revisiting her mother's experience, she intentionally misses her flight
to Canada. The lovers reunite at the end of the novel and plan to live together
– now in Toronto rather than Jude's hometown – but this missed connection
sours their happiness. Thus Donoghue, like Madhavan, suggests through these
cross-cultural romances that individual relationships are shaped by larger forces
– namely the systemic inequalities of gender, race, and geography. Their happily ever afters are plagued by problems that refuse to be solved at the novels'
endings, leading the reader to speculate on the fate of these characters and the
challenges of migration.

In addition to these allegorical representations of Irish multiculturalism,
the novels also depict in more straightforward manner the country's receptiveness towards cultural difference. *Landing* makes clear that Silé and Jude's
relationship could not flourish in Ireland. In contrast to *Paddy Indian*, which is
set in the 1980s, *Landing* depicts a very contemporary Ireland: Silé is active in
Dublin's thriving gay and lesbian community, and she and her friends bemoan
some of the effects of the Celtic Tiger, such as dramatic population increase and
sky-rocketing property prices. Yet a persistent subplot of the novel involves Irish
hostility and racism toward inward migration. Silé's school-age nephew is called
a 'nigger' by another boy in his class, and her friend Brigid, who has 'black hair,
tans easily, but [is] County Cavan all the way', is told on the bus, 'Go home, Paki
bitch!' (Donoghue, 2007: 35). Orla, who runs a welcome centre for immigrants
and refugees, comments that 'the Irish get more racist every year … those letters
in the paper about the need to *save our culture from being swamped!*' (original
emphasis; 79).

It seems unsurprising, therefore, that Silé chooses to leave Ireland, for in spite of
its superficially modern and liberal atmosphere, Dublin does not accommodate
difference. Silé's departure is especially significant because she herself represents
a rooted multiculturalism within Ireland: her ability to weave together different
affiliations – a tone point in the novel, she refers to herself as 'brown Irish' – suggests the potential of a multicultural future in Ireland (Donoghue, 2007: 122). In
this way, Silé resembles the character Declan in Doyle's story 'Home to Harlem'.
A mixed-race Irish college student, Declan embarks on a study-abroad trip
to New York City, where he hopes to find his African-American grandfather.
Though Declan misses his family and his homeland, he seems uncertain about
actually returning to Ireland. The story ends shortly before his semester abroad
is finished, but Declan has only begun his thesis and seems to have no intention

of leaving New York in the near future. That both of these characters leave their homeland suggests Ireland's inability to provide a supportive environment for those outside its cultural centre.

Finally we return to *Paddy Indian*, which offers one of the most complex representations of multiculturalism in contemporary fiction in Ireland. In particular, Madhavan skilfully uses humour to address the complicated and sometimes contradictory nature of Irish responses to cultural difference. Homi Bhabha asserts that humour can function as a 'minority speech-act' that creates new affiliations between dominant and marginalised communities and, at the same time, offers space to critique both groups (1998: xxvi). We see this multifaceted process occur during Padhman's first day at the hospital. When a deliveryman from Khyber Tandoori arrives at the hospital, Padhman's nervousness about his migrant status becomes overt as he converses with an imagined Irishman who ordered the takeaway:

> I was hoping you'd taste some of this curry – you know, tell me if it is the 'real' stuff. Ah, go on, there's plenty. The Khyber is better than the Rajdoot, you know. The Rajdoot buggers don't serve chips with their curries. There you go, try that. Oh Jesus – no wait! It's bloody beef ... I mean, shit. You know, Holy Cow and all that. (Madhavan, 2001: 26)

Through the hospitality suggested by the desire to share food, this monologue pokes gentle fun at popular Irish self-perceptions. Yet it indicates Irish ethnocentrism: the imagined speaker evaluates the success of the two Indian takeaways based on their inclusion of chips with their curries and mistakenly assumes that all Indians are Hindu and therefore cannot eat beef. As such, the humour behind this imagined encounter lies in its ability to suggest the goodwill of the Irish but also their ignorance – and lack of interest – in cultures outside their own.

Padhman's first meetings with an Irish colleague contrast markedly to this imagined encounter. After being introduced, Niall, another doctor, asks upon meeting, 'Padhman ... not short for Padhmanabhan, is it? From South India, are you?' (Madhavan, 2001: 31). Expecting a half-apologetic refusal to learn a 'foreign name', Padhman is astounded and delighted by Niall's knowledge of his home country. As Niall explains, he has worked at a clinic near Madurai, and another Indian doctor vouches for his ability to curse in Tamil, though 'the Irish accent dilutes the effect' (32). This exchange contrasts greatly with the previous imagined conversation, for it refuses to adhere to a strict binary between Irish and Indian. Instead it indicates that, rather than expecting assimilation to an adopted country, transculturation and hybridity have become normative as global migration is bidirectional – thus negating the uniform expectations of Irishness that the imagined speaker affirms.[7]

Not all Irish share Niall's background or perspective, and frequently Padhman's Irish acquaintances and friends rely on stereotypes and clichés in their interactions with him. For instance, Mrs. Fogarty, the convenience store owner, interprets his foreignness as a disability, speaking slowly and offering helpful advice like 'Keep ... in ... freezer' when Padhman buys ice cream (Madhavan, 2001: 52). Anxious under her suspicious eye, Padhman routinely divulges personal information; in this case, he has explained that the ice cream is to celebrate a friend passing her driver's exam. Exasperated, he wonders, 'after all that soul-bearing, did she really think he couldn't speak the language?' (53). Racial prejudice is more painful when it comes from a friend. After Maura, Niall's fiancée and a nurse at the hospital, expresses pleasure at the perceived 'normality' of another Indian doctor's wife, Padhman asks what criteria she uses to gauge normalcy. Oblivious to Padhman's growing discomfort, she lists drinking wine, wearing pants, and listening to Simon and Garfunkel. Padhman marvels that 'it is my perceived *abnormality*, my deviation from their idea of a defined norm for someone like me, which makes me one of them i.e. normal' (original emphasis; 195).

As these instances demonstrate, Madhavan is disinterested in establishing a fixed binary between one culture and the other, and to read the book as upholding a division between the ignorant, racist Irish and victimised immigrant is too reductive. No character becomes representative of the interaction between the Irish and the immigrants; instead they suggest the range of relationships possible between people. Indeed, the fact that Niall, whose relationship with Padhman suggests a more developed understanding of cultural norms, and Maura, whose prejudices are more damaging because they are unthinking and covert, marry one another suggests that both multiple, contradictory responses to cultural differences in one's own backyard frequently go hand in hand. Moreover, Madhavan suggests how Padhman himself operates under damaging racial ideologies. After Padhman vents to his best friends Sunil and Renu about his uncomfortable encounter with Mrs. Fogarty at the convenience store, he immediately imitates a well-worn, offensive version of Chinese-English: 'The flied lice and libs? ... Me takee the flied lice' (Madhavan, 2001: 54). With no irony whatsoever, Padhman reproduces Mrs. Fogarty's stance about immigrants and their inability to speak or understand 'proper' English.

It is impossible to view Padhman's speech as learned behaviour from his adopted country, for the novel clearly indicates the racial and ethnic prejudices that exist in India. This is revealed most readily through Padhman's relationship with his former girlfriend Annie. His mother had previously opposed the relationship because Annie is Anglo-Indian, and in Ireland, another Indian doctor asks Padhman about the 'dingo dame' (contemptuous slang for someone of Anglo-Indian descent). Although Padhman stands up for Annie by inventing a new lineage for her – daughter of a Brahmin and an English lord – he realises afterwards that, rather than defending her, he had merely 'implied breeding, by giving her what he reckoned was a more socially acceptable background. What a nation of bigots he came from' (115). These two instances are telling. First, they suggest that racial prejudice is not the sole domain of the Irish but rather a part of every culture. More importantly, they demonstrate that a wider context than an immigrant/native binary is necessary to truly grasp Irish multiculturalism.

The success of *Paddy Indian* and *Landing* can be explained in part because they position Irish multiculturalism in a global context: that is, they indicate that Irish multiculturalism cannot be contained or dictated by the nation-state. In countries like Ireland, where nationality and ethnicity are conflated, discussions of multiculturalism often assume that immigrants can or should eventually integrate into mainstream culture. Both Emma Donoghue and Cauvery Madhavan instead affirm the notion of transmigration, a phrase social scientists use to describe immigration that is multi-directional, open, and continuous. Transmigration provides the opportunity for multiple affiliations but also points to persistent and perhaps insolvable questions about both individual and collective identity (see Glick Schiller *et al.*, 1995). By revealing the struggles inherent in Irish multiculturalism – rather than resolving these complications – Donoghue and Madhavan demonstrate that for contemporary migrants, making a home in Ireland is not simply a national issue but a global one.

Notes

1   Of course, the most significant indication of these restrictions is the 2004 Citizenship Referendum; see Lentin and McVeigh (2006) for an insightful discussion of the law's transformation of the country from a racial state to a racist one.
2   One of the most significant early events in the American Civil Rights Movement was Rosa Parks' arrest for refusing to move to the back of the bus for a white passenger; in doing so, she challenged the racial segregation laws enforced at the time. For more detailed information on this historical event, see Kohl (2005).
3   I want to pay particular attention here to the collection's 'feel-good' stories, 'Guess Who's Coming for the Dinner?' and 'The Deportees'. Although not discussed here, 'Black Hoodie' and '57% Irish' work in a similar manner. Other tales in *The Deportees* do not fit into this model. For an insightful reading of 'The Pram', Doyle's horror story, see Molly E. Ferguson (2010). I discuss 'Home to Harlem', which I consider Doyle's most successful and complex presentation of Irish multiculturalism, in the section below.
4   The story clearly connects itself with the American film, *Guess Who's Coming to Dinner* (1967), but unlike the film, Doyle's story does not actually involve interracial marriage.
5   The *Oxford English Dictionary* characterises it as 'derogatory and offensive'.
6   Moira E. Casey (2011) offers a more comprehensive discussion of *Landing*'s reviews but draws the same conclusion.

7   'Transculturation' is most frequently used in Latin American Studies and describes the process through which oppressed and minority cultures appropriate and reinvent – rather than assimilate – a dominant culture's practices. Thus the term both indicates the power dynamic so often involved in cultural interactions and refutes the idea of an essential or static culture. See Spitta (1995).

References

Bhabha, Homi, K. (1998). 'Joking aside: The idea of a self-critical community', in Bryan Cheyette and Laura Marcus (eds), *Modernity, Culture and 'The Jew'*. Cambridge: Polity, xvi–xx.

Bogle, Donald (2001). *Toms, Coons, Mulattoes, Mammies, and Bucks: An Interpretive History of Blacks in American Films*. New York: Continuum.

Butler, Pamela and Jigna Desai (2008). 'Manolos, marriage, and mantras: Chick lit criticism and transnational feminism', *Meridians: Feminism, Race, and Transnationalism* 8.2: 1–31.

Casey, Moira E. (2011). '"If love's a country": Transnationalism and the Celtic Tiger in Emma Donoghue's Landing', *New Hibernia Review* 15.2: 64–79.

Cohen, Margaret (2010). *The Novel and the Sea*. Princeton, NJ: Princeton University Press.

Donoghue, Emma (2007). *Landing*. New York: Houghton Mifflin Harcourt.

Doyle, Roddy (2007). *The Deportees and Other Stories*. New York: Viking.

Fanning, Bryan (2002). *Racism and Social Change in the Republic of Ireland*. Manchester: Manchester University Press.

Ferguson, Molly E. (2010). 'Reading the ghost story: Roddy Doyle's *The Deportees and Other Stories*', *Canadian Journal of Irish Studies* 35.2: 52–60.

Forum on Migration and Communications (FOMACS). 'What We Do'. www.fomacs.org/index. Accessed on 15 January 2012.

Gilroy, Paul (2000). *Between Camps: Nations, Cultures, and the Illusion of Race*. London: Penguin.

Glick Schiller, Nina, Linda Basch, and Christina Szanton Blanc (1995). 'From immigrant to transmigrant: Theorizing transnational migration', *Anthropological Quarterly* 68: 48–63.

Keegan, Claire (2007). *Walk the Blue Fields*. London: Grove.

Kidd, Patrick (2001). '*Paddy Indian*', *The Times*, 6 October: n.p.

King, Jason (2009). 'Irish multicultural fiction: Metaphors of miscegenation and interracial romance', in James P. Byrne, Padraig Kirwan, and Michael O'Sullivan (eds), *Affecting Irishness: Negotiating Culture Within and Beyond the Nation*. Oxford, Bern and New York: Peter Lang, 159–78.

Kohl, Herbert (2005). *She Would Not Be Moved: How We Tell the Story of Rosa Parks and the Montgomery Bus Boycott*. New York: The New Press.

Lentin, Ronit and Robbie McVeigh (2006). *After Optimism? Ireland, Racism and Globalisation*. Dublin: Metro Éireann.

Mac Cormaic, Ruadhán (2007). 'Signs of new vitality in how film and drama treat immigrants', *Irish Times*, 23 May. www.irishtimes.com/focus/gageby/changingplaces/articles/230507_article.html. Accessed on 15 January 2012.

Madhavan, Cauvery (2001). *Paddy Indian*. London: Black Amber.

Markey, Alfred (2010). 'Beyond the commuter pale: Borderlands and authenticity in the recent short fiction of Claire Keegan and John McKenna', in David Clark and Rubén Jarazo Álvarez (eds), *In the Wake of the Tiger: Irish Studies in the Twenty-First Century*. Oleiros: Netbiblio, 93–102.

Murphy, Colin (dir.) (2008). *The Richness of Change*. Dublin: Forum on Migration and Communication.

Reddy, Maureen T. (2005). 'Reading and writing race in Ireland: Roddy Doyle and *Metro Éireann*', *Irish University Review* 35.2: 374–88.

Rushdie, Salman (1991). *Imaginary Homelands: Essays and Criticism 1981–1991*. London: Granta.

Spitta, Sylvia (1995). *Between Two Waters: Narratives of Transculturation in Latin America*. Houston, TX: Rice University Press.

4

'A nation of Others': the immigrant in contemporary Irish poetry

Pilar Villar-Argáiz

The changing face of Irish society and the new influx of immigration during the economic boom of the country have compelled Irish poets to rethink nationhood intersectionally, as modulated by race and ethnicity. Depictions of ethnic migrant communities in Ireland have appeared in the work of poets since the early 1990s. Eithne Strong, for instance, dealt with this topic in her poems 'Let Live', about the emotional impact the Indian community has on the native Irish population with its 'oddness' and 'alternative culture' (1993: 75–6), and 'Woad and Olive', which reflects on the difficulty of 'harmonious coexistence' among different ethnicities and cultures (113–15). However, it has not been until recent years that Irish poetry has dwelt more accurately on the drastic changes Ireland has undergone at the sociological level. This is observed in the increasing interest on the part of some writers in reflecting the multiethnic atmosphere of the country, expressing their openness to cultural diversity and their alertness to the voices of the marginalised.

This chapter examines this aspect by analysing depictions of interethnic encounters between the Irish host and the foreign 'guest' in the recent poetry produced by Colette Bryce, Mary O'Donnell, and Michael O'Loughlin. It has been regularly asserted that Ireland can be considered a truly multicultural country, as a consequence of the unprecedented immigration of the last decades. The poems selected for analysis by Bryce, O'Donnell, and O'Loughlin challenge this idealisation of Irish multiculturalism by revealing the various ways in which newcomers are marginalised in present-day Ireland. These poets tend to denounce the immigrants' lack of integration within Irish culture, the seemingly impenetrable boundaries existing between the majority and the minority, and the absence of genuine interaction between both groups. Only occasionally do they envisage a positive encounter between natives and newcomers and in such cases this is produced mostly at the abstract level. The implication seems to be that, whereas 'real' life is identified by social inequality and solitude, poetry can sometimes allow for positive encounters and healing, at least at the level of the imagination. As sociologist Breda Gray (2008: 68) puts it, '[t]he discourse of immigration as enrichment is an abstract discourse based on the *potentially* enriching contribution that immigrants might make to Irish society. These discourses are invariably articulated in the future tense. They point to possibilities rather than a return to some putative past state of harmony and homogeneity' (original emphasis).

Before analysing how this *potential* conviviality between natives and newcomers is envisaged by some contemporary Irish poets, it is important to note that immigrant voices in Ireland are starting to make themselves heard in the literary panorama, as the poetic anthology *Landing Places* demonstrates, enriching Irish culture with their distinctive rhythms, traditions, and images (Bourke and Faragó, 2010). One of these migrant poets is the Polish writer Kinga Olszewska, who came to live in Ireland in the early 1990s. Like the poetry of the Irish writers mentioned in this chapter, Olszewska's work illustrates the 'sharp and new poetic space produced by the joining, and sometimes collision, of Irish experience and immigrant experience' (Bourke and Faragó, 2010: xxii). This dual, but contrasting, process of 'joining' and 'collision' is observed in her poem 'Site for Sale'. Here, Olszewska describes Ireland through the eyes of a Polish woman who wants to buy a house. The poem draws upon the difficulties and prejudices this immigrant experiences in Ireland when trying to integrate herself:

> 'Site for sale to locals in the area'
> I go in to inquire.
> Are you local? the man behind the desk asks disbelievingly.
> I have been local for the last ten years.
> But you are not really Irish?
> So I recite: Irish passport, Revenue, Hibernian, Bank of Ireland,
> Áine and Saoirse, holiday house in Wicklow,
> I start quoting national heroes
> When the man interrupts
> In fairness, I don't think it's a site for you.
>
> (Olszewska, 2010: 144)

The persona finds it impossible to buy a house in an Irish urban neighbourhood, as this area is restricted to those who can prove their nationality only in terms of blood lineage and not in terms of other factors such as long-time residency or historical knowledge. This restrictive definition of nationality recalls the controversial 2004 Referendum on Citizenship, the implications of which are mentioned below. Olszewska addresses the segregation experienced in contemporary Ireland, with immigrant ghettoes on the one hand and exclusive, desirable residential areas for Irish nationals on the other. As Kuhling and Keohane (2007: 201) claim in the context of Celtic Tiger Ireland, 'town planning is over-ridden by ... practices that promote class and ethnic segregation and that support anti-cosmopolitan rather than pro-cosmopolitan lifestyles'. Such a defining line between Irish and newcomers reveals a xenophobic attitude towards immigrants which is, ironically, reminiscent of the colonial treatment of the Irish by the British.

Olszewska's poetry can be set beside the work of Colette Bryce, Mary O'Donnell, and Michael O'Loughlin, as all these writers also share this interest in recording the tensions involved in the interactions between the immigrants and the host community, although this time mostly from a native, and not migrant, perspective. Colette Bryce is particularly outspoken with respect to Ireland's multiethnic atmosphere. Like Olszewska, this critically acclaimed poet from Northern Ireland denounces the unequal position of ethnic and migrant minorities. In her poem 'Word', published in her 2005 collection *The Full Indian Rope Trick*, Bryce highlights the existence of racism not only at the individual, but also at the institutional level. As Ronit Lentin (2001) claims, the Irish government and media has tended to refer 'to asylum-seekers as "problem," "flood," and as "economic migrants" at best and "bogus refugees" and "illegal immigrants" at worst'. Bryce's poem denounces this tendency to demonise immigrants and other outcasts, particularly illegal migrants, vagrants, and drug smugglers:

> He arrived, confused, in groups at the harbours,
> walking unsteadily over the gangways;
> turned up at the airports, lost in the corridors,
> shunted and shoved from Control to Security;
> fell, blinking and bent, a live cargo
> spilled from the darks of our lorries,
> dirty-looking, disarranged, full of lies, lies,
> full of wild stories – threats and guns and foreign wars;
> or He simply appeared, as out of the ground,
> as man, woman, infant, child, darkening doorways,
> tugging at sleeves with *Lady, Mister, please, please* ...
>
> (Bryce, 2005: 24)

Bryce uses the capitalised masculine pronoun 'He' throughout the poem in order to include in a unifying category the heterogeneous reality of men, women, infants, and children arriving in groups at the harbours and airports. This stylistic choice might signify, on the one hand, the government's tendency to homogenise difference by considering all immigrants as one single group: that of the alien Other. On the other hand, Bryce uses this pronoun subversively, establishing a parallelism between the hardship and sufferings of Jesus Christ and the experiences of migrants in Ireland. Just as Christ in his time, Ireland's outcasts are demonised as 'dirty-looking, disarranged' and 'full of lies' and 'wild stories'. Furthermore, they are bound to bear the blame of all the 'incidents' happening around them:

> There were incidents; He would ask for it –
> His broken English, guttural; swaying
> His way through rush-hour trains, touching people,
> causing trouble; peddling guilt in the market place,
> His thousand hands demanding change, flocking
> in rags to the steps of the church, milking
> the faithful, blocking the porch, He was chased –
> but arrived in greater numbers, needs misspelt
> on scraps of paper, hungry, pushy, shifty, gypsy,
> not comprehending *No* for an answer.

> (*Ibid.*)

Bryce talks about immigration in terms of imagery of tides and floods of invasion: migrants arrive 'in *groups*', they are presented as 'a live cargo / *spilled* from the darks of our lorries', with '*thousand* hands demanding change' and arriving 'in *greater numbers*' every time they are chased (emphasis added). As pointed out by various critics (Kiberd, 2005: 311; King, 2008: 49), the Irish media of the last decade of the twentieth century tends to talk about inward migration in terms of 'floods' and 'invasions' which 'pour in and swamp the continent'. Such prevailing discourse constructs the view of Ireland as a passive, 'porous' and 'vulnerable' nation, an organic entity threatened to be 'drown[ed]' by the uncontrollable arrival of foreigners (King, 2008: 52). The inflammatory tone of Bryce's poem recalls this idea of immigration as a 'threat'. Implicit in Bryce's mimicry of such conventionalised discourses is the belief that Irish society should be as homogeneous and uniform as possible. Hybridity is discouraged and contact with Otherness might lead to 'contamination'.

Interestingly enough, Bryce's poem was published in 2005, a year after the Irish Citizenship Referendum, and hence her concern with the State's exclusionary attitude towards immigrants. This Referendum radically limited the parameters of citizenship to biological lineage. It stipulated that children who are born to non-Irish parents are not entitled to the same rights as those born to Irish parents. Consequently, many critics in Ireland, most notably Ronit Lentin, viewed the Referendum as a racist attempt to reinforce – at a legal and institutional level – monocultural, rather than multicultural, notions of Irishness. This homogeneous construction of national identity goes back to the essentialist pre- and post-Independent project of nation-building, which reified Catholicism, the Irish language, and the Gaelic Sports Associations (Lentin and McVeigh, 2006: 10; Kuhling and Keohane, 2007: 67).

In light of this interpretation, Bryce's use of religious discourse is highly significant. The myth of martyrdom has been intrinsically connected to the poetic discourse of the Irish motherland. An illustration of this is Pearse's poem 'A Mother Speaks', in its powerful invocation of blood sacrifice. This discourse of sacrificial martyrdom is also recorded in 'The Word', although its purpose and mode of articulation is radically different. In Pearse's poem, the national poet 'identifies his own martyrdom with that of Christ who also "had gone forth to die for men"' (Kearney, 1997: 118). In Bryce's poem, there is also a conjugation of national discourse and Catholic sacrifice. Nevertheless, the poet does not occupy the stance of the martyr, but that of the Pharisees who condemn Christ and send him to the cross. Thus, the persona sarcastically adopts the perspective of the nation-state, who, like the Pharisees in Jesus's time, advocates strict interpretation and observance of the law:

> What could we do?
> We returned to the Word; called to our journalists, they heard
> and hammered a word through the palms of His hands: *SCAM*.
> They battered a word through the bones of His feet: *CHEAT*.
> Blood from a bogus crown trickled down,
> ran into His eyes and His mouth and His throat,
> *OUT*: He gagged, but wouldn't leave.
> We rounded Him up with riot police,
> drove Him in vanloads out of our streets,
> away from our cities, into the tomb
> and left Him there, a job well done.
> We are safer now, for much has changed,
> now the Word is the law is a huge, immovable stone,
>
> should He rise again.
>
> (Original emphasis; Bryce, 2005: 25)

Supported by the journalists and the media, the 'law' of the State (which is further validated by the sacred 'Word') provides legitimisation for the present 'extermination' of immigrants. Like Christ, inward migrants are branded, crucified, and buried with 'a huge, immovable stone' above their graves, should they dare to 'rise again' and overstep the boundaries set up by the State. Immigrants also occupy the role of scapegoats dying for the sake of restoring the purity of an ethnically united nation. From this perspective, the poem records the Volk Utopia and 'the scapegoating mechanism' at the heart of nationalist ways of thinking, which Kearney explains as 'the sacrifice of the victim, on whom the evils of society are projected, being mythically experienced as a means of purging and restoring the community to unity' (1997: 109). Bryce's poem precisely records this process identified by Kearney. By relying on the 'law' and the 'Word', the State tries to restore the unity and sovereignty which has been lost by Ireland's postnationalist reality of cultural disunity and difference during the Celtic Tiger period.

Together with Colette Bryce, the Maynooth-based poet Mary O'Donnell also deals explicitly with the disadvantageous reality of migrant communities. She is, without doubt, one of the most outspoken Irish poets dealing today with what she calls the 'multi-ethnic' reality of twenty-first-century Ireland. As she claims, 'Ireland has had … a race "earthquake" … and it's good. We are not multi-cultural in my view, but we are multi-ethnic with a dominant Irish culture surveying the different ethnicities. If we were multi-cultural we would not have so many racist incidents' (Villar-Argáiz, 2010). O'Donnell's collections *A Place of Miracles* (2006) and *The Ark Builders* (2009) include a series of poems which precisely focus on the tensions produced by the encounter between the Irish population and immigrants of diverse ethnic origin. In line with Bryce's 'The Word', these poems clearly challenge idealised and harmonious representations of Irish society as multicultural and diverse, by foregrounding the economic and social inequalities between individuals on the basis of nationality.

This critique is observed in her sequence of poems 'Exiles' (2006: 150–6). In 'Girl from the East, Palmerstown Traffic-Lights', for instance, O'Donnell depicts a crippled girl from Eastern Europe delivering newspapers among 'snoozing cars'. This character becomes the starting point for the speaker to reflect on how '[h]ere [in Ireland], she is at war with deficit' (150). Her disadvantaged citizenship is strengthened not only by her physical, handicapped condition, but also by virtue of her economic class and ethnic background. O'Donnell denounces the unwillingness of Irish society to address such inequities. The sleepiness of Irish drivers recalls their utter indifference towards the personal tragedies of immigrants. While they sit comfortably in cars, this Eastern girl is exposed to the extreme external violence of '[a] squall of snow' and the 'bullets of hail'. The vicissitudes involved in walking with a crutch in such a stormy weather are also emphasised visually in the poem: 'Her forehead … knotted against such force / that shreds air   sky   time' (*ibid.*).

In 'An Amnesiac in Dublin', O'Donnell also depicts mainstream Irish society as openly inattentive to the reality of immigrants and outcasts. Here, the poet redefines the urban landscape of the capital city as a predominantly white setting, by describing a metropolitan milieu where 'taxis dodge O'Connell Street, / the Battle of the Burger, / Little Africa / and *Beijing Nua*' (2009: 34). The different fast food restaurants in this central Dublin street (from North-American multinationals such as Burger King and McDonald's to African and Chinese restaurants) are symbolic of the multiethnic composition of Irish society. Once again, the author defines the native community as oblivious to this present heterogeneous reality, because they are still consciously trapped in their colonial past:

> Amnesiac to the present,
> we avert our faces, try to recall older struggles:
> Lockout, Rising, the death of Collins;
> amnesiac, we remember the war we took no part in.
>
> (Ibid.)

The malady of the present world, the poet seems to imply, is amnesia: there is a partial loss of memory, a conscious withdrawal from the uncomfortable pain of others. The tragic story of the homeless, for instance, is overwritten by epic stories belonging to the past. It is more comfortable and less painful, the poet implies, to recall the past death of Michael Collins than to focus on the present anguish of vagrants and immigrants.

The main thematic concern underlying these poems by O'Donnell is to condemn the situation of exclusion affecting minority communities in Ireland. In line with Olszewska and Bryce, this poet denounces the existing segregation between natives and newcomers in the Ireland of the Celtic Tiger and the Irish indifference to the plight of others. Another important concern informing O'Donnell's poetry is to celebrate Ireland's new ethnic diversity as potentially enriching. In the second poem of the sequence 'Exiles', 'Alex in the Garden', this writer advocates a pressing need to engage in more genuine interactions with immigrants. This time, O'Donnell focuses on Alex, a Lithuanian gardener working for her mother in Monaghan. The pain and estrangement of exile for this figure, bound to leave wife and daughters behind, is strengthened by the linguistic barriers he finds in the new setting:

> His whiteness struggles
> for survival in the red speech of our North, he
> tries to match his landscape to the stranger's, pondering
> aloud, 'What is this number, this number *ee-yit*?'
>
> (2006: 151)

O'Donnell shows the cultural barrier that language can set up between interethnic encounters. However, the poem finishes by blurring all the national boundaries exposed in the previous lines, as the speaker praises the emotional connection between Alex and her Irish family: 'when my father died, he shed fat tears / at the wake, they flowed unashamed, / watering his roots and ours' (*ibid.*). The well demarcated divisions between natives and immigrants are weakened here symbolically by Alex's tears, which manage to dissolve national 'roots', disclosing the linking bonds of affection that unite families in the moment of death. Whereas in 'Girl from the East' O'Donnell stresses the inequality and solitude experienced by a migrant girl from Eastern Europe, this poem opens the possibility of healing, by envisaging a more positive encounter between the Irish host and the foreign 'guest'. As Gunn points out, recognising difference does not necessarily entail strengthening the chasm between cultures; it can result in a 'fundamental kinship' (2001: 47). It is this sense of 'kinship' fostered by the recognition of, and interaction with, difference that O'Donnell visualises as the poem draws to a close. Alex's 'fat tears', flowing 'unashamed' down the page, dissolve the damaging boundaries established between natives and immigrants and reveal the fallacy of contemporary bureaucratic attempts to maintain legal frontiers between both groups. By recognising the presence of migrants and engaging in an active process of interaction with them, O'Donnell carries out a 'subversive inscription of racialised spaces in white-settled-Catholic Ireland' (Lentin, 2001).

Another Irish poet who is interested in the interactions between natives and the so-called 'new Irish' is Michael O'Loughlin. Issues of multiculturalism and migration have been central to his work since his first book in 1980, and this subject matter is chiefly determined by his experience as an exile in Spain, the Netherlands, and France. His collection *In This Life* (2011) deals with the migration issue in a different fashion. When O'Loughlin settled back in Ireland in 2003, he found a country which was experiencing a sudden wave of immigration for the first time in its history. As he claims, '[f]or me personally it was particularly interesting. In my early work I had plundered the Eastern European experience for metaphors and imagery, and now the metaphors were made flesh' (Villar-Argáiz, 2011).

In This Life precisely reflects this changing landscape that the poet encounters on returning to Ireland. The second section of the collection includes a series of poems in which he adopts the perspective of an invented 'persona', a Latvian poet named Mikelis Norgelis who arrives in Ireland as a so-called 'economic migrant'. O'Loughlin claims on page 21 to have translated his work from this poet. As a translator of more than a hundred books, mainly from Dutch, translation is indeed an important mode for him. In this volume, this alleged translation allows him to adopt the masquerade of someone else, adopting more freely the position of an Other. By exploring multiethnicity from the perspective of the incoming migrant, O'Loughlin switches the centre's perspective for that of the periphery and consequently challenges what Kuhling and Keohane (2007: 84) call 'the monovocality of Irish society'. Another writer who has decentralised white Irish perspectives by imaginatively adopting the perspective of the migrant is Roddy Doyle, in his story 'I Understand'. Reddy's comment in relation to this story can be applied to O'Loughlin's poetry: 'White Irish readers are asked to look at the Irish context differently, to move outside their comfort zone to a place where whiteness and Irishness are neither central nor normative' (2007: 23). This interest in adopting the voice of the immigrant has also been shared lately by other male writers such as Hugo Hamilton (in *Hand in the Fire*) and Dermot Bolger (in poems such as 'On the 7 am Luas to Tallaght'). Interestingly,

Irish women writers have not used to date such a ventriloquist technique, probably because poetic identity itself has been a contested issue for them and they are more consciously aware of the dangers of objectification and simplification involved in the act of speaking on behalf of an Other.

Through this fictional Latvian voice, O'Loughlin imagines the dispossession of exile and the barriers that migrants experience when integrating themselves in the Irish community. The initial poem describes the very moment Mikelis Norgelis bids farewell to his beloved in Riga, an experience described in terms of spiritual agony and emotional death: 'I am travelling West / to bury my heart in an Irish bog' (O'Loughlin, 2011: 26). When arriving in Ireland, Mikelis is assailed by similar feelings, as he strives hard to maintain his personal integrity in an increasingly dehumanised capitalist world:

> How am I to praise
> The call-centre operative,
> The barista in the boutique hotel,
> The estate agent renting out boxes to Slovaks?
>
> (27)

In this aggressive, consumerist society, human relations are not fostered, and the distance between people widens. As Kirby, Gibbons, and Cronin (2002a: 13) claim, the Celtic Tiger period has fostered a change of moral values which prioritise competitiveness, consumerism, and individualism over other values concerning the family and self-sacrifice. This loss of solidarity and communal values is recorded in O'Loughlin's poem. In his description of the cheap labour of economic migrants, of which he forms part, Norgelis describes his solitude and isolation, not only with respect to the native Irish, but also in relation to other migrant co-workers in Tesco:

> I sit here eight hours a day in my blue uniform
> At the cash register in Tesco's
> Trying to think of a name
> For what I actually do.
> My co-workers are called Mariska or Mujummad
> I do not know where they live
> I do not know what they eat.
>
> All I know is we are low-caste priests
> In the greatest church that history has ever seen.
> The people come to the altar rail,
> We lay our hands on the fruits of the earth
> And give them back to the people who made them
> Blessed, sanctified, paid for.
>
> (O'Loughlin, 2011: 27)

The imagery of 'the fruits of the earth' placed outside its original, natural context symbolises the commodification of Irish society, a modern society of domesticated lives detached from nature. This food imagery, together with the supermarket metaphor, recalls the iconic poem of the Beat generation 'A Supermarket in California' by Allen Ginsberg. Like Ginsberg, this imaginary Latvian poet also situates himself and some fellow poets of previous generations in a supermarket. While Ginsberg begins his critique of mainstream American culture by contrasting the consumerist society of his generation with Whitman's, Norgelis compares this ruthless capitalist world with the more optimistic, truthfully revolutionary world in which Neruda, Mayakowsky, and other poetic comrades lived, writing 'their Odes to Labour' (*ibid.*). For Norgelis, these poets represent a value system that contradicts everything that Tesco represents: a globalised world of financial profit and neo-liberal values. In such a competitive setting, immigrants, as cheap labour, are forced to partake in Ireland's mainstream culture, fulfilling the demands of profit and payment of the supermarket. Working eight hours a day in their blue uniforms as Tesco cashiers, they are 'low-caste priests / In the greatest church that history ever seen'. In this regard, immigrants are treated by the nation as 'factors of production' rather than individuals (Kuhling and Keohane, 2007: 51).

O'Loughlin does not only denounce the dehumanising effects of capitalism. Like Bryce and O'Donnell, he also draws our attention to the invisible boundaries that separate natives from newcomers, revealing, as Bryan Fanning (2002: 179) would put it, a 'weak multiculturalism' which leaves untouched the embedded inequalities which separate both groups. Rather than emphasising intercultural connection, O'Loughlin describes a multicultural setting in which different ethnic minorities ignore each other, as they stick to their own people and culture. As we have seen in the previous poem, Norgelis does not know his fellow immigrant workers at Tesco. In 'A Latvian Poet does the Joycean Pilgrimage', ethnic segregation also predominates: the poetic voice continues buying his 'Latvian beer / In a shop called Booze2Go' while his fellow 'Russian' citizens chat among themselves at the entrance of hostels (O'Loughlin, 2011: 28). The exchanges between immigrants and the Irish population are also described in terms of estrangement and defamiliarisation. In 'A Latvian Poet Spends Xmas in Foley Street', for instance, O'Loughlin parodies normal Christian festivities. This period should be a time for charity and happiness; instead O'Loughlin portrays a cold setting, in which even human communication itself is portrayed in terms of forced articulation:

> The streets are strangely full …
> Outside the all-night Spar
> A girl pushes her tongue in my mouth
> Like a hungry fish.

'I'm out of the Joy for Christmas',
She says. 'Can you tell me
The price of a packet of fags?'

(35)[1]

One reason for this lack of genuine interculturality might stem from the in-
ternalisation of a colonial mentality, as O'Loughlin suggests in 'A Latvian Poet
Encounters Róisín Dubh'. In this poem, Norgelis addresses Róisín Dubh, the
nationalist image of feminised Ireland:

You make me rub your back till the skin is red and broken
you make me press your bones till they crack.
I want to reach my fist down
deep inside your chest
to pull out your heart, and hold it up to glisten in the light …
I want to fillet out your spine.

(29)

As in nationalist discourse, Róisín Dubh occupies the role of a passive national
symbol, one oppressed and colonised, in this particular case by the incoming
migrant and not by the British imperialist. The foreigner's relationship with
Ireland is one characterised by violence, hatred, and alluring Otherness: he
wants both to destroy the country that has accepted him, while discovering
its ineluctable secrets, reaching inside her heart, and 'hold[ing] it up to glisten
in the light'. In any case, O'Loughlin's poem blurs the historically assimilated
dichotomies between coloniser and colonised, conquerors and natives. In the
Hegelian master-slave dialectics O'Loughlin describes, Ireland is also portrayed
as a complicit participant. She '*make[s]* [the foreigner] rub [her] back till the
skin is red and broken' (emphasis added) and 'press [her] bones till they crack'.
This active role assigned to Ireland is confirmed in succeeding lines, where the
reader learns that it was Ireland herself who transformed the immigrant into a
violent 'butcher'. Róisín Dubh is no longer a passive victim, but an aggressive
monster like the Greek mythical Minotaur: 'Now you move like the Minotaur /
through my body's dark maze / to carve me like an invisible butcher' (31).

According to Edward Said, the stereotype of the Orient was invented by
Western scholarship in order to fulfil its own political and ideological needs to
create a dehumanised 'Other'. The coloniser dehumanised the Orient in order
to fulfil two purposes: on the one hand to strengthen his self-image and justify
his exploitation and domination of the Other; and on the other hand to provide a demoralising image which is partially internalised by the colonised (1995:
7). This process would explain the caricatured portrayal of the Stage Irishman,
promoted by English playwrights from the eighteenth century onwards. Such
a xenophobic attitude of the British colonialist towards the colonised is in turn

replicated by the Irish, who mimicking imperialist discourses, foster the stereo-type of the menacing, immigrant 'butcher'. Kuhling and Keohane have explained how the psychological legacy of colonialism still manifests itself in covert racist attitudes towards the migrants in Ireland (2007: 65–7). As they claim, 'Ireland's problematic relationship to immigration, migrant workers and refugees can be interpreted against this backdrop of [colonial] trauma and ambivalence' (66). This very same argument is put forward by Kirby, Gibbons, and Cronin (2002b: 197), who claim that the new Ireland of the twenty-first century is partly con-structed upon the suppression of historical memory and the negation of many aspects of Ireland's past, in particular, the experiences of colonisation and di-aspora. One of the results of this historical amnesia is that the ex-colonised unconsciously project this unresolved past trauma onto another alien Other, in this particular case, the immigrant. In O'Loughlin's poem, Róisín Dubh has unconsciously inherited these imperialist attitudes by fostering the stereotype of the migrant as a threatening figure.

Such a demonised portrayal of the foreigner is also recorded by Norgelis in 'A Latvian Poet Reads Yeats's *A Vision* in the Oliver St John Gogarty':

> Strange to think that all of us –
> The Poles, the Chinese and me –
> Once were children in shining white shirts …
> Not knowing we were the Beast
> They feared so much over here
> That we almost blotted out the light.
>
> But the Beast is dead and
> We have come crawling like vermin
> Out of its cold fur.
>
> (O'Loughlin, 2011: 33)

Immigrants are here perceived as threatening presences which might stain, or 'contaminate', the monolithic identity that the Irish nation has cultivated throughout the twentieth century. Nevertheless, as Norgelis reveals, Ireland's fear is unjustified: 'the Beast is dead' and subsequently the threat the immi-grant poses is just illusory. In this poem, and in others such as 'A Latvian Poet Encounters Róisín Dubh' with its references to the Great Irish Elk and the myth-ological Minotaur (29, 31), O'Loughlin uses constant imagery of dead, extinct or non-existent animals in order to talk about the Celtic Tiger period. The dead beast in this poem is a symbol of the corruption of prosperous Ireland, a coun-try in which human communication has demised and where immigrants are considered as destructive and injurious 'vermin'.

In this sense, the possibility of genuine intercultural mediation is problem-atised in the poetic accounts of Mikelis Norgelis. O'Loughlin seems to suggest, through this fictional voice, that a truly intercultural society in Ireland can only be conceived in the abstract form, because real life is characterised by this lack of truthful connection. Conscious of being an Other in a strange place, this Latvian poet battles his strong sense of 'foreignness' as he wanders through the streets of Dublin. In O'Loughlin's clean, well-crafted poetry, Norgelis narrates with sarcastic perceptiveness his 'Joycean Pilgrimage' throughout a multicultural city of 'Lithuanian cars', and 'Korean' and 'Chinese restaurants' (28, 53). In such a shifting landscape, the ability lies, as Norgelis suggests, in opening one's mind, in order to truly learn from the Other, creating a new atmosphere where hybridity between cultures is greatly encouraged. O'Loughlin records Norgelis's marvel at his discovery of iconic figures in Irish literature, particularly Yeats and Joyce. Rather than being uncritically assimilated by the majority culture, Norgelis strives hard to engage in a truthful dialogue with the Irish tradition, raising the possibility that people of Latvian ancestry can create an Irish identity that is much more fluid, dynamic, and hybrid. In this sense, this migrant character disrupts the taken-for-granted binary oppositions 'insider v. outsider' and 'Irish v. non-Irish', by appropriating key elements of Irishness and, in the words of Kuhling and Keohane (2007: 84), breaking open 'what tends to be a static, rigid and impermeable understanding of Irish culture as something frozen in the past and hermetically sealed off from active constructions by the "new Irish."'

This advocacy of new hybrid identities is observed in 'Parnell Street', where Norgelis expresses his delight at the prospect of listening to different languages and drinking different kinds of beer in the centre of Dublin: 'Now I hear again every language I ever heard / Drink beer I crossed a continent to taste' (O'Loughlin, 2011: 52). O'Loughlin's defence of intercultural conviviality is articulated through this recognition of a mongrelised self who moves beyond fixed identities. Whereas the 'real' life of Norgelis is determined by segregation and solitude, working as he does eight hours a day at Tesco, his creativity is constantly nourished by Dublin's hybridised culture and society. By revealing this immigrant's proximity to traditional icons of Irishness (Róisín Dubh, Yeats or Joyce), O'Loughlin challenges stable concepts of identity and nationality and consequently opens a new poetic space in which genuine conviviality can be truly envisaged.

This chapter has addressed how poets in Ireland reflect the new ethnic diversity by articulating specific aspects of crosscultural and interethnic exchange. The possibility of extending this analysis to a wider range of poems and authors (both Irish and non-Irish) makes these conclusions necessarily provisional. Furthermore, it is evident that the economic recession in the Ireland of the new millennium will have some sort of impact on debates around multiculturalism. We need time to assess the effects of this on the discourses of Otherness which are articulated by both Irish poets and the migrant minority. However, the poems studied so far clearly reveal both the flexibility and ability of contemporary poetry in Ireland to accommodate cultural diversity, in its advocacy of tolerance and the articulation of a new Ireland constructed around the interaction with immigrants. All in all, the issues raised and explored by Olszewska, Bryce, O'Donnell, and O'Loughlin are of key importance in the current context of the Republic: the legal handling of immigration, the working and living conditions of foreigners, their integration and assimilation, the stereotypes projected onto them, and the locals' sense of hospitality.

When dealing with all these topics, these writers seem to cultivate, in different ways, new modes of recognition for the so-called 'new Irish'. The general tendency in their work is to envision interethnic encounters in Ireland as spaces of collision and confrontation. Olszewska and Bryce, for instance, reveal the negative prejudices projected onto migrants by the host community and how their marginalisation is accentuated by Ireland's legislative attempts to handle immigration. This critique is continued in the work of O'Donnell and O'Loughlin; both poets draw our attention to the dehumanising effects of Celtic Tiger capitalism and the repercussion of these on widening social and economic inequities. In their aesthetic explorations of interethnic encounters, both writers re-imagine Ireland at times as a site of pluralism where cultural diversity is both respected and celebrated. This Ireland of the future will no longer be considered 'as a nation that … *includes* Others', but as 'a nation *of* Others' (original emphasis; Hickman, 2007: 23).

Notes

1   This lack of genuine interactions between natives and newcomers is also emphasised in 'The Cormorant' (O'Loughin, 2011: 10–12).

References

Bourke, Eva and Borbála Faragó (eds) (2010). 'Introduction', *Landing Places. Immigrant Poets in Ireland*. Dublin: Dedalus, xvii–xxv.

Bryce, Colette (2005). *The Full Indian Rope Trick*. Basingstoke and Oxford: Picador.

Fanning, Bryan (2002). *Racism and Social Change in the Republic of Ireland*. Manchester: Manchester University Press.

Gray, Breda (2008). 'Steering a course somewhere between hegemonic discourses of Irishness', in Ronit Lentin (ed.), *The Expanding Nation: Towards a Multi-Ethnic Ireland*, vol. I. Dublin: MPhil in Ethnic and Racial Studies, Department of Sociology, Trinity College Dublin, 60–72.

Gunn, Giles (2001). *Beyond Solidarity: Pragmatism and Difference in a Globalized World*. Chicago: University of Chicago Press.

Hickman, Mary J. (2007). 'Immigration and monocultural (re)imaginings in Ireland and Britain', *Translocations. The Irish Migration, Race and Social Transformation Review* 2.1: 12–25.

Kearney, Richard (1997). *Postnationalist Ireland: Politics, Culture, Philosophy*. London: Routledge.

Kiberd, Declan (2005). *The Irish Writer and the World*. Cambridge: Cambridge University Press.

King, Jason (2008). 'Porous nation: From Ireland's "haemorrhage" to immigrant inundation', in Ronit Lentin (ed.), *The Expanding Nation: Towards a Multi-Ethnic Ireland*, vol. I. Dublin: MPhil in Ethnic and Racial Studies, Department of Sociology, Trinity College Dublin, 49–54.

Kirby, Peadar, Luke Gibbons, and Michael Cronin (eds) (2002a). 'Introduction', *Reinventing Ireland: Culture, Society and the Global Economy*. London: Pluto, 1–19.

—— (2002b). 'Conclusions and transformations', *Reinventing Ireland: Culture, Society and the Global Economy*. London: Pluto, 196–208.

Kuhling, Carmen and Kieran Keohane (2007). *Cosmopolitanism Ireland: Globalization and Quality of Life*. London: Pluto.

Lentin, Ronit (2001). 'Responding to the racialisation of Irishness: Disavowed multiculturalism and its discontents', *Sociological Research Online* 5.4: n.p.

Lentin, Ronit and Robbie McVeigh (2006). *After Optimism? Ireland, Racism and Globalisation*. Dublin: Metro Éireann.

O'Donnell, Mary (2006). *The Place of Miracles: New and Selected Poems*. Dublin: New Island.

—— (2009). *The Ark Builders*. Nanholme Mill: Arc.

O'Loughlin, Michael (2011). *In This Life*. Dublin: New Island.

Olszewska, Kinga (2010). 'Site for Sale', in Eva Bourke and Borbála Faragó (eds), *Landing Places: Immigrant Poets in Ireland*. Dublin: Dedalus, 144.

Reddy, Maureen T. (2007). 'Reading and writing race in Ireland: Roddy Doyle and *Metro Éireann*', in Wanda Balzano, Anne Mulhall, and Moynagh Sullivan (eds), *Irish Postmodernisms and Popular Culture*. New York: Palgrave Macmillan, 15–25.

Said, Edward (1995) [1978]. *Orientalism: Western Conceptions of the Orient*. London: Penguin.

Strong, Eithne (1993). *Spatial Nosing. New and Selected Poems*. Swords: Salmon.

Villar-Argáiz, Pilar (2010). Interview with Mary O'Donnell, 8 April. Unpublished.

—— (2011). Interview with Michael O'Loughlin, 4 May. Unpublished.

5

Immigration in Celtic Tiger and post-Celtic Tiger novels

Margarita Estévez-Saá

The history of Ireland and of the Irish is full of stories of deprival, to the extent that they were, for a long time, divested of houses, estates, land, country, and nation, and forced to emigrate. Irish literature, inevitably, has bore witness to this history of deprivation recreating it once and again in an attempt to overcome that trauma, by means of the transformation, reorientation, or re-evaluation of the experience of loss (Balaev, 2008: 164). Recent examples by representative writers of the Irish literary scene are, among others, Joseph O'Connor (*Redemption Falls*, 2008), Colm Toíbín (*Brooklyn*, 2009), and Sebastian Barry (*On Canaan's Side*, 2011), writers who are still trying to come to terms with the hardships the Irish emigrants had to endure for centuries and the consequent intergenerational transmission of that traumatic legacy.

If emigration had been and still is a recurrent topic in the novels published in Ireland in the twenty-first century, immigration has progressively, although comparatively speaking more slowly, become a prominent concern of twenty-first-century Irish literature. The purpose of this chapter is precisely to study how contemporary Irish fiction depicts, and reflects on, the incipient multicultural Irish society. Declan Kiberd considers that it has taken Irish authors too long to offer an adequate literary response to the new social circumstances of the island (Kiberd, 2005: 276). Beyond the Irish context, some voices have also expressed the difficulties of writers in judiciously reflecting on and fairly representing the experience of the migrant. Thus, Ashley Dawson asserts that '[m]uch of what is classified today as the literature of migration does not reflect the conditions of extreme duress of those who are trafficked from one part of the world to another', and she recalls Amitav Ghosh's words when the Bengali Indian author argued that 'we do not yet possess literary forms to give true expression to the experience of global migrants' (Dawson, 2010: 178–9). Nevertheless, as we advance into the twenty-first century, we certainly detect Irish writers' concern with the presence of inward migrants in Ireland. In some of the novels analysed in this chapter, immigrants are even turned into protagonists – subjects of their own narratives – rather than mere participants in the background. Indeed, one can detect an evolution in the way Irish writers talk about immigration, from the mere representation of 'multi-culturalism' in Ireland – that for Edna Longley 'signifies cultural coexistence rather than cultural exchange' – to a progressive involvement with an 'inter-cultural' project that implies 'engaging with genuine differences and making them fruitful' (Longley, 2001: 5, 9).

Therefore, after a survey of the novels published in Ireland since the year 2000, it is plausible to recognise three main attitudes that respond to a progressive treatment of the issues mentioned above. We find a first group of novels that depicts the emigrant's or his/her descendants' return to Ireland; these novels also include references to the existence of a new population attracted by what I call the 'picturesque' of the island, that is, a highly idealised and romanticised image of Ireland and the Irish. This is the case, for example, in novels by Mary Rose Callaghan (*The Visitors' Book*, 2001) or Elizabeth Wassell (*The Things He Loves*, 2001). Both authors, as we will see, combine idealised visions of nationhood with scattered hints of racism, revealing the dark side of the culturally and economically attractive country that initially appeals to foreigners. A different group of novels, more openly focused on Celtic Tiger Ireland, presents a multiethnic and multicultural society in which migrants astonish the natives who still see this new social landscape with surprised eyes. Good examples are Éilís Ní Dhuibhne's *Fox, Swallow, Scarecrow* (2007) and Anne Haverty's *The Free and Easy* (2007). Finally, we find more recent works of fiction which manage to definitively give voice to the realities of immigrants in Ireland, in order to offer readers their own perspective and experience: Chris Binchy's *Open-Handed* (2008), Peter Cunningham's *Capital Sins* (2010), and Hugo Hamilton's *Hand in the Fire* (2010) are good examples.

Picturesque Ireland: 'How we'd get so fashionable?'

An exhaustive study of the Irish novels published since the 1990s reveals that it is not until the early twenty-first century that Irish writers begin to systematically include the representation of immigrants in Irish society. There are two general groups of new inhabitants in the island that are alluded to in this first group of novels. On the one hand, we find the figure of the returned emigrant who, without considering himself or herself a foreigner, feels almost like a stranger in his or her native land or in the country of his or her ancestors. On the other hand, we find people from different countries who come to Ireland attracted by the economic and cultural attractions of the island. Both groups appear in novels by Mary Rose Callaghan and Elizabeth Wassell.

Mary Rose Callaghan is a Dublin-born writer whose literary trajectory has been recently vindicated (Felder, 2010: 18). As Maryanne Felder has stated, 'Callaghan's fiction charts the movement of "old Ireland" into Celtic Tiger Ireland and exposes some of the limitations of the island's entry into the European Union' (19). Many of her novels deal with issues of emigration and immigration in Ireland. In *The Visitors' Book* (2001) or *A Bit of a Scandal* (2009), Callaghan offers a sound reflection on the experience of immigration and the new propitious circumstances of the island after the economic boom. *A Bit of a Scandal* narrates the story of Irish-born Art History Professor Louise, who returns from New York to her native Dublin (the opposite journey to that taken by Anne O'Brien in Callaghan's 1996 novel *Emigrant Dreams*). This voyage makes Louise recall an illicit love affair she had with a monk as a young woman in the 1970s. Twenty years later, on the occasion of her visit to Ireland, Louise meets a very different social landscape:

> Dublin had changed so much: faceless concrete buildings were everywhere and cranes crisscrossed the sky. The traffic alarmed me, and the new immigrants made the place reminiscent of New York, where I'd spent more than half my life. … Over lunch we agreed that Dublin had turned into a province of China, or Poland: you often met shop assistants who couldn't speak English. (Callaghan, 2009: 11)

This new socio-cultural landscape of the Ireland of the last decades of the twentieth century shocks Louise in her otherwise mainly mental recreation of her experience in the repressive island of the 1970s. More interesting for the purposes of this chapter is Callaghan's novel *The Visitors' Book*, a good instance of what has been described as this writer's 'continuing interest in transatlantic comic possibilities' (Felder, 2010: 24). *The Visitors' Book* is an illustrative and rather early example of what I have called the 'picturesque' attraction that Ireland exerts over foreigners attracted by the economic prosperity of the once-called Celtic Tiger island. This novel is narrated in the form of diary entries written by Peggy, a middle-aged Irishwoman who decides to return to her native country with her American husband Charlie. Once in Ireland, their house becomes the centre for various visitors – hence the title of the novel – who come attracted by the idiosyncrasy they associate with the island.

Peggy and Charlie explain their return to Ireland very differently. Whereas Peggy is of Irish origins but does not concede her roots too much significance, Charlie 'considers himself Irish. His mother was [from] New York, but his father was southern with Irish ancestry, so this haunts him. It hovers at his shoulder, beckoning like the ghost in Hugh Leonard's *Da*' (Callaghan, 2001: 24). As we later learn, '[l]ike most Americans, Charlie's in search of happiness. Dublin was the inspiration of his hero, James Joyce. And Ireland's a little bit of heaven fallen from out of the sky one day. He wanted a bohemian life' (25). We detect in Charlie's attitude the association he establishes between Ireland and an ideally bohemian cultural landscape that he projects and with which he wants to identify himself.

A similar romanticised vision of Ireland is held by Billy Boy, one of the couple's visitors, and a distant relative of Charlie's. Billy Boy is obsessed with an idealised, prejudiced vision of Irishwomen, and has come to Ireland precisely to look for and marry what he considers the 'traditional Irish girl': 'He's terribly romantic and talked non-stop of his future life with a "traditional" Irish girl. It's a fantasy out of *The Quiet Man*. He imagines he's John Wayne and he'll meet Maureen O'Hara, milking a cow outside a thatched cottage, preferably barefoot' (104). Billy Boy – in his misadventures with Irishwomen – comically illustrates a naive and prejudiced view of Ireland, of the Irish, and of Irishwomen.

Despite these comic outbursts, the novel also offers a brilliant and sound reflection on the economic and social follies brought about by financial prosperity: house prices rising, interest rates going up, overcrowded streets, and traffic jams. The narrator inevitably wonders how it is that Ireland has become such a fashionable place: 'A new thing in Ireland, now that everyone wants to come and live here – returned emigrants like me, Americans like Charlie, EU citizens, and all the new-age travelers, refugees, aliens, asylum seekers and what-have-yous. How'd we get so fashionable?' (11).

This idealised version of Ireland as a truly multicultural and financially prosperous society is counteracted by serious commentaries on racism. A significant example is that of the adopted daughter of a friend of Peggy's, a Chinese adolescent who comes to Ireland for a brief stay. Despite the multicultural community that Ireland has become – as Peggy tells the girl '[t]here're many Asians living in Dublin. Some run wonderful restaurants. Chinese food is Charlie's favourite' (91) – Shevawn is the object of other girls' abuse and Peggy has to acknowledge that racism unquestionably exists in that seemingly liberal society: 'God, what's Ireland coming to? What strange beast's stalking the land? They call it the Celtic Tiger, but it's some evil spirit of racism' (90). In this sense, Callaghan portrays two contradictory (or seemingly contradictory) views of Ireland: as an idealised multicultural society which is financially prosperous and open to the outside world, but also as a racist, deeply insular society.

Elizabeth Wassell can be considered alongside Mary Rose Callaghan. Of American origins and married to the Irish poet John Montague, Wassell established herself in County Cork, and similarly to Callaghan's, her work reflects on the spell that Ireland casts over people of different nationalities. The main plot of her first novel *The Honey Plain* (1997) revolves around the young painter Grania MacCormack, the daughter of an American senator, who comes to Ireland attracted by its allegedly special light, which she wants to capture on her canvas. In *The Thing He Loves* (2001), Wassell also focuses on a group of European and American artists who, fascinated by its cultural charm, decide to settle in the isle. In particular, the novel tells the story of Fleur York, a successful English painter, Gabriel Charles Phillips, a North American aspiring painter who used to spend the summers of his childhood in Ireland, and another North American Tony Daly, who wants to become a renowned painter. They all come to settle in the Irish valley of Glenfern and become part of the intellectual community there. They associate Ireland and its people with culture and art, reflecting a highly idealised vision of the hospitality of the region. Tony, for instance, 'was happier here than he had ever been in any other place, perhaps because it was the region's custom to embrace people like himself, bohemian types, wanderers, artists and renegades, outsiders in general' (Wassell, 2001: 68–9).

Although hospitality is idealised here as a particular trait of the Irish, racism appears as a counter narrative in some novels by Wassell. In the fashionable world of Dublin and its surroundings depicted in her 2011 novel, *Sustenance*, for instance, we also detect, as in Callaghan's novel, outbreaks of racism which significantly arise among the intelligentsia and glamorous Dubliners: 'Ireland ought to consider becoming a bit more vigilant in that regard as well, since all these immigrants have been pouring in – immigrants and Jews' (49).

Thus, both O'Callaghan and Wassell present a kind of privileged foreigner who comes to Ireland of his/her own accord, attracted by the cultural and social possibilities that the country offers them. At the same time, as we have seen, both authors reveal the existence of less favoured immigrants, more ethnically distinguishable than the previous ones (such as Chinese or Jews) and subjected to more racist and xenophobic attitudes on the part of the Irish. The coexistence of both types of migrants and the different ways they are regarded and represented by these authors should make us consider Nikos Papastergiadis's assertion in his seminal work *The Turbulence of Migration* that '[a] more subtle vocabulary on migration is necessary' (2000: 55). Papastergiadis vindicates the need to delimit the meaning of 'migrancy' and begins by distinguishing between voluntary and involuntary migrants (57), a distinction that, as we have seen, is provided by the novels considered here.

Multicultural Celtic Tiger Ireland: 'Nothing you wouldn't see in NY'

Éilís Ní Dhuibhne's *Fox, Swallow, Scarecrow* has been described by some critics as the Celtic Tiger novel everybody was waiting for (Houston, 2007: 13; Spain, 2010). Most of the action of the novel is set in twenty-first-century Dublin, a city crowded with, on the one hand, intellectuals (writers, publishers, editors) and successful businessmen who star in the fashionable meetings of the affluent city; and, on the other, immigrant characters who strive to earn their living almost anonymously: Spanish and Swedish au pairs, Lithuanian cleaners, and Romanian and Polish migrants begging in the street, among others (Ní Dhuibhne, 2007: 53, 61, 324). A similar multicultural landscape appears in Anne Haverty's novel *The Free and Easy*, which has been rightly described by Miles Dungan in an interview for the RTÉ as 'an antidote to the Celtic Tiger' (Dungan, 2007). This novel convincingly depicts prosperous Ireland, while humorously and shrewdly criticising its foibles. The city is visited by Tom Blessman, an Irish American sent to the island by his rich great-uncle with the mission of 'saving the country' (Haverty, 2007: 13). Once there, Blessman discovers that Ireland is no longer a poor dejected country but rather a prosperous modern nation composed of people from different nationalities. As he tells his great-uncle's secretary in America: 'I haven't met any of the Irish yet. ... A shoe-shine I spoke to turned out to be Hungarian and the cab driver was Latvian. We went through a few dodgy areas but nothing you wouldn't see in NY. The skyline is littered with construction cranes, looks like there's big money around' (30).

Both *Fox, Swallow, Scarecrow* and *The Free and Easy* analyse with realism as well as sharpness the economic, political, social, and cultural atmosphere of the island. They also show the attentive critical stance of Irish writers in general and of Irish women writers in particular towards the changes that Irish society was undergoing at the time. In both novels, the immigrants portrayed contribute to the welfare of the affluent Irish but without really interfering in or engaging with the host community. Thus, it is ignorance and aloofness that separates the Irish from their 'guests'. In *Fox, Swallow, Scarecrow*, for instance, Ulla, a Swedish au pair, cannot comprehend the Irish 'obsession' with public transport and property values (Ní Dhuibhne, 2007: 31) and Anna, one of the Irish protagonists of this novel, reflects on the distrust and lack of understanding that distances her from the Lithuanian cleaning lady she has at home:

> Ludmilla was a treasure; she cost very little and worked like a trooper. But there was something about her that Anna didn't like – like Ulla in Bray, Ludmilla was aloof, and, unlike Ulla, Anna sensed, disapproving. ... Ludmilla seldom revealed anything to Anna about her own life. She was Lithuanian and had let it be known that she came from a village fifty kilometres from Klaipeda and that she had been a teacher once, but that was about all. (39)

Overall, these two novels reflect realistically the initial attitude of Celtic Tiger Ireland towards its new settlers. Although immigrants were needed in the new economic context, they were not taken into account and were rather constructed as 'cargo' or 'alien' figures (Dawson, 2010: 190–1). Only when the Celtic Tiger began to collapse, and these communities of immigrants became redundant, did

Irish writers turn their gaze more attentively towards these members of their community. This is, at least, the message that their work seems to have sent us, since it is in novels that depict post-Celtic Tiger Ireland where we find Irish authors giving immigrants a more predominant role.

Intercultural post-Celtic Tiger Ireland: 'Too many people'

The narratives analysed above recreate the mainly disinterested attitude of the natives towards their new, culturally different neighbours. In all cases, the Irish are still the protagonists of these multicultural novels. In this sense, Irish writers offer what can be considered as the doubly privileged view of migration, that of the occidental writer and of his/her western protagonists. After the financial collapse of the country, Irish novelists have progressively begun to focus on the migrants' perspective as they try to reflect on their experience and recreate it as sympathetically as possible. Their new stance on the matter fulfils the demand expressed by Dawson in 'Cargo culture: Literature in an age of mass displacement':

> Much of what is classified today as the literature of migration does not reflect the conditions of extreme duress of those who are trafficked from one part of the world to another. In many instances, postcolonial theories of hybridity and the literary forms in which such theories are instantiated were the product of elite forms of migration that have little connection to the experience of working-class migrants. (Dawson, 2010: 178)

In recent years, however, some Irish writers have depicted the hard conditions of working migrants in Ireland. Good examples are found in Chris Binchy's *Open-Handed*, Peter Cunningham's *Capital Sins*, and Hugo Hamilton's *Hand in the Fire*.

In *Open-Handed*, Binchy proposes a detailed and profound reflection on multiculturalism, or rather interculturalism, in twenty-first-century Ireland. His narrative includes the perspectives of different human types with particular emphasis on the migrants' experiences. Thus, his protagonists are Polish, Russian, and Romanian men and women who are forced to accept low-paid jobs and live in poor circumstances despite their working experience or academic background. In this sense, the novel offers what can be considered an undoubtedly crude but certainly realistic and sympathetic representation of the experience of the economic immigrant in Ireland from the perspective of an Irish writer. The two Irish property developers, Sylvester and Dessie, share centre stage with Victor, Agnieszka, and Marcin, immigrants who hail from Romania, Russia, and Poland respectively. All have come to Ireland looking for a better future but end up working in low-paid jobs that turn them into second-class citizens in their host country. The novel presents a suffocating, overcrowded city in which the personal stories of these characters are inevitably intertwined. In this urban milieu, the immigrant finds it particularly difficult to survive, as is brilliantly depicted in the following passage:

> Where was the city? Everything was too small, like the backstreets of a country town struggling to cope. Narrow lanes where the map showed thoroughfares. The mad push and rush of the people, like spawning fish. The traffic that crawled along streets that couldn't take it, as if God had shrunk the city and left the people and the cars and the buses and the lorries the same size. … Everything and everybody on top of each other. Paths and shops and bars and cafés and supermarkets, all too small. No room to breathe. Too many people. (Binchy, 2008: 60)

In such an overcrowded place, natives and immigrants unavoidably interact as a result of the chaotic situation that Binchy describes, that of 'too many people' coexisting in a 'shrunken' city of 'narrow lanes' and bars and cafés which are 'too small'. At the beginning of the novel, and occasionally throughout the whole narrative, it is difficult to distinguish clearly who is the focus of the stories, as all narratives are more or less interconnected. This feature could very well answer to the author's conscious technique of representing the slippery, ghostly, and liminal condition of the protagonists who appear as spectral figures moving on the margins, a choir of voices that are suffocated by the crowd while earnestly striving to be heard in the text. Thus, we learn about Marcin's having acquired a university degree in his native Poland and his academic aspirations – 'He had talked about Ireland and archaeology, its ancient Celtic culture and the importance of its sites. How the booming economy meant there were huge resources for digs, research, college departments. It all seemed plausible' (16) – or about Victor's desire to earn enough money so as to go back to Romania and become an impresario (117). Despite their dreams and aspirations, the narrative realistically describes these immigrants' adverse circumstances as they are forced to work at night as pub porters and security guards. While Victor strives in vain to avoid the violence of Dublin nightlife, Marcin moves like a spectre around his flat the few hours of the day he spends awake: 'In the daytime Marcin moved like a ghost around the house, skin grey, eyes sunken, barely there, barely visible, while Basil and Andrzej and Arthur were out at work' (94). Marcin's tragedy is emphasised when he phones his parents and tells them lies about his present circumstances in Ireland.

A particularly moving episode in the novel concerns the female immigrant's experience, embodied by Agnieszka, a Russian barmaid. Binchy represents with great sensibility her hardships and the gender conditionings that inevitably turn her into a victim. Scholars such as Papastergiadis have shown the traditional oblivion in literature and academic criticism of the experience of the female immigrant, claiming that women are 'not seen as active agents in the great migration stories: they [are] either left behind, or taken along as part of the man's family' (2000: 52). Similarly, Dawson observes that '[w]omen migrants are … rendered invisible not simply by xenophobic public discourse but also by dominant academic accounts of migration' (2010: 182). Binchy overcomes such an omission by granting the female immigrant a place of her own in the novel. Ostensibly beautiful, Agnieszka works honestly and earnestly as a barmaid at a Dublin fashionable hotel but she is soon offered the chance to become a high-standing prostitute. Her desperation is hinted at when we discover after a phone call to her native country that she has left people dependant on her. Agnieszka provides some of the soundest reflections in the novel on the hiring of female immigrants as labour in Ireland:

> Could it be legal? She thought not, not here in the West, with its EU directives and honesty and cultures of excellence that must surely prevent employers making girls bend over in interviews, inspecting their haunches and teeth as if they were horses. … This was what they were all here for. She watched the new girls smile through it and then, as the weeks passed, she saw how their smiles faded and how the ones that lasted toughened up. (Binchy, 2008: 11)

Another novel in which the topic of immigration features prominently is Peter Cunningham's *Capital Sins*, which has been described as '[t]he first post-Celtic Tiger novel' (Myers, 2010). As a pioneering novel fictionalising Ireland's economic collapse, it could not avoid the issue of immigration. This novel scrutinises the progressive assimilation and integration of immigrants in the Ireland of the financial boom with all its positive as well as negative implications, by uncovering 'the roots of social malaise', namely political corruption, economic greed, and the manipulation of the media (Mac Anna, 2010). In particular, Cunningham, whose financial expertise is backed up by his work as an accountant prior to his literary career, offers a satirical account of the egotism and lack of scruples that led Ireland to the socioeconomic crisis. The protagonists of the novel are Albert Barr, a successful developer, and the young journalist Lee Carew; both characters embody the two most representative powers in twenty-first-century Ireland: economy and the media. Although the Ireland of the economic downfall is portrayed as crowded with immigrants begging in the streets or striving to make a living with low-paid jobs, there are also migrants in Cunningham's narrative who are more comfortably incorporated into the everyday life of the country. We find several allusions to their presence in the city centre as well as in the outskirts of Dublin, running their own businesses and even colonising whole areas: 'Rathmines, once a cosy village on the south side of Dublin, now a series of fast-food joints run by Indians, convenience stores operated by taciturn Chinese and a series of building sites in various stages of completion where the predominant language was Russian' (Cunningham, 2010: 31). No longer do we see isolated foreigners missing their families; by contrast, whole immigrant familial unities with financial potential are now part of the quotidian landscape of the capital city. As Lee Carew drags his girlfriend across a park in Dublin, he notices, for instance, 'closely knit groups of bespectacled Chinese and turbaned Sikh families with prams and heavily swathed Muslim women pushing replete shopping trolleys' (173).

The integration of these new citizens into Irish life is not carried out smoothly and easily in the novel. Albert Barr, for instance, strongly disapproves of their acquisitive power, illustrating a more generalised rejection of the incipient economic welfare of the once low and middle classes: 'People of no substance, Polish immigrants for God's sake, flipping Dublin apartments within six months of buying them. Bricklayers with properties in the sun, garbage-men driving brand-new cars, typists talking about three weeks in the Caribbean. Mares' tails in the blue skies of the Celtic Tiger' (199). Although Barr is not interested in the possibilities afforded by interacting with immigrants, interculturality is envisioned in the novel as a fruitful possibility. This is observed in a significant piece of dialogue, in which the journalist Lee meets an African man, known as Delicato, who sells newspapers at traffic lights. Lee learns about his difficult journey from Africa to Ireland as well as about his dreams and plans for the future. It is Delicato who advises Lee to write a novel about his own story. Both of them are similar liminal figures who do not fit into the scheme of a greedy corrupted society, as this leaves no room for honest hard-working people, be they Irish or immigrants:

> – You can do it, Lee. Tell your story.
> – I have no story. Sometimes I think I am dead.
> – Yeah, I know that feeling. The living dead. People look right through me. Like I is a ghost. Why do they do that?
> – They're scared of us, of our potential.
> – You think so?
> – I'm certain of it. Which is why we waft through life, you and me. Two phantoms, Lee said.

> (88)

Therefore, the perspective on immigration provided by *Capital Sins* includes the inevitable intercultural coexistence of natives and immigrants. Nevertheless, this coexistence is not unproblematic but rather mediated by interest. A good example is offered in a reference to the presence of a young Polish-Irish player in a hurling team. The media, instead of simply accepting the automatic integration of immigrants in Ireland, invents a story that relates the Polish immigrant family to well-known public figures such as Lech Walesa or John Paul II:

There's this new kid on the Dublin minor hurling team, name of Peader Petrowski. First generation Polish-Irish, parents came to Phibsboro from Krakow in the early 1990s. There's sure to be an angle on John Paul II; I think the dad knew Lech Walesa – he was the Solidarity trade union fellow? I'm thinking along the lines, 'John Paul II Family Friend is Dublin's Saviour'. (31)

Cunningham's overall message in relation to immigration seems to be that, whether accepted or questioned, immigrants are no longer mere statistical figures in Ireland, as they have taken an active part in the rise and downfall of the Celtic Tiger. This idea is clearly conveyed at a certain stage in the novel, when the narrative describes a report on a TV programme, the *Pat Kenny Show*, discussing rising property prices in Ireland: 'The support for the continuing upward price spiral in property was due to immigrants, Pat himself said. Rather than it being the immigrants who ought to be grateful to the Irish, it was the Irish who ought to be grateful to the immigrants' (25–6).

Notwithstanding, it is in Hugo Hamilton's novel *Hand in the Fire* where we find the most detailed account of impending interculturality in Ireland. Hamilton himself has said that '[t]he outsiders are going to rescue us' (Egan, 2010). Even though Hamilton refers to himself as Irish – 'us' – this writer knows first-hand what it means to feel displaced, as he was brought up by a mother who spoke German and an Irish nationalist father who only spoke Irish to his children. The hardships of his culturally mixed childhood were fictionalised in his 2003 novel *The Speckled People*. In *Hand in the Fire,* Hamilton focuses once again on the topics of the search for identity and the feeling of inadequacy. The novel tells the story of Vid Ćosić, a young Serb from Belgrade who has come to Ireland to work as a carpenter. He meets an Irish lawyer, Kevin Concannon, and Vid earnestly strives to become part of Kevin's circle of family and friends. Vid's efforts at friendship (which go as far as to compromise his own persona) symbolise his desire to belong, to become part of Ireland as a member of its community.

Anne Enright has described *Hand in the Fire* as 'the first [novel] in the Irish tradition that is written from an Eastern European point of view' (Enright, 2010). Hamilton and his protagonist Vid provide us with what it means to see the world 'in translation', revealing at last 'the voice of the migrant, the mongrel, … the person who is neither one thing nor the other, of the stranger and the traveller in us all' (*ibid.*). Indeed, the protagonist of *Hand in the Fire* is more than an immigrant, since Vid is, above all, a fictional reflection on the human dimension of migration, leaving aside economic and political interests.

Vid's problem is not an economic one: he is a hard worker who finds jobs easily as a carpenter and as he acknowledges, his desire 'was not just the money. … It was the friendship, the family, the idea of belonging that mattered to me' (Hamilton, 2010: 132). In order to fulfil this vital need, Vid does not spare means to comprehend Irish history, culture, and language: 'I wanted to forget about my own country and start again. I wanted to get a foothold here, get to know the place and the people … I was beginning to understand the way things are done here … I was working on the accent, learning all the clichés' (2–3). By means of this character, the novel dramatises the possibilities and limitations of a truly intercultural Ireland. It claims that the efforts made seem to rely only on the immigrant, with a passive attitude on the part of the Irish, who remain aloof and disinterested if their own interests are not at stake. And here is where Hamilton, by means of Vid, reminds the Irish of their own past as emigrants. The narrative includes the past history of the Concannon family and focuses on Johny Concannon, who was compelled to migrate to London and who returned years later to have the impression of being a foreigner in his own native land. Whereas the new generation of Concannons is not interested in recalling this figure and his past, Vid demonstrates concern and sympathy. The refusal of the Concannon family to face the father's tragic experience of unrootedness and displacement is symptomatic of a trauma that has not been assimilated and, consequently, cannot be healed. Irish literature, as claimed at the beginning of this chapter, is still trying to assimilate the trauma of massive Irish emigration by recreating and narrating it over and over again as a first response to an event that is ever-present and intrusive (Balaev, 2008: 164). The perspective of the migrant – in Hugo Hamilton's case, Vid's vision – can also act as a healing agent for Ireland and the Irish. Vid is not only concerned with his own process of becoming 'an ordinary inhabitant who belonged here' (Hamilton, 2010: 261) but he is also intent on forcing the Concannons, and by extension the Irish, to assimilate and come to terms with their own historical sense of dispossession and dislocation. Thus Hamilton offers the Irish reader a brilliant example of how the immigrant is able to enter 'into the story of the country at last', becoming 'a participant, a player, an insider taking action' (261). The writer's announcement that '[t]he outsiders are going to rescue us' acquires further significance here, as Vid offers a nicely polished looking-glass in which the Irish can look at their own fathers' and mothers' sense of displacement and need of belonging, recreating their own historical and identitary inheritance, a heritage the Irish are still nowadays assimilating.

All in all, the novels studied here are politically relevant in the present multicultural context of Ireland. In some way or another, they all denounce the existence of racism or the difficulties that immigrants face in genuinely integrating themselves within Irish society. As we advance in the first decade of the twenty-first century, we also detect an attempt from various Irish writers to represent not only the multicultural atmosphere of the country, but also the many intercultural relationships between natives and immigrants that characterise the country in the new millennium.

References

Balaev, Michelle (2008). 'Trends in literary trauma theory', *Mosaic* 41.2: 149–65.

Binchy, Chris (2008). *Open-Handed*. London: Penguin.

Callaghan, Mary Rose (1996). *Emigrant Dreams*. Dublin: Poolbeg.

—— (2001). *The Visitors' Book*. Dingle: Brandon.

—— (2009). *A Bit of a Scandal*. Dingle: Brandon.

Cunningham, Peter (2010). *Capital Sins*. Dublin: New Island.

Dawson, Ashley (2010). 'Cargo culture: Literature in an age of mass displacement', *Women's Studies Quarterly* 38.1–2: 178–93.

Dungan, Miles (2007). 'Interview with Anne Haverty', *Rattlebag*. Radio Telefís Éireann (RTÉ), 10 April. www.rte.ie/arts/2006/0410/rattlebag.html. Accessed on 10 August 2010.

Egan, Barry (2010). 'Help from the outside', *Independent*, 11 April. www.independent.ie/lifestyle/help-from-the-outside–2133575.html. Accessed on 25 August 2011.

Enright, Anne (2010). 'Review of *Hand in the Fire* by Hugo Hamilton', *Guardian*, 17 April. www.guardian.co.uk/books/2010/apr/17/hand-fire-hugo-hamilton-review. Accessed on 25 August 2011.

Felder, Maryanne (2010). *Crossing Borders: A Critical Introduction to the Works of Mary Rose Callaghan*. Cranbury: Associated University Presses.

Hamilton, Hugo (2010). *Hand in the Fire*. London: Harper Collins.

Haverty, Anne (2007). *The Free and Easy*. London: Vintage.

Houston, Nainsí J. (2007). 'Celtic Tiger Ireland: Free and easy?', *World Literature Today* 81.1: 12–15.

Kiberd, Declan (2005). *The Irish Writer and the World*. Cambridge: Cambridge University Press.

Longley, Edna (2001). 'Multi-culturalism and Northern Ireland: Making differences fruitful', in Edna Longley and Declan Kiberd. *Multi-Culturalism: The View from the Two Irelands*. Cork: Cork University Press in association with The Centre for Cross Border Studies, Armagh, 1–44.

Mac Anna, Ferdia (2010). 'The Celtic Tiger's Hemingway', *Irish Times*, 3 July. www.petercunninghambooks.com/reviews/Irish_Times_Ferdia_Mac_Anna.pdf. Accessed on 25 August 2011.

Myers, Kevin (2010). 'If there is to be a genre of Celtic Tiger fiction, *Capital Sins* will be the foundation stone', *Independent*, 1 July. www.independent.ie/opinion/columnists/kevin-myers/kevin-myers-if-there-is-to-be-a-genre-of-celtic-tiger-fiction-capital-sins-will-be-the-foundation-stone–2241241.html. Accessed on 25 August 2011.

Ní Dhuibhne, Éilís (2007). *Fox, Swallow, Scarecrow*. Belfast: Blackstaff.

Papastergiadis, Nikos (2000). *The Turbulence of Migration. Globalization, Deterritorialization and Hybridity*. Cambridge: Polity.

Spain, John (2010). 'Riding the Tiger: Review of *Capital Sins* by Peter Cunningham', *Irish Independent*, 12 June. www.petercunninghambooks.com/reviews/Irish_Independent_John_Spain.pdf. Accessed on 25 August 2011.

Wassell, Elizabeth (1997). *The Honey Plain*. Dublin: Wolfhound.

—— (2001). *The Thing He Loves*. Dingle: Brandon.
—— (2011). *Sustenance*. Dublin: Liberties.

PART II

'Rethinking Ireland' as a postnationalist community

6

'Who is Irish?':
Roddy Doyle's hyphenated identities

Eva Roa White

As a result of its Celtic Tiger brief economic boom, Ireland has experienced a significant increase in inward migration. With the new influx of immigrants comes the necessity to pose the question 'Who is Irish?' In an effort to answer this question, Roddy Doyle, the only one of his siblings who did not emigrate, recounts the change in the traditional relationship Ireland has had with the experience of immigration, now that the tables are turned and Ireland is playing the role of host country on a larger scale than ever before. The wave of inward migration of the 1990s seems to have taken Ireland by surprise. However, the popular notion that Ireland was a monocultural country before that period is inaccurate. For example, Chinese immigration to Ireland has been taking place since at least the late 1950s (Yau, 2007: 49). Furthermore, Mary J. Hickman, in discussing the erasure of Ireland's historical multiculturality and hybridity, poses a crucial question: 'Can the shift be made from considering Ireland as a nation that now *includes* Others to recognising Ireland as a nation *of* Others?' (original emphasis; Hickman 2007: 22–3). For her, this is not about immigration policies only, but about the 'opportunity to focus on what sort of society Ireland wants to become' (*ibid.*). Doyle comments on this very issue in his interview with Jody Allen-Randolph. Answering a question about the transformation of Ireland's idea of itself during the boom years, he refers to the new Ireland as 'a shift in the way we think about ourselves' (Allen-Randolph, 2010: 151–2). This 'shift' echoes Stuart Hall's definition of cultural identities as 'the unstable points of identification or suture, which are made, within the discourses of history and culture. Not an essence but a *positioning*' (Hall, 1994: 395). For Doyle, Ireland's new 'positioning' includes a larger definition of Irishness that encompasses hybridisation and its resulting hyphenated identities, that is, identities that encompass more than one nationality, ethnicity or culture. Diane Sabenacio Nititham is a good example of an Irish hyphenated identity, as her cultural identity encompasses two nationalities. In her article on Filipina hybrid identity in Ireland, she offers her own experience of double identity as a hyphenated 'Filipina Irish or Irish Filipina', while discussing the cultural intersections and 'in-between spaces that a hyphenated identity produces' and how these allow for the ethnic minority voices to be central (2008: 70).

In *The Deportees* (2007), Doyle chronicles these cultural intersections and tensions in eight stories that illustrate the encounters between the native Irish and the new immigrants. These stories promote a shift from 'multiculturality' (disconnected and passive coexistence with ethnic minorities) to 'interculturalism' (active exchange between different cultures and ethnicities). This movement from multiculturality to interculturalism is an example of what I term 'identity migration': the diaspora of the mind or inner voyage from one's state of origin into another that affiliates one to another culture, race, gender or ideology with which one feels a connection. Identity migrants rearrange their 'innerscape' (landscape of the mind) in order to accommodate their double identities. This diaspora of the mind reflects the adaptation of identity migrants to a new set of circumstances brought about by intercultural encounters arising from both physical and/or intellectual diasporas. As a result, these identity migrants construct for themselves a grafted or hybrid identity, which encompasses at least two worlds: the world of origin and the adopted world (White, 2010: 104). According to my definition, Doyle is a successful identity migrant who reaches out to the immigrant community in Dublin and claims it as his own. In the process, Doyle constructs new innerscapes for himself and Ireland by challenging and stretching the concept of 'Irishness' into hyphenated identities. This chapter focuses on the construction and defence of such an intercultural landscape of hyphenated identities in Doyle's short story '57% Irish', although general comments on this writer's oeuvre will be provided in order to further contextualise the issues mentioned above.

Doyle's reaching out for connection and affiliation to another ethnic group is not new. In his well-known novel *The Commitments* (1987), he introduces Jimmy Rabbitte as his first identity migrant character who claims an African American identity for his band, using the brotherhood of the oppressed as a bridge between white Irish identity and black American identity (Pirroux, 1998; McGlynn, 2004). Like Jimmy, Doyle moves across the boundaries of nationality and race to affiliate himself with other cultures and nationalities. His collaboration with Nigerian Irish playwright Bisi Adigun on a multicultural version of J.M. Synge's *The Playboy of the Western World* (2007) provides a good example of a hyphenated Irish identity. By casting a Nigerian immigrant in the role of Christy Mahon, Doyle and Adigun seek to bridge the cultural differences between Ireland and its inward migrants. One main criticism voiced by Karen

Fricker (2007) is that the new *Playboy* fails to address the racial tension in twenty-first-century Ireland. Indeed, the intercultural relationship between Pegeen and Christopher misses the opportunity to dramatise the real challenges of interracial couples in Ireland by treating race as a non-issue. As a result, the new intercultural Ireland that Doyle and Adigun are promoting remains one that avoids confrontation.

The theme of intercultural relationships is also at the heart of Doyle's short story collection, *The Deportees*. Initially written for the weekly immigrant newspaper *Metro Éireann*, these stories are another example of Doyle's crusade for racial tolerance. In her article about Doyle's collaboration with *Metro Éireann*, Maureen T. Reddy relates this writer's statement that the short stories would all 'be funny, optimistic stories that would bring people together' and that he saw the stories as his 'contribution' to antiracist work in Ireland (Reddy, 2005: 382).

In this collection, Doyle addresses the reality of several types of immigrants and the degree of acceptance (or lack thereof) they encounter in their dealings with their native Irish hosts. Most of the stories relate the successful acculturation and identity migration of their characters with racial harmony and positive immigrant experiences triumphing over racism and xenophobia. In 'The Deportees', for instance, Jimmy Rabbitte, former manager of the band The Commitments, rewrites the past by forming a Dublin multicultural band that is composed of immigrants and an Irish Traveller, thus bringing together old and new Irish hybridities (Doyle, 2007: 27–77). Jimmy's success with his new band is Doyle's model for an ideal intercultural Ireland. 'New Boy' is the story of Joseph, a nine-year-old African refugee, who finally bonds with Irish school bullies through his refusal to denounce them to his teacher (78–99). The result is the bond of schoolboys united against their teacher, thus transcending racial and cultural differences. Positive interculturalism is also envisaged in 'Black Hoodie'. Here, the narrator is an Irish teenager in love with a Nigerian girl, with whom he investigates racial profiling in retail stores, as part of a school project (130–53). Inspired by the strength of the character of 'Miss Nigeria' and her family, the teenager stands up to the racist Garda. By the end of the story, the two teenagers are holding hands after crossing a literal and metaphorical cultural bridge. A similar optimistic landscape is portrayed in 'I Understand'. This story features Tom, an isolated illegal immigrant from no specific country, who finally stands up to Irish thugs who want him to run drugs (215–42). His dream of having Irish children promises to come true when he falls in love with an Irish girl. The notable exception to the collection is 'The Pram', the story of Alina, a Polish au pair, who seeks revenge by terrifying the older children in her care with horror stories and murders her abusive employer when dismissed (154–78). Another story that veers from the rest is 'Home to Harlem'. It does not feature an immigrant/host encounter, but focuses on Declan O'Connor, a biracial Irish graduate student who goes to New York to do research on the Harlem Renaissance and reconnect with his American roots (179–214). He admires the ease with which Americans seem to accept racial hyphenated identities, unlike in Ireland, where being black precludes one from being fully Irish. By the end of the story, Declan has found the ideal title for his thesis: 'Who the Fuck Are We?', voicing the question many hyphenated Irish are still trying to answer today (214).

'Guess Who's Coming for the Dinner?' best typifies the inevitable encounter between Ireland and its immigrant community or, as Doyle puts it in the Foreword to *The Deportees*: 'the story – someone new meets someone old – has become an unavoidable one' (xiii). Set in Larry Linnane's home, and featuring the dinner table as the site of the domestic intercultural encounter, the story is remindful of the well-known American racial encounter over dinner, the film *Guess Who's Coming to Dinner* (1967). However, Doyle gives it a twist in that, unbeknown to her father, the Irish daughter has no intention of marrying the Nigerian man. The result is that although it initiates a necessary racial conversation and promotes interculturalism, much like Doyle and Adigun's new *Playboy*, the story stops short of a frank conversation about interracial marriage.

An easy-going Irish working-class father, Larry is forced to confront his racial stereotypes when his daughter Stephanie brings home Ben, a Nigerian refugee. Confused, bewildered, and defensive at what he experiences as an invasion of his home, Larry is also shocked by how uncomfortable he feels about this. When Larry's wife, Mona, confronts him with the question 'Is it because he is black?', Larry feels ashamed at the thought of being a racist (6). Reminded that one of his heroes was black, Larry retorts: 'Phil Lynnot was Irish! … He was fuckin' civilised!' (*ibid.*). Here is the moment where Larry begins his inner shift towards identity migration, as he realises that being Irish does not necessarily equate to being white. As for most Irish natives, the most difficult part for Larry is how to separate the two. After some soul-searching, Larry concludes that it must be Ben's status of refugee that upsets him.

The images of Africa that Larry summons up in his mind are those fed to him by the popular media, which depict Nigeria as a violent country riddled with AIDS and civil wars (8). Larry's ignorance of Nigeria adds to his confusion and his fear of the Other. This fear is an abstract one, based on the 'Idea of the Other' rather than on the concrete human experience of a face-to-face intercultural encounter. Confronted with a well-dressed, educated Nigerian, Larry has to readjust his ideas about race and Nigerian immigrants. He is won over by the obvious superiority (in looks, dress, profession, and moral stance as well as choice of cologne) of Ben, the Nigerian accountant who is so perfect that there is no way for Larry to find fault with him at all, outside perhaps of his self-righteousness. Larry is the Ireland who finally lets Ben's Nigeria in; thus, he is a successful identity migrant in that he accepts Ben as kin. Larry has come to admire the Other whom he no longer regards as an unwanted foreigner invading his country by way of his dinner table, but as a guest to whom he would gladly extend a hand of welcome, not only to his country but into his family. In Larry, Ireland is ready to share its wealth (dinner) with Nigeria as represented by Ben. Doyle's idealistic portrayal of the Nigerian immigrant is resonant of the zealousness of a new convert: the identity migrant whose self-assigned duty is to champion his new kinship with the Other. Though this is a positive effort, its delivery feels superficial.

The story '57% Irish' also addresses intercultural relationships but this time in the public sphere. Here Doyle uses his writing as a socio-political tool to satirise the amended 2004 Irish Nationality and Citizenship Act. Although Doyle tries to present Ireland as open to immigrants, the reality is that the country is experiencing a great challenge in sharing Irish citizenship with its inward migrants who are perceived 'as a threat to the national identity' (Piola, 2006: 54). The fear is that adding more hyphenated identities to Ireland's long-standing divisions such as religion, politics, and language might divide the country further. Understandably, for a country that has only obtained partial independence less than a century ago, the perceived new 'invasion' by foreigners is indeed a challenge, especially when they bring yet another dividing factor into play: race. Ironically, while restricting citizenship to inward migrants, Ireland has been reinforcing its cultural identity by welcoming the primarily white descendants of Irish immigrants (Piola, 2006: 47). By opening its cultural and national community to selected hyphenated Irish such as Irish Americans, Ireland opens itself up to the charge of discrimination. This is a central theme in '57% Irish', in which the Minister for the Arts and Ethnicity hires graduate student Ray Brady to devise a test that will keep immigrants out of Ireland. At first, Ray seems indifferent to the plight of these marginalised minorities, even though he has a son with Darya Alexandrovna, a Russian immigrant. The story ends well, however, as Ray, like Larry a successful identity migrant, mends his relationship with Darya, whom he first refers to as 'Stalin' and later renames 'Gorbachev' as a sign of the end of their private Cold War. This rapprochement inspires Ray to rebel against the government by manipulating the test, the Fáilte Score, in a way that allows him to grant Irish citizenship not only to his girlfriend, but also to over 800,000 Africans and East Europeans before he is caught.

In '57% Irish', the novelty of a multicultural Ireland is reflected in the creation of the position of Minister for the Arts and Ethnicity, which in turn acknowledges the necessity to revisit the issue of Irish citizenship and to pose the questions: What does it mean to be Irish in modern Ireland? How does one become Irish? In her 2006 article, 'The reform of Irish citizenship', Catherine Piola addresses this very issue: 'In the last ten years, the number of citizenship applications in

Ireland has risen, from about 150 in 1980 to over 2,800 in 2001, and the chang-ing population patterns … have brought the issue of Irish citizenship to the foreground in debates over an immigration policy' (2006: 41). Before one can become Irish, one needs to know what 'Irishness' is. To get to the heart of this matter, '57% Irish' has Ray Brady formulate two key questions: 'How do you measure nationality?' and 'How do you measure Irishness?' (Doyle, 2007: 101, 107). It does not take Ray long to realise the difficulty and near impossibility of answering these questions because of the constructed nature of nationality and, by extension, Irishness. The underlying question that Brady also needs to answer is: What are the markers of nationality? According to Piola these are difficult to specify, as the conditions added to the recent pieces of legislation (Irish Nationality and Citizenship Act, 2004, No. 38) 'do not intend to define Irish citizenship qualitatively' and 'there has never been any mention of cultural or linguistic requirements' (Piola, 2006: 55). Without a control mechanism and qualitative definition, Irish citizenship becomes a vague and slippery concept.

This problem of defining Irishness is central in '57% Irish'. Doyle plays with this lack of definition by placing the job of devising a test of Irishness in the hands of an incompetent and racist Minister, who in turn hires a graduate stu-dent to design it. The story opens with Ray monitoring a young man taking his Irishness test, devised as part of his research grant topic: "'OléOléOlé – Football and the Road to Irishness." He's designed and redesigned techniques that would let him measure love of country via football, ways that were new and sexy and beyond skepticism' (Doyle, 2007: 101). However, Ray is very well aware of the difficulty to pin down 'Irishness' based on one factor only, as he realises that basing Irish nationality on the love of the Irish football team does not work. What led Ray to investigate the roots of national identity was his intercultural experience with a Polish football fan who embraced him, deliriously happy at Ireland's victory over Iran in the 2002 World Cup playoffs:

> The idea – the thesis – had come to Ray in the minutes, three years before, just after Robbie Keane had actually scored that goal and Ray had hugged and kissed maybe fifteen people in the pub, and he'd found himself in the arms of a big lad from Poland. And he's wondered. Why was this guy hugging Ray? Kissing his forehead. Punching the air. Throwing his head back and singing:
> – YOU'LL NEVER BEAT THE EYE-RISH
> YOU'LL NEVER BEAT THE EYE-RISH –
> Why?
> Because his own team was shite? (Poland had been beaten the day before, by South Korea). Because he'd been in Ireland a while and felt that he was one of the gang? Because he wanted to feel that way?
> Why? (100–1)

Ray is bewildered by the Pole's quick identification with the Irish team. In spite of his relationship with Darya, he still experiences the immigrant community as Other. It is clear that at this point in the story Ray is not ready to have a full intercultural encounter with this Polish fan or with his girlfriend either. Although he lets them both embrace him, he remains aloof and feeling a bit superior. The Polish fan, on the other hand, has effected a full identity migration and thinks of himself as Irish.

Ray has experienced multicultural Ireland first hand through his relationship with his Russian girlfriend, whom he renames 'Stalin', as an indicator of their distant and troubled relationship. The act of renaming her is itself indicative of Ray's lack of acceptance of the mother of his child and of his general attitude towards immigrants. He is ready to accept multicultural Ireland, but only on his own terms. He is also the father of Vladimir Damien, who, as his hybrid name indicates, is a prime example of a hyphenated Irish identity: 'Russian ma, Irish da – what would that make the baby?' (101). Ray's brother's answer: 'German,' though playful, illustrates the difficulty of defining a hyphenated nationality as well as the fact that Ray's son is a foreigner to both parents: the member of a new category of identity that requires a hyphen, proof that the child does not belong completely to either one of his parents' nationalities.

Unlike Ray, who at least manages an intimate relationship with an immigrant, the new Minister of Arts and Ethnicity resists the multicultural reality of modern Ireland. He is not ready to embrace interculturalism as a viable, enriching possibility for both natives and immigrants. He experiences the encounter with foreigners as a threat to traditional Irish culture and values. Doyle's characterisation of the Minister for the Arts and Ethnicity as a thug with no cultural sensitivity poses the question of how genuine the Irish government is in terms of accepting the ethnic minorities in Ireland unconditionally. As we find out later, the Minister is a wolf in sheep's clothing who, far from representing and promoting cultural understanding, is actually in charge of keeping immigrants from obtaining Irish citizenship, without seeming to do so. The fact that he turns to a graduate student rather than an expert points to the unofficial goals he promotes. From the way Ray describes him, the Minister does not inspire confidence: 'He was a big man in a big suit. The smile was big too but it wasn't warm. It was the smile of a man who might have had a gun or a bread-knife hidden up one of the big sleeves' (103). Ray's assessment of the shadiness of this political figure proves to be correct. Although the Minister surrounds himself with artefacts such as 'Jack B. Yeats prints on the walls, a typed page of *Ulysses* ... an autographed photo of Ronan Keating ... The Proclamation of Independence, a U2 gold disc' as markers of Irishness (*ibid.*), he soon confesses to Ray his ignorance and lack of interest in his new job: 'I'll be frank with you, Raymond,' he said. – A week ago I was the Minister for Arts and Tourism. The arts came first in the job description but I was more at home with the tourism. The arts; grand, but a lot of it is bolloxology' (104). The Minister does not try to hide the fact that he has been stuck with ethnicity or that he has only recently found out the definition of the term 'ethnic': 'Ethnic. Of or relating to a human group with racial, religious and linguistic characteristics in common, from the Greek, *ethnos*' (105). It is ironic that a country that revived its own ethnic roots through the Celtic Revival chooses as Minister of Ethnicity someone who does not know the meaning of that term. When Ray questions the motivation behind this new Ministry, the Minister answers that it is the European shift to the left that has now forced a new stance of openness for Ireland (*ibid.*). He also explains that behind this front of cooperation with the EU, the Irish government's plan is very different:

> We're telling no one, especially not the wee lads with the sandals on the other side of the Cabinet table. No, we'll play ball. The walls must come down, says Brussel. So, fair enough. But …
> We want you to make it harder to be Irish …
> – But, said the Minister. – You have to make it look easier.
>
> (106)

His only guidance for Ray is: 'Go easy on the racial … We can't be showing anyone the door because of their skin. But the rest is up to yourself' (107). It seems shocking that the Minister of Art and Ethnicity would have such a free hand in devising ways to limit access to Irish citizenship to specific groups, but according to Piola (2006: 49), in real life the Minister of Justice in Ireland does have such freedom. As the official website for Irish Naturalisation and Immigration Service states, one of the ways one can acquire Irish citizenship is 'by naturalisation at the absolute discretion of the Minister for Justice and Equality' (see section 'Citizenship').

It is clear that Doyle is attacking such a state of affairs through his depiction of the Minister in '57% Irish'. Furthermore, the fact that this writer locates the Department of the Arts and Ethnicity in fictional Castletimoney, which he describes as a conservative stronghold with a definite anti-immigrant stance, is another jab at the Irish government, as it underscores the Minister's hypocritical stance: 'Castletimoney boasted two pubs, a monument, a Spar that stayed open till ten, and the country's fourth biggest lap-dancing club, the Creamery. ONLY GENUINE IRISH GIRLS USED ON THESE PREMISES, said the banner over the door, ALL HEADAGE CHEQUES CASHED' (Doyle, 2007: 106–7). Although Ray is given an official office there, 'the real work would be done in the shed in his parents' back garden', again emphasising the unofficial status of the test (106).

Ray does not seem to have any moral qualms about his role in the Minister's plan. In charge of constructing a test that measures Irishness in a way that helps restrict access to Irish citizenship, Ray only wrestles with the best way to measure identity: 'No, an old-fashioned quiz wasn't going to work. A Nigerian could become an expert on all things Irish without leaving Nigeria; he could be quiz-perfect Irish before he'd even packed' (108). Certainly, in a world of global internet access, information is at everyone's fingertips: 'Everyone on the planet was a fuckin' Irish expert, a citizen just waiting to pass'. (108–9). This new global connectivity blurs the boundaries of national identity and demands a 'post-national environment' for Ireland. As Richard Kearney posits, this type of society would acknowledge the fact 'that nationality may actually be strengthened by its decoupling from ethnicity and permitted to find more appropriate forms of expression than a centralist nation-state' (1997: 58).

Indeed, physical geography cannot contain by itself the markers of Irish identity. Rather, the relevant landscapes are now the innerscapes of each prospective Irish citizen. Conscious of this new glocal paradigm, Ray devises the Fáilte Score. The first week of testing reveals needs for adjustments: 'On day one, a Ghanaian crossed his legs during the test, and that action had delivered three minutes of hardcore Irish pornography, and sent his score soaring to 97 per cent' (Doyle, 2007: 123). This makes him the most Irish man in the country, in glaring contrast to the Minister's score of 57 per cent. It takes many tries before Ray finally realises that the key to the test is to match it to the test taker: 'A different test each time, hidden inside the official test – that was what Ray was after; he could burn all the variants onto the one CD. The Fáilte Score. Success and failure pre-preordained' (112). Ray's approach to the test illustrates the fact that nationality is a fluid, subjective condition rather than a monolithic, homogenous identity. It also acknowledges that nationality is expressed differently for everybody, and more importantly, it proves that it is constructed and arbitrary and no longer contained by physical borders. The old definition of ethnicity that Ray is working with ('The individual shares certain characteristics with other members of the ethnic group. Elements of the culture. Language ... And an attachment to a specific territory. Ireland' (113)) is no longer valid. Ireland itself is a vague term that cannot be contained within a geographical space only. It is a concept, a state of mind, and an imaginary community that can be expressed through a set of variable signifiers (like the artefacts in the Minister's office). To underscore this point, Doyle has Ray give the Minister a test designed just for him, using the markers of Irishness that he knows will resonate with the Minister:

> He pressed Play and let the Minister have it. The best and the worst of Ireland, a jagged line of green hills and bared arses, fiddle and feedback. Ray watched the shifting score of the Minister's Irishness. 'The Fields of Athenry' sent him into the 80s, but a quick blast of Joe Duffy dropped him back down. *The Riordans* picked him up, and the Chemotherapy Virgins kicked him in the bollix. Five minutes

later, the Minister was falling under the 40 mark – 'Teenage Kicks', *Disco Pigs* – but a pornstar's fanny dragged him over the finish line. (114)

This passage illustrates the construction of Irish identity through a shared Irish culture. However, factors such as age, class, gender, occupation, religion, and political views complicate this imagined or constructed cultural community and at times even subvert it. So much so that finding shared signifiers that denote Irishness is virtually impossible. Instead, Ray has to customise each test for each individual by adjusting the delivery of different markers of Irish cultural identity, in order to connect to each test-taker's subjectivity. Through this test, it becomes clear that no two Irish citizens inhabit the same Ireland. The Ireland that Ray devises for his test-takers is an imaginary and subjective one, tailored to their individual conception of Irishness and the Irish world.

Although Ray has until now seemed indifferent to the plight of immigrants, things become personal when the Minister wants him to tackle citizenship applicants from Eastern Europe. Darya is on the list and at risk of deportation in spite of having given birth to an Irish citizen:

> Ray looked at Stalin's name on the Fáilte list.
> – There's a woman here, he said. – And she has a kid born in this country.
> – We ironed out that difficulty some years ago, Raymond, said the Minister. – The child's nationality does not entitle his mother or father –
> I'm his fucking father, thought Ray.
> – to citizenship or residency rights.
>
> (125–6)

The Minister's statements in this passage explicitly direct readers to the IBC/05 Scheme which requires the foreign national parents of Irish-born children to apply for permission to remain in Ireland with their children. As the Citizens Information Board Website (see section 'Leave to remain in Ireland') explains:

> Prior to 2003, parents of an Irish-born child were … able to withdraw from the asylum process and seek leave to remain. Since February 2003, the Department of Justice and Equality no longer accepts applications for leave to remain, based on a person's parentage of an Irish-born child. In 2005 under the Irish Born Child Scheme (IBC/05) a number of foreign national parents of children born in the State prior to 1 January 2005 were granted leave to remain for an initial period of 2 years. In 2007 under the IBC/05 renewal scheme … many of them had their leave to remain extended for 3 years subject to certain conditions. In 2010 they can apply for a further 3-year extension of their leave to remain.

Ray's reaction to this information is to question and subvert the Fáilte Score. His reconnection with Darya marks a turning point in his life and initiates his identity migration. From that moment on, Ray is able to embrace his relationship with her as well as with the immigrant Other that she represents, establishing as a result a true intercultural connection. This is reflected in his deeper understanding of who Darya is, which allows him to construct a test that she can easily pass: 'She sat in front of a screen that delivered Behan and Chekov, Christchurch and the Kremlin. It was boring, but she still scored 83 per cent' (Doyle, 2007: 128). This test represents Ray's acceptance of Darya's hyphenated identity as Russian-Irish. The intercultural connection between both characters is illustrated by their exchange after the test: 'How did you get on? She answered the Irish way. – Grand. – Cool, said Ray' (*ibid.*). Thus, Ray's test functions as a bridge between the couple and solidifies their relationship. His new understanding of the immigrant psyche in turn allows him to travel through the new landscape of Ireland, both virtually through the designing of the Fáilte test, and concretely by interacting with the multicultural population of Dublin. Ironically, his reinvention of 'Irishness' helps reveal the real modern Ireland.

Ray's attempt to create a more inclusive test illustrates the gradual change in the official mindset of the country. One significant example is the introduction of formal citizenship ceremonies by the new Minister for Justice, Equality and Defence, Alan Shatter. This small but important gesture is a step towards interculturalism in that the ceremonies not only emphasise the visibility of hyphenated Irish citizens, but also help bring them in from the margins in what represents an official welcome to Ireland. As Shatter states: 'Chief among the initiatives already up and running in this area is the hugely successful Citizenship Ceremony which for the first time ever marks the grant of citizenship with an occasion befitting its importance to the recipient and to us as the host nation' (see official website for Irish Naturalisation and Immigration Service, section 'Immigration in Ireland 2011'). Whether this is the first step towards a greater appreciation of immigrants remains to be seen. One thing is clear: the wave of inward migration of the 1990s seems far from receding, as a significant reform in 2011 was the push to expedite (within six months) the greater number of applications, from 1,000 applications in the year 2000 to 25,671 in 2010 (*ibid.*).

Doyle promotes the acceptance of Ireland as a new hybrid country not only through the transformation of Ray's attitude towards migrants but also by having Darya introduce her Irish-Russian son to Ray's mother. The new intercultural future that is envisaged in the short story is also illustrated in the final scene between Ray and his brother on the afternoon of Ray's retirement:

– Look, said his brother.
– What?
– An Irishman.
Ray looked.
– Where?
– There, look; at the lights. Scratching his arse.
– Ah, yeah.

– Haven't seen one like him in years. What happened, Ray?
– Haven't a clue, said Ray.

(Doyle, 2007: 129)

Doyle's parting shot provides an interesting ending that refers back to the Foreword of *The Deportees* collection where the writer tries to explain what happened to Ireland during the Celtic Tiger years:

> It was about jobs and the EU, and infrastructure and wise decisions, and accident. It was about education and energy, and words like 'tax' and 'incentive', and what happens when they are put beside each other. It was also about music and dancing and literature and football. It happened, I think, some time in the mid-90s. I went to bed in one country and woke up in a different one. (xi)

Like Doyle, Ray's brother seems to be surprised by the new demographic landscape in Ireland, to the point that he experiences and comments on the sighting of an 'Irishman' much like one would react to the sighting of an endangered species. The fact that he refers to the man 'scratching his arse' as the one recognisable characteristic of a native points to the atavistic quality of such a specimen in such a new multicultural landscape. So what is an 'Irishman'? Doyle does not give an answer, but leaves it to the readers to create their own definition of Irishness, thus making the '57% Irish' story his particular version of the Fáilte Test.

References

Allen-Randolph, Jody (2010). 'Roddy Doyle', *Close to the Next Moment: Interviews from a Changing Ireland*. Manchester: Carcanet, 144–53.

Citizens Information Board. 'Leave to remain in Ireland'. www.citizensinformation.ie/en/moving_country/asylum_seekers_and_refugees/refugee_status_and_leave_to_remain/leave_to_remain.html. Accessed on 9 March 2012.

Doyle, Roddy (1991) [1987]. *The Commitments*. London: Minerva.

—— (2007). *The Deportees and Other Stories*. London: Jonathan Cape.

Fricker, Karen (2007). 'The Playboy of the Western World', *Variety*, 9 October. www.variety.com/review/VE1117935049.html?categoryid=33&cs=1. Accessed on 9 January 2012.

Hall, Stuart (1994). 'Cultural identity and diaspora', in Patrick Williams and Laura Chrisman (eds), *Colonial Discourse and Post-Colonial Theory: A Reader*. London: Harvester Wheatsheaf, 392–401.

Hickman, Mary J. (2007). 'Immigration and monocultural (re)imaginings in Ireland and Britain', *Translocations. The Irish Migration, Race and Social Transformation Review* 2.1: 12–25.

Irish Naturalisation and Immigration Service. 'Citizenship', 'Immigration in Ireland 2011'. Department of Justice and Equality. www.inis.gov.ie/. Accessed on 10 January 2012.

Kearney, Richard (1997). *Post Nationalist Ireland: Politics, Literature, Philosophy*. London: Routledge.

McGlynn, Mary (2004). 'Why Jimmy wears a suit: White, black, and working class in *The Commitments*', *Studies in the Novel* 36.2: 232–50.

Nititham, Diane Sabenacio (2008). 'Locating the self in diaspora space', *Translocations. The Irish Migration, Race and Social Transformation Review* 3.1: 69–85.

Piola, Catherine (2006). 'The reform of Irish citizenship', *Nordic Irish Studies* 5.1: 41–58.

Pirroux, Lorraine (1998). 'I'm black an' I'm proud: Re-inventing Irishness in Roddy Doyle's *The Commitments*', *College Literature* 25.2: 45–57.

Reddy, Maureen T. (2005). 'Reading and writing race in Ireland: Roddy Doyle and *Metro Éireann*', *Irish University Review* 35.2: 374–88.

White, Eva Roa (2010). 'From emigration to immigration: Irishness in *The Irish Short Stories* of *Sarah Orne Jewett* and Roddy Doyle's *The Deportees*', in David Clark and Rubén Jarazo Álvarez (eds), *In the Wake of the Tiger: Irish Studies in the Twentieth-First Century*. Oleiros: Netbiblo, 103–10.

Yau, Nicola (2007). 'Celtic Tiger, hidden dragon: Exploring identity among second generation Chinese in Ireland', *Translocations. The Irish Migration, Race and Social Transformation Review* 2.1: 48–69.

7

'Our identity is our own instability': intercultural exchanges and the redefinition of identity in Hugo Hamilton's *Disguise* and *Hand in the Fire*[1]

Carmen Zamorano Llena

In 1995 the then President of Ireland Mary Robinson gave an address entitled 'Cherishing the Irish diaspora' to the Houses of the Oireachtas in order to commemorate the 150th anniversary of the beginning of the Great Irish Famine. This historical event, which has been reworked as one of the founding traumas of the Irish nation, also marked a dramatic increase in the Irish exodus that made Ireland the only country in Europe to experience a decline in population growth in the second half of the nineteenth century (Kuhling and Keohane, 2007: 53). Significantly, Mary Robinson's speech did not delve into the representation of the Great Irish Famine and its consequences as being caused by the British indifference to its neighbouring island, an argument characteristic of the postcolonial discourse on which the twentieth-century construct of Irish national identity was highly dependent.[2] On the contrary, Robinson took the commemoration as an opportunity to show how the national 'great narrative of dispossession and belonging' could be transformed 'with a certain amount of historic irony [into] one of the treasures of [Irish] society', from which the Irish people could learn 'values of diversity, tolerance and fair-mindedness' (Robinson, 1995). As Richard Kearney notes, Robinson's definition of the Irish nation came under the rubric of the '*migrant* nation', where 'the nation remains partially ethnic, but is enlarged to embrace all those emigrants and exiles who live beyond the territory of the nation-state *per se*' (original emphasis; Kearney, 1997: 5). Thus, Robinson proposed a broadening of the definition of the phrase 'the Irish people', making it inclusive of the Irish diaspora, as a way of redefining past constructs of Irish identity. Similarly, in his seminal work *Postnationalist Ireland* (1997), Richard Kearney – who, incidentally, was Mary Robinson's speechwriter in the early days of her first term in power – also suggested the need to redefine the construct of the Irish nation by revising the cultural and politico-philosophical founding national narratives. Kearney's analysis suggests that traditional definitions of Irishness are overcome through an internationalisation of the cultural and political discourses. Thus, the 'obsession with an exclusive identity is abandoned' by bringing to the fore the 'network of relations extending from local communities at home to migrant communities abroad' (Kearney, 1997: 100). Through this globalisation of Irishness, Kearney and Robinson set the premises for a redefinition of the 'new Ireland' of the mid-1990s. However, their discourse was still flawed in that it persisted in maintaining an ethnocultural base to definitions of Irish identity. The dramatic socio-economic changes that Ireland had undergone since the mid-1990s added a new meaning to the internationalisation of 'the Irish people' and to the concept of the 'migrant nation' as defined by Robinson and Kearney, thus forcing a redefinition of traditionally ethnocultural definitions of Irish national identity.

The short-lived economic boom experienced by Ireland between 1995 and 2007 radically changed the social fabric of Ireland by attracting great numbers of Irish returnees, migrant workers, asylum-seekers, and refugees. This turned Ireland, for the second time in its history since the Famine, into a country of net inward migration (Immigrant Council of Ireland, 2005). By 2007 about 10 per cent of the Irish population had been born outside Ireland (Central Statistics Office, 2007), and according to a study by the National University of Ireland there are over 167 languages spoken by 160 different nationalities in the Republic of Ireland (O'Brien, 2006). The speed and intensity of these changes have led some analysts to claim that 'Ireland, north and south, has had a crash course in cultural diversity' (Wilson, 2008). Consequently, as Fintan O'Toole already suggested in 1999, the traditional definition of Irishness would necessarily have to be redefined under this radical multiculturalisation of Ireland. As several scholars have argued (Lentin, 2001; Hickman, 2007), one of the main contributions of this arguably 'new' multiculturalism is that it has forced a re-examination of the monocultural representation of Irish society, which already existed in pre-Celtic Tiger Ireland. This monocultural construct found its roots in the nation-building project of nineteenth-century Ireland, and was largely dependent on a 'falsely homogenising Irish culture and [on] excising cultural forms deemed to be Other' (Kuhling and Keohane, 2007: 67). It is precisely to this pre-Celtic Tiger multicultural Ireland that Irish-born writer Hugo Hamilton belongs.

In his article 'The loneliness of being German', Hamilton recalls a talk, while on a reading tour in Germany, where he discussed the topic of national pride with the students of a secondary school in Otterberg, a southern German town. To this audience Hamilton explained how his German-Irish background in an Irish socio-historical context where nationalism and its consequences were still predominant provided him with the literary language that dominates his writing:

> my German-Irish childhood in Dublin had been plagued by these questions of nationalism, the ebbing Irish nationalism on my father's side and the legacy of German nationalism which my mother experienced under Nazism. I had outlined [to the students] the language war into which I had been conscripted as a child, forced to speak only Irish and German, wearing Aran Sweaters and Lederhosen, forbidden from speaking English. (Hamilton, 2004)

This hybrid identity, though ridden with difficulties at a personal level, locates Hamilton in a strategically advantageous position from which to exert what Ronit Lentin, with reference to the Irish case, calls a 'politics of interrogation' of monological understandings of collective identity (2001). The main aim of this chapter is to analyse how in his two latest works of fiction, *Disguise* (2008) and *Hand in the Fire* (2010), Hamilton explores the limitations that monological, especially ethnocultural, constructs of collective identity impose on individuals, and how these are contested in a contemporary context of increased globalisation and intercultural exchanges. By examining this issue in the two different national contexts that influence his sense of identity, namely Germany and Ireland, Hamilton redefines Kearney's ethnocultural definition of the internationalisation of Irishness in postnationalist Ireland,[3] and suggests rather a civic-based understanding of collective identity that allows individuals to locate 'the others of our selves' (Bhabha, 1994: 56).

In his review of *Hand in the Fire* for the *Irish Times*, literary critic Liam Harte claims that 'a preoccupation with history's secrets [and] the mood of *heimatlos*', or homelessness, are two of the main themes that pervade Hamilton's oeuvre (Harte, 2010). To a certain extent, this is also true of the two novels under study. *Disguise* and *Hand in the Fire* are thematically more closely interrelated than his other works. This close interrelationship is observed in that both novels analyse how individual characters negotiate and try to overcome traditionally ethnocultural definitions of the national *Heimat*, thus exposing the damaging effects of such homogenising identity constructs on collective and individual identities.

In *Disguise*, the relevance of memory in the construction of individual and collective identities is underscored by the narrative structure, which moves between the events of a single day at the end of September 2008 in a farm outside the former East German town of Jüterborg, and the post-Second World War Germany that was utterly changed in the aftermath of the war. The process of remembrance and forgetting that this pendular movement between different times highlights serves to explore the identity formation of the main character Gregor Liedmann. He is a man in his sixties in 2008, who as a two-year-old orphaned refugee from the East was given to a German woman by her father to replace the son who had just been killed during one of the last bombings of Berlin. The mother, whose husband is still fighting on the Russian front at the end of the Second World War, is made to promise that she will never tell anybody about the replacement of her dead son, not even her husband, a promise that she maintains against all odds. Gregor's chance discovery of this event in his young adulthood makes him question his sense of identity, as it had been given to him, and forces him to reconstruct it on half-suspected truths.

The German political philosopher Jürgen Habermas argues that individual identity and collective identity cannot be equated, but that they exist in a 'complementary relationship' (1988: 9). Similarly, in the literary realm of *Disguise*, Gregor's individual narrative of identity formation bears a metonymic relationship with the identity (re)formation of the German national identity after the Holocaust. As critics generally agree (Habermas, 1988; Fullbrook, 2002), Auschwitz put an end to the German myth of national identity which, finding its roots in the romantic definition of *Heimat*, assumed its more strident ethnic overtones in the first half of the twentieth century and culminated with what Mary Fullbrook terms 'Hitler's conception of a "racially pure" ethnic community, or *Volksgemeinschaft*' (2002: 22). As Habermas remarks, 'Auschwitz altered the conditions for the continuation of historical life' (1988: 4); it rendered the historiographical work, which had been one of the founding pillars in the nineteenth-century construct of the German nation, unreliable, exposing the horrific consequences that the selection and interpretation of history from a specifically racist perspective could lead to. This, consequently, caused the loss of the traditional sense of *Heimat*, and the problematisation of definitions of collective identity in the post-Auschwitz German context, which left its people with an intense sense of *heimatlos* and with the need to redefine the basis on which a common sense of identity could be reconstructed.

In a similar sense, Gregor's *heimatlos* is a consequence of the disasters of the war. The war has left him without a *Heimat* in the broadest sense of this German term, namely, without his natural family, without a clear identification with his place of birth and origins, which are unclear, and, consequently, without a sense of belonging to a community that shares a common history, culture, and traditions. In this context, and after accidentally discovering his homeless condition, Gregor decides to reconstruct his sense of identity as a Jew in the German Federal Republic, based on traces of memory and hearsay. As a consequence, in his late adulthood Gregor comes to realise the unstable grounds of his identity, as the narrator notes, recalling an early memory of Gregor's childhood as a surrogate child: 'Sometimes he cannot distinguish between his memory and what he has been told, between what he experienced and what he has read in books. He is made up of all those things that he has heard about and read about' (Hamilton, 2008: 23). In his young adulthood, however, living in 1960s Berlin,

Gregor reimagines his identity reproducing the mistakes of the past, namely, trying to adopt those cultural traits that are associated with a traditionally ethnocentric understanding of collective identity, in this case, a Jewish identity. Thus, he decides to be circumcised and 'marked down his religion as Jewish on official documents. Dues were deducted from his pay packet each month which went directly to the Jewish community' (59). He also tries to join the Jewish synagogue, not because 'he had [any] great wish to attend the synagogue or to go through any religious customs. He merely wanted to belong to the Jewish community in Berlin' (60). However, he is denied access to this community precisely because of the impossibility to find 'solid evidence' of his Jewish parentage (*ibid.*). Thus, in an ironic historical reversal, the Jewish community denies him access due to their limited ethnocultural and racial interpretation of communal belonging.

Gregor's existence is doubly plagued, firstly by the state of homelessness caused by the war, and secondly by the traumatic impossibility of reconstructing his sense of identity on the terms that had been used before the war to define what Benedict Anderson termed 'imagined communities' (1991).[4] Thus, Gregor reproduces the mistakes of the past, just as East and West Germany, turned *heimatlos* by the war, fell back again into the selective use of history to reconstruct a sense of collective identity. As Fullbrook states, both East and West Germany 'sought to define and to anchor new partial identities … in differing reinterpretations of selected aspects of a common past. … The interpretation and presentation of the past became an integral and often hotly contested element of the present' (2002: 3). This obsession with the past hindered the healing of the open wounds of Germany's traumatic history and of its collective sense of identity. Similarly, Gregor's obsession with this old sense of belongingness, based on 'solid evidence' of his origins in the bygone past (Hamilton, 2008: 60), bars him from establishing significant relationships in the present with his adoptive parents, with his wife Mara, and with his son Daniel. It is only by the end of a late summer day outside Jüterborg, when he realises the damage that this obsession with a fixed form of identity has caused not only to him but also to those around him, that he gains a new insight into what composes his sense of identity: 'His identity is not what he was or what the Nazis thought he was. His identity is the people he's been living with, but he's denied them each time. He always ran away from anyone who gave him any sense of identity' (216).

Gregor's damaged sense of identity can only be healed in the context of contemporary Berlin, a city that, since the fall of the Wall in 1989, has been transformed from a symbol of confrontation to a contested symbol of cultural diversity and intercultural relations.[5] As Gregor reflects in his description of contemporary Berlin, '[m]any of the people around here have also travelled a lot, collecting cultural idiosyncrasies from around the world before returning to live in this semi-eccentric, semi-chic and ethnically mixed suburb of Berlin' (20). This new circumstance of interculturalism, facilitated by the current process of globalisation, makes him realise that the old obsessions with the past and fixed constructs of identity have been replaced by the utterly mobile population and the shrinking of time and space allowed by new technologies and low-cost flights:

> He has become part of this late-night shrine of rock himself now, the hall of has-beens, the place in which everything has gone by, eclipsed by cultural innovation accelerating into the future. The world has rushed on into a new set of obsessions. When Gregor was growing up, the planet seemed like an enormous place, full of sections all devoted to staying apart with their own culture and their own separate identities. North America was far away. Peru was unimaginably remote. The past was close behind, was the phrase from a song which described how everyone felt. Nowhere is far away now. Even the most distant places in Alaska are on everyone's doorstep. (250–1)

In this context of the new, post-1989 Berlin, Gregor's development becomes more clearly defined. The war had made Gregor a *heimatlos*, an eternal exile who 'had turned his life into a search for belonging', which, initially, he could only find in pre-war definitions of collective identity (218). However, that traditional understanding of the sense of pertaining to an imagined community is replaced by the new generation represented by his son Daniel, whose identity, as Gregor reflects, 'was not so much inherited any more. It had little to do with religion, with history or with geography, even less with his place of birth or his ancestors. His identity was something in the making' (175). Daniel's identity is not based on the old national topoi of shared culture, language, and history, but on current symbols of collective identity, such as popular sports like football, which can unite individuals living in the same locale, regardless of their cultural backgrounds, and which can bring them a 'feeling of belonging in the city, a family of inhabitants, a spooling of emotions into one large unlikely commune' (175).[6]

Like Gregor Liedmann in *Disguise*, the Serbian migrant Vid Ćosić, the main character and narrative voice in *Hand in the Fire*, has been deprived of a sense of *Heimat* by tragic historical and private events in his country of origin. The theme of immigration in contemporary Ireland and the experiences of the so-called 'new Irish' in the Celtic and post-Celtic Tiger context are themes that have attracted the attention of a number of contemporary Irish writers, including Roddy Doyle, Patrick McCabe, and Hugo Hamilton. A number of their fictional texts focus on the changes that Ireland has undergone under the influence of globalisation and mass migration. Thematically, their work can be considered to have initiated a new literary subgenre in Ireland, namely migration literature. Recent literary criticism has outlined migration literature as distinct from migrant literature (Rösch, 2006; Frank, 2010). Whereas the latter placed the emphasis on the migrant origins of the author writing on issues of migration, the former is defined by intratextual features, such as the thematic focus on the migrant experience and the narrative perspective (Rösch, 2006), as well as the interest in analysing the changes that the host society undergoes under the influence of migration. It is in this sense that Hamilton's *Hand in the Fire* can be regarded as a significant contribution to this subgenre in the Irish context.[7]

Vid is a Serbian migrant who arrives in Ireland trying to escape from the trauma of the ethnocultural conflict and subsequent fratricide war in former Yugoslavia, and the private trauma of losing his parents in a car accident, which he survived, sometime after the end of the war. His conscious desire to leave behind the past unconsciously blocks his capacity to recall previous events, and impels him to embrace an assimilationist approach to his new life in Ireland. As Anne Enright observes in her review of Hamilton's novel, 'Vid is slow to form opinions. An opinion is a form of ownership, and as a stranger both in the country and in the language, he owns very little' (2010). As a migrant, Vid does not feel entitled to form opinions in his new country, and the safest way for him to adapt to his new home is to adopt the ways of the host society, a choice that, as the novel progresses, proves to be sterile.

As Philip Watt states in his analysis of interculturalism and migration in Ireland, in socio-political discourses, the assimilationist approach 'promoted the absorption of minorities into a "shared" value system that was viewed as the only way forward' (2006: 155). In a similar manner, Vid dislikes being asked about his country of origin because this reminds him of his outsider status in the host country, and tries to mimic the language, manners, and cultural values of the new country of residence, as suggested by his reflections after his first encounter with the Irish lawyer Kevin Concannon:

> What does it matter where you come from? You could say it's irrelevant. I wanted to forget about my own country and start again. I wanted to get a foothold here, get to know the place and the people. I already knew some of the most famous names, like James Joyce and George Best and Bono and Bobby Sands. I knew the most important landmarks, like the GPO ... I was beginning to understand the way things are done here, the way you have of saying 'how's the man?' and 'what's the craic?' I was starting to pick up the jokes, trying not to take everything so seriously. I was working on the accent, learning all the clichés. (Hamilton, 2010: 2)

Like Gregor Liedmann, Vid's life is governed by his desire to belong, and he also initially aims to meet this objective by unquestioningly ascribing to the ethnocultural features that define the traditional Irish sense of communal identity, classically summarised by what the Irish poet Seamus Heaney has defined as a 'sense of place'.

As Heaney defines it, the sense of identity with the land and its community can only be achieved by exploring the 'silent ancestry' that is engraved in the geographical spaces of the country where the individual is born, thus attaining 'a marriage between the geographical country and the country of the mind', where the latter 'takes its tone unconsciously from a shared oral inherited culture' (1980: 132). Through the immigrant character in *Hand in the Fire*, Hamilton challenges this conservative understanding of the sense of place and outlines the manner in which it is to be redefined in the current globalised and intercultural Ireland. Through his troublesome friendship with Kevin Concannon, Vid gains access to Kevin's life story and to a dark family legend of discrimination and exclusion linked to the symbolically charged Aran Islands off the west coast of Ireland. Thus, Kevin's life story and the family's 'silent [or, rather, silenced] ancestry' are the two narratives that will enable Vid to find a different sense of place in his host country. By emphasising the connecting points between Kevin's and Vid's experiences of estrangement in Ireland, the novel fosters what Ronit Lentin has called a 'politics of interrogation' of the Irish 'we' instead of a 'politics of recognition' of new ethnic minorities, integrating them into an unquestioned existing Irish society (2001).

Kevin's life story provides Vid with some insight into the diversity and complex social reality of pre-Celtic Tiger Ireland. Kevin confides in Vid 'as an outsider who could be trusted' (Hamilton, 2010: 42), and tells him about how he was born in England of Irish émigrés. He confesses the difficulties that he underwent when his mother moved to Dublin with him and his two younger sisters when he was nine, and how he had struggled to eliminate his English accent so as 'to be Irish': 'At school, he learned what it was like to be excluded and tried to mix in and camouflage himself. He did his best to be Irish' (*ibid.*). Like Vid, Kevin opted to escape from the difficulties of the past and the sense of displacement derived from not quite belonging to the traditional Irish sense of place. Impelled by his motto 'never to look back' (*ibid.*), Kevin has suppressed the negative elements in the narrative of his life story, in the same manner as his family has suppressed the tragic family story of an aunt on his father's side that was found drowned in the sea after the priest in the local community in Inishmore, the biggest of the Aran Islands, denounced her from the altar for becoming pregnant out of wedlock. As Kevin recalls: 'He said that if the men in the area were not men enough to drown her, then perhaps she would have the decency to drown herself' (88). The actual causes of her death remained a mystery, but this action became inscribed in the 'memory of the landscape' (89), giving the name *Bean Bháite*, Irish for drowned woman, to the place where her body was found.

The secret story in the family provides Vid with another point of identification, since the inaction of the community towards the repressive power of the

Catholic Church reminds him of 'the way the secret police operated in [his] own country and the paralysis that people felt in the face of authority' (89). This Joycean paralysis also characterises Vid's attitude as a 'new Irish' in contemporary Dublin. He acts like a spectator of other people's lives and even of his own life, and does not take action when he intuits that Kevin has used him to cover up a physical aggression that may cost him his career as a lawyer. Vid's sense of unbelonging makes him withdraw from active participation in the life of his new country of residence. However, his awareness of the similarities between his migrant experience and that of Kevin and his father, as well as his own insights as a victim of racial discrimination, eventually shake him into action. Thus, when Ellis, Kevin's youngest sister and drug addict, is pressurised by her family to make the decision of having an abortion against her will – which resembles the secret family story repeating itself – Vid decides to come out of his paralysis as a migrant and help Ellis to overcome her life crisis. It is precisely his active involvement in what he perceives as an act of civic responsibility that turns Vid into an Irish citizen de facto:

> This was where I entered into the story of the country at last. I became a participant, a player, an insider taking action. Not letting things happen around me as if I was still only an immigrant and it was none of my business. I was not trying to make a name for myself or anything like that, but I was entitled to play my role as an ordinary inhabitant who belonged here. (261)

In this manner, Vid abandons the assimilationist approach to multiculturalism that he adopts at the beginning of the narrative. This approach initially relegates him into a passive, non-participatory existence in his host country, which in turn perpetuates his sense of *heimatlos*. As Hamilton's narrative shows, it is only by engaging actively and critically in the life and history of the adoptive country that Vid finds a sense of belonging and is able to transform Ireland into his own *Heimat*. This process suggests the need to overcome inherited nationalist and postnational ethnocultural definitions of Irishness so as to make them more inclusive of the Other communities existing in pre- and post-Celtic Tiger Ireland.

To conclude, Gregor Liedmann's and Vic Ćosić's life narratives expose the limitations of traditionally ethnocultural definitions of collective identities. History, a crucial tool in the selection of founding traumas with which to construct a sense of common origins, becomes for both a haunting presence to which they react in different ways. While Gregor identifies belongingness and a sense of *Heimat* with a past that the war has denied him, Vid, in his migrant condition, tries to elude his own past and assimilate into the host country. Despite their disparate reactions to the heavy weight of history and its traumas, each of them initially reverts to past forms of defining their own identity and liberating themselves from their imposed *heimatlos*. They try to artificially adopt those cultural features that are identified with a specifically ethnocultural sense of collective identity. However, the globalised and intercultural context in which they attempt to carry out this enterprise contributes to making them realise that collective and individual identities are characterised not by fixity, but by their own instability, as Gregor concludes in *Disguise* (Hamilton, 2008: 258–9). This new understanding of identities currently requires new definitions that ensure the transformation from a culture of identification with a common culture, ancestry, and history into a culture of diversity, where its members are united by symbols and actions that enable their active participation in their community regardless of their origins. The diversity of historical and cultural differences is not erased, as in the assimilationist approach, but incorporated so as to change contemporary understandings of the nation. Thus, as Hamilton's works suggest, the internationalisation of Irishness that former President Robinson and Richard Kearney fostered is transformed from its ethnic base, looking for Irish descendants abroad, into a process of acknowledging the Other within one's own community and making them active participants of the national *Heimat*.

Notes

1   I would like to thank the Swedish Research Council (Vetenskapsrådet) for financial support of the research project (ref. 2010-1820) in which this essay is included.
2   See, for example, Máire Ní Fhlathúin's essay 'The British empire' in *The Routledge Companion to Postcolonial Studies*, where she states that 'British laissez-faire economic policies were widely blamed for the catastrophic effects of the Irish Famine of 1845–51, which caused the loss of a large part of the population through death and emigration' (2007: 28–9). In *Daniel O'Connell, The British Press and the Irish Famine: Killing Remarks*, Leslie Williams analyses what he terms 'the violence that was done to the Irish people during the Famine' in the British press through a pejorative, stereotyped representation of the Irish (2003: 4). Williams's choice of words is representative of the Irish nationalist discourse in which the Irish Famine was incorporated.
3   In the 1990s, and for almost two decades, postnationalism was a concept that dominated politico-philosophical discourses, especially in the Western context. This was a highly debated concept, with its detractors considering it an 'assault' on national citizenship and the nation-state (Hansen, 2009) and its advocators arguing for the advantages of the postnational discourse, in which the pressures of globalisation forced 'a redefinition of the nation-state and the concept of social solidarity based on the cultural, historical and political constraints of national citizenship' (Gilsenan Nordin and Zamorano Llena, 2010: 2). Richard Kearney's use of postnationalism in the Irish context adheres to the latter understanding of this term. Thus, Kearney sees postnationalism as a discourse that enables the analyst 'to step back in order to rethink some of the prevailing ideas that have shaped the political understanding of most modern Irish citizens', characterised by monological nationalist understandings of Irish identity. As Kearney states, the aim of his text is 'not to denounce nationalism … but to reinterrogate its critical implications' (1997: 1).

4   In his seminal work *Imagined Communities: Reflections on the Origins and Spread of Nationalism*, Benedict Anderson used the title phrase to describe his understanding of what characterises nations. According to his definition, the nation is 'an imagined political community – and imagined as both inherently limited and sovereign', whose existence is possible because 'in the minds of each [of its members] lives the image of their communion' (1991: 6). Anderson's phrase is especially useful, since it underscores the constructed nature of nations, where the sense of collective identity is not inalterable, but socio-culturally determined and, therefore, varying depending on the changes experienced by the national community.

5   In any case, as argued by Bloomfield, there is still a clash between the cultural policies that present Berlin as a multicultural city, open to international influences, and a 'high cultural metropolis', and the difficulties that these policies imply in recognising and promoting the cultural diversity of the city and its 'intercultural mix' (2003: 167).

6   The role of popular sports as symbols of intercultural mediation is often present in contemporary Irish literary works, such as Dermot Bolger's play *In High Germany* (first performed in 1990) and Joseph O'Neill's *Netherland* (2008).

7   With regard to migrant literature in Ireland, it can be argued that it is a subgenre that started to develop recently with the new multiculturalism fostered by the socio-economic phenomenon of the Celtic Tiger. Some of the works in this emergent subgenre are Cauvery Madhavan's *Paddy Indian* (2001) and Marsha Mehran's *The Pomegranate Soup* (2006) and *Rosewater and Soda Bread* (2008). It will be interesting to observe how this subgenre develops in Ireland in the coming years, when recent changes in the social fabric of the country are consolidated.

References

Anderson, Benedict (1991) [1983]. *Imagined Communities: Reflections on the Origin and Spread of Nationalism*. London: Verso.

Bhabha, Homi K. (1994). *The Location of Culture*. London: Routledge.

Bloomfield, Jude (2003). '"Made in Berlin": Multicultural concept confusion and multicultural reality', *International Journal of Cultural Policy* 9.2: 167–83.

Bolger, Dermot (2000 [1990]. *In High Germany*, in *Plays I*. London: Methuen.

Central Statistics Office (2007). *The Statistical Yearbook of Ireland 2007*. www.cso.ie. Accessed on 10 May 2010.

Enright, Anne (2010). '*Hand in the Fire* by Hugo Hamilton', *Guardian*, 17 April. www.guardian.co.uk. Accessed on 27 March 2012.

Frank, Søren (2010). *Migration and Literature: Günter Grass, Milan Kundera, Salman Rushdie and Jan Kjaerstad*. London: Palgrave.

Fullbrook, Mary (2002) [1999]. *German National Identity after the Holocaust*. Cambridge: Polity.

Gilsenan Nordin, Irene and Carmen Zamorano Llena (eds) (2010). 'Introduction', *Redefinitions of Irish Identity: A Postnationalist Approach*. Oxford, Bern and New York: Peter Lang, 1–15.

Habermas, Jürgen (1988). 'Historical consciousness and post-traditional identity: Remarks on the Federal Republic's orientation to the West', *Acta Sociologica* 31.1: 3–13.

Hamilton, Hugo (2004). 'The loneliness of being German'. *Guardian*, 7 September. www.guardian.co.uk. Accessed on 18 February 2011.

—— (2008). *Disguise*. London: Fourth Estate.

—— (2010). *Hand in the Fire*. London: Fourth State.

Hansen, Randall (2009). 'The poverty of postnationalism: Citizenship, immigration, and the new Europe', *Theory and Society* 38.1: 1–24. www.springerlink.com/content/1203088206617280/fulltext.pdf. Accessed on 22 June 2009.

Harte, Liam (2010). 'A truth close to home', *Irish Times*, 20 March. www.irishtimes.com. Accessed on 23 June 2010.

Heaney, Seamus (1980) [1977]. 'The sense of place', *Preoccupations: Selected Prose 1968–1978*. London: Faber & Faber.

Hickman, Mary J. (2007). 'Immigration and monocultural (re)imaginings in Ireland and Britain', *Translocations: The Irish Migration, Race and Social Transformation Review* 2.1: 12–25. www.translocations.ie . Accessed on 17 May 2013.

Immigrant Council of Ireland (2005). 'Background information and statistics on immigration to Ireland'. www.immigrantcouncil.ie. Accessed on 2 February 2007.

Kearney, Richard (1997). *Postnationalist Ireland: Politics, Culture, Philosophy*. London: Routledge.

Kuhling, Carmen and Kieran Keohane (2007). *Cosmopolitan Ireland: Globalisation and Quality of Life*. London: Pluto.

Lentin, Ronit (2001). 'Responding to the racialisation of Irishness: Disavowed multiculturalism and its discontents', *Sociological Research Online* 5.4: n.p.

Madhavan, Cauvery (2001). *Paddy Indian*. London: Black Amber.

Mehran, Marsha (2006). *The Pomegranate Soup*. London: Arrow.

—— (2008). *Rosewater and Soda Bread*. London: Random House.

Ní Fhlathúin, Máire (2007). 'The British empire', in John McLeod (ed.), *The Routledge Companion to Postcolonial Studies*. London: Routledge, 21–31.

O'Brien, Carl (2006). 'From Acholi to Zulu, Ireland a land of over 167 languages', *Irish Times*, 25 March. www.ireland.com. Accessed on 2 May 2008.

O'Neill, Joseph (2008). *Netherland*. London: Fourth Estate.

O'Toole, Fintan (1999). 'Redefining Irishness within a mixed-race society', *Irish Times*, 23 July. www.ireland.com. Accessed on 5 May 2008.

Robinson, Mary (1995). 'Cherishing the Irish diaspora; on a matter of public importance. An address to the Houses of the Oireachtas'. www.rootsweb.ancestry.com/-irlker/diaspora.html. Accessed on 22 February 2011.

Rösch, Heidi (2006). 'Migrationslitteratur im interkulturellen Diskurs'. www.fulbright.de/fileadmin/files/togermany/information/2004-05/gss/Roesch_Migrationsliteratur.pdf. Accessed on 28 March 2012.

Watt, Philip (2006). 'An intercultural approach to "integration"', *Translocations: The Irish Migration, Race and Social Transformation Review* 1.1: 154–63.

Williams, Leslie A. (2003). *Daniel O'Connell, The British Press, and the Irish Famine: Killing Remarks*. Aldershot: Ashgate.

Wilson, Robert (2008). 'Time to take an integrated approach to cultural diversity', *Irish Times*, 9 May. www.ireland.com. Accessed on 9 May 2010.

8

'Many and terrible are the roads to home': representations of the immigrant in the contemporary Irish short story

Anne Fogarty

In *Fox, Swallow, Scarecrow* by Éilís Ní Dhuibhne (2007), Leo Kavanagh, the idealistic but struggling director of a small Irish-language press, muses about his most recent literary discovery. He dreams of the plaudits that await a volume of poems by Kambele Ngole, who is to the best of his knowledge the first black woman poet writing in Irish. The ethnic Otherness of this first-time author along with her gender, he conjectures, will be enticing selling points. Ní Dhuibhne's novel, which deftly skewers literary culture in Ireland during the Celtic Tiger period, exposes this dream of literary success to be an empty one. The Nigerian author who has mastered Irish to the degree of composing poetry in it is a phantom albeit not wholly improbable figure within the text. Her achievement is countermanded by the fact that publication in a minority language with a minuscule readership will only add to her obscurity. At the end of the novel, Anna, the central protagonist, modelled after Tolstoy's Anna Karenina, decides to abandon her fixation on commercial success and her desire to be the Irish J.K. Rowling to write genuine literary fiction. In her multi-layered fiction, Ní Dhuibhne thus disassembles the empty fantasy of an immigrant writer who will save the Irish from themselves, absolve them of their racism, and assuage their anxieties about the effects of a newly emergent multicultural community. She also reveals the degree to which the Irish literary scene is stirred by prognostications about the emergence of new immigrant voices but that it is not yet sufficiently attuned to take them on board. The crisis-ridden Irish writers she depicts are impelled, furthermore, by the pursuit of ideals of authenticity and cosmopolitanism that have become ever more difficult to live up to in the ethnically diverse society which they uneasily inhabit.

This chapter seeks to survey how immigrants are depicted in contemporary Irish short stories. A major premise of this analysis is that a depiction of the immigrant never occurs in isolation in fictional renderings of contemporary Ireland. Rather, such portrayals are always coupled with a scrutiny of Irish return migration and with a probing of the transnational dimensions of current Irish identity. The coming together with the immigrant goes hand in hand with a self-critique and a process of defamiliarisation. An interrogation of the value systems of Irish society is a concomitant in the stories analysed here with a readiness to imagine and on rare occasions give voice to the experience of immigrants. The confrontation with the ethnic Other involves a questioning of notions of belonging, an excavation of indigenous racisms, and a meditation on the role played by fantasy and empathy in cross-cultural communication. Hence, as will become evident, the delineation of the immigrant is bound up with a complex constellation of themes and never simply an isolated motif. The self is unmoored and problematised in current Irish narratives that set out to envisage ethnic outsiders.[1] The protagonists in the narratives examined here find themselves compromised and their belief systems confounded. Ironic insights, elisions, imaginative effusions, and trailing plotlines are used to signal many of the anxieties and conflicts in relation to what have been dubbed the 'new Irish'. These stories explore uncomfortable truths and uncover affective and ethical fault-lines in relation to the immigrant who is often rendered as a shadowy Other or a devastating void or absence. They aim, moreover, not to supply the momentary satisfaction of closure but rather to pinpoint the hazards of multiculturalism and to provide initial mappings of the altered imaginary through which we can gain a purchase on the unconscious realities of contemporary Ireland.

In exploring the symbolic patterns that emerge in these texts, I shall draw upon Paul Ricoeur's observations about the ethical imperatives which he contends should inform the links between self and Other (1992: 169–202). Ricoeur retools Emmanuel Levinas's formulation of the foundational necessity of the Other for intersubjectivity. In the latter's philosophy, the Other is entirely exterior to the ego and remains faceless and incapable of assimilation. Ricoeur is at pains to undo this condition of separation that defines the moral hold of the Other in Levinas's account of things. Building on Aristotle's hypothesis that friendship is a necessity, he argues instead for the primacy of the ethical in relations between self and non-self and conceives of these bonds in terms of ethical claims rather than binding moral duties. For him, solicitude and reciprocity are determining qualities of the friendships that interlink people. Moreover, self-esteem is posited by him to be a product of reciprocal exchange and adjudged to be a correlative of respect for others. Thus, self and Other are mutually constitutive in Ricoeur's eyes as there is a fundamental equivalence between esteem of the Other as oneself and the esteem of oneself as an Other. Injustice and dissymmetry occur when there is a refusal to accept the cycles of giving and receiving he sees as vital for cementing the relations between the ego and the non-self.

Political and sociological analyses of the impact of successive waves of immigration into Ireland from Africa, Asia, and the European accession states from the late 1990s onwards have pointed to the contradictions they have opened up within the reigning value systems in the country. Ronit Lentin has trenchantly argued that Ireland has moved in recent decades from a racial to a racist society (2006). Where once the Irish were denigrated within English colonial discourses as Others who – albeit white – were inferior and subaltern, they have become since the establishment of the Free State the architects of a racial state founded on principles of a bounded white Irishness that resolutely excludes outsiders and has racist underpinnings. For Lentin, as for many others, the 2004 Referendum which denied citizenship to the children of foreign nationals crystallised and reinforced the insidious values of a country that although agreeing to harbour immigrants and asylum-seekers has denied them crucial rights. Bryan Fanning, while also observing the historical continuities in the social inscription of racism in the country, has noted the widely disparate developments that have resulted from official handling of immigration in recent years (2011: 16–35). While citizenship was narrowed and redefined in 2004, the same year saw a remarkable revolution in government policy that allowed an unbridled embrace of immigration from within the EU to a level unparalleled in other member states. Two diametrically opposed attitudes to immigration thus manifest themselves in this signal year: a retrenchment of citizenship on the one hand and a large-scale diversification on the other. As Fanning demonstrates, the shift from a protectionist, monocultural Ireland to a multicultural, global economy has altered the rules for belonging in the country and also produced many inequities. Above all, discriminatory practices have been made systemic by governmental regulations that block access to welfare rights for immigrants. Drawing on the insights of Robert Putnam, Fanning contends that immigration by its very nature threatens social cohesion and produces imbalances (48–54). Not least of these imbalances is the lack of a national debate about racism and the difficulties faced by immigrants and asylum-seekers. Ireland, as many commentators have observed, is aberrant to the degree that it has largely ignored the problems that have been produced by recent social engineering in the interests of neoliberalism and global capitalism. The overt espousal of tolerance in Irish public discourse, moreover, glosses over many unsavoury realities such as the regular occurrence of racist violence throughout the country. Literary texts, it will be proposed here, mirror and reflect upon aspects of the problematic of immigration as enunciated by Irish sociologists and political theorists while also attempting to undo the silence frequently associated with this topic.

It has been suggested that the short story is a more flexible form than the novel and that as a consequence it has the capacity to register the effects of social change more rapidly than longer narratives.[2] It may also be that the suspensions and open endings peculiar to the modern short story endow it with the dexterity to explore contemporary flashpoints in a manner unsuited to the novel. If, as Frank O'Connor once mooted (1962: 13–45), the short story is particularly taken up with the portrayal of submerged populations, then it would seem no coincidence that many contemporary stories by Irish writers have begun to incorporate immigrant characters into their plots. Moreover, such characters are not merely mechanical super-additions. They feature in collections that portray transnational locales and Irish protagonists who lead international lives, moving between different countries and negotiating the challenges of a rootless migrant existence without any traditional nostalgia for home. Consequently, the phenomenon of the new immigrant is held in apposition to Irish figures haphazardly pursuing a global existence and to returned Irish migrants. The cross-over and points of connection between these categories are highlighted and notions of belonging, interdependence, political violence, and social inclusion tested in the process. The stories in Philip Ó Ceallaigh's *The Pleasant Light of Day* (2009), which are situated in numerous locales including Brazil, Egypt, Spain, Ireland, the US, and several unspecified Eastern European countries, undertake such interrogations as do the tales in Kevin Barry's *Dark Lies the Island* (2012), which shift between the UK, the midlands and west coast of Ireland, and Berlin, and foreground encounters between transient diasporic figures whose hostile but charged interactions are founded on their fleetingness.[3] With a view to pinpointing the commonalities between narratives that engage with the inequities of a migrant multicultural society as well as their individual aesthetic traits, this essay will briefly analyse six stories published in recent collections by writers who span several generations: Edna O' Brien's 'Shovel Kings', Colm Tóibín's 'The Street', Mary O'Donnell's 'Little Africa', Colum McCann's 'A Basket Full of Wallpaper', Anne Enright's 'Switzerland', and Éilís Ní Dhuibhne's 'The Shelter of Neighbours'. As will become evident, these works centre on the changed rules of belonging experienced in multiethnic communities and also draw out the silences and moments of deflection that exemplify the interaction between citizens and the out-groups in their midst. These fictions also self-reflexively weigh up the endeavour of depicting the Other as immigrant and the aesthetic and ethical quandaries that it entails.

'Shovel Kings' appeared in *Saints and Sinners*, a collection in which Edna O'Brien revisited many of the themes of her oeuvre overall and won from them fresh dimensions. The phrase in the title to this essay, 'many and terrible are the roads to home', is the final line of 'Plunder', an apocalyptic tale in the same volume which eerily recasts Irish history, condensing it into a nightmare narrative about the devastating invasion of a country by a nameless totalitarian force (O'Brien, 2011: 77–84).[4] This estranged retelling implicitly interfuses the atrocities of the Irish past with elements of the war in Bosnia. Ireland is conceived of not as a place apart but as a site of intersection between histories and cultures. The narrator who has been raped by marauding soldiers lingers on in her ruined house in a devastated landscape; the blood-stained lime-green dress to which she clings emblematises her forlorn hope expressed in the closing moments of the story that she might be able to undertake a journey in the future and find someone else like herself to talk to and thereby allay her pain.

Reciprocity and difference are also thematic concerns of 'Shovel Kings' (O'Brien, 2011: 1–36). The anonymous narrator – a young English woman of Irish descent – gets to know Rafferty, an elderly Irish immigrant, while on a visit to her analyst in North London on St Patrick's Day through a chance encounter in a pub. She befriends him and elicits his story through a series of further accidental meetings. It becomes clear that her conversations with him act as a substitute for the therapy that she is undergoing. Rafferty tells her of his life as a manual worker on the roads and building sites of London in the course of which he is toughened and brutalised. His father who has also emigrated to London turns to prostitutes and neglects the wife he has left behind in Ireland. Rafferty seeks solace in pubs and gradually turns into an alcoholic by way of reaction to the racist attitudes he encounters in England and to his father's harshness and emotional coldness. His own marriage to an Irishwoman in London repeats this cycle of failed relationships as it breaks down because he continues to drink despite his wife's strictures. O'Brien's story delicately captures the psychological impact of emigration and traces how the immigrant is moulded by his experiences. Rafferty, who had been too drunk to attend his mother's funeral and had avoided going home because of his hatred of his father, makes the decision to return late in life to take up a job as a carer for an elderly man. His inability to fit into a changed Ireland becomes symbolic of his double displacement. The taxi driver who drives him back to the airport in Dublin classifies him as a visitor thus reinforcing his sense of alienation. Celtic Ireland, it is intimated, rejects the returned migrant while feinting welcome.[5]

Rafferty's proud isolation is given sympathetic prominence by O'Brien but revealed to be at root an emotional stultification brought about by the difficulties of living as a migrant forever suspended between cultures. The narrator's coolly appraising interest in him also typifies the response of an observer who, although a second-generation emigrant, has acquired a studied cosmopolitanism. She makes vague overtures to Rafferty as he implicitly reminds her of aspects of herself and her heritage. But in the end she severs links with him to follow her therapist who has moved to Liverpool. Abandoned and broken connections thus strew this story; human involvement in a multicultural society is shown to alternate rapidly and arbitrarily between fascination and disengagement. The narrator's final enlargement of vision in the closing moments of the story when she reflects on and names all of the invisible and forgotten Irish men who have laid the buried but vital network of cables under the roads of London evinces the solicitude that Ricoeur has recognised to be an essential aspect of our dealings with the Other. Yet the story suggests that the bonds between people in a multiethnic society remain muffled, partial, and obscured. By the same token, the act of imagining the immigrant must necessarily recognise its incompletion and even ineffectuality.

Colm Tóibín's 'The Street', the concluding novella of *The Empty Family*, is a transnational story that focuses on the pathologies and silences of an immigrant Pakistani community in Barcelona and the strained forms of desire to which a ghettoised existence gives birth (Tóibín, 2010: 156–214). Even more intensely than O'Brien, Tóibín strives to fathom the unknowable psychology of the immigrant in following the fortunes of Malik, a young Pakistani man who has been sent to Barcelona by his family to work in a barber shop run by his fellow countrymen. Malik feels at once rejected by his harsh and uncommunicative father and ill at ease in this new environment in which he is completely at the mercy of Baldy, his controlling and repressive boss. Silence is the means by which Baldy enforces his authority and inspires fear. He picks up his new employee at the airport but proceeds to ignore him. The world Malik thereafter inhabits is an attenuated one, reduced to the single street in which he attempts to learn the new rules of survival and belonging. Desire and fear, it is shown, are the potent forces welding this Muslim community together. The men's longings fasten particularly on mobile phones and the different systems on which they play music. The consumerist objects and the forms of expression they permit offset the fears that underwrite their existence; their insulated self-enclosure is portrayed as a reaction to the scapegoating prejudices of Spanish society readily directed at them.

Malik is savagely beaten by his employer when he is discovered in a sexual act with Abdul, an older man whom he apprehensively lusts after and deeply desires. He discovers in the aftermath of this attack that his boss is also constrained by fear as he does not want his violence to be exposed or unnecessarily attract attention to himself. He locks Malik into an isolated apartment while he is convalescing and is persuaded to allow Abdul to sleep there too to keep him company. The latter's impenetrable silence and seeming disregard for Malik merely reinforce his erotic hold over him. The two men become lovers, their relationship transmuting the linguistic voids, loneliness, and unspoken dread of immigrant existence. Their happiness is dispelled by the arrival of Abdul's cousin, who unsuspectingly shows Malik a photo of his lover's wife. Surprisingly, this betrayal is cancelled out when Abdul overcomes his reticence, declaring to Malik that he is his real family and inviting him to join his extended household which includes his spouse, children, and other relatives in Pakistan. An unorthodox rewriting of the family thus emerges from the encounter between immigrants in Tóibín's tale. Even though the novella has minutely tracked the privations of immigrant life and the degree to which Pakistanis function as negative outsiders who are shunned and ostracised, an all-transcending love which overrides convention and mitigates the effects of social exclusion comes to the fore at the end. The immigrant as gay outsider and sexual Other, it is implied, can transform society from within and rewrite the terms of intimate, caring relationships. The fantasy of attachment is all the more beguiling because of its fragility. The dream of togetherness depends on the continued practice of the subterfuge and silence enjoined on immigrants by the communities in which they live but to which they never properly belong.[6]

Mary O'Donnell's 'Little Africa' also seeks to capture the viewpoint of the immigrant by tracking the story of Mosi, who moves to Ireland with his mother Angela after his father and siblings have been murdered in Nigeria (O'Donnell, 2008: 226–45). The story focuses on Mosi's process of adaptation to Irish society, his wary reactions to his Irish stepfather, and the lingering aftermath of the traumatic scenes he has witnessed in his homeland. His defamiliarising gaze exposes the Otherness of Irish culture. He reacts with horror to white skin, 'chicken pale, bloodless looking' (229), and has to learn how to distinguish Irish people from one another as they all look the same to him. He also notes the casual acceptance of racism in Dublin when security guards arrest a young African girl – who is reminiscent of his dead sister – for shoplifting. The harshness of their treatment of her fuses in his eyes with the violence of those who massacred his sibling. His emotive playing of the role of Balthasar, the black Magus, in the re-scripted nativity play in his school, marks a moment of acceptance as he is empowered to deliver a speech about freedom and equality. The ideological import of the Christian story which has been revised by his teachers as a tale about refugees, however, must cede to the pressing reality of the arrival of his new sister as his mother goes into labour at the end of the performance. In the maternity hospital, Mosi arrives at a guarded acceptance of his stepfather but only after he has given vent to his anger by punching him. As in the 'The Street', a renovated family unit emerges at the end of this story in which primacy is given to the difference of the African mother and her son. Pointedly, the immigrant child is given the licence to adopt his Irish father and not the other way round. O'Donnell's hopeful ending subtly implies that a renegotiation of value systems is needed in order for a workable multicultural community to emerge, as the superiority of white culture is challenged from within by Mosi, who retains his searing memories of life in Africa while acquiring a new identity in Dublin.

In contrast to Mary O'Donnell's story, Colum McCann's 'A Basket Full of Wallpaper' treats the immigrant not as a presence but as an alluring absence that fires the imagination of those he comes in contact with (McCann, 1994: 37–51). The story depicts the reactions of the inhabitants of a small Irish town to Osobe, a mysterious Japanese man who has taken up residence there in the 1950s in the aftermath of the Second World War. Osobe lives in isolation, never discloses his reasons for moving to Ireland, and refuses overtures to elicit his past history. The locals make good this void by spinning a proliferating series of conflicting stories which cast him variously as a former internee in a camp in Idaho where he had been a chicken-sexer, a kamikaze pilot, a refugee from Hiroshima, and a war-criminal who had brutally tortured US airmen. The immigrant thus serves as a phantasmatic space onto which they project their fear of and fascination with Otherness. Their extravagant musings and lurid pronouncements reinforce Osobe's difference. But they also signal the uncertainty and underlying anxieties of this apparently provincial community. The obsessively voiced distrust of Osobe, it is indicated, is coupled with the recognition of the pervasiveness of emigration and migrancy amongst the Irish themselves. The narrator, Sean Donnelly, takes up a job as an assistant to Osobe, who works sporadically as an interior decorator specialising in the hanging of wallpaper. Although he continues to embellish on his employer's putative experiences in Hiroshima and regales his friends with his inventions, he recognises that Osobe may have much in common with his 'uncle in Ghana, an older brother in Nebraska, a distant cousin who worked as a well-digger near Melbourne', none of whom he finds in any way remarkable (45). Indeed, it is Osobe's very ordinariness – his 'banality' (47), the sameness that he shares with the Irish rather than his Otherness – that ultimately inspire Donnelly's hatred. Despite being paid generously for his work, he maliciously steals £20 from his benefactor but is immediately guilt-ridden. Later, as an emigrant in London who is 'acquiring an English accent' (48), Donnelly receives a letter from his father which tells of Osobe's death and the funeral that had been mounted for him in the town.

A further disturbing story emerges in relation to this unknown man even after his demise. It is discovered that he had covered his house with layers and layers of wallpaper, 'gathering the walls into himself' (50). This cocooning is interpreted by the locals as a psychological after-effect of the trauma that he underwent in Hiroshima. Their domesticating rationale, however, as McCann suggests, is a further flight of fancy and papering over of surfaces. Osobe's wallpaper conjures up Orientalist stereotypes of inscrutability while also hinting at the layers of depth and complexity that remain hidden in the simplified cultural narratives into which he has been inserted. His imprisonment in his house is a poignant attempt to produce a home reminiscent of a Japanese dwelling, with its paper screens and a silent articulation of the self-narratives he never divulges. The narrator at the end of the story cross-associates his memory of the 'thin figure' of Osobe with an image of an Irish road that has vanished but which he has internalised and remains 'still within me somewhere' (51). His casting of a £20 note into the Thames late at night is a belated gesture of restitution and insight. Donnelly and Osobe, it is implied, have much in common: both are wanderers who eschew an essentialised self. Reciprocity is possible, however, only retrospectively. The febrile story-telling and exchange of rumours that have dominated the narrative pick up on the lack of fixity of Osobe as a figure, but this imaginative empathy holds other more deep-seated recognitions at bay.[7]

Anne Enright's 'Switzerland', in a similar fashion to McCann's story, considers the degree to which ethnic identities are imaginary constructs which we reinforce but which we are also in a position to deconstruct (Enright, 2008: 101–13). The story pits the fierce assaults on ethnic identity by an Irishwoman, Elaine, against the equally fervent preconceptions of her American boyfriend, Tim. Their cross-cultural liaison forces them to come to grips with exotic truisms about the Other and to refute them. They play out their relationship in their native countries and an assortment of other locales including Venice and Mexico. Their exchanges enact a mock warfare in which each ironically cites ethnic stereotypes to seduce the other and quibbles with the fabricated identities with which they find themselves associated. Elaine teasingly asks Tim to relate his family history and to tell her about coffin ships and potatoes, while he avers that he likes Irishwomen because of their accents and the 'weather in their hair' (106). Their romance seems founded on immutable legacies which are enshrined in their very bodies. She is enamoured of his size, irrepressible healthiness, and 'fresh white teeth' (103), while he falls for her 'dark lipstick, and all the history flowering up [her] back' (106). Stereotypes are shown to be enduring and to be as much the stock-in-trade of global as of traditional cultures. In Mexico, Elaine mounts a polemical attack on Swiss tourists she has met as she links them with the depredations of Nestlé who have commandeered all the local coffee plantations. But she rises to their defence when Tim too takes it on himself to denounce them. Later that night, she recognises that a lasting détente is not possible in interpersonal relations no matter how cosmopolitan they may be and that 'certainly she would hurt him, over time' (112). Although he succumbs to the blandishments of her family, 'he loved them all and they loved him' (113), she persuades him to leave Ireland as she cannot stand 'this fucking country' any longer (112). His needling but open questions to her which conclude the story - 'Where do you want to go? … Where do you want to go, now?' (113) - suggest that romantic views of the outsider tethered to essentialist traits and exotic preconceptions have been scotched. The childhood image that she has drawn on the underside of the table, '[a] green boat with a blue sail' (113), becomes symbolic of their onward journey with its embrace of the uncertainty of migrant existence. The pursuit of a cross-cultural relationship is depicted by

Enright as an unfurling process that must be prepared to challenge and jettison fixed perceptions about self and Other.[8]

'The Shelter of Neighbours' by Éilís Ní Dhuibhne also scrutinises the links between intimacy and estrangement. The story takes its bearings from the Irish proverb, quoted by Mitzy, one of the characters, *ar scáth a chéile a mhaireannna daoine*, we live in each other's shadow (Ní Dhuibhne, 2012: 107–28). The traditional adage underscores our interdependence and need for neighbours. But it also permits the alternative view that neighbours cast a shadow on our lives and trouble our assumptions about ourselves.[9] Ní Dhuibhne's multi-layered narrative recounts the story of Martha, following her through the different phases of her life in Dunroon Crescent, a Dublin suburban housing estate. The story treats the intimacy and distance between neighbours and the degree to which prejudice colours social interrelations and defines degrees of belonging and the boundaries between groups. It shows how internal self-divisions are perpetuated in order to shore up a sense of belonging. The residents of Ní Dhuibhne's fictional housing estate, Dunroon Crescent, construe their middle-class values in contradistinction to the uncouth behaviour they see as characteristic of Lourdes Gardens, a working-class area that abuts their own.

Due to her full-time job as a civil servant and her liberal beliefs, Martha has felt herself to be an outsider in her neighbourhood and at variance with her female neighbours who stay at home to take care of their families. However, over time she befriends Mitzy, a woman she had been wary of because of her doctrinaire middle-class values. The two women become especially close when Mitzy tends Martha's fatally ill son in hospital while she is at work. The story concentrates on a moment in the present after the economic collapse, a period at which Martha has become estranged from Mitzy once again because the latter has voiced her distrust of public servants, thus thoughtlessly insulting her. In aping the prejudices that have dominated Irish public debate since the bank bailout, she shows her readiness to accept lazily chosen scapegoats. On the pivotal night on which the narrative hinges, Martha, suffering from insomnia, gets up and puts out the bins in front of her house; while doing so she spots a suspiciously muffled-up figure who gives her a momentary scare. She is relieved, however, to recognise that it is Siobhán, Mitzy's adult daughter. Her sense of reassurance is later dispelled when she learns that a Polish woman, Katia Michalska, has been stabbed in Lourdes Gardens. Piecing information together, she chillingly realises that the murder victim was the new partner of Siobhán's former boyfriend. Mitzy, unaware of the dead woman's involvement with her daughter's ex, in a gossipy exchange denounces her to Martha and insinuates that her loose behaviour had caused her violent end. Her reinforcement of racist assumptions is shocking because it is automatic and all the more ironic as she is oblivious to the fact that her own daughter may well be guilty of the murder of this Polish woman. The story ends in *medias res* while Martha is being interrogated by police; it draws to a halt as she is about to respond to the question as to whether she saw anyone on the street on the night of the murder. The pointed suspension and incomplete action serve to emphasise the internal social friction in a Dublin community that has been vividly delineated throughout the story. The hiatus of the ending points to that space in which our ethical obligations to the Other must be reviewed. Ní Dhuibhne's narrative unearths the animosities and tragedies that underpin carefully maintained social facades and the manner in which scapegoats are sought out for local economic woes. The murder of a Polish immigrant is symbolic of the insidious silences of Irish society and of the damaging effect of the tacit rules of belonging that hold sway in multicultural communities. Further, the story, by turning the spotlight on the internal workings of a seemingly cohesive Dublin suburb, underscores the Otherness of the self as it depicts the instability of this middle-class world and the violence which it can engender and harbour at its core.

Contrary to a frequently iterated opinion that contemporary Irish writing is narrowly monocultural and has obtusely ignored the presence of diverse population groups in the country, the stories considered in this chapter evidence the conjoint concern of a wide range of writers with the figure of the immigrant and with the aesthetic problem of the representation of the ethnic Other. Thematically, the issue of the 'new Irish' is coupled with a constellation of intertwined subjects including Irish return migration, transnationalism, the still occluded histories of Irish emigration, and the problematic of social inclusion for all in-groups and out-groups in global communities. Kwame Appiah has argued that cosmopolitanism consists of twin strands: the recognition that we have obligations to others and a respect for legitimate difference (2006: xi–xvi). The stories examined in this investigation fulfil these dual ethical principles by scrutinising the ways in which outsiders are outlawed and turned into racial Others, and tracking the failures in empathy between the multiethnic figures that they represent. In attempting to depict the viewpoint of the Other, they dislocate Irish pieties about self, family, and community, and indicate that indigenous beliefs must be defamiliarised and opened up to question in order for the inequities and racist norms of Irish society to be exposed. Above all, they reveal that the immigrant operates troublingly as a phantasmatic excess, silence, void or elision within current imaginings. In making these absences and repressions resonant, these stories counter the failure of politicians to reflect adequately upon the exclusionary policies advocated by the State, resolutely raise the spectre of Irish racism, and pinpoint the resistance to integration as well as its possibilities for an altered and expanded sense of community.

Notes

1   Declan Kiberd has contended that self-alienation and a crisis with respect to the fundaments of Irish identity lie at the root of anxieties about immigrants as well as the conspicuous failure of governments to develop social policies to cope with an ethnically diverse population (2001: 50–2).
2   On the adaptability of the short story, see Ingman (2009: 225–66).
3   Ó Ceallaigh's first collection of short stories, *Notes from a Turkish Whorehouse* (2007), was largely set in Romania where he lives. Kevin Barry's initial works, the short story collection *There Are Little Kingdoms* (2007) and the novel *City of Bohane* (2011), concentrated on giving voice to a hidden non-metropolitan Ireland.
4   In 'My Two Mothers' in this volume (2011: 169–81), O'Brien returns to the theme of her mother's emigration to Brooklyn, which she had earlier treated in *The Light of Evening* (2006).
5   See Ní Laoire (2011) for an appraisal of recent reactions to the return migrant in Ireland.
6   For another short story in which a discovery of the Otherness of the self proves transformative see Emma Donoghue's 'The Sanctuary of Hands' (2006: 128–41). An Irishwoman, on holiday in France to recover from a broken love affair, is altered when she forms an involuntary bond with a young man with disability.
7   See Eóin Flannery (2011: 45–51) for a perceptive interpretation of this story.
8   For an account of the unsettling strategies of Enright's short fiction see Elke D'hoker (2001).
9   Several of the stories in the volume have transnational settings, including 'Illumination' (Ní Dhuibhne, 2012: 27–45) and 'It is a Miracle' (67–94). 'The Shortcut Through IKEA' focuses on a Swedish immigrant in Ireland (129–38).

References

Appiah, Kwame Anthony (2006). *Cosmopolitanism: Ethics in a World of Strangers*. London: Allen Lane.
Barry, Kevin (2007). *There Are Little Kingdoms*. Dublin: Stinging Fly.
—— (2011). *City of Bohane*. London: Jonathan Cape.
—— (2012). *Dark Lies the Island*. London: Jonathan Cape.
D'hoker, Elke (2011). 'Distorting mirrors and unsettling snapshots: Anne Enright's short fiction', in Claire Bracken and Susan Cahill (eds), *Anne Enright*. Dublin: Irish Academic Press, 33–50.
Donoghue, Emma (2006). *Touchy Subjects*. London: Virago.
Enright, Anne (2008). *Taking Pictures*. London: Jonathan Cape.
Fanning, Bryan (2011). *Immigration and Social Cohesion in the Republic of Ireland*. Manchester: Manchester University Press.
Flannery, Eóin (2011). *Colum McCann and the Aesthetics of Redemption*. Dublin: Irish Academic Press.
Ingman, Heather (2009). *A History of the Irish Short Story*. Cambridge: Cambridge University Press.
Kiberd, Declan (2001). 'Strangers in their country: Multi-culturalism in Ireland', in Edna Longley and Declan Kiberd, *Multi-Culturalism: The View from the Two Irelands*. Cork:

Cork University Press in association with The Centre for Cross Border Studies, Armagh, 45–74.

Lentin, Ronit (2006). 'From racial State to racist State?: Racism and immigration in twenty-first-century Ireland', in Alana Lentin and Ronit Lentin (eds), *Race and State*. Cambridge: Cambridge Scholars Press, 188–210.

McCann, Colum (1994). *Fishing the Sloe-Black River*. London: Phoenix.

Ní Dhuibhne, Éilís (2007). *Fox, Swallow, Scarecrow*. Belfast: Blackstaff.

—— (2012). *The Shelter of Neighbours*. Belfast: Blackstaff.

Ní Laoire, Caitríona (2011). 'Return migrants and boundaries of belonging', in Bryan Fanning and Ronaldo Munck (eds), *Globalization, Migration and Social Transformation*. London: Ashgate, 21–33.

O'Brien, Edna (2006). *The Light of Evening*. London: Weidenfeld & Nicolson.

—— (2011). *Saints and Sinners*. London: Faber & Faber.

Ó Ceallaigh, Philip (2007). *Notes from a Turkish Whorehouse*. London: Penguin.

—— (2009). *The Pleasant Light of Day*. London: Penguin.

O'Connor, Frank (1962). *The Lonely Voice: A Study of the Short Story*. London: Macmillan.

O'Donnell, Mary (2008). *Storm Over Belfast*. Dublin: New Island.

Ricoeur, Paul (1992). *Oneself as Another*, trans. Kathleen Blamey. Chicago: University of Chicago Press.

Tóibín, Colm (2010). *The Empty Family*. London: Viking.

9

Writing the 'new Irish' into Ireland's old narratives: the poetry of Sinéad Morrissey, Leontia Flynn, Mary O'Malley, and Michael Hayes

Katarzyna Poloczek

It is a relatively recent development that, as Tom Inglis notices, there have been more people arriving in Ireland than leaving the island, transforming the country into 'a multi-racial, multi-ethnic, multi-religious culture' (Inglis, 2008: 86). The progression of those changes has been so immense that even the Irish-born citizens returning to their country after years of living abroad look at the new Ireland with astonishment:

> It's a startling new Ireland, but why shouldn't it be? I myself left the best part of twenty years ago and the finest thing about coming home is the rawness and the newness. I dislike what has been lost, but why whine about it? Why hold tight to the past when we have this sort of future? (McCann, 2007: viii)

Commenting upon the recent wave of immigration to Ireland, John Brannigan (2009: 3) outlines its distinctive features. Among these, he enumerates its extensive scope ('the scale of contemporary migratory movement'), the creation of diverse ethnic localities ('the formation of particular ethnically perceived communities'), and the triggering of new legal regulations ('Irish governments since the 1990s have felt compelled to react with political and legal measures either to limit immigration or to dictate the terms of "integration"').

The cultural potential of immigration should also be taken into account. Justin Quinn (an Irish poet who has lived in Prague for the last fifteen years) observes that '[i]t is a fundamentally new immigration pattern that can only invigorate the monoculture that has held sway since 1922' (2009: 159). Consequently, Quinn conceives of the current immigration phenomenon as fertile in terms of the new opportunities for the development of Irish poetry. He envisages 'the hope of new engagements and collisions' between the old and the new Irish that will create new subjects and new perspectives in the contemporary Irish poetic landscape (*ibid.*). Moreover, the encounters with the polyphonic ethnic migrants result in 'awareness of the borders of English as a means of expression, inducing gold-leaf shifts of awareness and aspect' (*ibid.*). Last but not least, Quinn perceives a potential for liberation in abandoning the bygone, nationalist rhetoric in modern Irish discourse:

> This is not to say that Irish poetry will somehow get *better* in the years ahead; rather with the decline of nationalism, both as a political force and as an aesthetic ideology for poetry, language issues – primarily Irish ones, and secondary European – will perhaps lead towards a new enabling aesthetic ideology. (Original emphasis; *ibid.*)

Very much in the same vein, the poet Mary Montague recognises the need for 'contemporary Irish poetry to look beyond historic and national borders' (2009: 109). Montague's suggestions as to the way in which modern Irish poetry should advance, together with Quinn's arguments, seem to indicate that intercultural encounters with foreign, migratory Others might diversify the frame of reference and widen the prospective panorama in Irish poetry. As Declan Kiberd states, '[t]he fear of the outsider is often a version of the fear of the future' (2005: 317). Bearing this in mind, this chapter will look into Ireland's future, which is today shaped by the 'new Irish', 'mingled with the old Irish' (McCann, 2007: viii). The first section depicts poetic representations of economic migrants, mostly from the new EU member states, and other major groups of European visitors to contemporary Ireland. The opening passages, rendered from the standpoint of the world-travelled, migratory 'old Irish', examine European emigrants' arrival and their life in Ireland. The section probes poems by Sinéad Morrissey, Mary O'Malley, and Leontia Flynn. The latter part, on the other hand, focuses on portraits of refugees and asylum-seekers from African countries. More specifically, it examines Michael Hayes's poetic collection (2007) *'Survivor' – Representations of the 'New Irish': Dúchas Dóchasach*, published together with the paintings of an African artist Jean 'Ryan' Hakizimana. What Hayes's poems attempt is to write the African narratives into the Irish landscapes and ancient stories, without losing their distinctiveness. In addition to creating poetry and fiction, Michael Hayes conducts research and lectures at the University of Limerick on, among other topics, minority groups, Irish Travellers, asylum-seekers, migration, and oral tradition. Two books Hayes co-authored with Hakizimana are a part of the University of Limerick 'Sanctuary' project, whose purpose is 'providing ... spaces of genuine meeting and hospitality between old and new communities in Ireland' via 'music, dance, painting, poetry, drama [and] story-telling' (Phelan, 2008: xvi).

In the above-quoted essay 'Baggage reclaim', Quinn argues: '[t]he other side of the coin is the outward journey, when the Irish poet goes abroad, bringing with him or her a whole lot of baggage. How is one to make sense of the world one encounters out there, through an Irish literary lens?' (2009: 159). To some extent, what this chapter's opening section does is to try to respond to Quinn's rhetorical question. Justin Quinn, Mary O'Malley, and Sinéad Morrissey have lived and worked for some time abroad, and then come back to Ireland 'burdened with presents from being away', as Sinéad Morrissey puts it in the opening poem of her second volume *Between Here and There* (2002: 9). In this untitled poem, the persona's 'flexible throat full of a foreign language' compassionately signifies the alien Other, both feared and misunderstood (*ibid.*). Considering the above, the poets' perception of modern, multicultural Ireland – composed of people of different backgrounds, nationalities, and cultures – is shaped, to a large extent, by their own migratory experiences. This affects their empathetic understanding of the immigrant Other, in both aspects of this phenomenon: as subjects and objects of the bilateral multicultural interactions.

On her return to Ireland, Sinéad Morrissey captures her amazement with the country's 'rawness and the newness' (McCann, 2007: viii) in her 'baggage reclaim' collection, *Between Here and There*. The Ireland that Morrissey returned to has been in the process of transition into a different, multicultural country, vibrant with the energy of numerous newcomers. In spite of its title, Morrissey's poem 'Tourism' appears to explore not just one but many kinds of migratory movements to Ireland which have taken place over recent years. As Brannigan warns, '[t]here is no state, no "home", without the foreigner, without the one who is defined legally and culturally as other' (2009: 145). Questioning this binary thinking, Morrissey's 'Tourism' aims to deconstruct the alleged oppositions between the insider/outsider perspective, playing aptly upon the foreign v. home connotations. Welcoming foreigners and the 'new Irish' in her own country, the speaker subversively blurs the perspective of the Irish world-traveller and that of a local inhabitant. In doing so, Morrissey achieves a comparable effect to what Kiberd observes about Joyce: 'Joyce was one of the first artists ... to imagine "a world without foreigners", a world possible once men and women begin to accept the foreigner in the self and the necessarily fictive natures of all nationalisms, which are open to endless renegotiation' (Kiberd, 2005: 313–4).

Morrissey's narrative begins ironically with the mocking of Ireland's financial opportunities in the large-scale migratory business. The persona seems dismissive of the very notion of the itinerant human flows, referring to them as 'a manufactured prophesy of spring – / the Spanish and the Dutch are landing in airports / and filing out of ships. Our day has come' (Morrissey, 2002: 14). Equally double-edged is a derisive vision of the homogenous, impersonal migratory crowd of 'the Spanish and the Dutch', arriving in Ireland, motivated by their search for globetrotters' adventures, or seeking a place to live. The self-ironic statement 'Our day has come' indicates that during the Celtic Tiger prosperity Ireland is perceived by migrants as an attractive place with better living opportunities and a much appreciated excursionist destination. What is more, the speaker observes that not only the economically surging South but also the recovering, post-Good Friday Agreement North is beginning to draw, with the irresistible Irish 'off-beat, headstrong, suicidal charm', both short-term visitors and immigrants.[1] The persona enumerates all the gifts that the Irish receive from migrant Others: 'They bring us deliverance, restitution, / as we straighten our ties, strengthen our lattés, / polish our teeth' (*ibid.*). The first present seems to be derived from the religious and emancipatory discourse, meaning redemption and free expression; the latter signifies compensation and reimbursement. In this intercultural exchange, the native Irish seem to hospitably bestow multinational visitors with the best version of themselves,[2] together with other attractions ('We take them to those streets / they want to see most', (*ibid.*)).

The persona's 'fearing summary' also discloses how the Irish would rather avoid reviewing in a nutshell the last few centuries of their own history and the English colonial past (Morrissey, 2002: 14).[3] They would prefer to gloss over the background behind the Troubles, after showing newcomers around the 'splintered city', having drunk an obligatory pint of Guinness beer, and paid a visit to a Belfast shipyard (*ibid.*). Such a stereotypical marketing strategy might come dangerously close to the '"stage-Irish" approach' (Inglis, 2008: 104). Nonetheless, in other fragments of the poem, Morrissey's speaker self-derisively and self-effacingly lays bare the sore places in Irish history that might be addressed with catharsis, when exposed to foreign Others.

The poem's final fragment is addressed directly to the potential newcomers and migrants. Hence, the concluding passage constitutes a mixture, a subversively performed, provocative love–hate attitude. On the one hand, it renders the need for Ireland to become a modern, open, multicultural country. On the other, it discloses the suspicion of losing the self-contained, national idiosyncrasy, associated with the island's isolated developing communities. The poem terminates with a mockery of eurosceptical and euroenthusiastic approaches. Both become the target of the persona's derision: either because of their clinging to the old sentiments and xenophobia, or their attempt to transform Ireland into one more EU-identical country, with a more or less homogenised character.[4] Accordingly, the speaker records the moment of Ireland's opening to the world as follows:

> So come, keep coming here.
> We'll recklessly set chairs in the streets and pray for the sun.
> Diffuse the gene pool, confuse the local kings,
>
> infect us with your radical ideas; be carried here

on a sea breeze from the European superstate
we long to join; bring us new symbols,
a new national flag, a xylophone. Stay.

(Morrissey, 2002: 14)

Overtly, the female speaking voice uttering the above-quoted invitation seems to be ironically distanced from this declared, welcoming invitation. The blatant, performatively provocative sarcasm of her words is juxtaposed with the content's implied politeness towards migrants. The passage abounds with all sorts of national stereotypes. The catalogue embraces the foreigners' complaints about the Irish weather, Irish self-containment and self-absorption in their own local context, the xenophobic attitude towards newcomers, distrust in 'foreign' ideas and values, and scepticism towards EU politics. What is more, the list is amplified to the level of ridicule by the speaker's subversively assuming the self-important plural and collective voice ('We'll recklessly', 'we long to join; bring us'). As argued above, what is being derided is the Irish people's fear of multiculturalism as a subversive and radical movement ('your radical ideas; be carried here'), intoxicating the 'essence' of Irishness with 'new symbols' and new ideas, like the poisonous foreign puffer fish in the opening poem of *Between Here and There*. The in-between, self-ironic signification seems ridden with mocked clichés concerning the emerging Irish multiculturalism, perceived by some as a dangerous contagious disease (see 'infect us with your radical ideas'). Hence multiculturalism is sarcastically implied to constitute a threat to the Irish State's own independence ('bring us new symbols, a new national flag'), a danger to the continuity of Irish historical and cultural heritage ('confuse the local kings'), and even to Irishness itself ('Diffuse the gene pool'). Inglis's words might elucidate the roots of the xenophobic attitude ridiculed so aptly by Morrissey in 'Tourism': 'There are many cultural guardians who see the mixing of the global with the local as a form of foreign contamination that will eventually destroy traditional Irish culture' (Inglis, 2008: 63). In the end, Morrissey's speaker succeeds in subverting the aforementioned views, by mocking and challenging them with her own 'foreignising', world-traveller's attitude.[5]

As in Morrissey's 'Tourism', the female voice in Mary O'Malley's poem 'Dublinia' belongs to a worldly-wise migrant 'whose capitals were Lisbon and New York' (O'Malley, 2006: 67). This poem similarly brings to the surface the ambivalent and disowned feelings towards 'foreignised' Others. To address this disquieting issue, O'Malley's speaker does not detach herself with a self-ironic stand: apart from depicting her subjects of enunciation, the female speaking voice appears to empathetically co-experience their fate with them. The persona, having returned to Ireland after living abroad, seems dismayed with her visit to the country's capital city. What unsettles her most is a view of the 'discarded people' who occupy Dublin's pavements. One might argue that the Irish streets have always been populated with various musicians, performers, and people asking for some spare change, and that citizens most probably were accustomed to this view. Nonetheless, the modifier 'discarded' renders additional passivity, immobility, and helplessness. Thus, it excludes a colourful and cheerful performers' crowd. Moreover, *A Perfect V*'s publication date (2006) and the reference to the Millennium Spike indicate that the speaker means twenty-first-century Ireland, yet still before the Irish economic decline. In the light of the above, it seems plausible to assume that the abandoned and forgotten people (beggars or homeless), lying in Dublin's streets, could be conceived of as the 'new Irish', or at least as 'foreigners' in their exclusion from the 'normative' social order. For Dubliners, their acquiescent 'street' existence has become first 'domesticated' and then passed over. Nonetheless, the migratory speaker does acknowledge the 'discarded' people's presence. She can see them, as she chooses not to turn her eyes from that disquieting view.

One might further speculate as to whether O'Malley's poem implies here immigrants for whom the Irish dream has ended in the street, because of a lack of work, a lack of necessary adaptive or language skills, or the development of some addiction. 'Dublinia' does not give any definite resolution to that question. What the narrative does state explicitly is that, to some, the 'discarded people' might signify the dispensable human rubbish that needs to be removed (demonstrated by the expression 'the sidewalks / littered with discarded people'). That is why, as the speaker empathetically notices, these people's conspicuous, yet ignored, pavement presence pierces like the Millennium Spike the heart of Dublin – being its puncturing prick of conscience:

> Even those of us that never liked it,
> …
> didn't want it to come to this, the sidewalks
> littered with discarded people and a spike
> driven through its pot-holed heart.
>
> (O'Malley, 2006: 67)

Thus, the undesirable encounter with the migratory, 'foreign' Other (destitute, resigned, and vulnerable) might breed discomfort, embarrassment, consternation ('didn't want it to come to this'), and compassion. The present-day 'discarded people' might even irritate passers-by because they awaken the memories of Ireland's own times of poverty and deprivation (Kiberd, 2005: 318). Accordingly, Kiberd notes that '[t]he fear of hybridisation is really a terror in the face of potent but repressed forces within one's own culture' (310). On the linguistic level, the title of O'Malley's poem constitutes a peculiar hybrid with its surprising, foreign-sounding, un-English '-ia' suffix. On the other hand, the capital's foreignised designation, through a vowel finale, appears to mellow the signifier's consonantal-cluster root into a more feminised and softer endnote. Hence the harshness of the previously elaborated image is subdued by its soothing vocal representation. One might wonder whether the diminutively tender 'Dublinia' has been coined (inclusively) by immigrants or by the Irish themselves (as a means of foreign exclusion).

As these examples demonstrate, poetic representations of the 'new Irish' by Irish writers tend to be full of lyrical, pensive but, sometimes, also stereotypical depictions. There are a few poets who dare to break the cliché pattern with an audaciously unconventional account of immigrants. Such is the case of Leontia Flynn's playfully original poem 'The Vibrator' (Flynn, 2009: 55). The narrative relates the story of an unexpected gift, left behind by a hurried, forgetful lodger, to Polish immigrants. Together with a rented apartment, the flat's new tenants are to inherit an erotic gadget. The poem opens with the lament of the vibrator's rightful owner:

> … where was the vibrator?

> Oh cruel Gods! Oh vulgar implement
> that was stowed discretely on some shelf or cupboard
> but has almost certainly not been boxed away …
> Oh dirty gift of doubtful provenance
> Oh gift – surprise! – for the next week's settling tenants.

> Oh nice surprise for next week's settling tenants,
> four Polish men paid peanuts by the hour
> – for in Belfast too world history holds its sway –
> to find alone in some nook or niche-hole the vibrator
> still beats, in the dark, its battery-powered heart.
> (Flynn, 2009: 55)

As can be clearly seen, in Flynn's poem the multicultural encounter is accidental, unintentional, indirect (not in person), and yet it *does* happen. What is more, it takes place on several grounds. First, it occurs on the acknowledgement level, as the persona recognises the immigrants' presence as subjects in the future interaction. Secondly, it involves the dimension of social injustice, when the speaker admits that economic migrants work for lower wages than ought to be paid to them (the alliterated 'four *P*olish men *p*aid *p*eanuts by the hour'). In the poem's new version, included in Flynn's 2011 volume *Profit and Loss*, the author has altered two words: 'for in Belfast too *world history* holds its sway' becomes 'for in Belfast too *The Market* holds its sway' (Flynn, 2011: 15, emphasis added). Though not extensive, the poet's word change is very significant. It points explicitly to the source of immigrants' economic exploitation: the market economy thriving on a cheap(er) labour force. Thirdly, in 'The Vibrator' the personal stories of immigrants are mingled with Irish people's private narratives.

The intimate object inherited from the previous lodger allows the 'new Irish' to be let in on a shared secret. As a result, the unintentional (object) exchange creates a thread of familiarity between the Irish persona and the Polish economic migrants. By the accidental self-exposure of the speaker's privacy, the persona herself becomes vulnerable. Hence the dialectic of host–immigrant power relations is undermined. Additionally, what is usually kept in secret and away from Others' eyes becomes displayed publicly.

The final aspect of this object-mediated encounter is realised via its (tragic-comic) inter-subjective context. The poet skilfully balances between mockery and gravity. At first, the prophesised tragedy signifies solely the speaker's future shame when an embarrassing erotic gadget is discovered by the flat's new lodgers. The archaic-stylised language ('Oh dirty gift of doubtful provenance') sparkles with humour and distance from the looming misfortune. On the surface, Flynn's poem might even look like a derisive pastiche of stilted, neo-classical decorum (in line with Alexander's Pope 'The Rape of the Lock'). It abounds with pretentious exclamations, emphatic, highly emotive expressions, and hyperbolic tone ('Oh cruel Gods! Oh vulgar implement', 'Oh dirty gift', 'Oh gift – surprise!' and 'Oh nice surprise'). Line by line, the persona self-mockingly construes the impending calamity, aptly envisaging the harbingers of doom.

The derisive mood prevails until the concluding stanza, where the real-life rhetoric takes over. Once the speaker's hyperbolically imagined personal misfortune has been contrasted with the collective grim existence of the vibrator's potential finders, the poem's tone alters. It is then that the narrative marks a shift from the self-centred, solipsist, purely egoistic perspective to a broader, inter-subjective panorama, including migrant Others. Separated from their life partners, four badly paid male Polish immigrants, crammed in one studio, share the limited space and equally limited life options. That is why in the last line, the persona seems to (self-derisively) rejoice that it is they who will inherit her left-over gift ('Oh *nice* surprise for next week's settling tenants'; emphasis added). To put it bluntly, the vibrator's beating heart ('still beats, in the dark, its battery-powered heart') self-ironically renders a message of human solidarity, transferred on the level of understanding the immigrants' solitude in exile, their emotional longing, and sexual deprivation. Ultimately, the poem introduces a truly subversive reassurance without resorting to a consolatory mood.

As shown in this poem, the literary encounters with foreign Others might be humorous and practical, but also grievous and disconsolate. This happens because immigrants' multifarious experiences are not easily, or unanimously, transcribed into the vernacular discourse. Following this line of thinking, Michael Hayes's volume *'Survivor' – Representations of the 'New Irish': Dúchas Dóchasach* constitutes a daring attempt to write African asylum-seekers' stories into the Irish ancient narratives, familiar scenery, local imagery, and native idiom.

Hayes's collection is inspired by the life of an African refugee who was a survivor of ethnic genocide and an asylum-seeker in Ireland: Jean 'Ryan' Hakizimana.[6] Hakizimana's middle name 'Ryan' comes from the Irish missionary Fr. Ryan, who helped his family to stay alive in 1972, during the first phase of the Burundian bloodshed. Paradoxical as it may seem, what used to be a one-sided charitable mission in developing countries has turned into a true intercultural exchange in contemporary times. This is possible because Irish missionaries 'brought with them radical new ideas about democratising parish life or applying the principles of liberation theology, learned out in Africa or Latin America. Ireland, which had once given a lead to other decolonising peoples, now seemed to be following their example' (Kiberd, 2005: 305). Considering this, in the modern multicultural world the roles of tutors and disciples are never permanently fixed and constantly alternate. That is why, writing about the first Hakizimana-Hayes co-authored project, *Postcolonial Identities: Constructing the 'New Irish'* (2006), Helen Phelan argues: 'The collaborative voices of Jean and Michael weave in and out of a creative dialogue, surrounding Jean's paintings with history, story, and shaman-like journeying. … [T]his many-voiced story offers Irish, Burundian/ Rwandan reflections, with shared threads of history and a shared human story in Jean's journey' (2008: xv–xvi). Furthermore, Phelan elaborates that this thought, '[t]he doing of art – of song, story-telling, poetry and painting – … opens up a space around suffering and loss and surrounds it with vision, understanding, expression, acknowledgement and hope' (xv).

Unlike in *Postcolonial Identities*, the speaking voice in the *'Survivor'* (2007), nonetheless, ought not to be mistaken for the words of Hakizimana himself. Although in their 2006 project, Hakizimana's personal testimony was fused with Hayes's academic knowledge,[7] in *'Survivor'* Hayes's poems and Hakizimana's paintings co-exist side by side on equal and autonomous terms. As explained by these authors, 'Jean Ryan uses his paintings to tell the story of his troubled past and the difficulties experienced by asylum-seekers throughout the world' (Hayes and Hakizimana, 2007: 44). Despite the fact that Hayes's writing mode differs much from Hakizimana's art,[8] they both constitute mutually complementary, yet artistically independent, sides in this intercultural exchange.

Bearing this in mind, *'Survivor'* is the utterance of an Irish witness who listens to the voices of those who survived and those who did not make it during their immigrant journey to Ireland. The speaker in Hayes's collection does not usurp the right to explain let alone translate the anguish of the living immigrants or the silence of the deceased. He does not pretend to be speaking on behalf of the dispossessed asylum-seekers. Taking advantage of their stories and appropriating their pain would be an additional abuse done to survivors.[9] What Hayes does by intertwining the African narratives with the Irish oral story-telling tradition corresponds to Hakizimana's writing Irish landscapes, colours, and images into his own paintings. In other words, Hayes's volume renders the hybridisation of Irish heterogeneous identities, in the best sense that Kearney advocates:

> Contemporary Irish identity is most at ease with itself, it appears, when the obsession with an exclusive identity is abandoned. Irish culture rediscovers its best self, not self-consciously, not self-regardingly, but in its encounter with other cultures – continental, British, American, etc. For as long as Irish people think of themselves as Celtic Crusoes on a sequestered island, they ignore … the … truth that cultural creation comes from hybridization, not purity, contamination not immunity, polyphony not monologue. (Kearney, 1997: 101)

The hybridic volume *'Survivor' – Representations of the 'New Irish': Dúchas Dóchasach* is complemented by Irish translations of Hayes's poetry, done by Irish-language writers. One might interpret Hayes's decision to translate his poems into Irish as a decolonising gesture, aimed to make English be perceived as a 'foreign' language, one of the many alien, migratory idiolects. Paradoxical as it may seem, the new wave of immigration, with its proliferation of languages and cultures, has led to the revival of the readiness to study Irish. Quinn claims that '[t]here is evidence that the influx is subtly changing Irish attitudes towards Gaelic, with many people now actually trying to learn the language instead of saying how beautiful it is' (2009: 159). Considering the above, Hayes's persona assumes the position of intercultural mediator between the 'old' and the 'new Irish', between African narratives and the ancient Gaelic lore, between the English and Irish languages. Accordingly, *'Survivor'* seems to embrace at least two types of ancient story-tellers: *sgéalaí* and *seanchaí* (Kiberd, 2005: 44). This fusion between the international and local oral story-telling traditions blurs the boundaries between the foreign Other and the local self.

'Survivor' begins in Africa, before the asylum-seekers' arrival into Ireland. Then the poetic narrative follows the refugees through their dangerous sea voyage, and it accompanies immigrants during their stay in Ireland. Kiberd notices that '[i]n both Ireland and Africa, … the central role of the artist was to question the assumption that culture arises only when imperialists arrive' (2005: 133). That is why it is around a drummer-man, a symbolic African artist, that the commencing sections of Hayes's narrative are organised. In Hayes's poetry, the drum expression seems to signify artistic freedom, which begins with tenderness ('Caress, the drum he says'), and then progresses into a fierce cadence (Hayes, 2007: 3).[10] The middle section of 'Drum' introduces a note of sensuality: the rhythm penetrates the player's body and provides the orgasmic discharge of creative energy ('Then you come down hard / Until the rhythm is inside you / Right there' (*ibid.*). In 'Fever', the drummer-man is portrayed as a community leader who conducts the village celebrations with hallucinating visions and trance dances: 'The drummer-man gave the signal / And everybody bent to

smoke / They inhaled its texture' (11). The narrative 'Shack ("Teach")' implies a foreshadowing of Ireland as the immigrants' future destination. As the cycle proceeds, the poem 'Journey' indicates the unavoidable necessity of undertaking the asylum-seeking voyage: 'The old ones make out you / should always be ready / Your flask full, your bag packed / Spit and polish' (13).

Unlike the elusively symbolic 'Journey', the poem 'Survivor' appears to be firmly founded on realistic grounds. The nearly mythological quest referred to earlier turns out to be a deadly marine expedition to the shores of Ireland. During this journey, refugees might die of starvation, illness or extreme exhaustion. The narrative is filled with the sea voyage's specific details, as if the speaking voice intends to supply the missing pieces that fill in the gaps from 'Journey':

> It was the thirty-first day for the living
> They got the smell of the land
> and crawled forward from the shadows
> Leather-skinned men,
> Emaciated.
> The teeth-rattle in their heads.
>
> (Hayes, 2007: 17)

When the African asylum-seekers finally reach Ireland, having been on the boat for over a month, they are too weak to walk on their own: 'Fifteen of them it took / to lift the lifeboat' (*ibid.*). Moreover, their anguish is rendered in the subversive, and overtly provocative, dehumanising idiom of the following expressions: 'got the smell' and 'crawled forward' (*ibid.*). The signifier 'leather' associated with people ('Leather-skinned men') deconstructs human v. non-human binaries. The modifier 'emaciated' makes an obvious pun on 'emancipated'. One cannot fail to notice how, in today's world, poverty, famine, and terror demean and subjugate people. Starved nearly to death men may as well eat the sea weeds and 'pieces of the moon' (*ibid.*). Nevertheless, they know that unlike those who did not make it, they are the lucky ones: the survivors. As the speaking voice in *Postcolonial Identities: Constructing the 'New Irish'* explains, 'How to describe the life of a refugee? The lives of the limbo-people! The people who are trapped. The people who can neither go forward into the future nor backwards into the past ... Survival is the aim' (Hakizimana and Hayes, 2008: 33).

The poem 'Survivor' emanates with the immigrants' inner strength and dignity. The fact that all the Africans speak different languages shows them not as an impersonal, homogenous crowd but as individuals:

> Later – each man swore different,
> One man said the bladder-wrack was cake
> Another ate pieces of the moon.
>
> (Hayes, 2007:17)

In other poems such as 'Butterfly', and especially in 'An Fear Marbh: Homage to the Dingle-Man Himself', quoted below, what strikes one immediately is the ambience of peaceful serenity that emanates from the narrative. The anxiety of the earlier poems is replaced by safety when one does not have to fear physical extinction: 'Stretched out / Relaxed / Snoozing / as a summer-cat' (30). The final exclamatory utterances ('Just imagine that! / Asleep on edge of the world!' (*ibid.*) seem to express relief and pride in successfully accomplishing one's journey.

Nevertheless, the aforementioned security of the newly arrived immigrants is gradually transcribed into their need for belonging – being recognised as the 'new Irish'. In all the previously related poems, African immigrants are on their own: either when arriving in Ireland at night, or later while admiring the countryside or beginning to make their homes on the island. Commenting upon the situation of the refugees and asylum-seekers in Ireland, Hakizimana observes that:

> Many are segregated not only from their only families and countries but also from the local population in which they are living. This leads to feelings of exclusion and marginalisation ... [T]he refugees frequently remain segregated from the Irish people that they have chosen to make their new lives with. This leads to feelings of alienation and suspicion on the part of both the asylum-seekers and the Irish people. (Hakizimana and Hayes, 2008: 82)

The isolation and separation of the African asylum-seekers in the Irish community is foregrounded in Hayes's volume. 'Warrior' is ultimately the first narrative in '*Survivor*' where the African asylum-seekers are mentioned in the context of an encounter with other Irish people:

> The Irishmen stood at the counter
> ...
> They were young and old
> Munstermen and Connachtmen
> Northerners and Jackeens.
>
> > (Hayes, 2007:35)

During the pub celebration, the Irish-born citizens 'dug for common ground / And the names tripped off their tongues / Like the gods of the harvest' (*ibid.*). The speaker recounts the Irish men's surnames preserved in loving memories: 'Ring, Mackey, Carey / Doyle and English / Cooney and Kelly' (*ibid.*). Nonetheless, the search for 'common ground' turns out to be a rather exclusionary process.[11] The Irish surnames' catalogue does not embrace foreign-sounding designations. None of the immigrants or the new ethnic communities are brought to mind in the pub litany, regardless of the fact that immigrant stories, like those of the African survivors, are the narratives of journeys into Ireland:

A great man to ...
A deadly man to ...
A power of a man ...
A horse of a man ...
The Litany went on.

(Hayes, 2007: 35)

Suddenly, during the pub's remembrance of the dead, the African immigrants hear their name written into the Irish narrative of the departed and recalled. The elusive phrase 'one man mentioned the "Warrior"' does not disclose by whom the Warrior is commemorated. What has changed through this inclusion is the Irish people's awareness. The Irish pub customers are being confronted with the fact that contemporary prayers for the dead also include immigrants who either died on Irish soil or are called to mind by the 'new Irish':

Then they paused
and pulled deep from their porter
They had only just licked their lips clean
when one man mentioned the 'Warrior'.

(*Ibid.*)

The final poem from 'Survivor', entitled 'Inlets', evokes a point that tends to be forgotten these days, namely that 'people from all sorts of ethnic and cultural backgrounds have called Ireland 'home' and have been doing it throughout Irish history' and that these people 'made immeasurable contributions to Ireland's culture and prosperity' (Richardson, 2005):

Three inlets
Related all,
The stories they'd tell
if only they could talk!
First came the Stone people
Then the Bronze
Vikings and Normans
Jews, Gentile and Moor
Saxon and Celt.

(Hayes, 2007: 41)

With its bygone frame of reference, the allegedly all-embracing conclusion of the whole volume ('Come day, go day / The inlets welcomed them all' (*ibid.*)) might appear bleak. By employing the past tense of the verb 'welcomed' Hayes seems to imply that present-day Ireland does not always receive incoming immigrants with open arms. Instead of stating it explicitly, Hayes reminds the Irish of their hospitable attitude in the previous centuries. It happens implicitly because Hayes's succinct, haiku-like poems, operating upon the imagist tradition, are full of restraint, understatement, and ellipsis. Declan Kiberd articulates Hayes's innuendo more directly:

> The seductive charm of Irish culture no longer seems to work in quite the old way. A *céad míle fáilte* is not extended to all new arrivals any more. Yet the historical capacity of the Irish to assimilate waves of incomers should never be underestimated … Who is to say that the latest group of arriving Nigerians might not know the same destiny? (2005: 303)

Considering this, true intercultural exchanges happen when immigrants and hosts learn from one another. Although '[a]t the most rudimentary level, the presence of black Africans in the streets of Dublin is a reminder of a colonial past of shame and shared humiliation which some might prefer to ignore', 'the new immigrants are providing a priceless service, reconnecting people with their own buried feelings' (Kiberd, 2005: 318). Moreover, immigrants' own voices are needed in modern Irish discourse as a reminder that 'We, refugees, are human too! We are not a burden!' (Hakizimana and Hayes, 2008: 82).

Notes

1   Margaret Ward (2004: 239) and Andrew Finlay (2006) analyse respectively the sociological and socio-political dimensions of the current changes in the North. Taking into account the recent migratory flows, Finlay distinguishes the old, Northern Irish 'stubbornly bicultural' approach from the multicultural, 'new pluralist agenda opened up by the arrival of immigrants'. He admits, nonetheless, that 'extending the old pluralist agenda to include those who do not fit into either one of the two specified communal identities has proved problematic' (Finlay, 2006).
2   Brannigan suggests sarcastically that the notion of Irish hospitality has been developed quite recently for marketing and publicity purposes: 'The idea of Ireland as specifically a culture of hospitality was marketed aggressively by the Irish Tourist Board as a way of countering the association of the country with political violence' (2009: 155).
3   As Kiberd reminds us, '[t]he official self-image of the Irish State is Eurocentric, but the cultural and the social realities are more often post-colonial' (2005: 255).
4   This contradictory attitude towards foreign nationals has been addressed by Inglis, who claims that '[m]any see [foreigners] as a threat and believe that they can never become truly Irish. And yet, on many occasions, there was a national outpouring of sympathy and concern for particular individuals. It may well be that such concern emerges when people relate to the "other" as an individual rather than as a member of a group. In other words, the individual does not take on the stigma of the group' (2008: 110).
5   The concept 'foreignising' is evoked in Vona Groarke's poetic journal '"Foreignism": A Philadelphia Diary', published in the *Dublin Review* (2005).
6   Hakizimana's whole family – his father, two sisters, his elder brother, and his beloved mother (all of them of Burundian origin) – were murdered in the Hutu–Tutsi ethnic fights that began in 1993. Hakizimana (himself Rwanda-born) survived the bloodshed, took shelter in refugee camps, was imprisoned and tortured, and finally escaped to

Tanzania. Six years later he arrived in Ireland, not on a life-boat like the asylum-seekers depicted in *'Survivor'*, but on a ferry from England.

7 The co-authored *Postcolonial Identities* identifies Hakizimana as a 'narrator and artist', and Hayes as the one who 'transcribed and edited' the book (Hakizimana and Hayes, 2008). Some of Hakizimana's paintings from *'Survivor'* were previously included in *Postcolonial Identities*. Hayes's poem 'Survivor' preceded their earlier project.

8 Hakizimana explains that his 'paintings have three principal qualities – a sense of colour, a sense of joy and a sense of freedom' (Hakizimana and Hayes, 2008: 89). Indeed, his paintings are expressionist, dynamic, and vibrant with vivid colours and un-familiar images. Some of them, like those preceding the poems 'Unborn' or 'Butterfly', tend towards the fauvist style, abandoning their literal accuracy in favour of symbolic ambiguity.

9 In this respect, Kiberd warns about the tenacity of the postcolonial standpoint, which writers might easily abuse: 'Bolger does have something in common with Rushdie – a skill in using the rhetoric of an oppressed minority when in fact he is securely empow-ered as a leading figure in the dominant code' (2005: 256).

10 The ending of the poem 'Fever', like 'Drum', culminates with a premonition of blood: 'The drummer-man got carried away / He hit the drum so hard / – his fingers bled' (Hayes, 2007: 11).

11 The cover illustration of *'Survivor'* features a skinny African man, sitting on the floor in front of the Immigration Office's door, with a red plate reading 'Closed' on the latch. The painting is not so far-fetched, considering that '[t]he citizenship amendment es-tablished racial identity as the foundation of Irish citizenship' (Brannigan, 2009: 224). Brannigan reminds that '[r]acism did not simply arrive with the immigrants in 1996, but emerged in different forms ... long before' (3). See also Brannigan's reference to Ardagh (1995) and his drawing upon Rolston's 1999 essay 'Are the Irish Black?' (182).

References

Ardagh, Johh (1995). *Ireland and the Irish: Portrait of a Changing Society*. London: Penguin.

Brannigan, John (2009). *Race in Modern Irish Literature and Culture*. Edinburgh: Edinburgh University Press.

Finlay, Andrew (2006). 'Multiculturalism after the Good Friday Agreement', *Irish Journal of Anthropology* 19.3: 8–17. www. tara.tcd.ie/ … /Multiculturalism%20After%20the%20 Good %20Friday%.2006. Accessed on 19 January 2012.

Flynn, Leontia (2009). 'The Vibrator', in Joan McBreen (ed.), *The Watchful Heart: A New Generation of Irish Poets: Poems and Essays*. Cliffs of Moher: Salmon Poetry, 55.

—— (2011). *Profit and Loss*. London: Jonathan Cape.

Groarke, Vona (2005). '"Foreignism:" A Philadelphia diary', *The Dublin Review* 18: 4–72.

Hakizimana, Jean 'Ryan' and Michael Hayes (2008) [2006]. *Postcolonial Identities: Constructing the 'New Irish'*. Newcastle: Cambridge Scholars Publishing.

Hayes, Michael (poems) and Jean 'Ryan' Hakizimana (paintings) (2007). *'Survivor' – Representations of the 'New Irish:' Dúchas Dóchasach*. Newcastle: Cambridge Scholars Publishing.

Inglis, Tom (2008). *Global Ireland: Same Difference*. New York and London: Routledge.

Kearney, Richard (1997). *Postnationalist Ireland: Politics, Culture, Religion*. London and New York: Routledge.

Kiberd, Declan (2005). *The Irish Writer and the World*. Cambridge: Cambridge University Press.

McCann, Colum (2007). 'Introduction', in Michael Hayes (poems) and Jean 'Ryan' Hakizimana (paintings), *'Survivor' – Representations of the 'New Irish:' Dúchas Dóchasach*. Newcastle: Cambridge Scholars Publishing, viii.

Montague, Mary (2009). 'Contemporary Irish poetry', in Joan McBreen (ed.), *The Watchful Heart: A New Generation of Irish Poets: Poems and Essays*. Cliffs of Moher: Salmon Poetry, 106–9.

Morrissey, Sinéad (2002). *Between Here and There*. Manchester: Carcanet.

O'Malley, Mary (2006). *A Perfect V*. Manchester: Carcanet.

Phelan, Helen (2008). 'Introduction', in Jean 'Ryan' Hakizimana and Michael Hayes, *Postcolonial Identities: Constructing the 'New Irish'*, xiii–xvi.

Quinn, Justin (2009). 'Baggage reclaim', in Joan McBreen (ed.), *The Watchful Heart: A New Generation of Irish Poets: Poems and Essays*. Cliffs of Moher: Salmon Poetry, 158–60.

Richardson, Sally (2005). 'Multiculturalism is nothing new', *Irish Democrat*, 19 May. www.irishdemocrat.couk./featues/multiculturalism. Accessed on 19 January 2012.

Rolston, Bill (1999). 'Are the Irish black?', *Race and Class* 41.1/2: 95–102.

Ward, Margaret (2004). 'Motherhood in Northern Ireland', in Patricia Kennedy (ed.), *Motherhood in Ireland: Creation and Context*. Cork: Mercier, 228–40.

PART III

'The return of the repressed': 'performing' Irishness through intercultural encounters

10

'Marooned men in foreign cities': encounters with the Other in Dermot Bolger's *The Ballymun Trilogy*

Paula Murphy

In *The Townlands of Brazil*, the second play in Dermot Bolger's *The Ballymun Trilogy*, multiculturalism in Ireland is explored by focusing on the small community of Ballymun, in Dublin city. The first act takes place in the 1960s and explores the fate of an unmarried pregnant woman, Eileen, who escapes having to give up her baby for adoption by fleeing to England. Her experience of being an emigrant in a foreign city echoes that of her baby's father, Michael. Eileen and he met and conceived their child while he was at home in Ireland on holiday from his job in England. In Act Two, the play jumps forward in time to the 2000s. Ballymun is changing, undergoing regeneration, and its population has changed too. In this act, the main characters are migrant workers who are building lives for themselves in that community. The first and second acts echo each other in many ways in terms of story, language, imagery, and physical movement, and by having the same actors play Irish characters in the first act and immigrant characters in the second. In these ways, Bolger encourages the audience to view the present multiculturalism of Ireland through the long history of Irish emigration. In this chapter, this idea will be analysed through the themes of racism, the persistence of intolerance over time and space, the alienation of the migrant at home and abroad, and the shared experience of migrants which can overcome this isolation. Other aspects explored are the staging of the play and the importance of including migrants within the narrative of the nation.

As a middle play in the trilogy, *The Townlands of Brazil* is book-ended by plays that also analyse encounters with the Other. The first play, *From These Green Heights*, explores the lives of the original inhabitants of the tower block of Ballymun, who were initially strangers in the newly built suburb and feared by the local residents. The final play, *The Consequences of Lightning*, based around the death and funeral of the first inhabitant of the tower blocks, examines how

151

the community can deal with its past, its identity as Other in contemporary Dublin as an area of socio-economic disadvantage, and its present and future regeneration. By situating the encounter with ethnic alterity in *The Townlands of Brazil* in the context of local definitions of and encounters with the Other, Bolger presents the experience of 'marooned men in foreign cities' as one with which all can empathise (Bolger, 2010: 169). All of the plays were initially staged in the Axis Arts Centre in Ballymun to a primarily local audience. The second play was conceived of as a challenge to the audience, who, in the first play, had seen a play which told the story of the challenges they faced in creating a sense of community in a place with so few social amenities. As Bolger explains, 'there is a certain ... fear and suspicion. And there's also curiosity. I thought it would be interesting to give them a play where nobody's from Ireland, not to mind from Ballymun and they responded to that really, really well' (Murphy, 2008: 12). Bolger's play presents a challenge not only to the residents of Ballymun but also to Irish society, in the way that it asks its audience to re-imagine their personal and national histories in new historical, social, and cultural frameworks.

Despite the apparent careful construction of the Ballymun plays as a trilogy, they were not initially envisioned as such and evolved organically. As Bolger states,

> [w]hen I wrote *From These Green Heights*, I didn't know it was a trilogy, because it was just a play. And then it was actually very successful and Axis asked me to do a trilogy. But if I was writing a trilogy, I would have said, I'll make that one decade. But I'd already told everything about Ballymun so the only way I could figure to do it was to write something that was a sequel and a pre-sequel ... Ballymun before the towers were built and Ballymun after the towers had been pulled down. (Murphy, 2008: 11)

The Townlands of Brazil is both prequel and sequel to *From These Green Heights*. The story of Act One goes back before the time span of the first play in the trilogy, before the towers were built and the first tenants arrived and settled in. When Eileen is growing up in Ballymun, and when she leaves at eighteen for England, this community is 'only a scatter of cottages hugging the back road to Swords with cross-eyed young heifers staring over the hedges' (Bolger, 2010: 110). By Act Two, it has become an urban community, associated with socio-economic disadvantage, and is in the middle of a regeneration project that will see the infamous tower blocks, which defined its landscape for so long, pulled down. This rapid change from a rural community to an urban one is something that Bolger experienced himself growing up in nearby Finglas. Bolger's knowledge of and affinity with the community of Ballymun depicted in the trilogy is perhaps why he was chosen to read at the real-life demolition of one of the towers, when he read 'Ballymun Incantation' which appears at the start of the trilogy's first play.

Migration (both outward and inward) constitutes a central theme in the play. The rural community of Ballymun in the 1960s is an impossible place for an unmarried mother to live. For Eileen, a life in England offers an escape route that will enable her to mother her unborn child. In Ireland, the options offered to her are to work in a Magdalene Laundry and give up her baby for adoption, or work as a servant for employers who take in unwed mothers as part of a charity organised by a priest. In this case too, her baby would have to be given up for adoption. The option to live and work as a single mother in Ireland in 1963 does not seem to be available to Eileen because of the stigma and shame that would be attached to her family, herself, and her child. This is certainly not the first time that Bolger has dealt dramatically with the social oppression of women in Irish society. Mireia Aragay points out that in *The Holy Ground*, for example, 'Bolger effects a deconstruction of the submissive, suffering, maternal Irish woman' (1997: 61). Eileen does suffer for her motherhood, but she is certainly not submissive, taking matters into her own hands and leaving the country when the country will not allow her to live the life she wishes with her child.

The migratory experience is also central in Act Two. Here, the characters are mainly migrant workers. Anna is from Moldova, Monika from Poland, Oscar from Turkey, and Matthew, Eileen's son, is from England. All are working in or near Ballymun: Anna and Monika as mushroom pickers, and Oscar and Matthew on a demolition site. At the start of Act Two, Monika relates the story of how she came to Ballymun. Her lover Thomas was working in Ireland and died in a car crash when she was approximately five months pregnant with their child, the same stage that Eileen was at with her pregnancy when her lover died working abroad. Unlike Eileen, she has emigrated without her child, who is in the care of her father's parents, supported by the money she sends back from Ireland.

At first sight, migration is conceived in the play as a liberating alternative, both for the Irish emigrants in the past and the present newcomers in contemporary Ireland. For Eileen's lover Michael, his adopted city of Liverpool offers an opportunity for escape. While she is escaping social condemnation and repressive religious attitudes to unmarried mothers, Michael is escaping more mundane and localised socio-economic discrimination. He comes from a poor family and wants to make a change for himself and his future children. If he stays in Ireland 'they'll always simply be another bunch of Bradys reared in a labourer's cabin in the townland of Brazil' (Bolger, 2010: 126). In Liverpool however, 'I'm judged on my hands alone and not on who my people were. I've no history in Liverpool. I'm free to become whoever I want to be' (*ibid.*). Liverpool liberates him from being defined by his family, and offers opportunity for social and economic advancement that would be impossible in Ireland. Oscar, the Turkish character in Act Two, relates how Monika's lover Thomas felt the same way: 'In Poland, he would always be his father's son. But here he was simply himself, no better or worse than any other man' (173).

When Michael embarks on a relationship with Eileen, an incident that occurred in the family history of each provides an example of how difficult it is to break out of prejudices associated with one's family. During the Civil War, Michael's uncle was beaten to death after locals found out that he intended to join the newly formed Free State police. Eileen's uncle was one of those involved in the attack. Mirroring this family feud, in Act Two, Monika relates how her father and Thomas's father 'stood together during the workers' strike of 1976' but with the onset of martial law, she suspects that Thomas's father betrayed hers. Emigration provides an opportunity to break away from being defined by these family histories in the 1960s and the 2000s.

In spite of the liberating alternative that migration offers, Bolger portrays characters who still experience alienation in their new countries of destination, as a result of racism and xenophobia. In Act Two, the immigrants Anna, Oscar, Matthew, and Monika all experience the antipathy of some Irish towards them. For some characters, such as Anna, this antipathy turns into virulent racism. Rather than exploring racism as a twenty-first-century phenomenon, brought about by the unprecedented immigrant population of the Celtic Tiger, Bolger shows that fear of the Other is an age-old problem that merely takes different forms in shifting socio-cultural situations. In Act One, Eileen's mother is anxious about the new tower blocks that are planned, and the people from inner-city Dublin who will be moving out to Ballymun: 'I've nothing against Dubliners, a few at a time … but we'll be swamped by outsiders … They'll never belong in Ballymun' (Bolger, 2010: 114). However, Bolger shows that even those who fear strangers the most like Eileen's mother could have been a stranger in a strange land themselves. For Eileen's mother, at nineteen, all her older siblings had emigrated and she herself had a ticket purchased for Boston when her husband proposed and she remained in Ireland to marry instead. Eileen's mother is the character who is most conservative in her views, most fearful of the Other, most determined that Eileen must leave when she becomes pregnant. Bolger shows that she too could have been an emigrant like Eileen, Michael, and the immigrant characters of Act Two, had her life taken a slightly different turn. The marriage proposal was put to Eileen's grandfather through a matchmaker, who argued that it should be accepted on the basis that 'if your daughter takes the boat to Boston, then God knows what class of a Chinaman or black fellow she could end up marrying' (120). Thus, Bolger shows that the discrimination towards foreign races that is seen in Act Two in 2006 was present in the 1960s when Eileen leaves Ireland, in the 1940s when her mother stays, and, we can imagine, throughout the social history of the country. As Lentin and McVeigh argue, ethnicity is always founded in relation to a dialectical Other: 'ethnicity is quintessentially dialectical because it never *is* except when it simultaneously is *not*' (original emphasis; 2002: 5). In order to define who the ethnic group includes, it must define who it excludes.

Fear of the Other is not only directed towards differing ethnic groups however. Carmel O'Rourke is an Irish character who knew Eileen when she was a young woman and now runs the glasshouses in which Monika and Eileen work as mushroom pickers. She relates how she has inherited her mother's fear of those who were different from themselves, first the local girls, then the girls from the Ballymun towers, and the suppliers. Now, amongst the multicultural mushroom pickers in her glasshouses 'I feel like I'm the true foreigner and the only words I can make out are my mother's, "Watch them or they'll rob us blind"' (Bolger, 2010: 179).

Bolger introduces this racism in Act Two with the ethnic group that is closest to home. Matthew's English accent attracts some insulting remarks when he comes to Ireland: 'Feck off, mister, back to where you belong. We bombed your sort out of Ireland' (Bolger, 2010: 151). However, the unconscious, unthinking racism seen in Act Two is just as offensive to the migrant workers. The Irish attitude towards migrant workers is portrayed as devoid of the traditional Irish welcome. Oscar feels that the requirement for his labour fails to conceal resentment at his presence: 'This country only needs me until my shift ends. Once I put down my shovel, strangers think me a leech' (124). Anna concurs with this view, saying '[w]hen the Irish have no more use for me, I'll be put on the first plane' (167). Anna's and Oscar's experience of the Irish is that they dehumanise them, treating them as a commodity. As Bill Ong Hing argues, 'dehumanization commodifies the immigrants … [it] silences the immigrants. Dehumanization allows the public to ignore their faces' (1998: 83). It is Anna who experiences the most powerful racist hatred, when she is followed by a group of girls, hastily assembled via text message, who physically intimidate her and chant 'foreign bitch' (Bolger, 2010: 177). Her response is to shoplift shampoos, the variety of scents and brands available to her a symbol of the prosperity she is desperately searching for, this prosperity the thing that is supposed to make her stay in Ireland and the racism she has to endure worthwhile.

The experiences of Irish emigrants to England in the first act are closely linked to those of the immigrants to Ireland in the second act. For both sets of characters, their status as economic migrants detaches them from their original home and hinders them from feeling at ease in their adopted country. Eileen describes the emigrants who returned to Ireland on the 'builder's holiday', the first two weeks in August, as follows: 'Every year, you sensed that this place felt a little less like home for them. People looked forward to them coming home but felt an unspoken relief when they left again' (Bolger, 2010: 124). Oscar in Act Two is also caught between two countries, at home in neither. He has left behind two wives in Turkey, '[t]he one I left behind the first time I went away and the one I married when I tried to fit back in. Both said the same thing, packing my bag. You don't belong anymore' (172). Matthew's experience shows how this sense of dislocation can transfer to second-generation emigrants too: 'I only felt truly English the day I flew into Dublin and saw how Irish people viewed me as a foreigner. Before then, I thought I looked obviously Irish' (187). Like Michael and Oscar, he is an outsider in both places. As such, these migrants are operating within the 'Third Space', which according to Bhabha, 'though unrepresentable in itself … constitutes the discursive conditions of enunciation that ensure that the meaning and symbols of culture have no primordial unity or fixity' (1994: 37). Bolger's 1990 play, *In High Germany*, also explores the relationship between Ireland and Europe and the destabilising Third Space between them. As Damien Shortt suggests, in this play, Bolger 'offers evidence that the traditional modes for understanding and defining Irishness no longer resonate with the new, European Irish' (2010: 123). In *The Townlands of Brazil* however, while he is dealing with the same axes of movement between Ireland and England and Ireland and Europe, he shows how Irish identity in the twenty-first century must be understood and defined in relation to immigration as well as emigration – the experiences of those who have come to Ireland as well as those who have left.

In this sense, the life of the migrant, though it promises and often delivers social and economic opportunity, is associated with painful loneliness, both for the emigrants of the 1960s and the immigrants of the 2000s. This loneliness is sometimes alleviated by working excessively hard to accumulate money. Michael's mother blames overwork for his death. She tells Eileen '[i]t was money that killed him, working in a flooded trench. All autumn they say he worked like a man possessed' (Bolger, 2010: 135). In Act Two, Oscar tells Monica that her lover Thomas worked double shifts because he missed her intensely, and the audience wonder if the same was true of Michael. Oscar himself has more than enough money, but is entirely without companionship. He states '[a]fter twenty-five years chasing work across Europe, I trust no-one' (157). Oscar, like Michael, dies on a construction site, when he is looking for a missing baby at the end of Act Two. The female immigrants in this play work in the safer environment of a mushroom farm rather than a construction site, but the life of the migrant worker can be a precarious one for them too. Anna relates how her cousin Maria was the presumed victim of sex-trafficking and has not been heard from since she left home.

Thus, while loneliness is common for individuals, Bolger constantly points out that there is a vast shared experience amongst migrants across decades and nations. As Lentin puts it, '[i]nterrogating the Irish "we" cannot evade interrogating the painful past of emigration, a wound still festering because it was never tended, and which is returning to haunt Irish people through the presence of the immigrant "other"' (2002: 228). For Bolger, this painful wound that links migrants across time and space can be seen positively, as something that offers comfort, albeit temporarily. When Eileen leaves Ireland she says 'I didn't feel lonely because the ghosts of a thousand emigrants surrounded me, carrying suitcases and sacks, striding out in search of new lives' (Bolger, 2010: 144). In the play's 'overture' and 'finale' too, we see this sense of shared experience break down barriers between individuals in terms of time and geography, when the characters' voices come together, finish each other's sentences and create a unified narrative from the divergent characters' words, as argued below. In the context of a discussion on Bolger's *In High Germany*, Aidan Arrowsmith argues that '[i]n the twentieth-century negotiation of discourses of essentialism and anti-essentialism, counter-revivalism and revisionism, postmodernism and "post-nationalism", "Irishness" is discredited and seemingly discarded' (1999: 177). *The Townlands of Brazil* refutes this argument, as the play does not discredit the idea of 'Irishness' but rather shows its elusive, ever-shifting, multi-faceted nature as it moves through the experiences of residents, immigrants, emigrants, and second-generation emigrants.

When a baby goes missing at the end of Act Two, it unites the characters of this act in shared concern: 'That night all Ballymun held our breath for that baby. Locals and foreign workers like ourselves' (Bolger, 2010: 182). The incident specifically links the experiences of the female characters of Act Two. It reminds Carmel O'Rourke of the 'local girls who disappeared years ago' (*ibid.*), girls like Eileen. The lost baby links obviously to Monika, who feels the pain of separation from her child who she left behind when she emigrated to Ireland. Monika's child's name is Teresa, the same name as the woman that Eileen met at the adoption clinic in Act One. We discover that the baby resonates with Anna too, who reveals that she has had an abortion, after becoming pregnant by a man called Michael, the same name as Eileen's lover, who 'went away and never wrote' (*ibid.*). Weaving this complex web of connections and intersections, between characters of disparate origin and experience, defeats the accusation that Bolger is simplistically revisionist in his attitude towards the nation. Writing of Bolger's earlier work, Liam Harte argues that 'from the rigid referents of territory and the nation state, Bolger merely replaces an essentialising nationalism with an equally essentialising revisionism' (1997: 20). In contrast to this view, *The Townlands of Brazil* presents its audience with a nuanced, inclusive, and open perspective on the nation that is shown to have the potential to embrace Otherness and difference.

The act of telling stories is seen to be enormously significant for the characters themselves, their relationships with each other, and their place in public memory. The isolation felt by many of the emigrant characters, combined with their underrepresentation in national histories, meant that telling their stories is essential to orientate themselves as individuals and to re-instate them in the story of the nation. For example, Matthew's mother Eileen seems to have been erased as far as official documents are concerned. He has been unable to find any trace of his mother, though he has been searching for about twenty years. In Act One, Eileen herself is aware that the fate of unwed mothers who flee the country is to be erased from official public memory: 'I've joined the Ballymun girls who've disappeared from history' (Bolger, 2010: 112). Alone with her unborn child as the ferry sails further away from Dublin, Eileen must reiterate her own life story to remind herself of who she is, to locate herself when she feels as though her identity is slipping away: 'My name is Eileen Redmond. I was born in Ballymun on Whitsuntide, when the Holy Spirit descended' (148). Anna feels a similar sense of dislocation, saying '[s]ometimes I feel that a gust of wind will sweep me away with nobody noticing' (169). At the end of the play, when Matthew writes his mother's name on the wall of the Ballymun tower block, it has a symbolic function. He is writing her into existence by telling a piece of her story in his graffiti. He is writing her name alongside the names of those who moved to Ballymun and grew up there, 'the Antos and Tomos and Jacintas' (194), and reinstating her rightful place as part of the story and history of that community. The names of Monika, Anna, and Oscar are also written on the wall of the tower block before it is demolished. As Monika says to her daughter, '[i]t's a long story, Teresa, but we're going to be a part of it' (195).

Indeed, characters in this play often echo each other's words and images, creating linguistic resonances or patterns that highlight the similarities within their stories. This is particularly true at the beginning and end of the play in which characters from different time periods and geographical locations within the story create an 'overture' and 'finale' to the play. I use these musical terms rather than prologue and epilogue which commonly apply to drama because the verbal echoes and patterns create a poetic musicality within these parts of the play. Speaking of his mother, Matthew states that '[a]fter the age of eighteen, she never felt able to return here. So, for her, the townlands of Ballymun remain suspended in 1963' (Bolger, 2010: 108). In the next monologue, Monika's, she states that 'the farther we go, the more home becomes frozen in our minds' (*ibid.*), her experience echoing that of Eileen's forty years before. Monika's monologue flows seamlessly from Matthew's, her first line finishing his last sentence: the tower blocks of Ballymun, Matthew says, 'are withering, their innards ground down into petals of asbestos by foreign workers to make space for a gleaming New Jerusalem … [Monika] … A wondrous chance to wash away the sins of the past, a new start for Ballymun' (107–8). Underscoring the link between the first and second acts, when Monika and Matthew's intersecting monologues introduce Act Two, they repeat some of their lines from the beginning of Act One, alerting the audience to the fact that although this act is set forty-three years later, the situations, characters, and themes are similar.

The word and concept of Brazil is also used to link the first and second acts of the play. When Eileen's mother tells her about this place, Eileen assumes it is Brazil in South America. She is corrected however: it is 'the townland of Brazil near Swords where people are too busy picking spuds to dance any fandangos' (Bolger, 2010: 123). Swords is a village near Ballymun, and so the word Brazil functions to connect the local and knowable and the foreign and strange. Speaking in the context of the first play in the trilogy, *From These Green Heights*, Victor Merriman notes the importance of its local dimension, stating that 'in dialogue with the experiences of local people, cultural workers may generate prophetic narratives, enabling social visions alternative to those generated and distributed globally' (2005: 496). In this second play in the trilogy, *The Townlands of Brazil*, Bolger goes a step further and incorporates the local and global dimensions of Ballymun within the play. In Act Two, Monika gives the word Brazil another connotation, when she refers to 'our Hy-Brazil of jobs and euros' (Bolger, 2010: 181). Hy-Brazil is a mythical island, similar to Atlantis, of unknown location. It is purportedly a hospitable island of good fortune. The concept of Hy-Brazil links the local and international dimensions of Brazil in the play, overriding both with a symbol of the common desire for prosperity, peace, and happiness. In relation to the theme of migration, the metaphor destabilises the boundaries between insiders and outsiders, local and global, natives and immigrants.

The historical comparison that Bolger establishes between past Irish emigration and present immigration in Ireland is also reflected by the staging of the play itself. As is typical of Bolger's style, *The Townlands of Brazil* requires minimalist staging. There is no attempt at realism with backdrop or props, Bolger preferring instead to allow the audience's imagination to create the physical world of the play. The stage directions at the beginning of Act One specify only the following: 'Lights rise on empty stage furnished only with a succession of boxes, which the cast may use to build certain shapes to create spaces' (Bolger, 2010: 107). The simplicity and versatility of these boxes, which can be constructed and deconstructed at will, has a symbolic as well as a practical function. Their changing structure in the play reverberates with the transience of the play's characters, which move geographically in the story, from Moldova, Poland, Turkey, and England to Ireland, and from Ireland to England. They may also relate to the lack of rootedness of the characters, often referred to in the dialogue. In this sense, the boxes can be seen as storage boxes, indicating movement without settling, impermanence, and lack of a stable home base. The boxes also reflect the play's flexible attitude towards time, in which we see characters from the past enter into the dialogue and action of the play without concern for verisimilitude. For example, in the 'overture' to Act One, the stage directions tell us that Matthew looks at his mother Eileen, who, according to the story, he has not seen since he was a child.

In common with the first play in the trilogy, *From These Green Heights*, all the actors remain onstage for the duration of the play. Bolger specifies that as Eileen enters singing at the start of Act One, '[t]he rest of the cast enter during the song and spread out, standing as silent figures watching. They will remain seated on the boxes to either side on the stage when not directly engaged in the action, functioning as a sort of internal audience' (Bolger, 2010: 107). As with the boxes, there is a practical benefit to having all the actors onstage. It means that they can easily make brief verbal or physical interjections without distracting from the main dialogue and action with entrances and exits. He also uses the assembled cast for sound effects, such as when they count down from ten to one when Matthew is describing how he detonates buildings at the beginning of Act Two, or when they make the sound of Anna's alarm clock.

Having all the actors present on stage throughout the play also allows them to act as a type of Greek chorus, becoming the voice of the community at certain points. In this sense, like the chorus of ancient Greek drama, they are partly the audience's representative onstage, and as such implicate the audience in the play's action. Moreover, because the audience look at these actors and see the Irish and immigrant characters they play as well as the anonymous chorus they represent, it suggests that any of the individual characters could be part of the judgemental community that persecutes the characters, narrowing the distance between the characters and the communities from which they feel alienated. Finally, the actors' continuous presence onstage gives the impression that the characters that they play are bearing silent witness to each other's stories: listening, observing, and supporting in a way that they often will not or cannot do within the story itself. When Eileen speaks the long monologue of her mother's story in Act One, we are told that '[t]he Cast shift boxes to clear a space around Eileen and gather behind her' (Bolger, 2010: 115). They listen supportively and, at one point, help Eileen to enact the story she tells, as they swing her around the stage when she is describing her mother at a dance.

Each actor in *The Townlands of Brazil* plays more than one character and usually, an actor plays an Irish character and an immigrant character. Eileen, the pregnant Irish girl who flees to England with her unborn child is played by the same actress who plays Anna, a Moldovan immigrant in Act Two. The same actor plays the Irish Michael, Eileen's lover and Matthew, her son, a first-generation emigrant. The actor who plays Eileen's father, a mild-mannered pensioner, also plays Oscar, a Turkish immigrant to Ireland in Act Two. Eileen's mother, Michael's mother, and Anna's mother are all played by the same actress. The part of Carmel O'Rourke, the owner of the mushroom farm, is paired with the part of her mother, Mrs. O'Rourke. Finally, the actress who plays Monika, the young Polish woman central to Act Two, plays Theresa too, a young woman who Eileen meets in Act One, who is also planning to give up her baby for adoption. The web of relationships that Bolger creates between these characters is complex. Often, there are straightforward comparisons drawn between the two or more parts played by the same actor. At other times, the most striking parallels are between characters played by different actors, emphasising that the ostensible boundaries that separate immigrants from natives are in fact unstable, capable of shifting, and changing.

Sometimes multiple parts played by the same actor show the audience the common experience of seemingly disparate characters. The audience is aware of the old Civil War tensions that exist between Eileen's family and Michael's family. Yet, the fact that her mother and his mother are played by the same actress alerts us to their shared sorrow at being the mothers of emigrant children. In Act Two, this same actress also plays Anna's mother, representing the loss of children to emigration that connects parents across national and cultural divides. The most overt swap that one actor has to make between two characters occurs at the end of Act Two when the actor playing Anna removes her blonde wig and speaks as Eileen. It occurs when Michael is narrating the story of his short time with his mother, and how she resorted to prostitution in an effort to make money for herself and her son. Anna, speaking as Eileen, interposes a few lines into his narrative, representing his memories of his mother's voice. The fact that it is the character of Anna who speaks these lines draws the audience's attention to a parallel between Anna and Eileen. Anna has earlier suggested that prostitution would be the only way to make the kind of money in Moldova that she does in Ireland.

All of the actors participate in the chorus, which functions to unite the characters from different countries and cultures, and show that they could all be part of a judgemental community in different circumstances and implicate the audience in the action, as outlined above. In Act One for example, the cast as chorus chant 'no blacks, no dogs, no Irish' as Eileen travels towards Liverpool, reciting the infamous racial slur that Irish emigrants to England encountered. At the end of this act, when Eileen leaves the adoption centre, they shout 'Catch the slut before she steals God's child!' (Bolger, 2010: 148). The prejudice faced by Michael and Eileen, emigrants to England in the 1960s, is linked with the prejudice faced by immigrants to Ireland in the 2000s, because the actors playing the chorus are also the actors playing the Irish and immigrant characters, uniting the characters from all the nationalities represented in their shared understanding and experience of discrimination.

In conclusion, in *The Townlands of Brazil*, these migrant characters from the 1960s and the 2000s literally become part of the story of Ballymun. The play has made them part of the fictional life associated with this community and its cultural history. The fact that the play was first staged in the Axis Arts Centre in Ballymun physically locates these fictional characters in this place. Just as within the play, they strive to make a physical mark on the wall of the tower, albeit a transient one that will remain only until the towers are blown up. In the play's 'finale' at the end of Act Two, the voices of the characters intermingle, spanning time and nationalities, taking up each other's phrases to create a unified narrative stream, expressing the commonalities of experience that Bolger has highlighted through language, imagery, character symmetry, and story throughout the play:

> Monika: Just wait till I fly home …
> Anna (as Eileen): And I'll tell you about when I kissed the only man I ever truly loved …
> Monika (looks at Matthew): And I'll tell you all about your new life …
> Anna (as Eileen): … in my old home.
> Monika: In your new home …
> Matthew: … In this place called Ballymun.
>
> (Bolger, 2010: 196)

References

Aragay, Mireia (1997). 'Reading Dermot Bolger's *The Holy Ground*: National identity, gender and sexuality in postcolonial Ireland', *Links and Letters* 4: 53–64.

Arrowsmith, Aidan (1999). 'Debating diasporic identity: Nostalgia (post)nationalism, "critical traditionalism,"' *Irish Studies Review* 7.2: 173–81.

Bhabha, Homi K. (1994). *The Location of Culture*. London and New York: Routledge.

Bolger, Dermot (2010). *The Ballymun Trilogy*. Dublin: New Island.

Harte, Liam (1997). 'A kind of scab: Irish identity in the writings of Dermot Bolger and Joseph O'Connor', *Irish Studies Review* 20: 17–22.

Lentin, Ronit (2002). 'Anti-racist responses to the racialisation of Irishness: Disavowed multiculturalism and its discontents', in Ronit Lentin and Robbie McVeigh (eds), *Racism and Anti-Racism in Ireland*. Belfast: Beyond the Pale, 226–39.

Lentin, Ronit and Robbie McVeigh (eds) (2002). 'Situated racisms: A theoretical introduction', *Racism and Anti-Racism in Ireland*. Belfast: Beyond the Pale, 1–48.

Merriman, Victor (2005). 'A responsibility to dream', *Third Text* 19.5: 487–97.

Murphy, Paula (2008). 'Interview with Dermot Bolger'. Unpublished, 1–17.

Ong Hing, Bill (1998). 'The immigrant as criminal: Punishing dreamers', *Hastings Women's Law Journal* 9.1: 79–96.

Shortt, Damien (2010). '"Who put the ball in the English net?": The privatisation of Irish postnationalism in Dermot Bolger's *In High Germany*', in Irene Gilsenan Nordin and Carmen Zamorano Llena (eds), *Redefinitions of Irish Identity: A Postnationalist Approach*. Oxford, Bern, and New York: Peter Lang, 103–24.

11

'Like a foreigner / in my native land': transculturality and Otherness in twenty-first-century Irish poetry

Michaela Schrage-Früh

Ireland in the Celtic Tiger years saw an unprecedented influx of ethnically diverse migrants to a nation formerly perceived as comparatively monocultural. Sketching the two dominant representations of post-Celtic Tiger multiculturalism, Amanda Tucker notes that the first of these 'emphasizes that fear and hostility continue to characterize Irish responses to inward migration since the Gaelic Catholic monolith remains' at the heart of twenty-first-century Irish identity, thus reinforcing 'the idea of Ireland as a monocultural rather than multicultural society' (Tucker, 2010: 107).[1] The second type of response claims that, despite the legal situation of immigrants, Ireland is a country traditionally open and genuinely hospitable towards its newcomers, not least of all by virtue of its own history of colonisation and emigration (108). Both of these representations of Irish multiculturalism reinforce the centrality of national identity as well as the myth of separateness between internally homogenous cultural groups. However, the recent demographic changes have increasingly given rise to renegotiations of the concept of Irishness, including a necessary dismantling of the myth of Irish homogeneity both past and present.

In view of these changes, Julia Kristeva's notion that we need to recognise the foreigner 'within ourselves' so that 'we are spared detesting him in himself' (Kristeva, 1991: 1) has become particularly relevant. Taking his cue from Kristeva, the cultural philosopher Wolfgang Welsch has developed the concept of 'transculturality', arguing that 'the recognition of a degree of internal foreignness forms a prerequisite for the acceptance of the external foreign. It is precisely when we no longer deny, but rather perceive, our inner transculturality, that we will become capable of dealing with outer transculturality' (Welsch, 1999: 201). In Welsch's view, concepts such as 'interculturalism' and 'multiculturalism' fail to address the overall hybridity of today's cultures, instead wrongly assuming interactions between 'clearly distinguished, in themselves homoge-neous cultures' (196). In contrast, the concept of 'transculturality' suggests that contemporary identities, both at the cultural macro-level and at the individual micro-level, are inevitably constructed of components from various cultures and that '[w]ork on one's identity is becoming more and more work on the integra-tion of components of differing cultural origin' (199). In the Irish context, then, the acceptance of internal Otherness helps to forge not only a more welcoming stance towards the migrant Other, but also a more complex understanding of what it means to be Irish.

Kristeva's notion of the 'foreigner … within' and Welsch's concept of 'inner transculturality' are by no means unprecedented in discourses of Irish identity. Thus, in *The Irish Writer and the World* Declan Kiberd points to James Joyce as 'one of the first artists … to imagine "a world without foreigners", a world possible once men and women begin to accept the foreigner in the self and the necessarily fictive nature of all nationalisms, which are open to endless renego-tiation' (Kiberd, 2005: 314–15). As Kiberd elaborates,

[i]f everyone recognises her or his own strangeness, the very notion of the *foreign* dissolves, to be replaced by the *strange*. … That recognition needn't be as difficult as it might seem, for the whole object of British colonialism in Ireland throughout the nineteenth century was, in the words of Friedrich Engels, 'to make the Irish feel like strangers in their own country'. That ordeal is something which even the stay-at-home Irish have in common with refugees and asylum-seekers. (Original emphasis; 2005: 317)

The realisation that we are ultimately all 'strangers to ourselves' is explored in various ways in the poems analysed in this chapter.[2] Thus, Mary O'Malley's 'In the Name of God and of the Dead Generations' views the recent demographic changes in Ireland through the lens of Irish history, especially language loss, en-forced outward migration, and dispossession. Similarly, David Wheatley's poem 'Misery Hill' links present-day refugees to former Irish outcasts whose presence still haunts the speaker during his nightmarish descent into Dublin's neglected underworld. More obviously autobiographical, Dermot Bolger's poem 'Travel Light' is sparked by childhood memories that turn out to be emblematic of the situations of contemporary guest workers' families, a realisation which facili-tates his adoption of one such worker's voice in 'On the 7 am Luas to Tallaght'. Alongside Bolger's poetry, this chapter will also focus on works by lesser known poets included in his *Night and Day* collection, notably Betty Keogh, Eileen Casey, Siobhan Daffy, and Adenice Adedoyin, who likewise choose to explore Irish multiculturalism through the lens of personal experience. Finally, this chapter will conclude with a discussion of Pat Boran's poem 'Bread' and its vision of an Irish multicultural garden of Eden in which the foreign is acknowledged and embraced as an enriching variety of the familiar.

In *The Irish Writer and the World* Kiberd points out that James Joyce 'was also highly astute in locating the racist impulse in those who have an impoverished sense of history' (2005: 314). It is in accordance with this realisation that many poems more or less explicitly dealing with Irish multiculturalism serve as reminders that Irish history has been one of painful, economically enforced outward migration. These poems deliberately highlight parallels between those Irish migrants and present-day refugees or economic migrants from Africa, Asia, and Eastern Europe. Such analogies clearly aim to incite a more welcoming stance towards Celtic Tiger inward migrants, suggesting that in times of economic prosperity it is all too easy to close one's eyes to the past. This is the theme of Mary O'Malley's 'In the Name of God and of the Dead Generations' (2001: 25–6), in whose title O'Malley tellingly appropriates the opening phrase of address from the 1916 'Proclamation of the Republic', thereby suggesting that her poem can be read as an alternative Celtic Tiger manifesto. The poetic speaker reminds the reader that there were 'new Jews in Brooklyn, new Irish / in the Bronx a hundred years ago' (26), thus placing Irish migrants in a cross-cultural position with other diasporic groups such as the Jews. She also evokes these migrants' language loss, by highlighting the image of '[a]n old man from the Gaeltacht at a wedding / "Excuse me, miss, I don't speak English so good" / the Miss a branding iron. / In Irish the sentence would have sung' (*ibid.*). As the poem suggests, contemporary migrants to Ireland are linked to the 'old man from the Gaeltacht' by engaging in a similar struggle with language, by producing the same 'sound the wounded make':

> Vowels that rise out of slashed throats
> Will be somewhat strangled
> And inelegant in our Hiberno English –
> The gurgled speech of Kosovo
> Ringed with hard Dublin argot
> From the inner city or drawn out by tender vowels in Clare
> Sounds uneducated as well as broken.
>
> (*Ibid.*)

O'Malley's poem, however, moves beyond the clear-cut parallel between the living and the 'dead generations' of migrants in that she highlights internal differences, unmasking the myth of a homogeneous Irish identity. Thus, the speaker informs us that she herself 'was born outside the pale / and am outside it still. I do not fit in' (25). References to the 'Gaeltacht' on the one hand and 'the pale' or 'Dublin' on the other highlight the differences in language, lifestyle, and cultural heritage represented by the two geographical areas. Similarly, the 'hard Dublin argot / from the inner city' and the 'tender vowels in Clare' indicate the spectrum of native Irish diversity at the level of 'Hiberno English'. The poem further suggests that the traditional 'Céad Míle Fáilte' may well embrace the French beau 'Andre' whose 'sexy' accent wins over a young Irishwoman's parents in the 1990s Kerry Gold commercial. He, indeed, is welcomed into the family circle (and, by implication, the nation) with the now much parodied words 'Put a bit of butter on the spuds Andre' (26). The same welcoming hospitality, however, is not extended to those refugees speaking 'the gurgled speech of Kosovo', even though they are the ones whose story of displacement most parallels that of 'the ones that got away / from Mother Machree and the ancient order / of Hibernians, the black Irish' (*ibid.*). Alluding to the Irish emigrants who had to leave 'in the darkened holds of coffin ships' to escape from the Great Famine of the 1840s, O'Malley recognises their present-day counterparts in the illegal refugees who 'arrive sealed in the holds of containers / wounded, sometimes dead, between the jigs and the reels / and the Céad Míle Fáilte' (*ibid.*). The poem thus simultaneously disrupts the myth of Irish homogeneity and suggests that the past (here the Irish Famine) should not just be commemorated for its own sake (remembered 'in Universities all over America' (*ibid.*)) but that the awareness of past sufferings should create a 'welcoming place / into which strangers may come' (25).

A similar strategy is employed in the surrealistic title poem of David Wheatley's collection *Misery Hill* (2000). Zooming in on a Dublin area which is off the beaten track of tourist routes and out of sight of the bustling commercial city centre, the poem conjures up 'the lepers and plague victims of the Middle Ages or the slum dwellers that used to populate Misery Hill until the recent past' and illustrates how they 'have been replaced by the new social outcasts, namely, the illegal immigrants whose reality does not enter the tourist brochures of the city' (Zamorano Llena, 2010: 151). At the beginning of the poem, a container ship full of refugees from Romania and Kosovo arrives, one of these refugees reporting about the 'week he'd spent as a stowaway': 'It was as much as I could do to cross over. / The sailors spat at me, called me a dirty Arab. / Remember me, if you find her, to my daughter' (Wheatley, 2000: 62). In the course of what turns out to be a nightmarish dream journey, the speaker himself experiences 'Misery Hill' as though he were a refugee himself, taking a 'holiday' from the 'underworld':

> We drifted past the Kish still waiting for dawn,
> helpless before the unfamiliar stars.
> Was this really the town I'd called my own?
>
> Nemo didn't know. We traded stares.

I'd nothing to declare and nothing to lose.

(60)

In the course of the long poem, then, Wheatley uses the speaker's unsettling nightmare phantasms as an apt image for the refugees' dislocating experiences in a harsh and unwelcoming host country.

In contrast to O'Malley's and Wheatley's historical vantage points, Dermot Bolger's poem 'Travel Light' (2008a: 20–1) has its speaker draw from his own childhood memories to explore the theme of families regularly torn apart by economic necessity. In this poem the father's, a ship's cook, frequent absences from home during journeys 'bound for Hamburg, Le Havre and Rotterdam' are rendered emblematic of the lot shared by other migrants' and guest workers' families across the globe:

> How many men were needed before the Port Tunnel was complete,
> How many daughters helped mothers pack a holdall or travel-light,
>
> How many sons carried suitcases to the corner of a street,
> And waved until their fathers had long passed beyond sight?

(20)

It is thus only a small imaginative step for the speaker to focus on 'the many workers [who] have reached this land, from which many once left' (*ibid.*). These include the ones who helped build the Dublin Port Tunnel, which was opened in December 2006 and enables trucks and other heavy vehicles to speedily traverse the distance from Dublin Port to the M50. In the course of building what the official website describes as 'the longest road tunnel in an urban area in Europe' a total of 5,000 workers were employed and the international make-up of the construction crew is suggested by the sheer abundance of Asian and Eastern European names included in the comprehensive list of all workers involved. Generally, however, these workers and the individual sacrifices made in return for economic prosperity and progress are ignored by the wider public. Bolger's poem, in contrast, aims to draw attention to all the 'factory hands', 'hauliers', 'stevedores and crane drivers, fork lift operators and ship-hands' involved in en-suring 'the everyday miracle of the consignments that arrive / When the world is asleep' (*ibid.*). All these guest and migratory workers share the same 'yearn[ing] for distant homelands' and while the individual destinies 'behind any shipment' are all too easily forgotten or ignored, the speaker's memory of his own father's frequent absences helps him envision the anonymous worker as 'a father, like my father, forced to miss his son's birth' and to imaginatively grasp the reality of 'a family in a foreign land awaiting a money transfer; … calls from Internet cafés and hostel steps; / … a son at a corner watching his father's departure' (21). The family homes across the globe are connected by the fathers' absences, symbolised here by the 'empty hook … / Waiting to hold a rucksack, a suitcase or a battered travel-light', their lighted travel routes resembling a 'patchwork of absences crisscrossing the globe at night' (21).

While in 'Travel Light' Bolger has his autobiographical speaker juxtapose his own childhood memories with those of the workers whose corresponding experiences he imaginatively evokes, in 'On the 7 am Luas to Tallaght' he adopts the voice of a Polish construction worker riding the Luas every morning at dawn on his way to work (Bolger, 2008b: 18).[3] This poem is included in Bolger's *Night and Day* collection, which was the result of the poet's two years as resident artist with South Dublin County Council's In Context 3 Per Cent for Art Programme. According to the collection's cover blurb, '[d]uring this time he created a series of poems about everyday life that were displayed in unusual locations – as murals on Luas stops and walls of community centres or as posters in libraries or tax offices'. As Bolger explains in his 'Introduction', his aim was to 'strip away the "I" from [his] poetry and use instead the "eye" through which we perpetually observe fellow commuters, strangers we pass on streets, people with whom we share busy lifts or supermarket check-out queues, the others whose lives we find ourselves unconsciously speculating about' (Bolger, 2008c: 10). The collection thus demonstrates poetry's unique capacity for taking vignette-like 'snapshots … on the run' (2008c: cover blurb), if not 'clear photograph[s]' (Kiberd 2005: 276) of a fast-changing 'ethnoscape'[4] such as Ireland's.[5]

In 'On the 7 am Luas to Tallaght' Bolger puts himself into the position of one of these others frequently speculated about in passing. Here, outward observation remains in the background: the speaker, a Polish worker on the Luas, is 'trying to sleep' and only briefly registers his fellow passengers who 'stare out, barely able to yawn' (Bolger, 2008b: 18). Their multicultural set-up is hinted at with the reference to their swapping words in 'ten languages for tiredness'. The speaker's liminal existence as guest worker is strikingly illustrated by the perceived split between his body and mind. Thus, his tired body (aching with loneliness, the 'mouth so dry' he 'can no longer taste [his wife's] kiss') is tied to the physical location of Dublin as well as to his work routine consisting of riding on the tram on his way to and back from the building site where, '[a]ll day I will shovel cement'. In contrast, his mind is 'unable to stop thinking of home', 'yearning to caress' his wife's neck. The one precarious physical connection is the telephone, but the long-distance phone calls only deepen his sense of growing distance, suggesting that he is neither here nor there; a stranger in his host country, who is turning into a stranger to his family back home:

> Last night on the phone I could sense your stress,
> Our children no longer asking when will I come:
> I never thought that the West would be like this.

> To them I'm now a cheque from a foreign address,
> A man who builds apartments we could never own,
> My mouth so dry I can no longer taste your kiss.

The form of the villanelle is ideally suited to capture the tired refrains produced by a half-asleep mind torn between its response to a far from promised land ('I never thought that the West would be like this') and its sense of loss for a home left behind ('My mouth so dry I can no longer taste your kiss'). The speaker's experience of 'the West' (i.e. Ireland) is reduced to physical labour, pay cheques, overwhelming tiredness, and his constant yearning for home. The locale of the moving Luas with its chance community of '[f]ellow passengers' highlights the migrants' geographical and communal uprootedness, emblematically reflected by their shared 'journey' which 'compounds every ache of loneliness'.

It needs to be stressed that Bolger's series of poems comprises only half of the *Night and Day* collection. The other half consists of poems written by residents of the South Dublin Council area in response to or inspired by Bolger's work so that, as the blurb puts it, 'Bolger's poems would merge into a symphony of other voices creating a tapestry of lives as lived today in Ireland'. Bolger's exploration of foreignness as a physical reality and as a state of mind in 'On the 7 am Luas to Tallaght' can be usefully compared to some of these 'other voices' that explore encounters with the ethnic Other from the native Irish speakers' perspectives.

The first one to be discussed here is Betty Keogh's short poem 'Reflections', which likewise uses the Luas as setting, but, unlike the almost meditative intro-spection presented in Bolger's poem, creates a sense of fleetingness and rapidity by means of the observer's perspective from the moving tram:

> Through the window
> Their features look familiar,
> Yet I don't understand their tongue.
>
> Luas stop after stop
> People board and alight,
> Dusk turns into dark.
>
> We whiz past streetlights:
> Factories, houses, the Square,
> Apartments climbing skyward.
>
> I feel like a foreigner
> In my native land.

> (Keogh, 2008: 88)

The poem creates a dialectics between familiarity and foreignness: the passengers, waiting outside at the Luas stop and observed by the speaker from inside the tram, bear familiar-looking features, while the languages in which they converse are foreign. Although this is not spelled out in the poem, they are part of the changing urban landscape, most likely migrants or guest workers from Poland, Latvia or other Eastern European countries, waiting to catch the Luas on their way back from one of the countless construction sites to their most likely provisional Dublin homes. The initial opposition between 'them' and 'I' is suspended in the third stanza, when the moving tram creates a temporary community of fellow passengers, as highlighted by the pronoun 'we'. Finally, in the poem's closing couplet, the relation between native Dubliner and migrant Other collapses for good, as the speaker admits to feeling 'like a foreigner / In [her] native land'. At first glance, the poem's ending could suggest a sense of dispossession, possibly even defiance, on the speaker's part. It can, however, also be read in more affirmative terms. By feeling like a 'foreigner' herself, the speaker is united with the actual migrants; she shares or reflects their sense of strangeness and discovers aspects of her self that would otherwise go unnoticed. The ambivalence of the final two lines deliberately points to the sense of overwhelming confusion local Dubliners may well experience in view of the radical changes in their 'native land', which, at worst, might find an outlet in the defensive stances of xenophobia and racism. The poem thus skilfully undermines any clear-cut binary between native and foreigner, since here the emphasis on *feeling* like a foreigner suggests the lack of stability and security surrounding the precarious notions of home and belonging as well as personal and cultural identity in a fast-changing globalised and increasingly transcultural world. After all, the Luas itself is a modern emblem of Dublin's changing cityscape as suggested by 'the / Apartments climbing skyward'. As Balzano and Holdridge aptly point out, with the introduction of the Luas (the Irish for speed) in 2004, '[t]he strategic value of the non-place of speed has supplanted that of place, and, with the movements of the masses, the old imperialist saying of the Romans, "ubi pedes, ibi patria" ("where the feet are, there is the homeland") has a new, urgent meaning in Dublin's contemporary transnational scene' (2007: 110).

Eileen Casey's poem 'Warriors' (2008: 22), too, uses the Luas as setting for an intercultural encounter that puts the speaker in touch with her own foreignness. The poem conjures up a sense of the exotic as the speaker, comfortably seated and 'thinking of nothing in particular', observes an unspectacular incident: a man is running, trying to catch the tram. To the speaker, however, he seems 'swift as an antelope' as his '[l]egs, long as spears, gather speed'. In the speaker's imagination the ordinary winter surroundings are magically transformed by the man's exotic presence. Despite the fact that he is appropriately dressed in a 'winter coat, shirt and navy trousers', in the speaker's imaginative perception his clothes 'dissolve to gorgeous Maasai colours', thus suggesting his African origin, and the Luas itself is transformed into 'a metal beast', 'a wild one / broken free from the herd'. Unlike Bolger's poem, 'Warriors' refrains from exploring the man's state of mind. His principal function is to trigger the speaker's own imagination, which, interestingly, does not transport her to a foreign exotic place in Africa, but carries her back to 'the Midland Streets' of her own Irish hometown, where '[a] cow breaks from a loose bunch, / is chased by a farmer in breeches / held up with braces, his face berry red, / legs akimbo'. In the speaker's imagination, then, she and the man she calls 'my warrior' are connected by belonging to their own respective 'tribe'. They are both migrants to the city, bringing their own memories to the urban space towards which they journey, possibly using their 'warrior' qualities as best they can in the urban jungle of Ireland's capital. The poem, thus, illustrates and corroborates Kiberd's argument that '[e]ven those people who have moved from country to city in the past two generations have an experience which gives them something in common with that of immigrants' (2005: 317). Unbeknown to the running man, his presence thus contributes to the speaker's increased self-awareness of being foreign to the city in which she lives and works, removed from her childhood world in the rural Midlands. At the same time the urban surroundings are transformed by the 'mirage' of the 'warrior', whose presence fuels the speaker's imagination and forges a sense of community. After all, not only is the poem's title in the plural ('Warriors') but the initially isolated 'I ... on the Luas' turns into the plural pronoun 'we' in the poem's concluding line. The poem thus powerfully illustrates how the Luas turns into 'an urban illusion that allows the voyeur-voyager to project his/her own fantasies beyond the screen on the windshield, as in cinemascope' (Balzano and Holdridge, 2007: 111).

Siobhan Daffy's 'Nigerian Lady on Tallaght High Street' (2008: 50) may well be written from a similar 'voyeur-voyager' perspective, although the Luas is not explicitly mentioned in the poem. The speaker, at any rate, forges a similarly positive image of the migrant Other, as she admiringly sketches a Nigerian woman's exotic looks and describes their appeal to the senses in their colourful and sundrenched opulence: 'She wears indigo, / Oniko blue. / ... Sun dark skin / On her smiling cheek bones'. In the course of the poem the African woman is, however, somewhat problematically mythologised as a mother goddess, the final line suggesting that she may suitably replace outdated versions of the Mother Ireland figure:[6]

> Her feet hug the ground
> Her hips at one
>
> With the ebb and flow
> Of the moon and the sun.
>
> One child at her breast,
> Another by the hand.
>
> Queen of this land.

In both Daffy's and Casey's poems, then, images of Africa are positively connoted, pictured as fuelling the speakers' imagination and as enriching the host culture. However, these are outside perspectives which tell us nothing about the immigrants' own viewpoints, experiences, and emotions. What is more, in their valorisation and iconisation of the exotic such representations clearly run the risk of patronising or even exploiting the ethnic Other for the sake of their own personal and national identity constructions. The depiction of a Nigerian mother as 'Queen of this land' uncomfortably brings to mind the gendered representation of Irish nationhood, the 'fusion of the national and the feminine which seemed to simplify both' (Boland, 1996: 128) and which has been successfully revised by women poets such as Eavan Boland from the 1970s onward. In Bolger's collection a necessary corrective is thus provided by what could be considered and is most certainly intended as a companion piece to Daffy's poem, namely 'I am a Nigerian from West Africa' (2008: 52). In this short and unadorned poem Adenice Adedoyin lets us in on her everyday experiences as citizen of Tallaght – both the positive and the negative sides: 'Tallaght has been good – I can work / And call myself part of the community, / … And Tallaght has been bad – There were attacks from adults and teenagers'. In contrast to the iconic images of a 'warrior' or a 'Queen', this speaker creates an image of herself as ordinary citizen concerned with everyday problems and obstacles: 'When I first came to Tallaght it was difficult. / The buses were not regular'. She also stresses the importance of being 'part of the community' and of being allowed to work, explaining that '[m]y job helps me know more about Irish people, / Their needs and feelings and beliefs'.

As this chapter has aimed to show, twenty-first-century Irish poetry interrogates notions of transculturality and Otherness from various angles. While encounters with the 'external foreign' can bring us in touch with our own 'internal foreignness' and 'inner transculturality', this awareness of our own heterogeneity in turn facilitates a more open and compassionate stance towards the migrant Other's feelings of uprootedness, homesickness, and displacement. As Alice Feldman puts it, '[i]n the current Irish context, the immigrant-other exposes the uncertainties, contradictions, anxieties underpinning Irish people's own taken for granted assumptions – but at the same time inspires openness with regard to being able to be as Irish as one wants to be' (2008: 272). However, while the acceptance of one's own 'internal foreignness' might render one more welcoming to encounters with the 'external foreign', it might ultimately also alert one to the shared human core underneath. This shared human core is poignantly explored in Pat Boran's poem 'Bread' (2007: 222–3). The poem's second part consists of a long list of 56 different types of bread including 'ekmek from Turkey, lavosh from Armenia', 'Polish paska', 'Pan de Muertos from Mexico', 'Ethiopian injera, taka hallah, talladega, / fillipino biblingka, Irish sliced pan' (223). Bread is basic to human survival; it is a universal kind of food even though it may come in ever so many shapes, sizes, textures, and flavours. The poem's first part explores how, for instance, 'the smell / of warm bread cooling near a window' is '['t]he only working time machine' (222) not only because baking bread is a truly universal, cross-cultural activity, but because a comforting smell like freshly baked bread can carry us back to our childhood homes. As the speaker poignantly describes in the third stanza, it can also make an immigrant child from Africa feel at home in a foreign host culture like Ireland: 'The child begins to sing / forgotten songs. It makes her feel at home, / this beating, this kneading, this rolling, this baking of bread' (*ibid.*). The poem also subtly undermines the black and white dichotomy, suggesting that the baking of bread transcends cultural, ethnic, and racial differences, when

> a man born in a distant land
> stops a moment to dust his hands
> with white flour then bends to leave
> white hand-prints on a child's dark cheeks;
> ... while outside
> an Irish garden slowly comes to life.

(Ibid.)

The utopian 'Irish garden' envisioned here is a truly multicultural Eden, which extends its Céad Míle Fáilte to all the 'new Irish', announcing to them, as the speaker puts it in the poem's soothing refrain: *'The journey's over, rest your weary legs, / join us now at table, share our bread'* (original emphasis; *ibid.*). However, as Boran acknowledges, the vision of such an 'Irish garden *slowly* comes to life' (emphasis added; *ibid.*). For the garden to finally stand in full bloom much may depend on the capacity of both the native Irish and the 'new Irish' for recognising the foreigner within themselves and the self in one another.

Notes

1   This hostile stance towards inward migration is manifest in twenty-first-century Irish State legislation such as the 2004 Citizenship Referendum, which denies children born in Ireland to foreign parents the birthright of citizenship. It is also addressed by some 'new Irish' poets dealing with autobiographical experiences of ethnically motivated discrimination and racism. One such example is Adenice Adedoyin's poem 'I am a Nigerian from West Africa', in which the speaker mentions 'attacks from adults and teenagers' (2008: 52).

2   Kristeva's and Kiberd's theories of the inner foreigner have also been applied in Pilar Villar-Argáiz' detailed study of Paula Meehan's poetry with reference to the multicultural atmosphere of the country (2011).

3   The speaker's Polish identity is suggested by the fact that in *Night and Day* the English original is followed by its translation into Polish.

4   The term 'ethnoscape' was coined by Arjun Appadurai and can be defined as 'the landscape of persons who constitute the shifting world in which we live: tourists, immigrants, refugees, exiles, guest workers, and other moving groups and individuals [that] appear to affect the politics of (and between) nations to a hitherto unprecedented degree' (1996: 33).

5   Commenting on the hesitation with which Irish writers have addressed the Celtic Tiger changes in their literary works, Declan Kiberd has suggested that 'it is never easy to take a clear photograph of a moving object, especially when you are up close to it' (2005: 276).

6   A similar strategy is employed in Rita Ann Higgins' title poem of her collection *Ireland is Changing Mother* (2011). Here, however, it is the sons rather than the iconic mother figure that are replaced, as the speaker, referring to an intercultural football match, scathingly informs her addressee: 'Now the Namibian Gods and the Bally Bane Taliban / are bringing the local yokels / to their menacing senses / and scoring more goals than Cú Chulainn. / Ireland is changing mother / tell yourself, tell your sons' (Higgins, 2011: 10).

References

Adedoyin, Adenice (2008). 'I am a Nigerian from West Africa', in Dermot Bolger (ed.), *Night and Day: Twenty Four Hours in the Life of Dublin City*. Dublin: New Island, 52.

Appadurai, Arjun (1996). *Modernity at Large: Cultural Dimensions of Globalization*. Minneapolis: University of Minneapolis Press.

Balzano, Wanda and Jefferson Holdridge (2007). 'Tracking the Luas between the human and the inhuman', in Wanda Balzano, Anne Mulhall, and Moynagh Sullivan (eds), *Irish Postmodernisms and Popular Culture*. Basingstoke: Palgrave, 100–12.

Boland, Eavan (1996). *Object Lessons: The Life of the Woman and the Poet in our Time*. London: Vintage.

Bolger, Dermot (2008a). *External Affairs: New Poems by Dermot Bolger*. Dublin: New Island.

—— (ed.) (2008b). 'On the 7 am Luas to Tallaght', *Night and Day: Twenty Four Hours in the Life of Dublin City*. Dublin: New Island, 18.

—— (ed.) (2008c). 'Introduction', *Night and Day: Twenty Four Hours in the Life of Dublin City*. Dublin: New Island, 9–12.

Boran, Pat (2007). *New and Selected Poems*. Dublin: Dedalus, 2007.

Casey, Eileen (2008). 'Warriors', in Dermot Bolger (ed.), *Night and Day: Twenty Four Hours in the Life of Dublin City*. Dublin: New Island, 22.

Daffy, Siobhan (2008). 'Nigerian lady on Tallaght High Street', in Dermot Bolger (ed.), *Night and Day: Twenty Four Hours in the Life of Dublin City*. Dublin: New Island, 50.

Dublin Port Tunnel Website. www.dublinporttunnel.ie/about/. Accessed on 22 February 2012.

Feldman, Alice (2008). 'Facing all the Others: The legacy of old identities for new belongings in post-emigration Ireland', in Borbála Faragó and Moynagh Sullivan (eds), *Facing the Other: Interdisciplinary Studies on Race, Gender and Social Justice in Ireland*. Newcastle: Cambridge Scholars Publishing, 259–74.

Higgins, Rita Ann (2011). *Ireland is Changing Mother*. Tarset: Bloodaxe.

Keogh, Betty (2008). 'Reflections', in Dermot Bolger (ed.), *Night and Day: Twenty Four Hours in the Life of Dublin City*. Dublin: New Island, 88.

Kiberd, Declan (2005). *The Irish Writer and the World*. Cambridge: Cambridge University Press.

Kristeva, Julia (1991). *Strangers to Ourselves*, trans. Leon S. Roudiez. New York: Columbia University Press.

O'Malley, Mary (2001). *Asylum Road*. Cliffs of Moher: Salmon.

Tucker, Amanda (2010). '"Our story is everywhere": Colum McCann and Irish multiculturalism', *Irish University Review* 40.2: 107–28.

Villar-Argáiz, Pilar (2011). '"A stranger to herself": The pedagogical presence of the Other in Paula Meehan's poetry', *White Rabbit. English Studies in Latin America* 1: 1–16.

Welsch, Wolfgang (1999). 'Transculturality – The puzzling form of cultures today', in Mike Featherstone and Scott Lash (eds), *Spaces of Culture: City, Nation, World*. London: Sage, 194–213.

Wheatley, David (2000). *Misery Hill*. Loughcrew-Oldcastle: Gallery.

Zamorano Llena, Carmen (2010). 'Glocal identities in a postnationalist Ireland as reflected through contemporary Irish poetry', in Irene Gilsenan Nordin and Carmen Zamorano Llena (eds), *Redefinitions of Irish Identity: A Postnationalist Approach*. Oxford, Bern, and New York: Peter Lang, 141–58.

12

Irish multicultural epiphanies: modernity and the recuperation of migrant memory in the writing of Hugo Hamilton

Jason King

At the height of the Irish economic boom on St. Patrick's Day 2007, the *Irish Times* editorialised that 'we are all the speckled people today. Confident, wealthy, forward-looking, internationalist, we can afford to define our identity in terms that celebrate our overlapping multiplicity of allegiances and diversity' (Anon., 2007). In its allusion to Hugo Hamilton's memoir *The Speckled People* (2003), the newspaper envisioned the author as the embodiment of a culturally diverse, inclusive, modern Irish nation. Its emphasis on the affordability of a more fluid and plural form of identity was obviously short-sighted in light of Ireland's subsequent economic collapse, but the metaphor of the 'speckled people' also became a shorthand for an Irish multicultural self-image. Hamilton himself is more self-effacing, claiming not to be a spokesperson but rather to have found his voice as a result of the profound cultural and socio-economic changes and influx of immigrants that occurred during the period of the Celtic Tiger. In a 2010 interview, he acknowledged that although he 'grew up with Joyce and Beckett', Hamilton's own artistic inspiration 'came from trying to understand [his] hybrid situation … [and] that difficult issue of belonging' (Allen-Randolph, 2010: 14). Unlike his modernist predecessors, his creative impetus derived not from a sense of alienation, literary experimentation, and an artistic self-image of exile, but rather a desire for acceptance in Irish culture. It was from the struggles of recently arrived immigrants that he 'discovered that there was a moment for me, also, to speak my very intimate and awkward story of being an outsider in Ireland[:] … I'm not the representative Irish person, but one of these newcomers, one of the new Irish' (15).

This chapter examines such representations of self-discovery of Irish multicultural identity and the ways in which contemporary writers like Hugo Hamilton position themselves as outsiders in relation to their literary predecessors, and as intermediaries between 'new Irish' migrants and communities and Ireland's host culture. More specifically, it will be argued that Hamilton deliberately recuperates emigrant memory and transforms Joyce's modernist idea of the epiphany as a profound moment of artistic self-revelation into one of cognisance of cultural difference as a prelude to self-acceptance. Through his repeated employment of an anachronistic narrative perspective – whether it be the arrested development of the autobiographical subject in his memoirs, retracing the journey of Heinrich Böll in his travelogue *Die Redselige Insel* (*The Island of Talking*, 2007), or his immigrant protagonist Vid Ćosić's quest to recover the story of his host family's ancestor, the 'drowned woman', who perished a century before in *Hand in the Fire* (2010) – Hamilton conflates and juxtaposes the experiences of Ireland's migrants in the imagined past and historical present into palimpsestic figures whose self-discovery of a multicultural identity becomes emblematic for the nation at large. That is, his texts tend to split the subjectivity of his protagonists between contemporary and historical Irish migratory storylines that become reconciled in an epiphanic moment of self-realisation: one that is precipitated by the former's reclamation of his or her predecessor's past experience.

From his early novel *Sad Bastard* (1998), Hamilton has not only represented the arrival of immigrants in Ireland in terms of 'the return of the national repressed' (Lentin, 2002: 233), but also as catalysts for the evocation of a more expansive form of memory that recalls marginalised figures like former Irish emigrants as integral members of the nation. 'Here they were at last, the emigrants returning to Ireland', observes Coyne, the protagonist in *Sad Bastard*, as a group of Romanian immigrants become merged in his imagination with the memory of '[t]he Blasket Islanders. The Famine people coming back in their coffin ships' (Hamilton, 1998: 115). It is this sense of remembrance of former migrants as unacknowledged predecessors that Hamilton explores in his fiction, memoirs, and travel writing. Indeed, his repeated premise is that the immigrant's recuperation of the emigrant experience provides a vehicle of acculturation and integration into contemporary Irish society. Thus, he recalls his own 'hybrid' childhood as a harbinger for a 'new Irish' identity.

The question of whether an established author like Hamilton can adequately represent 'new Irish' immigrants and communities is, of course, a vexed one that has been examined earlier in this volume. As Pilar Villar-Argáiz notes in her Introduction, writers such as

> Dermot Bolger, Michael O'Loughlin, and Hugo Hamilton ... openly take some risks in their explicit, conscious adoption of the immigrant voice, placing immigrants at the centre of their work as protagonists. Of course, such ventriloquism is not unproblematic, as it raises inevitable issues concerning entitlement, simplification, and misrepresentation (problems which are eased in the case of Hamilton, as a 'new Irish' writer of hybrid German-Irish identity).

Elsewhere, Maureen Reddy argues convincingly that Roddy Doyle has struggled to render the voices of African immigrants in Ireland in his short story collection *The Deportees* (2007). According to Reddy, 'Doyle's own positionality – white, Irish, settled, male, economically secure – cannot be ignored: he is the one ventriloquizing blackness, so to speak. … From that perspective, the Other remains silent' (2005: 386). This question of when voice appropriation occurs in representations of the 'new Irish' has not yet been sufficiently addressed in Irish cultural criticism. In the case of Hamilton's memoirs, however, he does not simply 'speak for the Other' but also seeks to recover the memory of his own 'intimate and awkward' childhood as 'an outsider in Ireland': one whose experiences can only be fully recollected and given voice from the later perspective of an adult in a more propitious cultural context. Indeed, both *The Speckled People* and *The Sailor in the Wardrobe: A Memoir* (2006) (or, in the USA, the *Harbor Boys: A Memoir*, 2007) comprise biographical narratives of self-discovery of the author's own alterity which reconceptualise his 'hybrid situation' from being a locus of anxiety and stigmatisation into a more fluid form of identity.

As such, Hamilton's memoirs also afford a unique perspective on the historical period when he was raised, in de Valera's Ireland in the 1950s, which has been compulsively revisited by contemporary Irish novelists and playwrights. Like many works of contemporary Irish writing, *The Speckled People* can be considered a generically complex narrative that combines the forms of the memoir and *bildungsroman* with a historical chronicle that registers the occurrence of important national and international events through the eyes of a child. It is also resolutely set in the past, as a story about coming to terms with personal and familial trauma, especially the sexual abuse that the narrator's mother Irmgard suffered in her native Germany at the hand of Herr Stiegler. Yet Hamilton does not offer a retrospective account of de Valera's Ireland so much as a prescient glimpse of the damaging effects that the denial of cultural difference has on the nation's children, who, like Hamilton himself, might have been born in Ireland, but 'still end up living in a foreign country because we're the children from somewhere else' (Hamilton, 2003: 33). As Pilar Villar-Argáiz also notes in her Introduction to this volume, the subject matter of contemporary Irish literature often appears disengaged with the social concerns of the present, because 'Irish writers need to acquire the perspective afforded by time, as the reality of multicultural Ireland is too recent to be completely understood'. Joe Cleary has argued, on the other hand, that there is a great deal of complacency in the repeated elision of contemporary social reality to be found in recent Irish writing (2006: 162).[1] Where Hamilton's memoirs differ from contemporary works is in their imaginative reconstruction of Ireland's past from the vantage point of a 'new Irish' perspective: a historicised as much as a hybridised self-image, cultivated 'partly from Ireland and partly from somewhere else' (Hamilton, 2003: 7).

Each of Hamilton's memoirs is thus structured around his increasing cognisance of cultural difference which he comes to embrace rather than eschew in epiphanic moments of self-revelation. In both *The Speckled People* and *The Sailor in the Wardrobe*, he brackets personal, familial, and historical memories together to gradually develop a fluid, culturally hyphenated 'German-Irish' self-image that construes Ireland to be at once an emigrant place of origin and immigrant destination. He also adopts the voice of a child to recount his experiences of being raised in an Irish and German-speaking household in which the English language was forbidden, and of trying to adjust and fit into an Irish cultural mainstream from which he is doubly excluded for being too Irish and not Irish enough at the same time. His memoir thus offers an extended meditation about the meaning of displacement in modern Irish culture. Through his increasingly anachronistic, deceptively simple, and naive narrative perspective, he effectively defamiliarises the historical and literary landscape of de Valera's Ireland to convey his own experience of feeling doubly dislocated from the dominant culture in which 'Irish speakers in Ireland were being treated like people from a foreign country, from another planet' (Hamilton, 2003: 181). The child's repeated expressions of bewilderment about the inculcation and imposition of various forms of Irish identity in his homestead and the country at large call into question such normative configurations of a national self-image as much in the past as in the present. His feelings of exclusion from the mainstream of Irish society as an Irish language speaker and a second-generation German immigrant, for being too much of an insider and too much of an outsider at the same time, lead Hamilton to imagine a shared experience of marginality.

In his memoirs Hamilton also has to come to terms with different burdens of German and Irish historical memory, in which he is paradoxically implicated as 'victim and perpetrator at the same time', bullied and stigmatised by his peers as a Nazi and Eichmann yet conscripted into 'making sacrifices for Ireland' when his father's 'language war went indoors' (2006: 112, 184). He thus learns to negotiate between his mother's and his father's distinctive modes of remembrance, which intertwine ideals of passive resistance and a desire for vengeance for the violations of the past, and come into conflict when he discovers his father's youthful anti-Semitism that was premised on the incommensurability of hybrid identities in Ireland, the impossibility of 'such a thing as an Irish Jew' (Hamilton, 2003: 254). Hamilton's rejection of anti-Semitism thus becomes a moment of self-revelation, one in which he learns 'that you have to be on the side of the losers … those who are homesick' and subject to 'more than one story' in Ireland (282–3). Empathy rather than enmity is revealed to be the object of historical memory, his realisation that 'we don't just have one language and one history' the fruit of his self-discovery.

Ultimately, the metaphor of 'the speckled people' comes to symbolise Hamilton's acceptance of his own culturally hybridised form of identity in a rhetorically charged moment of self-revelation that takes place near Sandymount Strand not far from where Stephen Dedalus experienced his own epiphany almost a century earlier. Although Hamilton acknowledges that he 'grew up with Joyce and Beckett' (Allen-Randolph, 2010: 14), his autobiographical subject differs markedly from his modernist predecessors in his mode of self-discovery, which is not inspired by his sudden realisation of an artistic vocation but rather his acceptance of his own alterity. There is, in fact, a fundamental distinction that can be made between the forms of self-revelation experienced by Joyce's and Hamilton's autobiographical subjects on the Dublin shoreline, both of which are precipitated by their perceptions of cultural difference. In *A Portrait of the Artist as a Young Man* and *Ulysses*, Stephen Dedalus cultivates a sense of historical consciousness to imagine himself as a native inhabitant of medieval Dublin on the cusp of colonial subjection – 'the ghost in the kingdom of the Danes'; 'from the starving cagework city a horde of jerkined dwarfs, my people' (Joyce, 2007: 148; 1992: 66) – who must transcend his condition of cultural degradation through artistic flight. His epiphany that he will forge within the 'smithy of [his] soul the uncreated conscience' (2007: 224) of his race is preceded by a moment of historical awakening: one that equates an artistic with an indigenous sensibility, and takes shape in the shadow of the coloniser. By contrast, Hamilton deliberately identifies with the figure of the threatening outsider and transforms Joyce's liminal setting of the Dublin shoreline from a site of artistic self-discovery and defiance into a place of self-acceptance of cultural difference. Thus, whereas Joyce's protagonist declares that 'I do not fear to be alone or to be spurned for another or to leave whenever I have to leave' in order to express himself as freely as he can (Joyce, 2007: 218), Hamilton's states: 'I'm not afraid anymore of being Irish or German, or anywhere in between ... I'm not afraid of being homesick and having no language to live in. I don't have to be like anyone else' (Hamilton, 2003: 295). Unlike Stephen Dedalus, Hamilton's self-image is inspired by the evanescence of the Dublin shoreline – 'so full of bouncing light ... like a piece of silver paper in the sun' (*ibid.*) – which engenders a liminal mode of consciousness associated with this fluid sense of place, a singular revelation about the protean nature of cultural rather than artistic identity. Joyce's heroic ideal of redemptive displacement and detached vantage point of the artist in exile differs profoundly from Hamilton's unassuming self-image and style. The modernist sensibility of transcendental homelessness is transformed into a less elitist susceptibility to feelings of homesickness, linguistic confusion, and anxiety about belonging that become registers of a 'new Irish' identity.

Nevertheless, for all of the cultural confusion they express, Hamilton's memoirs conclude in an affirmative manner with the declaration that 'I was going to stay the way I was, speckled' (Hamilton, 2006: 263). At times, it is difficult to discern whether his hybrid self-image is more fixed or fluid in its configuration, a product of the renunciation or repossession of national identity in Ireland. His hybrid sensibility is both contorted and shaped by his need to reconcile his parents' distinctive German and Irish modes of remembrance, which are defined by their disavowal and exaltation of ideals of national belonging. In 'The loneliness of being German', Hamilton surmises that 'maybe there is no such thing as a German national consciousness' (2004), a feeling that is expressed by his mother Irmgard in *The Speckled People*, who laments that 'the Germans would never be able to go home again … They cannot be themselves' (2003: 227). These sentiments precipitate Hamilton's embrace of a postmodern identity of disconnectedness which finds expression in the metaphor of dwelling 'underwater where there's no language' (290), a condition of submersion beneath the flow of cultural, familial, and national currents. Yet the maternal disavowal of national identity does not determine Hamilton's hybrid self-image any more than his father's patriarchal glorification of it. His desire to escape his father's strictures does not negate but complicates his sense of cultural affiliation.

In a similar manner, the tension between his parents' German and Irish modes of remembrance informs patterns of literary influence in Hamilton's memoirs and travel narratives. He writes sensitively about the evocation of different forms of memory in relation to the distinct features of German and Irish history and topography. In 'The loneliness of being German', Hamilton reflects upon the legacy of Heinrich Böll, whose *Irisches Tagebuch* (1957; translated as *Irish Journal*, 1994) records impressions of Ireland that were largely shared by his mother. 'Unlike the Irish, Germans abroad tend to forget where they come from', Hamilton writes (2004). He notes that 'Seamus Heaney's exploration of digging, for instance, would mean something else altogether in Germany. In Ireland, the bog reveals things that connect us to the past, whereas the German forests are full of self-accusing landmines' (*ibid.*). In his allusions to Seamus Heaney and Heinrich Böll, Hamilton elicits the creative tension between the evocation and elision of his mixed cultural heritage that is evident in his writing. More to the point, his own impressions of contemporary Ireland are mediated by literary predecessors like Böll, whose sense of enchantment and estrangement from Irish culture provides the same formative influence in Hamilton's travel narratives as his mother's reminiscences in his memoirs. In *Die Redselige Insel: Irisches Tagebuch* (*The Island of Talking*, 2007), Hamilton retraces Böll's 1957 journey to Achill Island, where he was struck by an abandoned village that resembled the 'skeleton of a human habitation' (Böll, 1994: 31). Yet where Heinrich Böll finds peace in his contemplation of ruins, Hamilton seeks to repopulate the village in his imagination, to summon to memory the previous generations of emigrants who once inhabited its now skeletal remains (Hamilton, 2007: 48). He recasts

Böll's romantic impressions to fleetingly recreate a sense of communal vitality in a landscape that bears testament to rural desolation. Hamilton's evocation of the Irish past does not replace but rather is filtered through the prism of Böll's romantic impressions: his reminiscence of the landscape is compounded against his predecessor's obliviousness to its loss. As he retraces Böll's journey, Hamilton treads a pathway of memory: he recollects his predecessor's experiences of being enthralled and estranged from Irish culture as he endeavours to rediscover it anew. In acknowledging such literary influences, Hamilton also affirms his hybrid identity. He does not seek to repudiate but expand the limits of Irish national consciousness beyond the confines of his own alterity.

This theme of self-discovery through the recuperation of migrant identity also features prominently in Hugo Hamilton's 2010 novel, *Hand in the Fire*. Its protagonist, the Serbian Vid Ćosić, chooses to immigrate to Ireland because he perceives it to be 'quite neutral' and 'a very friendly place' to escape from a partially remembered traumatic experience in his native land (Hamilton, 2010: 20). In Dublin, he is befriended by Kevin Concannon, a hyperactive lawyer who himself has grown up between England and Ireland and become embittered towards his absent father: 'a classic emigrant, the person who walked away but kept on singing about going home'. As Ćosić reflects, Kevin's 'father had written himself out of the family history. I was being written in' (43–4). A moment of crisis occurs early in the narrative when Kevin Concannon violently assaults a drunken man accosting Ćosić and then, to preserve his legal career, makes him become a scapegoat and claim responsibility for the incident. In doing so, Vid Ćosić not only appears culpable for Kevin's crime, but he also solidifies his place within the Concannon household and makes it his mission to reunite its disparate family members. In a figurative sense, his gradual acceptance into the Concannon family becomes a metaphor for the integration of immigrants in Ireland, who symbolically take the place and fill the role of former Irish emigrants. The dysfunctional Concannon family also stands in for the larger Irish society that has repressed the memory of its lost emigrant generations.

In his search for Irish role models, Hamilton's protagonist does not become acculturated by walking in the footsteps of literary predecessors. Rather, his acts of literary pilgrimage serve only to underline the extent of his estrangement from mainstream Irish culture. Soon after his arrival in Ireland, Vid Ćosić and his Moldovan girlfriend Luida make a self-conscious attempt to embrace what they perceive as Irish cultural activities but 'end up only preventing each other from integrating and moving ahead'. In his own words,

one day I brought her to a place called Howth. It's meant to be beautiful out there. Famous too, because this was the location where the writer James Joyce first made love to his future wife Nora, something which is commemorated publicly on the sixteenth of June every year in a national celebration of sex and literature and first love. People told me that Ireland used to be sexually repressed, but you'd never think it now …

Howth was just another hill, basically with a big golf course and some wealthy villas and gates and planes landing nearby at the airport. It didn't really mean anything to us … It was a mistake to bring her out there because it already belonged to somebody else. We were the latecomers. (Hamilton, 2010: 59)

From Vid Ćosić's perspective, the hill of Howth is less a literary touchstone than a suburban landscape in which the protuberances of modernity reinforce his sense of disconnection from Irish cultural norms. In a similar vein, his visit to the pier in Dun Laoghaire is less an occasion for 'commemoration of the writer Samuel Beckett' than confusion about the significance of his epiphany in *Krapp's Last Tape*, which Ćosić declares 'didn't mean very much to me' (87). As in Howth, the literary landscape of Dun Laoghaire proves an alienating setting for him to find his place in Irish culture.

Yet it is precisely in his failure to identify with literary predecessors like Joyce and Beckett that Hamilton's protagonist learns to empathise with the ordinary Irish emigrants who left in their multitudes from the very same pier in Dun Laoghaire. In his endeavours to bring the Concannon family back together, Vid Ćosić discovers that the absent father has in fact returned to Ireland only to become 'more of an exile here on his own doorstep than he had ever been abroad' (129). At first, he tries to restore Johnny Concannon into his family's affections, but when rebuffed Vid Ćosić comes to realise that his own place in the household is equally tenuous. 'What a touching mission this was, stepping into the shoes of a returning emigrant trying to make contact with his own son. I understood exactly how he must have felt, not knowing where to fit in', Ćosić declares (119). After his own expulsion from the Concannon home, he identifies even more closely with the former Irish emigrant, noting 'how similar we were, in between places, neither here nor there' (169).

It is from this liminal perspective that Vid Ćosić not only empathises with Irish emigrants of the past, but he also positions himself as their descendant whose integration is dependent on the recovery of their memory. Thus, Hamilton's protagonist casts his imagination back to what he perceives to be the original root of Concannon familial dysfunction that is embodied in the figure of their ancestor: the 'drowned woman', the pregnant, unwed Máire Concannon, who was denounced from the altar in Furbo, Connemara, and then washed up on the shores of the Aran Islands, a century earlier. As Hamilton makes clear in his afterword to the novel, the story of the drowned woman is neither fictional nor literary but a vestigial folktale 'about her death which entered into the memory of the landscape' (89). From Vid Ćosić's perspective, it is the protrusions of modernity on this landscape of memory that prevent the Concannon family and community at large from comprehending and mourning her loss.[2]

Hence, Vid Ćosić travels to Connemara to conjure an image of Máire Concannon and acknowledge her as his predecessor, to express contrition on behalf of her family and her nation for repressing the memory of her existence. 'We were standing only a few feet away from the hastily dug grave into which Máire Concannon had been put to rest', he exclaims, yet 'it seemed like only yesterday that she was found on the rocks and brought here on a board, all bashed by the sea. And maybe you could say this was her real funeral, only in delayed time' (Hamilton, 2010: 275). In presiding over the 'real funeral' of would-be emigrant Máire Concannon who perished over a century before his arrival in Ireland, Ćosić implies that he is uniquely placed to empathise with her plight. As he stares out to sea from the shoreline in Furbo, he imagines himself in her shoes and observes that

> the place must have changed quite a bit in recent times. There is a big hotel situated right on the shore now which seems to have come from a different country and been dropped on the landscape ...
>
> What was the view worth in times of hardship? Because I was from somewhere else, I had the ability to censor the big hotel from the map. The only thing that didn't change was the sea and the waves still pounding with the same rhythm after all this time ...
>
> What would it have been like for a young woman to become pregnant? An unmarried mother, denounced as unfit to live among her own people. She had become a stranger overnight. Her residence permit has run out, you might say. Faced with deportation, only in her case she was forced out into the sea. She had lost her rights and had become an alien in a place which she had grown up thinking of as home. (173)

From this anachronistic narrative perspective, Hamilton's protagonist imagines the complete and utter disempowerment of the would-be emigrant – who has lost any hold on her community and is confronted with expulsion – to be akin to the predicament of the illegal immigrant on the threshold of deportation. His comprehension of her feelings of vulnerability is enhanced by his ability to excise from the landscape all traces of modernity and to reconstruct it from Máire Concannon's point of view. On the site of the big hotel, he envisions the plight of previous generations who were driven out of Ireland 'in times of hardship'. It is the prerogative of the alien 'from somewhere else', he implies, to see through the veneer of modernity to recover the memory of emigrant predecessors and make clear the proximity of their past.

Yet it is also a mark of Vid Ćosić's acculturation and integration into Irish society that he identifies not only with the would-be emigrant but also her distant descendants who had repressed her memory and failed to acknowledge her loss. In claiming her as his predecessor, he does not only seek to make amends to the emigrant generations of the past; he also asserts his place within her present family and defines his role in contemporary Irish society. In raising and laying the ghost of Máire Concannon to rest, Vid Ćosić pays tribute to the figure of the Irish migrant in a delayed time of both past and present. He endeavours to fill the void occasioned by her loss and that of countless other former emigrants whose disappearance he makes it his mission to mark. He also provides a catalyst for both the Concannon family and the wider host society it represents to do the same. Ultimately, in developing this anachronistic narrative perspective in which immigrants view modern Ireland through emigrant eyes, Hamilton's protagonist Vid Ćosić adopts the same palimpsestic self-image and 'new Irish' vantage point as the autobiographical subject in his memoirs and travel writing. His imaginative encounter with a migrant predecessor provides the impetus for self-discovery of an Irish multicultural identity.

Throughout his writing, Hugo Hamilton represents this moment of self-acceptance of cultural difference in Ireland as the climactic occurrence of a multicultural epiphany: a profound experience of self-realisation that provides a form of narrative resolution as well as personal and national self-recognition. As a second-generation German-Irish author who was raised during a formative period in the nation's history, he becomes a cultural intermediary between 'new Irish' migrants and communities and the literary traditions of the host society. In his memoirs and travel writing, he cultivates a hybridised and historicised self-image that could provide a model for other forms of immigrant self-expression in Ireland. This is not to claim Hamilton as a spokesman for the 'new Irish' or to suggest that his own struggles to belong in the nation of de Valera and those of recent migrants and new communities are one and the same. A recent theatrical adaptation of *The Speckled People* at the Gate Theatre in 2011 received mixed reviews in part because of the seeming obsolescence of his child persona on stage. 'The complex plurality of Irish identity that Hamilton's memoir explored', according to Sara Keating, was 'sidelined in service of self-congratulation: a sort of "look how far we've come" smugness that neglects deeper questions of repressed psychology for an easy sentimental end' (Keating, 2011). Nevertheless, if Hamilton found his voice as a result of the influx of 'new Irish' migrants and the establishment of new communities in the late 1990s, then his contemplation of his hybrid situation also gave expression to this emergent Irish multicultural society. At root, Hamilton's narrative method brings together past and present migratory storylines that gradually intersect as the contemporary protagonist becomes aware of a historical predecessor whose experiences prefigure his own. The reconciliation of these narrative perspectives culminates in a climactic moment of self-recognition. His cultivation of a 'new Irish' identity also has implications for the wider host society insofar as his sense of self-recognition is based on coming to terms with the realisation that, in Kristeva's words, 'we are foreigners to ourselves' (Kristeva, 1991: 170). Hamilton documents this struggle to incorporate the unacknowledged Irish Other into not just a personal but also a national self-image that is explored in the contributions to this volume.

Notes

1   'In many ways, the recurrent return in the 1990s to the dark age of de Valera's Ireland acted as a backhanded validation of the present, which was clearly understood as a lucky escape from "all that business"', Cleary contends in *Outrageous Fortune* (2006: 162).
2   In a 2009 article entitled 'Reading the ruins: How Ireland is losing its memory', Hamilton declares that 'in the rush to place the history of famine and emigration behind us, ... parts of Connemara [have been converted] into a suburban landscape, as if the map is out of register' (Hamilton, 2009).

References

Allen-Randolph, Jody (2010). *Close to the Next Moment: Interviews from a Changing Ireland.* Manchester: Carcanet.

Anon. (2007). 'The rebranding of ourselves', Editorial *Irish Times*, 17 March. www.irishtimes. com/newspaper/opinion/2007/0317/1173880425466.html. Accessed on 20 April 2012.

Böll, Heinrich (1994). *Irish Journal*, trans. Leila Vennewitz. Evanston: Northwestern University Press.

Cleary, Joseph (2006). *Outrageous Fortune*. Dublin: Field Day.

Hamilton, Hugo (1998). *Sad Bastard*. London: Secker & Warburg.

—— (2003). *The Speckled People*. New York: Harper Collins.

—— (2004). 'The loneliness of being German', *Guardian*, 7 September. www.guardian.co.uk/ books/2004/sep/07/germany.society. Accessed 20 April 2012.

—— (2006). *The Sailor in the Wardrobe: A Memoir*. London: Fourth Estate.

—— (2007). *Die Redselige Insel: Irisches Tagebuch (The Island of Talking)*. Munich: Sammlung Luchterhand.

—— (2009). 'Reading the ruins: How Ireland is losing its memory', *Scottish Review of Books*. www. scottishreviewofbooks.org/index.php?option=com_content&view=article&id=75:reading-the-ruins-how-ireland-is-losing-its-memory-hugo-hamilton&catid=10:volume-4-issue-3-2008&Itemid=52. Accessed on 20 April 2012.

—— (2010). *Hand in the Fire*. London: Fourth Estate.

Joyce, James (2007) [1916]. *A Portrait of the Artist as a Young Man*. New York: Norton.

—— (1992) [1922]. *Ulysses*, London: Penguin.

Keating, Sara (2011). 'The Speckled People', *Irish Times*, 6 October. www.irishtimes.com/ newspaper/features/2011/1006/1224305320137.html. Accessed on 20 April 2012.

Kristeva, Julia (1991). *Strangers to Ourselves*, trans. Leon S. Roudiez. New York: Columbia University Press.

Lentin, Ronit (2002). 'Anti-racist responses to the racialisation of Irishness: Disavowed multiculturalism and its discontents', in Ronit Lentin and Robbie McVeigh (eds), *Racism and Anti-Racism in Ireland*. Belfast: Beyond the Pale, 226–39.

Reddy, Maureen T. (2005). 'Reading and writing race in Ireland: Roddy Doyle and *Metro Éireann*', *Irish University Review. A Journal of Irish Studies* 35.2: 374–88.

13

The Parts:
whiskey, tea, and sympathy

Katherine O'Donnell

There is a history of Irish empathy for black people. It can be argued that a key component in the construction of Irish political and cultural identity is the practice of emotion of 'feeling with' and standing in the same place with black Others. From the end of the eighteenth century we can see the articulation of Irish national identity being formulated (at least partially if not centrally) in terms of an ability to share in and hence represent the political and cultural sufferings and triumphs of the racialised Other. The location and ethnic identity of these Others fluctuates over the centuries: from the colonised Indians of Edmund Burke and Richard Brinsley Sheridan's long campaign to impeach Warren Hastings, the first Governor General of India, to the enslaved African that preoccupied the politics and speeches of Daniel O'Connell; from the Congolese and Putumayo who were the focus of Roger Casement's humanitarian efforts, to the global 'missions' of Irish religious orders in the mid-twentieth century; from the African American Civil Rights Movement which was the model for the political and cultural strategies of the Northern Irish Civil Rights Association, to those oppressed under apartheid rule in South Africa, who were the focus of the Dunnes Stores' workers' strike, and famine-stricken, debt-ridden Africa, the subject of Bob Geldof and Bono's interventions in more recent decades.

The function of this empathic performance for black people has a shifting register: it can be used to shame the British establishment, to launch a critique of colonial capitalism, to claim a superior morality of feeling and purpose, or to highlight the shared experience of dispossession, oppression, and a claim to sovereign independence. This empathetic identification can also be used to disavow the imputation of shame in being Irish, and to transcend the confines of nationalism and imagine that nationalism as part of an international solidarity movement for a more liberated, humane world. In the mid-twentieth century

Irish people have gone into exile among other races, in order to make home in sharing Christ's love, drawing on a heritage of solidarity with the oppressed and suffering. Irish empathy for the colonised, enslaved, recently liberated or starving black people has had a long and dynamic history. Its longevity and centrality to modes of feeling Irish has perhaps been in part due to the fact that the imagined black people lived far away (or like Olaudah Equiano or Frederick Douglass, they were passing through) and were therefore more amenable to poetic fantasy and symbolic projection. It is in the turning of the twenty-first century, with immigration occurring for the first time in hundreds of years of Irish history, that we saw this empathetic identification encountering actual dark-skinned people.[1]

Before the years of Celtic Tiger economic boom, the Republic of Ireland had been economically depressed, socially restrictive, and culturally and politically mired in how to address the war in the six counties of Northern Ireland without destabilising the 26-county Irish State. Joyce's *Dubliners* has ritually been read as an exposition of the 'paralysis' of pre-revolutionary twentieth-century Dublin. Roddy Doyle's first novel, *The Commitments*, self-published in 1987, similarly depicts the static of a stagnant city, but with the added bitterness of being capital of a failing project of national self-determination. When asked by a Social Welfare officer why he was two years drawing the dole, the protagonist Jimmy Rabbitte replies: 'We're a Third World Country. What do you expect?' (Doyle, 1989: 11). The novel's constant refrain of casual disdain for the nebulous 'culchies' who inhabit the rest of the country marks the capital city apart from any identification with the nation. This segregation is further underscored by a depiction of the city partitioned by class inequity. When northsider, working-class Jimmy Rabbitte advertises for musicians to join his band, he states that 'culchies' and middle-class southsiders need not apply, and in making the argument that the band should play African American soul music he asserts: 'The Irish are the niggers of Europe lads. ... An' Dubliners are the niggers of Ireland. The culchies have fuckin' everything. An' the northside Dubliners are the niggers o' Dublin' (31). Rabbitte's argument is that Irish identity is not so much in crisis but is a chronic disorder and because his community is segregated, reviled, and alienated by even the Third World Irish State, they are the blacks' blacks' black. This is not a practice of empathy but a position from which to launch a '"reverse" discourse' as Michel Foucault (1980: 101) might describe it: a language of identity politics used by the marginalised to speak back with pride against the shaming taxonomies and surveillance of the dominant, though in this case even the governing class are 'niggers'.

The stagnant Dublin of *The Commitments* is, at first glance, a world away from the Dublin of Keith Ridgway's second novel, *The Parts* (2003a), a fat, comic novel set in 'boom town' Dublin. Yet, the novels share some crucial similarities:

both repeatedly underscore that Dublin is Dublin and perhaps only distantly related to 'Ireland' (whatever that might be); both novels lovingly describe the city, yet it is depicted as an uncanny space and the lead characters are different-ly-abled melancholics; and both texts are realist novels that revel in the human voice, in humorous dialogue and soliloquy that banters between pugnacious rant and poetic lyric. Ridgway's virtuoso aesthetic depiction of *unheimlich*, comi-tragic Dublin and grief-struck misfits, struggling with shame, anxiety, and ineptitude, renders for us a place and characters that we recognise as inher-ently, convincingly, essentially, as Dublin, and despite the novel's protestations as Irish. Ridgway's rendition is a consummate presentation of cultural tropes prevalent in Irish literature, art, and popular culture, and the dominant 'struc-tures of feeling' (to cite Raymond Williams, 1985: 21) by which the specificity of 'Irishness' is conveyed and received. Ridgway's Dubliners know the Dublin of *The Commitments* as a part of the city and are kin to the wandering loquacious Dubliners of Joyce, O'Casey, Behan, Beckett, and na Gopaleen/O'Brien.[2]

Declan Kiberd cites *The Parts* as evidence that the reality of a recently 'multicultural' Ireland is too new to be fully grasped by novelists at the turn of the twenty-first century. The very title, *The Parts*, he says, points to the inevita-bility of an 'incomplete and partial' assessment of the cultural impact of diverse groups of immigrants as they arrive in large numbers to Ireland. Irish novelists, Kiberd argues, needed more time to assimilate the changes (2005: 277). I read Ridgway's novel as brilliantly conveying not only 'multicultural' Ireland but the *zeitgeist* of that Celtic Tiger period, in all its *manga* frenzy and dragging under-belly. The focus of this chapter is on the encounter with the migrant, which is no more than a few riffs in the jazz symphony of this novel, but these moments reveal such a lot about the practices of Irish identity and culture that they bear a forensic attention. Kiberd's commentary on the 'incomplete and partial' as-sessment is truer of the academic than the artist. Cultural critics need time for the gathering and sifting of evidence and percolation time for our processes of contemplation and argument. I think it might be fair to say that many of us who work in Irish Studies were often quite unsure of what to say during the economic boom. Our professional focus was on a culture of emigration and diaspora, the toll of clerical repression, the slow advent of modernity, the distinctive hybridity of Irish and English languages and cultural forms, or the postcolonial hangover of partition and sectarian conflict; thus, we needed time to adjust to the new re-alities. Irish literary writers were far ahead of the critical curve, and none more so than Ridgway who got nothing like the attention he deserved besides that of the *Irish Times*'s Eileen Battersby (2003), who described *The Parts* as the 'most convincing Irish comic novel since *At Swim-Two-Birds*'.

There are six main characters in the novel: Barry, a melancholic gay radio producer; his boss, Joe Kavanagh, a late-night radio talk-show host, recently separated from his wife and young daughter; Kitty Flood, an increasingly obese novelist who had some success with her only novel over a decade previously; Delly Roche, Kitty's erstwhile lover and widow of a billionaire pharmaceutical engineer; Dr George Addison-Blake, an American who was the adopted son of Delly's late husband; and sweet, poetic, and beautiful Kez, a rent boy and the moral centre on which the novel turns. The characters are Dickensian in their vivid hyper-reality: quasi-symbol and wholly human. Ridgway's novel is 'a wonderful study that caught the frenzy of [the] bogus Tiger moment' (Battersby, 2010). He brilliantly captures that 'free fall' as Battersby (*ibid.*) terms it – the strange anomie of that period where a country previously saturated in generations of poverty found itself in the money. The boom is depicted as just that: a new loud noise, a cacophony of busyness, traffic, loud conversation about prices, properties, foods from other places, trips and travel, with all values being subordinated to the measurement of material wealth. Ridgway's prescience on perceiving the Celtic Tiger period as a transitory noise comes from the perspective he establishes for the omniscient narrator whose gaze incessantly ranges over a multiplicity of synchronous realities. This roving perspective is grounded in a sense of Dublin as a timeless, massive constancy with its winds, weather, light, hills, river, and sweep of bay.

The 'poor, the really poor' that Barry sees '*everywhere*' (original emphasis; Ridgway, 2003a: 208) are occluded in the noise of economic boom – repressed from the dominant social imaginary – and they haunt the text. Ridgway depicts Dublin's criminal class without any of the glamour that is the usual patina in the slew of movies, novels, and TV series that take 'gangland Dublin' as a theme. There is a sublimated menace that rumbles through the novel and occasionally ruptures, especially when Dr George is making his peregrinations through this underworld. He becomes a subterfuge doctor for a criminal called Mr Martin, who 'needed a doctor who could look after his "little family" whenever they needed it' (193). In a remarkable passage Ridgway describes a house party that Dr George attends with Mr Martin and associates. The passage is a gothic enactment of violent racism:

> There was so much noise that a silence built. The air ruptured, buckled, gave. The house bled profusely. In the hall the host was in his boxer shorts, swinging wildly with a golf club. He hit nothing but a porcelain dog and a carriage clock. In an upstairs bathroom a Romanian girl was set upon by three men, her clothes stuck to the bath as if left over from an old fashioned wash day, her dignified terror lost on most, but a treat for those who noticed. In the kitchen, where the weapons always are, a woman was stabbed, her thigh split, and her chest punctured, and a black girl was blamed. (193)

Dr George knows that the black girl is innocent and he ruminates: 'these Irish guys … they were real ground floor racists, cartoon racists, unevolved, old fashioned racists. They saw a black face and they found they knew the script' (194). Dr George watches as the crowd 'beat her partner first', before attacking the anonymous black girl.

Such violent racism may be read as a response to one of the paradoxes of the economic boom: while absolute poverty levels decreased, inequalities of income and wealth became more obvious in the popular consciousness. Irish people were being told that they lived in one of the richest countries in the world, yet significant portions of the population had low-paid work, poor housing conditions, and marginal access to healthcare. In research carried out by the Irish Refugee Council in 2000, asylum-seekers (mostly African in origin) described the hostility they met with from other marginalised groups. They felt that such indigenous excluded groups often perceived asylum-seekers in competition with them to gain access to scarce social resources (Fanning, Loyal, and Staunton, 2000: 21).[3] One asylum-seeker described it thus: 'I think the racist people are from Ireland's cities, the people who are getting Social Welfare. I really think that educated people are not racist … even if in their roots they have some racism they learn to control it or they learn what it is to be racist' (20).

The marginalised Irish found racist discourse to be a 'script they knew', to paraphrase Ridgway, a script that offered an explanation for the crises they experienced in housing, healthcare, and jobs. For their part, the upper middle class was able to enjoy the creation of buffer zones in terms of legislation and social policy whereby they could remain remote from regular interaction with those seeking asylum, or indeed from having migrants as neighbours.[4] Ridgway's depiction of the random violence visited on the 'black face' is not the only reaction of those alienated from social and economic power. We see that for Kez race does not signify a distinction that makes a difference: when he rhapsodises a list about how closely interconnected everyone is in Dublin, Kenyan Billy is just another chap who hustles the quays when his rent is due (Ridgway, 2003a: 82).

Between violent racism and Kez's lack of distinction between races, are there narratives of empathy for the black 'Other' in *The Parts*? We can see the exploration of tropes of sympathy, identification, objectification, and projection in relation to the black Other in Ridgway's character Joe Kavanagh, and his relationship with his Nigerian neighbours. Joe Kavanagh ('Joe K' or the Joke as Barry privately calls him) is an Irish Everyman. His personality is familiar as a typically Irish radio talk-show host, an everyday feature of Irish domestic space: garrulous, querulous, entertaining, irreverent, charming, miscellaneous. Joe provides an interactive forum for story-telling, endlessly posing the question of what it is to be Irish ('do you think the Irish are fascists?'), for revealing the 'Hidden Ireland' (141). This feature of Irish radio programmes' fascinated self-regard with the mystery of what it is to be Irish was noticed by Joep Leersen, who termed this mentality as 'auto-exoticist' and as having a long genealogy in

Irish culture (1996: 67).[5] Joe is grief-struck at the recent ending of his marriage and Barry, who produces Joe's show, is scathing of the Joke's emotional investment in revamping the radio show to reveal a *societal, communal depression, which no one had noticed before, and which he would expose, as if it were something purposely hidden, obscured, by such things as advertising, materialism, the establishment's obsession with traffic* (original emphasis; Ridgway, 2003a: 103).

Joe is treating his grief with large doses of whiskey. One particular night he is at home with an old 'tape mix' at full volume, dancing 'in his best 80s *can't dance* style (a kind of stuttering hinge), with his hand full of genitals and his hat pulled slightly forward' (original emphasis; Ridgway, 2003a: 51). He hears a dim knocking but nothing seems amiss with the tape player, so he pulls down his shorts and scratches. On pulling up his pants he glances at the window and '[a] black man stood on the other side – staring at him, his fist raised knuckles forward, the glass shuddering slightly … He was a big black man at Joe's window. He seemed to be wearing a boxer's robe' (*ibid.*). When Joe opens the window, the black man politely addresses Joe as Mr Kavanagh and tells him that it is nearly 4 am, and that his wife and sons are trying to sleep. Joe is astonished that the man knows his name and disbelieving to hear he has lived next door 'for nearly two months' (*ibid.*). When Joe asks him his name, he is told it is Albert. All that Joe is capable of doing is staring at this black man's skin and mumbling an apology: 'I'm sorry. I'm drunk. I'm having a party but there's no one here. Where are you from? Do you like whiskey?' Albert manages to smile and gently says:

> 'I am from Nigeria'.
> Joe nodded.
> 'I am from Drumcondra', he said. 'Originally'.
> Albert clutched the neck of his robe.
> 'Will it be quiet now for a while?'
> 'Yes. Sorry'.
> 'Thank you'.
> He stepped back and turned. The robe was a dressing gown. It was navy blue, collared, comfortable looking.
> 'Call in sometime', said Joe. Leaning out the window. 'Come and have some whiskey'.
> Albert waved a hand vaguely, hopped the low bushes that divided the gardens. He disappeared.
> 'My name is Joe', called Joe. 'I'm your neighbour'.
>
> (52)

While Joe's encounter with the immigrant reverses the racist stereotype of the barbarian black disrupting the civilities of the white man's culture and society, it confirms the cultural stereotype of the perennially drunk Irish man: maudlin, raucous, infantile, and stupefied. The comedy of crass, Irish, whiskey-drinking

Joe's attempts to make friends with dignified, Nigerian, tea-drinking Albert continues for the rest of the novel. The next morning Joe tells Barry about the black man living next door, and recounts his confusion: 'I thought he was an American heavyweight boxer at my window. I am deeply embarrassed by myself. … What kind of man am I? What world am I living in? … I don't know my neighbours … I have no friends' (65). Joe's shame seems to be at least partially based in an inchoate sense that assuming a black man in a dressing gown must be an American heavyweight boxer is a crude stereotype that reveals provincial unworldliness. His embarrassment is also rooted in his failure to know his neighbours, an old-fashioned Irish phrase which connotes the value of cultivating good reciprocal relationships: Joe has failed a test of 'common decency' and moreover he has no friends. Joe is patently not capable of being empathetic. Empathy depends on a secure assurance in one's own position in the world, and a confidence in the capacity to grasp the feeling of what the Other suffers. Joe's emotional capacity extends only to self-pity. It is Albert who bestows sympathy on Joe, in the courtesy he extends to his drunken, boorish neighbour. Yet, we can never be sure that Albert's gentleness with Joe comes predominantly from sympathy or whether he is practised in the arts of appeasement and patience that subordinated groups are expected to deploy.

We can see how careful Albert is when Joe calls around to his house to apologise. Joe presents a bottle of whiskey and Albert thanks him while his wife raises her eyes and mutters under her breath (125). Albert invites him to drink tea and Joe is soon talking in grandiose terms about his radio show; he is expansive, elated, and high on egotistical bombast: '"I need to rediscover the fear. The source of the fear. You know?" Albert nods but Joe is disappointed in him: Albert seemed to possess none of the wisdom which Joe had assumed would be inherently his' (124). Joe is caught in the thrall of another racial stereotype: he wanted a sage primitive who was in touch with knowledge lost in the whorl of late-modernity. However, Joe sees that Albert is 'a modern man', who drives a small Audi, has polite children and books on cookery, photography, and American crime novels. Albert is not poetic, magical or feral, but mundane, domestic, and kindly. Joe realises that Albert's beautiful wife (whose name he 'just couldn't hold, something sibilant and leaking') does not like him: 'He was the problem from next door. The volume and the peeling paint' (125). Joe's failure to learn Albert's wife's name is a failure born out of a lazy complacency in being part of the dominant culture that will not put itself in the place of being a stuttering student of another language, even if that is to learn just one word: your neighbour's name. However, Albert's wife's shrugs, muttering, and silence do begin to teach Joe something. In realising how she sees him as 'the problem from next door', Joe starts to have an objective awareness of himself as someone who should be taking more care rather than wallowing in introspective self-pity.

Joe's initial racial stereotypes of Albert – that he is a champion boxer and must possess ancient wisdom – are not racist in the sense that they do not work from the assumption of a white superiority. Quite the reverse, they assume that black bodies and culture possess a glamour and richness lacking in Joe's world. In cultural studies we are sensitive to representations of the exotic Other and wary of romanticised generalisations and how they might serve as implicit justification for colonial domination and imperial ambitions. Yet Edward Said (1978) qualifies this perspective with the point that all cultures have views of other cultures that may be exotic but these do not necessarily presume an inferiority in the Other nor underpin a dominant–subordinate relationship of power.[6] There is also nothing in Joe's actions or musings that suggests he thinks of Albert as having a 'tremendous sexual power' as Frantz Fanon describes whites' projection onto black male bodies (1967: 157). When Joe does fantasise about being seen with a 'tall beautiful black woman with a lap top', his fantasy is not a white racist male fantasy about possessing a black female body; it does not assume this body to be hyper-sexualised (she is carrying a lap-top after all). In truth, he wants the reflected glamour of being seen with an attractive, exotic, powerful, materially successful woman so that his wife will engage with him: 'all in order to somehow get back at, or make jealous, or somehow, one way or another, to prod, poke, provoke, make sad or sorry or sick, his abandoning, absent, all together missing, wife' (Ridgway, 2003a: 203).

Joe tries to forge some common ground with Albert, relying on the classic opening gambit of Irish conversation between strangers, in asking him where he comes from: 'So whereabouts in Nigeria exactly … ?' (124). Albert's wife claps her hands and laughs in anticipation at Joe's inevitable ignorance. Albert smilingly asks Joe if he knows the country and Joe has to admit that 'he hasn't a clue' about Nigeria. Albert and his wife are clearly used to the question and presumption that by saying where they hail from, they will be rendered intelligible to their Irish-born inquisitors, who are used to using this enquiry to 'place' people, as the idiom goes. The answer of 'Lagos' invariably renders Albert and his wife more opaque to this 'placing'. 'Lagos' is a barrier to the follow-on questions, assertions, and stories that people in Ireland routinely deploy once they know where someone comes from – they determine if they can find people they know in common and they tell what they know of the place and the people. Joe's question points to his unfamiliarity in meeting strangers who are not Irish-born or part of the familiar geography of the Irish diaspora. Albert and his wife's humorous reaction points to their bemusement that Irish people routinely ask this question, when they 'haven't a clue' about Nigeria. This moment points to the fact that old scripts by which strangers in Ireland forged connections have to be rewritten to accommodate the foreigner who comes from a territory unknown to the interlocutor. Irish-born people like Joe will have to become conscious that the world is larger and stranger than the small island of Ireland and even the wider cities of the diaspora.

Joe's attempts to establish bonds with his neighbours become undermined by his anxiety at the tea-drinking domesticity and his desire to talk about his radio show. When he learns that Albert is an urologist he is delighted with the potential presented for two areas to exploit for the show. He does not elaborate on his second proposition – which is to use Albert as a contact for people with sexually transmitted disease, sex addicts or fetishists (127). Instead Joe launches into proposition one: he asks if Albert and his wife have encountered any racism, 'and if so at what level, … you know interfering, nasty, even fearful' (126), so that they tell their stories to him on air. Albert replies with gravitas and a dignified generosity:

> 'Most people', said Albert, 'are very kind. I have been here for most of the last ten years. Since I was a student. But there have been moments of horror and abuse'.
> 'We don't want to be on the radio'.
> She looked at the table, and then up at Joe, and smiled politely.
>
> *(Ibid.)*

Though we never do learn Albert's wife's name and her presence is slight, her shoulder shrugs, laughs, and shared looks with Albert speak eloquently of her derision of Joe, her good humour, and her close bond with her husband. Ridgway's depiction of her intervention in this instance is masterful: her pause to look at the table, collect herself, and then 'smile politely' point to the practised skills of impeccable manners, patience, and appeasement that marginalised people are often called on to deploy to manage social interactions when their feelings and their interests are not being considered. The words 'Horror and abuse' speak volumes in their tight-lipped brevity. 'Horror' points to the ongoing threat of random violence, and 'abuse' to a more systematic ingrained prejudice or bias. Albert continues by deflecting from the trauma to minimise their own personal experiences of racism: 'We are only two people. We are well off. We have friends and a nice house to live in and we are lucky and we are happy here' (127). Albert advises Joe to talk to people more qualified, such as relevant NGOs for refugees and asylum-seekers who are on welfare and 'have more trouble' (*ibid.*). This deflection, minimisation, and gratitude for safeties or privileges are hallmarks of oppressed peoples' survival strategies. Yet, Joe still remains crass and self-involved:

> 'What kind of abuse?'
> The wife laughed. Albert smiled.
> 'What kind would you like?'
> Joe felt himself redden a little as they looked at him.

'Well, I mean, what have you got? Sorry I mean. Well I'm just curious. Appalled. Sorry. Embarrassed'.

(Ibid.)

Joe is once again embarrassed and feels sorry for himself: 'He was, he told himself, too raw, cut too close' (*ibid.*). However, his self-pity gives way to an epiphany: 'But the truth, and he knew it, was that he was an asshole' (*ibid.*). The glimpse of self-awareness is immediately swallowed by the shamed realisation that he has made a fool of himself and the stabbing self-pity that 'his wife had left him'. The scene ends here with Joe asking: 'Are you going to open that whiskey or not then?' (*ibid.*).

Joe has proved himself an insensitive fool, wallowing in melancholia, ashamed and unable for mature conversation. Ridgway's presentation of Joe is of a classic stage Irishman: a drunken buffoon, paralysed in self-pity. He is a mirror by which native-born Irish people can begin to recognise how ill-equipped the culture is in considerately encountering the migrant. The readers' sympathies are entirely with Albert and his family as Joe proves himself incapable of empathy or understanding. He does not have a shard of sympathy: he wanted to use the stories Albert and his wife had of racism as fodder to feed his show. He would exploit their suffering to have the native Irish audience gasp in 'auto-exoticist' horror (Leersen, 1996: 67) at the fascinating spectacle of how racist Irish people actually are. Albert and his wife's story would be consumed as shocking entertainment with the frisson of recognition that 'the Irish' are as stupid and violent as the colonial stereotype and are the inveterate sinners that the Catholic Church has tried to minister. Joe does show a glimmer of self-awareness but that awareness is so uncomfortable he needs to saturate it in whiskey.

The final extended scene between Joe and his neighbours occurs after Joe 're-mained as drunk as long as he could' but eventually he sobers up and visits next door. This time he chooses to bring a gift of a tin of biscuits 'and it seemed to go better' (241). Joe meets Albert's children for the first time and describes them as 'two shy and very beautiful creatures who spoke in Dublin accents'. When Joe hears their accents, he says: '"You're putting that on," he said. "Wha?" "You're putting that on. You're imitating me or something. It's very good"' (241–2). Joe is so blinded by these exotic 'beautiful creatures' that he does not comprehend that they are Dubliners. Their blackness, beauty, and gentleness are not something that he identifies with Dublin. While this is a racial stereotype, it is not racist as Joe's implicit assumption is that the boys are too refined to share his culture. However, he is immediately thankful that the boys did not understand the point he was making and that their parents did not hear him. He realises, even without reflection, that to imply that the boys do not belong in Dublin is, however well-intentioned, potentially hurtful and if such an implication was maintained, it could result in fostering a strong culture of discrimination against the black people who the white people assume 'don't really belong'.

Joe recovers by trying to bond with the boys and asking them to the radio station; although they are not enthusiastic they agree. He says that he wants to introduce them to his daughter, assuring them that she is very nice, quiet, not 'materialistical', and would make a very good girlfriend. The boys are polite at the suggestion, shrugging and smiling. Joe asks Albert what he thinks of the proposition: 'My daughter and your son? Will we splice the families, form an alliance?' Albert replies with his usual *politesse*: 'That would be good Joe. But maybe they will think differently'. Joe does not understand Albert's subtlety, and he jocularly replies: 'That's kids for you isn't it. They think differently' (242). Albert is signalling that the children might not only think differently of Joe's proposal but they might also think differently from each other. Joe remains happily oblivious to any potential cultural differences or any racist attitudes that his daughter may have or that his potential grandchildren may suffer. Joe's white-skin privilege enables him to choose to ignore the effects of racism on the racially marked. He wants to bond with the neighbours; their black skin causes no offence to him, and so he does not acknowledge that their perceived Otherness might mean they live lives negotiating the threat and reality of 'horror and abuse'. Joe has no empathetic identification with his neighbours' position in Irish society; he does not acknowledge his myriad of material and symbolic privileges in his whiteness and native-born nationality; he does not acknowledge the power differential. Can there be honest engagement and friendship without this acknowledgement?[7] Joe intends to be cordial in his playing with the notion that his daughter and Albert's youngest son might be romantically linked. However, this unconscious or studied lack of awareness of what his neighbours face is also allied with an assumption that Nigerians will assimilate to Irish cultural norms and this assumption has a potential, at least, to give rise to discriminate against those who do not comply.

Joe's self-satisfied complacency is disturbed in watching Albert and his family sit down to eat, while he is 'offered nothing':

> He thought that this was strange. He felt hurt. They did not, it seemed, like him. But they did not dislike him enough to bar him from their house. Maybe he was on probation. Perhaps he was being tested, and if he behaved well enough he would be welcomed more fully into their home. (242)

Joe has a breakthrough from his self-absorption with hurt and pain, and he resolves to 'become best friends with Albert and his wife, whatever her name was, and their two boys. Their houses would be open to one another. Their meals would be shared, their stories mingled, their troubles halved' (243). As Joe leaves quietly, thanking them for their hospitality, he invites them to his house 'for supper' the following weekend. Albert's wife says nothing and Albert promises to check his work schedule to see 'whether he would be free' (*ibid.*). In an inversion of what we might expect, it is the migrant who will decide if he can bear to take up hospitality from the native-born. Joe goes home, gets drunk, and watches television but he is now so anxious about annoying his new friends that he turns the volume down further and has to move nearer the screen: 'Eventually his cheek was pressed to the static and he could hear nothing but the dimmest hiss, as if his inner audience was booing him at last' (*ibid.*). Joe is seeking redemption in being a good neighbour and cultivating friendships. He is no longer caught in exotic fantasies, racial stereotypes or spinning salacious stories; he is steeped in the reality of his own loneliness and his desire for connection. He does not seek to make a connection based on his empathetic understanding of Albert and his family, as he does not perceive Albert as in need of empathy. Joe wants mutuality: a sympathetic sharing. The final glimpse we have of Joe at the end of the novel suggests that he might make friends with his neighbours. We see him in his back garden trying to chat to Albert's wife 'over the wall' that is as symbolic as it is real. He does not objectify her; he does not assume a knowledge about her; he does not try and use her for his own ends: 'He wants her to like him. It's so simple that it makes a stuttering sob rise in his throat which he has to swallow back. He asks about her children, and she asks about his' (456).

Notes

1   The study of affect in general and empathy in particular is currently the focus – or indeed the locus – of a dynamic interdisciplinary conversation where scholars are talking with and to each other from fields as diverse as neuroscience and literary studies. See for example the special section 'Empathy' of *Emotion Review* (Russell and Barrett, 2012). Feminist thinkers have been at the forefront of this current wave of affect studies; see Gray (2004) for an overview of this field and a brilliant discussion of how empathy might be ethically deployed in a multicultural Ireland.

2   My argument for including Beckett rests with Ridgway's (2003b) reading of *Mercier and Camier* and his appreciative recognition of the city of Dublin in the text.

3   Similar results are found in an Amnesty International survey (O'Mahony *et al.*, 2001) and the ESRI (Economic and Social Research Institute) survey (McGinnity *et al.*, 2006).

4   See, for example, Mullally (2001). While Vang is positive about the levels of housing integration in Dublin between Africans, Asians, and East Europeans with native Irish due to the availability of private rental accommodation, his maps show no presence of Asian or African immigrants among the 'higher neighbourhood income levels' – most notably Howth, Malahide, and south County Dublin (Vang, 2010: 2998).

5   This bifurcation can be explained as a legacy of colonialism, where the shamed 'Irish' identity is in constant oscillation with internalised derision and an anxious assertion of national pride. My favourite exploration of this Irish cultural *modus operandi* is to be found in Myles na Gopaleen's plan to '*Hide Ireland again!*' (1975: 133).

6   See for example Said's discussion of German and Russian Orientalism which he sug-
     gests had 'clean' pasts (1978: 2–4).
7   Moreton-Robinson (2000: 186) has challenged white feminists to theorise 'the relin-
     quishment of power'. For an excellent response see Probyn (2004).

References

Battersby, Eileen (2003). 'The top twenty-one: Critic's choice; Eileen Battersby, Literary
     Correspondent, gives her assessment of her favourite fiction of the year', *Irish Times*,
     13 December: 62.
—— (2010). 'Finding the present in the past', *Irish Times*, 16 March: 18.
Doyle, Roddy (1989) [1987]. *The Commitments*. London: Vintage.
Fanning, Bryan, Steven Loyal, and Ciaran Staunton (2000). *Asylum Seekers and the Right to
     Work in Ireland*. Dublin: Irish Refugee Council.
Fanon, Frantz (1967). *Black Skin, White Masks*. London: Pluto.
Foucault, Michel (1980) [1978]. *History of Sexuality. An Introduction*, vol. I, trans. Robert
     Hurley. New York: Vintage.
Gray, Breda (2004). 'Remembering a "multicultural" future through a history of emigration:
     Towards a feminist politics of solidarity across difference', *Women's Studies International
     Forum* 27: 413–29.
Kiberd, Declan (2005). *The Irish Writer and the World*. Cambridge: Cambridge University
     Press.
Leersen, Joep (1996). *Remembrance and Imagination: Patterns in the Historical and Literary
     Representation of Ireland in the Nineteenth Century*. Cork: Cork University Press in as-
     sociation with Field Day.
McGinnity, Frances, Philip J. O'Connell, Emma Quinn, and James Williams (2006). *Migrants'
     Experience of Racism and Discrimination in Ireland*. Dublin: Economic and Social
     Research Institute (ESRI).
Moreton-Robinson, Aileen (2000). *Talkin' up to the White Woman*. St Lucia: University of
     Queensland Press.
Mullally, Siobhán (2001). *Manifestly Unjust: A Report on the Fairness and Sustainability of
     Accelerated Procedures for Asylum Determinations*. Dublin: Irish Refugee Council.
na Gopaleen, Myles/Flann O'Brien (1975) [1968]. *The Best of Myles*, Kevin O'Nolan (ed.).
     London: Picador.
O'Mahony, Eoin, Steven Loyal, and Aogán Mulcahy (2001). *Racism in Ireland: The Views of
     Black and Ethnic Minorities*. Dublin: Amnesty International.
Probyn, Fiona (2004). 'Playing chicken at the intersection: The white critic of whiteness',
     Borderlands e-journal 3.4: n.p.
Ridgway, Keith (2003a). *The Parts*. London: Faber & Faber.
—— (2003b). 'Knowing me, knowing you: It annoys the scholars, but Beckett's *Mercier and
     Camier* gives Keith Ridgway a thrill of recognition', *Guardian Review*, 19 July: 28
Russell, James A. and Lisa Feldman Barrett (eds) (2012). *Emotion Review. Special Section:
     Empathy* 4.1.
Said, Edward (1978). *Orientalism*. New York and London: Vintage.
Williams, Raymond (1985) [1977]. *Marxism and Literature*. Oxford: Oxford University Press.
Vang, Zoua M. (2010). 'Housing supply and residential segregation in Ireland', *Urban Studies*
     47.14: 2983–3012.

14

Hospitality and hauteur: tourism, cross-cultural space, and ethics in Irish poetry

Charles I. Armstrong

Tourism tends to be observed as an indispensable but regrettable epiphenomenon. For many states it provides a major source of income, facilitating commerce and jobs that make up an important part of the national economy. At the same time, there is a tendency to see tourism as involving a pernicious commodification of space, culture, and people's lives in general. Common conceptions of tourism tend to circle around cliché and stereotype. In an increasingly globalised economy, tourism is seen as bringing with it particularly reductive and restrictive forms of interaction across national and cultural borders. Relatedly, it is interpreted as being an ignoble descendant of a venerable ancestor, the Grand Tour, whereby young aristocrats developed their own characters (and art collections) through lengthy journeys to places where the classical heritage was felt to be still accessible. Around the turn from the eighteenth to the nineteenth century, a sea-change occurred whereby travel became available to a larger spectrum of the population. With this change, however, a distinction between tourists and more sophisticated travellers also ensued. As James Buzard puts it:

> The class-specific ideals of the Grand Tour were refunctioned to suit that atmosphere in which 'everybody' seemed to be abroad: the desiderata of travelling turned inward and created the honorific sense of 'traveller', which means essentially 'the one who is not a *tourist*'. Through varieties of what the sociologist Erving Goffman has called 'rôle distance', modern travellers and travel writers identified themselves as anti-touristic beings whose unhappy lot was to move amidst and in the wake of tourists, *for one of whom they might even be mistaken*. (Original emphasis; Buzard, 2002: 49)

Two important value-judgements, crucially important for the interpretation of tourism even to the present day, were being consolidated. Firstly, tourism was established as something unworthy or plebeian. The common tendency to belittle tourists – swiftly dismissing them as crassly dressed crowds more interested in taking photographs and sampling *ersatz* experiences, fitting pre-packaged notions of the native, than truly discovering anything new or noteworthy – was put into place. Secondly, a crucial differentiation between tourists and true travellers was set up. Even if those who aspired to the latter position were typically middle-class, they inherited – in their own perception at least – something of the distinction, individuality, and leisurely perceptiveness formerly associated with the upper classes. When on the road, writers and critics still typically identify themselves as this kind of traveller – in a movement akin, say, to the way in which Canadians define themselves as non-American – even as they inherit something of the anxiety of association (how can they set themselves apart from mere tourists?) mentioned by Buzard. The aspiration to be a kind of aristocrat *manqué* is especially tempting for the poet, perhaps, since poetry frequently is identified as being both a challenging and non-functional – and, as a result (at least in modernist inflections), elitist – endeavour.

Irish poetry from the 1980s to the present has typically seen fit to either follow or contest this schematics. The tendency, in the Republic of Ireland in particular, to foster close links between tourism and art makes tension all the more inevitable. At a governmental level, the imbrication between these phenomena has been confirmed by the existence of the Department of Arts, Sport, and Tourism from 2002 to 2010.[1] In the globalised book market, poets are interpreted within the framework of specifically 'Irish' associations and stereotypes that are also selling-points of tourist industry, even as they feel the need to distinguish their own activity from the mass-produced kind of pseudo-experience believed to be the pernicious hallmark of modern holidays. One is pitched perilously close to the kind of cultural consumption criticised by Henri Lefebvre:

> the sight-seer in Venice does not absorb Venice but words about Venice, the written words of guide-books and the spoken words of lectures, loudspeakers and records; he listens and looks, and the commodity he receives in exchange for his money, the consumer goods, the trade value, is a verbal commentary on the Piazza San Marco, the Palazzo dei Dogi, or Tintoretto; but the experience value, the thing itself (the work of art) eludes his avid consumption which is restricted only to talk. (Lefebvre, 2000: 133–4)

Understandably, the poet wishes to avoid becoming a mere tour-guide of this order. The kind of struggle between discourse and place outlined by Lefebvre is often at stake for poetry that articulates a critique of tourism: unless there is a sense of fatalistic dejection, it tends to seek either to side-step discourse (as Lefebvre implicitly envisages) or find a truer, more authentic form of expression that will provide a more productive relation to the native space.

One can observe the desire to debunk the mechanics of sight-seeing at work in Irish poetry dealing with tourist visits abroad. When Peter McDonald, in 'The Road to Rome', portrays a poet discomfited by the complacency of 'our guide's too zealous overview' (McDonald, 2004: 39), this is evidence of a legitimate desire to distinguish his own tentative, probing art from not only tour guides, but indeed everyone and everything that is self-confidently 'beaming and bursting with the truth' (*ibid.*). In a different vein, several of Ciaran Carson's Japanese poems poke fun at the Western desire to find a unique and unalloyed Eastern essence on trips to Asia. 'Fuji Film', for instance, throws together 'lobster samurai' with 'the icy blue of Northern fjords' and 'the signs for Coke' in a mesh of global images (Carson, 1998: 66). Carson is exploring the imaginative possibilities of this world order, rather than lamenting the loss of some presumed, original identity, and as such he avoids any simple dismissal of the possibilities of tourism. As Michael Cronin and Barbara O'Connor have pointed out, seeing tourism as a purely negative thing is no more nuanced than inverse celebrations of tourism as an unalloyed good (2003: 3). Certainly neither stance can provide a poet with an innovative or arresting theme: quite to the contrary, both would seem to take for granted a conception of what Lefebvre calls 'the thing itself', existing somehow outside of historical contingency and discourse, which is at best an impossible goal and at worst a credulous construction.

This chapter will look at a selection of poems written by Derek Mahon, Sinéad Morrissey, Mary O'Donnell, and Seamus Heaney, to scrutinise what happens when the poetic muse meets the touristic ruse. The focus will be exclusively on poems dealing with tourist visits to Ireland: as a result, the poets' critical focus on projections of Irish identity will be a key theme. This focus should, in theory, open for an emphasis on the needs, dreams, and identity of visitors to the Emerald Isle: how do Irish poets respond to tourists as individuals in their own right? In the poems discussed, however, there seems to be little interest in the personal stories and character traits of these travellers, and the ethical dimension of these encounters is not easily grasped. At most, there is an interest in national clichés that can mirror the clichés concerning Irish identity pandered by the tourist industry. On the other hand, more than one of these poets seems to suggest that there can be something of a true encounter between native and visitor: if the tourist is no mere stooge for the values and dreams of modern capitalism, it might just be possible to pursue deeper forms of questioning. In any case, it becomes evident that what is at stake in this poetry is neither a factual description of actual tourists nor a championing of their cause, but a self-reflexive exploration of the ideology of Irishness once it is exposed to a cross-cultural space of questioning and encounter.

The tourist may be seen as a representative of modern capitalism and the commodification of contemporary culture. Insofar as the tourist is subject to such overwhelming forces, though, he or she is reduced to a mere cipher: a faceless signifier without any identity necessary to dwell upon. Julia Kristeva's claim that 'the foreigner has no self' is especially true of the tourist (1991: 8). Although the stereotype tells us that tourists are so caught up in prejudices tied to their country of origin that they cannot delve beyond the surface of the sites they visit, the inverse is also true: no one has any interest in the personality of the tourist. Such a reduction of tourist identity is especially pointed in Derek Mahon's 1997 volume of poetry, *The Yellow Book*. Consisting of twenty numbered poems and a prologue (headed 'Context: Baudelaire' in parentheses), the book launches a swingeing attack on the perceived decadence of the Celtic Tiger. Although some scholars distinguish between an initial, more sustainable phase of the Celtic Tiger, lasting up to about 2002, and a second boom that was speculative and out of control (see Böss, 2011), *The Yellow Book* represents a wholesale critique of the way the Irish lived and did business already in the mid-1990s. The perceived decadence of the period is at times simplistically contrasted to visions of Ireland in the 1950s and other periods representative of 'the days before tourism and economic growth' (Mahon, 1999: 230),[2] but a more complex and productive parallel is established through repeated conjurings of the artistic milieu of the 1890s *fin de siècle*. Mahon's approach to the movement is centred upon its Irish, English, and French representatives, as he focuses on its bases in London and Paris. The Decadents' ambiguous position as both a symptom and a critique of modern society provides Mahon's verse with some nuance and ambivalence. An 1890s journal provides him with the title of *The Yellow Book*. The period marking the heyday of Oscar Wilde and the consolidation of the poetry of the early W.B. Yeats also vouchsafes him a contrast between art and society, or elitist aestheticism and the values of the bourgeoisie.

The tourist enters at a particularly crucial stage of the book, providing a contrast to Mahon's own artistic seclusion in the first of the numbered poems, 'Night Thoughts'. Against the commodification of central Dublin – now 'a Georgian theme-park for the tourist' (Mahon, 1999: 224) – Mahon holds his own memory and sense of artistic vocation up as almost heroic counterpoints. If Mahon is a poet 'haunted by the possibility of belonging' (Brown, 2003: 138), any semblance of belonging can here only come about in the midst of a feeling of extreme alienation and resistance. The depths of his aesthetic meditation become accessible through a haughty negation of the daytime trivia surrounding his capital lodgings: 'Night thoughts are best, the ones that visit us / where we lie smoking between three and four / before the first bird and the first tour bus' (Mahon, 1999: 224). If the raw material for art is to be enabled to 'visit', then the latter visitors must be decisively embargoed by the resilience of the poet. And, as it happens, Mahon's solitary poet never encounters the tourist crowds face-to-face. The closest one comes to such a meeting is through an experiential ellipsis included in the same opening poem:

> Soon crocus, daffodil, air-brake and diesel-chug,
> those rain-washed April mornings when the fog
> lifts and immediate 'coaches' throng the square,
> even in the bathroom I hear them shouting out there –
> aliens, space invaders clicking at the front door,
> goofy in baseball caps and nylon leisurewear.

(224–5)

Here the ironic scare-quotes provide a winking reminder that modern 'coaches' are a far cry from the 'horse-drawn cab out of the past' previously evoked by the poet's nostalgic imagination (224). Tellingly, there is no face-to-face encounter of the kind emphasised in the thought of Emmanuel Levinas (1999: 89–93): nothing, in this episode in Mahon's poem, can confront the speaker with an ethical dilemma or the singular humanity of the visitors. An auditory impression is sufficient, though, for the speaker to create an imaginary cliché. The tourists' presumed, phantasmal attire elicits the poet's derision, and their shouts contrast with the stillness of his own muse. The 'baseball caps' may signal that the visitors are North American (Haughton, 2007: 277). This would interestingly implicate Mahon himself, since the book signals his return to Ireland after a lengthy stay in the US as (in the words of his preceding, book-length poem *The Hudson Letter*) 'an undesirable resident alien' (Mahon, 1999: 190). Certainly, there is an anxiety throughout the poem, including some less-than-subtle hints that Mahon may be unable to transcend the very phenomena he vilifies: 'Geared up in Klein and Nike, Banana Republic, Gap, / we are all tourists now and there is no escape' (254). We are not too far removed from the kind of self-reflexive realisation of one's own uprootedness that Julia Kristeva prescribes as an antidote to xenophobia: 'By recognizing *our* uncanny strangeness we shall neither suffer from it nor enjoy it from the outside. The foreigner is within me, hence we are all foreigners' (original emphasis; 1991: 192). But whereas she identifies a psychological insight into our fundamental alienation from our unconsciousness as the lever that will bring about a welcoming receptiveness to the foreigner, *The Yellow Book* is instead preoccupied with what is conceived of as a profound, but not irrevocable, form of cultural and economic alienation. Like an erring ascetic, the Mahonian self is tainted but redeemable.

Whether or not the tourists are North American, the poet is keen to deny them any nativeness of their own: being 'aliens' they are effectively robbed of any home. Mahon's muse is anxious to turn its back on that which is not of his own native earth. The visitors from afar desecrate what is a holy space for the poet: a town inhabited by history and the remnants of Ireland's great literary past. The poem embraces what Doreen Massey has termed 'the imagination of defensible places, of the rights of "local people" to their own "local places", of a world divided by difference and the smack of firm boundaries, a geographical imagination of nationalisms' (2005: 86). Local space is here understood as a negation of global space, even if Mahon's fascination for links between French, English, and Irish literatures of the past militates somewhat against the more rigid implications of this rhetoric. There is no opening for any such thing as a cross-cultural space, unless it is conceived of as a global infraction upon the integrity of the local. Perhaps the reference to 'space invaders' has another dimension, too. In the original version of the poem, Mahon links the invasion of tourists to Britain's colonial possession of Ulster: 'Do we give up fighting so the tourists come / or fight the harder so they stay at home?' (Mahon, 1997: 27). What seems to be hinted is an underlying identification of tourists with the more immediately oppressive spectacle of weapon-carrying forces from abroad. Is there a reflex of past fears at work here, a preconscious or tacit assimilation of unwelcome, modern visitors to historical narratives of oppression and foreign dominance?

In Sinéad Morrissey's 'Tourism', included in her second volume *Between Here and There* (2002), the link between tourism and the conclusion of the Troubles in Northern Ireland is brought even closer to the fore. One of the more predictable benefits of the Peace Process in the North has been the increased attractiveness of the region as a holiday venue. Morrissey takes a characteristically skewed glance on this change, building upon the kind of view from the outside her extended travels abroad have made possible: the preceding poem in the collection, 'In Belfast', describes someone who has 'returned after ten years' and now feels, rather ambiguously, 'as much at home here as I will ever be' (Morrissey, 2002: 13). 'Tourism' takes a somewhat different approach: the poem depicts a local population desperate for foreign input. The vulnerable position of that population can be measured by their 'fearing summary' (14). Whereas Peter McDonald's 'Road to Rome' spoke out against the reductiveness of the tourist industry's 'too zealous overview' (2004: 39), here there is instead apprehensiveness about how the same industry might lay bare the fragile position of the locals. With humorous exaggeration, the tourists are portrayed as bringers of blessings from afar rather than the agents of desacralisation lamented by Mahon: 'They bring us deliverance, restitution' (Morrissey, 2002: 14). At the end of the poem, the call for them to 'Stay' is in part a tongue-in-cheek allusion to the departure of the gods in traditional faiths, but also an underlining of the tentative nature of the gains of the Peace Process. Morrissey has described the occasion of the poem as being 'the dissolution of the new Northern Ireland Assembly over the stalled issue of IRA decommissioning. I was furious that this had been allowed to take place, and saw it as a threat to the stability of the peace process' (Grima, 2003). The poem transcends these circumstances through its fascination with the strange, almost surreal conversion of Troubles history into tourist commodity:

> We take them to those streets
> they want to see most, at first,
>
> as though it's all over and safe behind bus glass
> like a staked African wasp. Unabashedly, this is our splintered city,
> and this, the corrugated line between doorstep and headstone.
> (Morrissey, 2002: 14)

There is a sense, here, of how the transformations of history present ready-made material for the poetic imagination: the tension between past and future, co-existing in one fraught but passing present, is equal to that between tenor and vehicle in any daring, poetically construed metaphor. A parallel to this over-laying of different temporal moments is also present in the lone image of the tourists in the poem: 'the Spanish and the Dutch are landing in airports / and filing out of ships. Our day has come'. In the distant past, military forces from Spain and Holland battled on Irish soil in crucial historical turning points such as the Nine Years' War and the Battle of the Boyne. Here Morrissey's enjambed line brings a subtle reminder of that past, smuggling in traditional transport by sea in the slipstream of modern air travel. As a result, a kind of palimpsest is created, where images of past and present visitors are overlaid. 'Tourism' does not mention the English, perhaps because the poem actually seems to imply that Northern Ireland more needs to be saved from itself than from any imperial power from across the Channel. In any case, the concluding stanza's evocation of a 'European superstate' and the bathetic image of the xylophone as a national symbol suffice to alert the reader to an element of irony, suggesting that also the new arrivals may bring with them mixed blessings.

Morrissey's poem registers some uneasiness about the natives' attempts to project an accessible and inviting image of themselves. To a certain degree, this uneasiness issues out of the specific location at stake. What is the true urban space of Northern Ireland? Since the tourist industry tends to highlight rural landscapes, part of the fun of the poem stems from the obvious awkwardness of any attempt to construct a convincingly authentic tourist venue out of contemporary Belfast. Tables and chairs are arranged outside cafés, even if the Belfast weather is not conducive to the kind of out-of-doors activities indulged in by visitors to more southern metropoles. Caffe latté also makes an appearance, as a global commodity enjoyed by tourists everywhere, but hardly representative for any innately Irish identity. The same beverage makes a similar appearance at the beginning of Mary O'Donnell's 'Les Français Sont Arrivés, Die Deutschen Auch': there, tourists are served 'lattes / and espressos our forebears sipped / before the hay was in' (O'Donnell, 2009: 28). The obvious lack of any real link between this icon of contemporary consumer culture and the Irish past is however quickly affirmed, as the early catalogue of tourist impressions are dismissed as 'visions of the way we never were' (*ibid.*). Like Morrissey's poem, O'Donnell's is primarily interested in the effect tourism has on local identity, as well as the tensions of a particularly fraught historical moment. Both consistently address a local 'we' and deploy injunctions to suggest a possible way of circumventing an anxious state of disarray. But there are also important differences: whereas 'Tourism' portrayed Belfast natives as being badly in need of some form of transcendence and transformation, 'Les Français Sont Arrivés, Die Deutschen Auch' portrays Irish hosts as being potentially exposed to a more active process of self-questioning. The tourist forces a self-reflective moment of recoil on the Irish 'we' of O'Donnell's poem. This is partly a result of the different historical narratives of Northern Ireland and the Republic of Ireland where the North's tourist narratives have been thrown into a fresh, if disconcerting, shape by the rapid historicisation of the Troubles; the collective representations of the Republic have long since arrived at more well-established patterns. O'Donnell's poem reacts by querying familiar stereotypes, opting instead to unearth more uncomfortable images of Irish identity and place. There is a parallel to Eavan Boland's poem 'Imago', though the latter's dismissal of nationalist imagery – 'Old Tara brooch. / And bog oak. / A harp and a wolfhound on an ashtray' – is more self-consciously preoccupied with the postcolonial heritage of Irish subjection to Britain (Boland, 2005: 249). The speaker of O'Donnell's poem is poised between resuscitating the past and banishing it to the dust-heap of the past. She tells her interlocutor to forget and leave behind the past even as she brings it to attention. For the falsifications of the tourist industry are, it is implied, much to be preferred to the harrowing truths and experiences left behind: 'just thank the times, / forget the memory of mists and mires' (O'Donnell, 2009: 29).

Even if O'Donnell's poem may appear to exist in a completely different context than the tourist poems of Mahon and Morrissey, it too is marked by the Northern Irish Troubles – albeit in a more subtle way. This influence is alluded to at the conclusion of its fourth and penultimate stanza. There, a discourse of evasive nullity comes to the fore: the experience of tourism is portrayed as a 'long note', served up to 'life-smudged innocents', that is 'cast out as if to say / whatever you sing, sing nothing' (O'Donnell, 2009: 29). Seamus Heaney's 'Whatever You Say Say Nothing' depicted the impotence of both journalistic and everyday responses to the conflict in Northern Ireland, indicting a dislocation of language and feeling from the harrowing reality to which they were unable to face up. The poem – published in *North* at the height of the Troubles – casts a cold and uncomforting eye on a state of paralysis: 'Competence with pain, / Coherent miseries, a bit and sup: / We hug our little destiny again' (Heaney, 1975: 55). In O'Donnell's poem the stakes are not quite as high, but the basic lack of empowerment and agency is the same: lost among the fragmentary delusions of a constructed, tourist image of themselves, her Irish are both unable and unwilling to face the darker realities lying below the surface.

O'Donnell's poem depicts the trap of an ideologically constructed Irishness that is as mythological as the national identity Roland Barthes exposed at work in a 1960s spaghetti advertisement: '*Italianicity* is not Italy, it is the condensed essence of everything that could be Italian, from spaghetti to painting' (Barthes, 1977: 48). Irishness, according to this view, is not Ireland, and O'Donnell's poem suggests that there is reason to embrace the simulacrum rather than to push on towards any purported deeper reality. In this respect, the psychoanalytical tendency to speak of the Imaginary rather than ideology is apt, whatever one might think of its political implications: psychoanalysis captures how a narcissistic immersion in images can be a tempting preventive measure, in order to exclude the fearful Real.[3] In O'Donnell's poem, there is no escape from the realm of illusion that is the collective Imaginary: the travellers from afar do not present a viable alternative to the falsifications of Irish identity. Instead, O'Donnell subjects also the French and German visitors mentioned in the title of the poem to the rule of cliché: 'Fish-loving français gobble / all the salmon, the Germans / cannot walk enough beneath / cloud-sailed skies' (O'Donnell, 2009: 28). The foreign nationals are here denied the kind of individual subjectivity and agency that is to be found in poems, included in the same volume, which deal with holiday experiences abroad, such as 'Considering Puccini's Women' (which addresses a visit to Puccini's home in Torre del Lago) and 'The Sisters of Viareggio' (20, 24). Any suspicion that the voracious appetite of the French visitors is about to present any sinister threat is dispelled by the more innocent reference to the manic hiking habits of the Teutonic travellers: unlike the tourists evoked by Mahon and Morrissey, these southern guests exist in a trivial space untainted by recent trauma. As such, they are also more easily redeemed. In the preceding poem of her collection *The Ark Builders*, O'Donnell is therefore able to present a more generous and descriptive study of a tourist. Interestingly, 'Explorer' starts off by describing the single visitor encountered in the poem as 'Forensic as a palaeontologist' (27). While Michael Cronin has argued that Irish travellers abroad seek to transcend the label of 'tourists' by aspiring to be writers (2003: 179), the more elevated status is here associated with science rather than literature. O'Donnell's explorer is, however, neither a distanced viewer nor restricted to external facts: he 'peers patiently into our hearts'. Although his is an expressly secular view, it nonetheless infringes upon the sacred, as he

> Loves our language
> as much as the bog. His gaze, his ear,
> bless the black crumble of both,

though the people keep faith with neither.
(O'Donnell, 2009: 27)

This is tourism taken to a higher level, reminding the local population of the virtues of their own lives that they are prone to forget. If 'Les Français Sont Arrivés, Die Deutschen Auch' shows tourism's ability to provoke both self-questioning and complacency, this poem shows a higher type of traveller – a version of the 'anti-touristic' traveller evoked by Buzard – that keeps burrowing away at the deeper challenges of life. The traveller is transformed into an existential hero, questioning the very nature of habitation: as the end of the poem puts it, he is 'here, among us, still seeking home' (*ibid.*). The echo of Morrissey's 'In Belfast' is significant: both poets seek to bring about a self-reflective return upon the self, whereby the simple dichotomy of home v. away (or native v. tourist) is challenged. This does not mean, however, that the tourist attains individual status in O'Donnell's poem, which remains happy to dwell upon stereotype, even if it is a challenging stereotype: 'His archetypal face you recognise – large-nosed, / unfreckled, deep-eyed – pushing on, at ease / with his search' (*ibid.*).

The explorer can be said to make Ireland strange to the native glance. In this respect, he is not unlike the ideal host portrayed in Seamus Heaney's celebrated poem 'Making Strange' (Heaney, 1984: 32–3). Heaney's speaker is placed between a visitor with a 'travelled intelligence' and a native Irish man who is 'unshorn and bewildered / in the tubs of his wellingtons'. This is effectively a symptom of the 'collision culture' of modern Ireland, which Keohane and Kuhling have described as being torn between 'old and new, global and local, the principles of traditional community and modern society' (2004: 4). The ensuing relationship between these tendencies in Heaney's poem is not without its tensions, both of a tacit and a more obvious kind. The hospitable speaker wishes to mediate between visitor and native, and portrays his own discovery of a common ground between them as the result of a sudden inspiration: 'a cunning middle voice / came out of the field across the road' (32). This voice conveys both a linguistic competence and a deep familiarity with the land. Contrary to the image conveyed by 'Les Français Sont Arrivés, Die Deutschen Auch', this time the encounter with the land is not hindered by discourse, but facilitated by it: language opens up to the Otherness of the natural landscape. It is precisely by being placed in the disorienting prism of the cross-cultural negotiation of discourses, that space is made accessible. Language does not merely copy; it reveals. Thus 'all that I knew' is allowed to 'make strange / at that same recitation', at the end of the poem, by the speaker's inspired disclosure of the surrounding landscape (Heaney, 1984: 33). By that stage the speaker has long since replaced the local man clad in wellingtons. After the beginning of the poem, we do not hear any more of the latter figure. This can be interpreted as showing a tacit scepticism concerning a too simplistic privileging of the local and native, in line with the 'decentring of place' Eugene O'Brien has identified in Heaney's work (O'Brien, 2003: 123). The linguistic utterance decontextualises the place from its original understanding, 'reciting' it in new verbal surroundings. This is also a 're-siting': a rediscovery of a locality that has become all too familiar and subject to a stereotypical understanding.

In rather mischievous fashion, Heaney's poem thus suggests that the ideal tour guide operates in a manner not unlike that of an inspired poet. Certainly the aesthetics conveyed in 'Making Strange' concur with the poetic ideals found elsewhere in Heaney's works. Oona Frawley has noted that Heaney is 'aligned with the Irish pastoral tradition', and when she claims that his 'international appeal and marketability suggests not only the strength of his poetic, but also the coincidence between his work and defined ideals of Ireland as a rural space' she is alluding to a potential problem (Frawley, 2005: 138). Is it not worrying that Heaney's conception of landscape, and its communicability, can so seamlessly be appropriated to the commercial interests of the tourist industry? After all, readers who first came across 'Making Strange' in the *Selected Poems, 1966–1987* edition, would be reading it in a book whose cover was provided by the Irish Tourist Office. The pastoral nostalgia of Heaney and much other Irish poetry is aligned with 'the retreat from modernity that is the objective of many tourist encounters' (Kuhling and Keohane, 2007: 81). This is the inverse risk accompanying the ethical commitment of 'Making Strange': this poem seems to take the tourist seriously as an individual in his own right, in a way which is not evident in the other poets discussed here. Privileging the encounter with an Other, Heaney's poem allows the tourist's desire for experience its own legitimacy. This involves, however, a bracketing out or forgetting of the entire framework that threatens to commodify and devalue the encounter between the tourist and the visited space.

The readings made in this chapter have striven to uncover the mechanics and presuppositions of the encounter with the tourist, as enacted in a group of recent Irish poems. There has been no desire to look at tourism in itself: instead, there has been an attempt to explore some of the consequences of the fact that 'tourism is a prism through which we can see other social, cultural and political scenarios being played out' (Cronin and O'Connor, 2003: 1). A key concern of the poems discussed has been to contest imaginary constructions of Irishness, which are the staple of the tourist industry. As a result of this interest in national identity, the identity of the visitors from abroad is also conceived of in ways that either confirm or displace national stereotypes about French, German, Dutch, Spanish or American visitors. Interestingly, there are no Asian tourists – or other non-western visitors – in sight in these poems, and as a result ethnicity is not a concern. The concluding reading of Heaney proved a rare attempt to prioritise the ethical dimension of the encounter with the visitor from afar. Even if Heaney's poem does not dwell on the personal circumstances of his visitor – we need to delve into the accompanying secondary literature to unearth the fact that the poem was spurred by a visit by the Jamaican-born poet Louis Simpson (Parker, 1993: 189; O'Driscoll, 2008: 113–14) – a spirit of generosity and responsibility is given primacy. Perhaps this ethical dimension would have been harder to uphold, were the poem to deal with a bus-load of strangers rather than one intimate visitor from afar. Where the latter often elicits a sense of hauteur inherited from tourism's class-related origins in the eighteenth century, a personal connection with a single visitor (or small group of visitors) is more inducive of an attitude of hospitality. Nevertheless, the singularity of Heaney's contribution is undeniable and exists, moreover, in strong opposition to the imaginary association – evident (to different degrees) in Mahon, Morrissey, and O'Donnell – of tourists with invading forces from foreign countries. If one is to welcome the foreigner, one cannot conceive him or her as a potential oppressor. But there are several alternatives to the ministry of fear. If Morrissey's poem perhaps has just a whiff of this fear, it also features an abject sense of dependency upon the visitors from afar. It is hard to read her poem as not involving some irony, implying that the EU and the influx of foreign travellers should not be read as a panacea for local paralysis. This kind of scepticism, expanded into a rather remorseless and predictable reduction of tourism in Mahon, is the flipside of Heaney's gesture of welcome. Insofar as tourism pitches us between critical analysis and an unflinching ethical receptiveness, the choice cannot be a simple one.

Notes

1 The current Fine Gael government has redubbed it the Department of Arts, Heritage, and the Gaeltacht.
2 Unless otherwise is specified, all references to Derek Mahon's poetry in this chapter make use of his 1999 edition of *The Collected Poems*.
3 On the Real and Imaginary orders in psychonalaysis, see Sarup (1992: 101–19).

References

Barthes, Roland (1977). *Image, Music, Text*, trans. Stephen Heath. London: Fontana.
Boland, Eavan (2005). *New Collected Poems*. Manchester: Carcanet.
Böss, Michael (2011). 'The collapse of the "Celtic Tiger" narrative', *Nordic Irish Studies* 10: 119–35.
Brown, Terence (2003). 'Mahon and Longley: Place and placelessness', in Mathew Campbell (ed.), *The Cambridge Companion to Contemporary Irish Poetry*. Cambridge: Cambridge University Press, 133–48.

Buzard, James (2002). 'The grand tour and after (1660–1840)', in Peter Hulme and Tim Youngs (eds), *The Cambridge Companion to Travel Writing*. Cambridge: Cambridge University Press, 37–52.

Carson, Ciaran (1998). *The Twelfth of Never*. Oldcastle: Gallery.

Cronin, Michael (2003). 'Next to being there: Ireland of the welcomes and tourism of the word', in Michael Cronin and Barbara O'Connor (eds), *Irish Tourism: Image, Culture and Identity*. Bristol: Channel View, 179–95.

Cronin, Michael and Barbara O'Connor (eds) (2003). 'Introduction', *Irish Tourism: Image, Culture and Identity*. Bristol: Channel View Publications, 1–18.

Frawley, Oona (2005). *Irish Pastoral: Nostalgia and Twentieth-Century Irish Literature*. Dublin and Portland: Irish Academic Press.

Grima, Adrian (2003). 'Dislocation and words', *Sunday Times*, 23 November. www.inizjamed. org/sinead_morrissey_in_malta.htm#Sinead%20Morrissey%20in%20Malta. Accessed on 23 January 2012.

Haughton, Hugh (2007). *The Poetry of Derek Mahon*. Oxford: Oxford University Press.

Heaney, Seamus (1975). *North*. London: Faber & Faber.

—— (1984). *Station Island*. London: Faber & Faber.

Keohane, Kieran and Carmen Kuhling (2004). *Collision Culture: Transformations in Everyday Life in Ireland*. Dublin: The Liffey Press.

Kristeva, Julia (1991). *Strangers to Ourselves*, trans. Leon S. Roudiez. New York: Columbia University Press.

Kuhling, Carmen and Kieran Keohane (2007). *Cosmopolitan Ireland: Globalisation and Quality of Life*. London, Dublin and Ann Arbor: Pluto.

Lefebvre, Henri (2000). *Everyday Life in the Modern World*, trans. Sacha Rabinovitch. London and New York: Continuum.

Levinas, Emmanuel (1999). *Otherwise than Being: Or, Beyond Essence*, trans. Alphonso Lingis. Pittsburgh: Duquesne University Press.

McDonald, Peter (2004). *Pastorals*. Manchester: Carcanet.

Mahon, Derek (1997). *The Yellow Book*. Oldcastle: The Gallery Press.

—— (1999). *Collected Poems*. Oldcastle: The Gallery Press.

Massey, Doreen (2005). *For Space*. London: Sage.

Morrissey, Sinéad (2002). *Between Here and There*. Manchester: Carcanet.

O'Brien, Eugene (2003). *Searches for Answers*. London, Dublin and Sterling: Pluto.

O'Donnell, Mary (2009). *The Ark Builders*. Todmorden: Arc.

O'Driscoll, Dennis (2008). *Stepping Stones: Interviews with Seamus Heaney*. London: Faber & Faber.

Parker, Michael (1993). *Seamus Heaney: The Makings of the Poet*. Basingstoke: Macmillan.

Sarup, Madan (1992). *Jacques Lacan*. New York: Harvester Wheatsheaf.

PART IV

Gender and the city

15

Towards a multiracial Ireland: *Black Baby*'s revision of Irish motherhood

Maureen T. Reddy

In the late 1980s, when Clare Boylan wrote *Black Baby*, few Irish thinkers were writing about race or about the role of race in Irishness and therefore in ideas of womanhood (and motherhood) in Ireland. Race remained transparent in prevailing definitions of Irishness until open expressions of racism pushed it into visibility in conjunction with the first wave of African immigration in the 1990s. Public debates on the 2004 Citizenship Referendum, disturbing as they often were, had the salubrious effect of making clear that one crucial task of Irish writers and cultural theorists in the twenty-first century is to rethink Irishness in a multiracial and multicultural context. Boylan's specifically feminist engagement with and revisions of dominant constructions of race and motherhood in *Black Baby* offers an especially useful roadmap for that necessary work. Boylan's novel makes a case not for multiculturalism or interculturalism per se, but instead for a thoroughgoing reassessment of Irishness and womanhood themselves, separately and together, positing antiracism as the requisite foundation for that reassessment.

The conceptual framework for an antiracist Irish feminism that *Black Baby* sketches centralises Irishwomen's not only double, but multiple, colonisation and the need for strategies to understand those interlocked systems of oppression. At the centre of this framework are the fraught issues of motherhood, as both experience and institution, and racialisation. Motherhood has certainly been deployed to control women in Ireland, as elsewhere. Writing in 1994, Gerardine Meaney notes the established argument that 'women only exist as a function of their maternity in the dominant ideology of Southern Ireland', with the mother positioned in Irish culture as 'an all-powerful, dehumanized figure' (Meaney, 1994: 230–1). Siobhan Kilfeather, in 'Irish Feminism', traces the modern history of the valorisation of motherhood above all other possible roles for women back to the early twentieth century, when 'leaders of the Catholic Church in Ireland repeatedly entwined discourses of racial purity, national pride and patriarchal authority' (Kilfeather, 2005: 106). That influenced in turn the 1937 Constitution's emphasis on women's roles within marriage and the family, with several articles designed ostensibly to protect mothers, such as those keeping them out of the workforce (107).

Reimagining motherhood is the central personal project for both of the main characters in *Black Baby*; neither is a biological mother but both are ensnared by the cultural conflation of woman and mother and both also suffer from lack of mothering in the sense of love and care. In having Alice think through her life as she lies in a coma during the second part of the novel and imagine it outside the discourses – of church, capitalism, patriarchy, race – that have previously defined it, Boylan suggests a possible trajectory for Irish feminist thought. Central to the progress and promise of this thought is reconceptualising race and including race seriously in any attempt to undo the colonisation of Irishwomen. That is, Boylan implies here that the oppression of race is not a parallel to the oppression of Irishwomen by gender, but a constitutive component of it. In its recognition of that constitutive role of race in twentieth-century ideas of Irishness, *Black Baby* thereby also offers a vision for the foundational requirements of a truly multiracial Ireland in the twenty-first century.

Cora/Dinah's[1] arrival at Alice's door early in the novel begins a complex fictional exploration of female sexuality, interracial sexual desire, the role of race in Irishness, maternal subjectivity (v. the objectifying construct of the Irish mammy), positionality (especially deconstruction of a One/Other racial binary), white fantasies of blackness, religion v. spirituality, nuclear/postmodern family configurations, and dozens of other intriguing possibilities, all refracted through a feminist lens. The reader's early suspicion that we are not in the world of realistic fiction gets both confirmed and undermined numerous times in the novel but most directly at the end, when the narrative makes clear that more than half of the book has taken place in Alice's head as she lies dying in hospital ('undermined' because of course what is in one's head is as 'real' as events in the world). That conclusion seems to me to underscore Boylan's insistence throughout the novel on the potential richness and power of the usually ignored subjectivity of a completely ordinary – and therefore culturally silenced and invisible – older woman who has 'neither chick nor child', in Alice's repeated formula (Boylan, 1989: 13).

Despite pre-dating the Celtic Tiger boom and the associated waves of migration to Ireland, *Black Baby* depicts the interaction of Irish host(s) and foreign guest(s) that became a focus of some Irish fiction and drama in the 1990s and 2000s. It begins, however, not in Ireland but in an unnamed African country in an unspecified past, where an Irish missionary nun is in the position of foreign guest, preaching to local women. The nun, like other missionaries, does not behave like a guest but like a coloniser, in this case 'here to save their souls for Jesus' (Boylan, 1989: 1); without Jesus, she tells the gathered women, they are 'savages'. Savagery is gender-specific and has a different valence for the nun, who takes for granted its undesirability, than for the women, who perceive it as an achievement, not a natural condition: 'The men must fight and kill to be savage. The boys suffer pain and trial; but women are savage only because they do not save their souls for gentle Jesus, meek and mild' (1–2). This description of the gender binary – men do, women be – is a European, patriarchal one. The nun shows round a picture of a white woman and girl and tells the assembled women that those in the photo are 'White ladies': 'when you are saved you will be like them', she says, neatly equating Christianity with whiteness (2). The rest of the novel plays with the terms of the opening chapter, as Cora/Dinah arrives in Ireland as a missionary from the world of feeling and warmth, saving Dubliners in general from their own lack of 'facility for intimacy' (153) and Alice in particular from her lifelong project of forgetting.

The opening chapter, which is hilarious in its deft juxtaposition of the Irish nun's assertions and the African women's interpretations of her 'Jesus juju', not only establishes the key terms for the rest of the novel, but also inaugurates the problems of point of view and mode that *Black Baby* foregrounds. Whose story is this? Are we meant to read it as realistic? The chapter makes most sense if we read it as a fantasy created by Cora/Dinah at the novel's end, interweaving her imagined version of her mother's childhood and Alice's story of the picture she sent to the black baby she 'bought' with her First Communion money. Alice assumes Cora/Dinah is African from their first meeting, but in fact she is from Brixton, the daughter of an African mother now long dead and a white British father who abandoned them both when Cora/Dinah was small. We first hear that Cora/Dinah's mother was African in a chapter that begins with Cora/Dinah talking her way into a Dublin B&B called 'Chez Nous'. The landlady at first tells her 'no coloureds', but Cora/Dinah offers to pay in advance and is allowed in to 'our house', a bleak and cold place, 'bare of human history' (Boylan, 1989: 23). In her room, Cora/Dinah thinks of nuns, who are not quite human to her, but 'like the talking animals of children's stories, awkward and powerful, wise, poetic, prejudiced' and then thinks of her mother as a little girl, who was surely 'not quite a person' to the nuns because 'people were white' (24). Significantly, the nuns are other-than-human to Cora/Dinah because they do not fit into normative, heterosexual, and nuclear familial categories. Cora/Dinah herself begins to break free of these restrictive categories while in Ireland, defining herself outside of the equally restrictive ideologies of race and gender that bind the nuns and that entrapped her mother.

Virginia Woolf's metaphoric claim about writers that 'we think back through our mothers if we are women' is literalised in this novel (Woolf, 1991: 76). Boylan's Alice, who is sixty-seven as *Black Baby* opens in about 1987, is roughly coeval with the modern Irish State and, we learn, was raised by a mother who fully internalised the entwined discourses of race, nation, and gender described by Kilfeather. Alice's mother continues to control her daughter decades after her death, with that enduring control demonstrating the power of the maternal role as constituted patriarchally. Interestingly, the first facts we learn about Cora (which she first says is her name, but then accepts and indeed prefers 'Dinah', Alice's name for her) are that she is a 'foreigner' in Dublin, 'unmistakably so', as the narrator says, and is 'starting off again [at age thirty-five or so], shedding the history her mother had bequeathed to her' (Boylan, 1989: 8). That maternal history is a history of colonisation and oppression, shaped in part by Irish missionary nuns. As several social analysts have noted, the Irish missionary tradition contributes to contemporary Irish racism (see, for example, Gretchen Fitzgerald, 1992), a genealogy of thought and often-unconscious attitudes this novel stresses. Most pertinent to understanding what Boylan is doing in this novel is *how* Cora/Dinah sheds that history, which is through constructing an alternate story for herself that incorporates her own reimagining and retelling of her mother's story. In other words, Cora/Dinah narrates her way out of the trap of her mother's history by thinking back through her mother while imaginatively altering the known facts of her mother's life. In so doing, she finds a way to forgive her mother for her shortcomings while providing for herself the mothering she needed but did not have, by freeing her mother in fantasy from the actual constraints of her life within a masculinist and racist paradigm.

Cora/Dinah's rewriting of her maternal history points us to the work that Alice must also do and that the novel implies all of Ireland must do if the future is not to replicate the past. Alice, we learn, has spent much of her adult life deliberately forgetting her own past, which she begins to recover through her relationship with Cora/Dinah. To dismantle oppressive structures, one must first see them clearly; to set oneself free from the constraints of an illegitimate authority (symbolised in this novel by Alice's patriarchal mother), one must first recognise its illegitimacy *and* its authority. Forgetting is unhelpful, the novel shows; what is helpful is remembering and re-narrating, analysing past events in order to assign them a more accurate meaning and then to incorporate them into a better, more liberatory story. This work is very close to what Ronit Lentin suggests is prerequisite to undoing Irish racism, which continues to operate within the official discourse of multiculturalism (2001). Lentin describes multiculturalism as 'the return of the national repressed. In the Irish case, my sense is that the national repressed is the pain of emigration, returning to haunt the Irish, through the presence of the immigrant "other"'. As Lentin concludes, '[t]he "other" threatens the newly regained national voice of contemporary Ireland not only because her/his habits, rituals and discourses interfere with the nation's enjoyment of itself. It also threatens this regained national voice because it reminds it of its not-too-distant past pain' (*ibid.*). What is needed, then, is 'intercultural interrogation' in which the past Irish trauma is recuperated and the foundational terms of Irishness interrogated in order to move towards true multiracialism and integration. In similar fashion, Cora/Dinah reminds Alice of the real losses in her past that deserve grieving; it takes Alice some time and some serious mistakes to begin to face those losses.

The day after Cora/Dinah's first appearance at her house, Alice does some research in the ancient copies of *National Geographic* stored in her attic: 'As she thumbed and discarded the aged periodicals she made the disturbing discovery that blacks were not safely contained in one scorching continent. They seemed to be everywhere' (Boylan, 1989: 27). Alice focuses on women: 'The women's breasts, suspended at all angles, told more than their faces did. You could tell, after careful study, which breasts had been sucked on by children. You could almost tell which had been touched, and which were no longer touched' (*ibid.*). Following her mother's precepts, still-virginal Alice has until this point in her life lived in near-total denial of not only her own body, but of any body and all bodies. The widespread somatophobia, especially in relation to female bodies, inculcated by patriarchal ideology and given the force of religious belief through cults of the Virgin Mary, reinforces denial of the embodied experience of motherhood. Alice initially recognises motherhood as a bodily experience by looking at the bodies of black women, displayed as anthropological curiosities, in a familiar pattern of projecting all bodily experience onto the racial Other. However, Alice does not complete the typical One/Other move, as looking at these maternal bodies does not reinforce her sense of difference from black women, but instead prompts a reconsideration of her own body in relation to other female bodies. The need for feminism to rethink continually the meaning(s) of female bodies and to insist on women's ownership of their own bodies gets a pointed reminder here. Alice subverts a masculinist, racist text – a magazine published by a US society founded by elite white men interested in global travel – by using it to begin setting herself free, in a microcosmic example of her growth in the novel. Alice's nascent identification with other women through their bodies is an extraordinary leap for her, as is her assumption of readerly authority. It seems to me significant that the knowledge Alice finds was available to her all along – those magazines in her attic – but she never before sought it or even was open to it. That openness, that new willingness to learn and to believe she can make her own judgements, results from her encounter with Cora/Dinah, who challenges Alice's limited ideas. We see here an example of intercultural interrogation, then, with Cora/Dinah prompting Alice to turn a critical lens on her own previously unquestioned, received beliefs about race and racial difference.

Cora/Dinah meanwhile is doing her own research, observing the denizens of a seedy pub – mainly 'two old men who watched her with hate over pints of stout' (Boylan, 1989: 38) – and thinking about Ireland. She is disappointed in how she has been received thus far in this 'favorite country of Jesus', as she puts it, and muses: 'No one had flung out the welcome mat, it was true, but that was a temporary state of affairs. Once they knew she was a baptized Christian and the protégée of a white lady, there would be smiles all round' (39). Cora/Dinah's naive view that religion will trump race in Ireland is quickly disproved, but she does find a better welcome from some Dubliners. In that same pub, immediately following a telephone conversation with Alice, Cora/Dinah experiences 'that most unlikely and delightful of occurrences, a friendly encounter with a stranger' (41). This stranger, Figgis, buys her a drink and teaches her to sing 'Kevin Barry', serving from their first meeting as Cora/Dinah's guide to the ways of the Irish. That 'Kevin Barry' is the first Irish song Cora/Dinah learns seems important, as the song romanticises republicanism, celebrates martyrdom, and includes a verse about Barry's 'broken-hearted mother / Whose grief no one can tell'; it is thus a highly economical encoding of precisely the overlapping discourses that both Alice and Cora/Dinah must struggle against. Figgis turns out to be 'adamant on the subject of mothers', insisting they are 'above reproach no matter what they do' (65). Figgis's own mother seems to have resembled Alice's in her role as an enforcer of social rules, as she made it clear to Figgis that he was a disappointment to her ('it is only human if they [mothers] sometimes reveal to us the dropped jaw' (64)) and he believes he 'drove [her] to an early grave, at the age of ninety-one' (65). One consequence of this mammy worship is that Figgis remains childlike, irresponsibly hanging about in pubs when he has a wife and children at home, and attempting to conduct a sexual affair with Cora/Dinah, thwarted only by drink-induced impotence. His view is that '[i]t is given to each man to have as many women as he can handle, but he only gets one mother' (*ibid.*). Cora/Dinah sees Irish men as 'nice' and 'child-like', 'thirsty and eagerly self-critical' (46). Dublin, she thinks, is 'full of churches and children and charming, romantic men who liked to laugh and drink' (*ibid.*). Missing from Cora/Dinah's perception of Dublin are women, an omission that serves to underscore Irishwomen's invisibility except in their prescribed role as mothers; even then they are not publicly visible as individuals but strictly as reified, dehumanised symbols.

In the parallel narratives of Alice and Cora/Dinah that constitute the first part of the novel, Alice begins rethinking her past – including quite a lot that she has up until now deliberately worked on forgetting – while Cora/Dinah tries to sort out her present, especially how she will survive economically in Dublin.

The relationship between these two women is rooted in two essentially fraud-ulent economic interchanges. Cora/Dinah planned to cheat or perhaps even directly rob Alice, having got her name and address from a con man who sold Alice a bad television set, but in the event, face to face with Alice, cannot bring herself to do it. Alice's interest in Cora/Dinah comes from the fantasy that she is the adult version of the black baby she 'bought' with her First Communion money. In one of the few chapters of the novel's second part not imagined by Alice in hospital, Cora/Dinah tells Figgis the truth of how she met Alice; when he asks why she did not go through with her plan to steal, she says she does not know but then adds: 'Something happened. She gave me tea and sherry. She thought an old record player was a coffin. Besides, we had a lot in common. Both of us had spent long years looking after our mothers' (Boylan, 1989: 156). The 'something' that happened was a moment of mutual human recognition outside the usual constraints of commodified relationships. Cora/Dinah's re-counting of that moment suggests that the colour line can only be crossed by acknowledging simultaneously both differences and similarities. Alice is slower than Cora/Dinah to see that their commonalities are rooted in their experiences as dispossessed daughters of mothers who could not offer the care the daughters needed, but required (demanded, even) care from the daughters for themselves. Alice instead thinks of Cora/Dinah as the daughter and herself as the mother.

When Cora/Dinah hears from Alice about the 'penny for the black baby' con-vention, she describes it as 'a bit of a swindle' and Alice begins to wonder if she is right (Boylan, 1989: 49). The black babies are supposed to remain far away as part of a 'spiritual' family, not turn up in the flesh expecting to be part of a real one. To many white Irish people, distant black people are acceptable; black people in Dublin are not. At the time of her First Communion, when she happi-ly gave all her money 'to purchase a savage soul' (50), Alice did not understand that the baby she named Dinah after paying out two and sixpence would not ac-tually be sent to live with her. The child Alice readied the little cradle her father had made for her and waited, but no African infant arrived. As a child, Alice did not perceive skin colour as signifying anything beyond itself. The only doll she owned was black; she named the doll Dinah and 'practiced her maternal skills on it'. At twelve, Alice 'wanted to use the same endearments, the same name on a doll whose fingers clutched, whose mouth laughed' (51). In the intervening five decades, however, Alice learned that skin colour does signify and thoroughly internalised that racist teaching. She acts on her understanding of the 'proper place' of blacks – in photographs in *National Geographic*, in other countries, but not in Ireland and certainly not on an equal footing with white Irish – by offering Cora/Dinah a disused maid's room as a bedroom. Cora/Dinah express-es her rejection of that placement/containment by leaving angrily. In order to have the relationship she craves with Cora/Dinah, Alice's necessary task is to unlearn the social significance of skin colour in a racist context. The hierarchy of race is imbricated with a hierarchy of relatedness in dominant ideology, as reflected in Alice's being 'brought up to believe that family came first' (5), a belief she also must unlearn. Alice instinctively resisted her mother's condemnation of strangers as 'dangerous' people who 'poked their noses into your business and then stabbed you in the back', but was always 'too timid' to stand up to her mother and express her own belief that 'strangers were the sugar of the earth, as those more familiar and more worthy were its salt' (34). The white/black and family/stranger binaries powerfully contribute to the reproduction of racism and of women's oppression by persistently reinscribing current social conditions as both norm and ideal. The distrust of strangers Alice's mother acts upon keeps Alice at home, caring for her parents, instead of leaving to strike out on her own or even with one of the two strangers who wanted to marry her.

Alice temporarily 'replaces' Cora/Dinah – whom she calls her daughter – by joining a Catholic group dedicated to reclaiming prostitutes from the streets. She gives money to the one prostitute she meets, Verity, and then feels guilty because she 'was supposed to have mentioned Christ's blood and the saving tide of the precious wounds. Instead she had handed over hard cash and sympathy' (Boylan, 1989: 73). Alice has also handed over her name and address, and wonders if she had 'been bribing Verity, in the hopes that she would someday come and see her' (*ibid.*). Verity gives the address to two boys who then break in to Alice's house to rob her, a connection Alice seems not to make. Like Cora/Dinah, Verity enters Alice's life through a desire for money, seeing Alice as a potential source of funds; unlike Cora/Dinah, Verity first accepts money from and then goes through with robbing Alice, so that their relationship is thoroughly commodified, part of a corrupt capitalist system. Alice's substitution of cash for religious proselytising in her approach to Verity, like 'pennies for a black baby', is a logical shift between the two closely bound together systems of capitalism and Catholicism, neither of which serves women's freedom. Alice's offer of sympathy could move Verity and herself toward a relation that might subvert these systems, but Verity is incapable of taking that imaginative leap into identification with another woman. The structural paralleling of Cora/Dinah and Verity emphasises their outsider status, their Otherness, with race and sexuality placed in homologous hierarchies. At the same time, the key distinction between them – their different decisions about Alice's subsidising them – points up the need to separate money from relationships if those relationships are ever to be authentic and caring. Alice has considerable trouble learning this lesson. Boylan repeatedly places the character in relationships vexed by money and although Alice never quite grasps the ways in which the norms of capitalism have stunted her experiences, the reader certainly cannot escape the centrality of money in Alice's self-limiting view of the world.

The masculinist bias that divides women from each other by seeing them as important only in their relation to men, and that contributes to relationships being commodified, plays out repeatedly in this novel. For instance, while in hospital recovering from the injuries she sustained during the robbery, Alice strikes up an acquaintance with her neighbour, the widowed (and childless) Mrs. Willoughby, who comes to visit her. Alice sees Mrs. Willoughby as a good-time girl whose husband thoughtfully bequeathed her a social life. Significantly, Mrs. Willoughby, who serves as Alice's more cheerful but also more desperate double, has fully embraced the demand that women exist only in relation to men; she believes whites are superior to blacks and sees others largely in relation to their ability to provide her with money. Like Cora/Dinah and Verity before her, Mrs. Willoughby judges Alice as a meal ticket – quite literally, as she persuades Alice to take a taxi from the hospital to an expensive French restaurant, where Mrs. Willoughby orders champagne, flirts with the waiter, and then drops dead.

Mrs. Willoughby is so committed to the sexist, racist status quo that she cannot be reclaimed; the death of this anti-model/double sets the second part of the book in motion. At Mrs. Willoughby's funeral, Alice at first imagines her own long-dead parents standing by the grave but quickly realises it is some other old couple; she also understands that the seemingly exotic widow's relatives are 'no more interesting than her own' (Boylan, 1989: 98). These twinned epiphanies contribute to Alice's feeling a 'mild pang' and then a 'burst of pure fury' that feels like 'a banging on her chest – like the fist of God' (*ibid.*). What sparks this fury is Alice's realisation that two of the mourners are wearing Mrs. Willoughby's clothes, with one woman dressed in one of the dead woman's suits and the other sporting her fox stole. Their appropriation of these garments before their owner is even buried may remind Alice of her own niece-in-laws' apparent attitude toward her as the future heirs of her house. Alice's fury not only releases her from her mother's patriarchal precepts but also brings on a stroke that leads to a coma. Obviously, then, it is not an unmixed good. Mrs. Willoughby's funeral, a precursor to and image of her own, is what sends Alice down the rabbit hole, so to speak, and into an alternate universe in which she can remember what she has spent decades trying to forget and can rethink the proper relation of women to the world. Alice never has an opportunity to live according to what she learns while comatose, a fact that calls into question how hopeful we are to be about the possibilities of freedom for women the novel sketches. Alice's coma is a liminal condition that connects this novel to other feminist *bildungs*, as Jeanette Roberts Shumaker notes, with Alice's 'carnivalesque fantasy' made plausible in order to emphasise 'the supremacy of imaginary experience compared to actual life' (Shumaker, 2006: 105).

This second part of the novel demonstrates the necessity of unlearning racism and all its imbricated ideologies (including nationalism and Catholicism) *before* one can reimagine womanhood outside patriarchal definitions. The figure of Cora/Dinah serves as Alice's principal guide; Cora/Dinah moves from being the reclaimed 'pagan baby' from what Alice thinks of as a 'savage' and 'heathen' place to being a prophet, acclaimed for her gospel of love. Reimagining herself as open and willing to learn from intercultural exchanges, Alice begins to accept Cora/Dinah's worldview that 'we live with ghosts and miracles; that in the natural world nothing is strange before God and nothing quite known to man' (Boylan, 1989: 161). 'Strapped up in religion all her life, she [Alice] had never believed in God' (*ibid.*) but she begins to believe now. She also remembers a second lover – she has previously thought about a Mr. Gosling, whom her mother drove off – who she did not even consider bringing home because he was black. Although even in this fantasy Alice briefly acts her mother's part in relation to Cora/Dinah, trying to control her and punishing her when she 'defies' this mother (and that defiance is all tied up with sexuality and ownership of the female body), she soon abandons that pose in favour of a more egalitarian relationship with her 'daughter'. In her fantasy, Alice gets a chance to re-mother herself through caring for Verity's abandoned baby; this baby is also a new saviour, brought to Alice's house on Christmas Eve. When Verity puts on Alice's mother's clothes, we see that Verity *is* the mother: harsh, judgemental, racist, and angry, accepting precisely the patriarchal precepts Alice's mother upheld although violating some of them in practice if not in philosophy. Verity's occupation as a prostitute is structurally identical to Alice's mother's position as wife, with both logical corollaries of patriarchal capitalism, as many feminist theorists of the 1970s and 1980s suggested in their analyses of compulsory heterosexuality (e.g. Adrienne Rich's 'Compulsory heterosexuality and lesbian existence' (Rich, 1980) and Alison Jaggar's *Feminist Politics and Human Nature*). Verity abandons her baby while Alice's mother stayed on the scene, but the institution of motherhood required that Alice's mother emotionally abandon Alice, as it requires that *all* mothers abandon their daughters in loyalty to patriarchy.

The life Alice lives in her head while in hospital is warm, loving, full of caring people and kindness. It is the opposite of Cora/Dinah's view of the Irish. As she tells Figgis in one of the few later chapters not in Alice's head, '[t]he people of this country are full of kindness, but always to strangers. When a relationship is required – landlady, mother, husband, wife – complications and hostilities arise. They do not have the facility for intimacy' (Boylan, 1989: 153). The novel suggests otherwise, but illustrates the impossibility of true intimacy when relationships are colonised ones, shaped by a capitalist (money figures in all the relationships Alice has in her waking life), sexist, and racist ideology. If the institution of motherhood exists primarily to prop up the State and to reproduce a dominant ideology, then relationships between mothers and children, especially daughters, cannot ever be intimate. The mother serves the function of the police in this formulation and achieves power only through disavowal of her own class (if we think of gender as a class) interests. One possible feminist solution that the novel outlines is to separate mothering from biology (thereby dissolving the family/stranger binary) and to reconfigure mothering so that attentive care as opposed to service to the State takes priority.

In Alice's dream, Cora/Dinah accepts Alice's fumbling attempts at mothering and also mothers Alice, even renovating her house so that it is no longer a cold repository of parental relics but instead a warm, inviting place with a beautiful, lush garden. Alice imagines that Cora/Dinah is acclaimed as a prophet by Dubliners, running a café that becomes a gathering place not only for the men that Cora/Dinah first attracts but also for their wives, some of whom 'struck up warm relationships with other wives and plotted to abscond to Greenham Common', site of a feminist encampment (Boylan, 1989: 149). Shumaker, like other readers of the novel, takes for granted that the prophet-café story is part of Alice's fantasy (Shumaker, 2006: 104–6; St. Peter, 1997: 36–7), but the novel's final chapter undermines that assumption in ways that leave the reader with something of a puzzle: the chapter takes place after Alice's death, yet in it Cora/Dinah thinks about her new friends from the café and has several thousand pounds in her suitcase as she prepares to leave Dublin. Are we to think Cora/Dinah really did enjoy some celebrity as a prophet? Perhaps. Or perhaps not: the penultimate chapter also takes place after Alice's death, but in it we learn of Alice's reunion with her father in the garden Cora/Dinah created.

Whether we are to read it as part of Alice's fantasy or not, the novel's final chapter pointedly recapitulates Boylan's invitation to read this book as a kind of parable of liberation with Alice as an every Irishwoman. That chapter focuses on Cora/Dinah's post-café plans, which initially include going 'home' to Africa to offer herself as a kind of spokesperson for the dispossessed, a possibility frustrated by her realisation that her mother never specified a country, never mind a specific village. Cora/Dinah's belated realisation serves a parallel function to Alice's fury at Mrs. Willoughby's funeral. Sitting on a bench in Stephen's Green, Cora/Dinah faces how her own life was stunted by a lack of maternal care and an excess of maternal control, remembering her mother's forcing her to have an abortion when she was just sixteen for reasons having nothing to do with Cora/Dinah and everything to do with her mother, who 'could stand no more misfortune' (Boylan, 1989: 208). As Cora/Dinah sits desolate and crying, an elderly white Irishwoman joins her on the bench and soon calls her 'Elsie', crying out 'It's my daughter!' (209). Cora/Dinah moves away rapidly, but soon apprehends that this 'mother' has made off with her suitcase and therefore turns back. The novel closes with Cora/Dinah beginning 'to stalk after her mother' (210), which implies that the whole cycle we have just read about has begun again, once more with a commodified mother/daughter relationship that starts with an attempted swindle and that presumably brings a lonely white Irishwoman into intimate contact with a black visitor.

The sharpest limitation of *Black Baby*'s case for redefining Irishness and motherhood is that it apparently treats the black visitor as the bringer of wisdom to Irishwomen, with the Irishwomen benefitting in obvious ways but the benefit to the immigrant less obvious. Placement of a black woman in a purely instrumental role reproduces the existing racial hierarchy and should therefore be seen as a case of the master's tools, which can never dismantle the master's house. However, the novel is not so simple. In fact, Cora/Dinah also benefits from the relationship with Alice, a benefit that is particularly striking if we read the final chapter as taking place outside of Alice's head, in 'reality'. It is, after all, her relationship with Alice that brings Cora/Dinah to a truthful and therefore painful analysis of her own past; without Alice, Cora/Dinah would not be able to re-narrate her mother's story in a way that makes it useful for her own life. Then, too, a familiar argument against immigration and integration casts the benefits all on one side (the immigrant's), whereas this novel shows that in fact the Irish are likely to gain more than they give in intercultural exchanges. Indeed, Boylan's *Black Baby* suggests that a true intercultural interrogation could gain Irishwomen real freedom and therefore the possibility of true intimacy, which is not a bad bargain, to use the language of capitalism.

Notes

1   I use the admittedly awkward 'Cora/Dinah' throughout because using 'Cora' alone is confusing, since everyone in the novel calls her Dinah; yet using 'Dinah' alone suggests acceptance of the arrogation of the right of naming the novel critiques.

References

Boylan, Clare (1989) [1988]. *Black Baby*. London: Penguin.
Fitzgerald , Gretchen (1992). *Repulsing Racism: Reflections on Racism and the Irish*. Dublin: Attic (LIPS series pamphlet).
Jaggar, Alison M. (1983). *Feminist Politics and Human Nature*. Lanham: Rowman & Littlefield.
Kilfeather, Siobhan (2005). 'Irish feminism', in Joseph N. Cleary and Claire Connolly (eds), *The Cambridge Companion to Modern Irish Culture*. Cambridge: Cambridge University Press, 96–116.
Lentin, Ronit (2001). 'Responding to the racialisation of Irishness: Disavowed multiculturalism and its discontents', *Sociological Research Online* 5.4: n.p.
Meaney, Gerardine (1994). 'Sex and nation: Women in Irish culture and politics', in Ailbhe Smyth (ed.), *Women's Studies in Ireland: A Reader*. Dublin: Attic, 230–44.
Rich, Adrienne (1980). 'Compulsory heterosexuality and lesbian existence', *Signs* 5.4: 631–60.

Shumaker, Jeanette Roberts (2006). 'Accepting the grotesque body: Bildungs by Clare Boylan and Éilís Ní Dhuibhne', *Estudios Irlandeses* 1: 103–11.
St. Peter, Christine (1997). '*Black Baby* takes us back', *Canadian Woman Studies* 17.3: 36–8.
Woolf, Virginia (1991) [1929]. *A Room of One's Own*. Orlando: Harcourt, Brace.

16

Beginning history again: gendering the foreigner in Emer Martin's *Baby Zero*

Wanda Balzano

In Ireland, especially in the post-Celtic Tiger era, we are witnessing a radical move toward a new historicity and a new feminism. It is almost as if we were given the chance to record time on a new scale and thereby, still resisting patriarchal and capitalistic systems, begin history again, starting from zero. As Alice A. Jardine had anticipated over two decades ago in her ground-breaking critical study *Gynesis: Configurations of Woman and Modernity*, the master narratives of history, religion, and philosophy at the turn of the millennium have been placed under close scrutiny, while what was left out of history is now re-valorised in critical and artistic contexts. In criticism and the arts, 'the putting into discourse of "woman,"' today often seen as nomad and migrant, develops 'as that *process* … as intrinsic to the condition of modernity; indeed, the valorization of the feminine, woman, and her … historical [and geographical] connotations, [are increasingly seen] as somehow intrinsic to new and necessary modes of thinking, writing, speaking' (original emphasis; Jardine, 1986: 25).

The comprehensive value of Jardine's *Gynesis* consisted of a proposed rapprochement of Franco-American feminist debates in order to explore how 'woman', or the metaphorised concept of the 'feminine' as a set of cultural and libidinal constructions, appears in the important configurations of modernity. Since that book was written, we have witnessed numerous reconfigurations of modernity, where women have increasingly been studied as foreigners and as migrant and nomadic subjects (see Kristeva, 1991; and Braidotti, 1994). In Ireland, the reconfigurations of modernity and the rearticulation of feminist debates have taken place in the midst of a major intercultural change with the influx of numerous minority cultures from both EU and non-EU countries. The impact of this change is becoming more discernible today in the output of new artists who are either from multiethnic, multi-faith backgrounds themselves or have had significant contact with different cultures. In light of this, we need therefore to reevaluate women's individual lives and stories against the backdrop of a variety of multicultural issues of race, language, religion, and culture if we are to resonate with the present intercultural changes and recognise fully the impact of this new artistic production in Irish society and culture as a whole.

The Other as our unconscious: mirroring the challenges of religious nationalism

Emer Martin's *Baby Zero* (2007) traces the vicissitudes of a family caught between the East and the West. At the beginning of the narrative, a pregnant Irishwoman named Marguerite is imprisoned for taking a stand against the fundamentalist government of Orap, a fictional Middle-Eastern land where, with each new regime, the year is turned back to zero, as if to begin history again. Here the notion of self-perpetuating patriarchies clashes with the notion of feminist reinventions. Whose time begins again? Whose history is erased into a blank slate? The fact that each girl in this family is born in the year zero, during alternating fundamentalist regimes, points to a never-ending cycle of (patriarchal) oppression and (feminist) resistance.

In Part I, Marguerite – born to Orapian parents in a refugee camp and later granted Irish citizenship – is portrayed while visiting her mother in her country of origin, where an oppressive regime imposes the full veil on its female population and forbids women from venturing onto the streets if unaccompanied by men of their family. Marguerite's aunt, a former dentist who feels responsible for a hospital that is overflowing with hopelessly agonising women, asks her niece to drive a truck full of the dying women from the hospital to the government buildings and leave them there as a protest. She believes that Marguerite's foreign passport will protect her, but she is wrong: as a result, she is herself publicly stoned to death while her niece is incarcerated. In prison, Marguerite comes into contact with other Orapian women whose faces have been melted by acid, thrown at them by their family members as a form of punishment, and whose bodies have been repeatedly beaten and violated by the guards, leaving many of them pregnant. Soon, and brutally, Marguerite learns that she, too, will share the fate of these jailed women. As she finds herself pregnant in prison, she decides to narrate her own story to the child in her womb: 'Baby Zero, listen carefully, for this is your story too. Your messy inheritance. I know, I am baby zero too' (Martin, 2007: 30).

Martin's novel effectively explores how contemporary religious nationalism has brought new patriarchies into power in Islamic states, which are driven to find new legitimising ideologies and power bases. Of course, for Martin the notion of religious nationalism in Islamic states mirrors the question of religious nationalism in the West and, more specifically, religious nationalism at home, both in the past and in the present. Martin started *Baby Zero* in the year 2000, while she was living in the US and where she witnessed, first-hand, the September 11 attacks in 2001 that transformed the site of the World Trade Center into Ground Zero. She also witnessed the American military response to these attacks in the name of nationalism and religion (McKay, 2009). Those were also the years in which great scandal about the Magdalene Asylums culminated in Ireland. In the 2002 Peter Mullan film entitled *Magdalene Sisters*, the central character, named Margaret, fights an oppressive national and religious system that, during the 1960s, keeps her and other girls imprisoned in the Magdalene Laundries, just like Marguerite and the other women are imprisoned by the equally theocratic Orapian regime. East and West mirror each other. Orap is a construction of the West and a mythical place, yet it is also ourselves: not only the 'O' of Orap resembles the oval of a mirror but, while suggestive of the Orient, 'Eoraip' in Irish means 'Europe'. In Martin's words, 'Orap is a creation of the West. It is the nightmare of Orientalism. It has been forced into existence through repeated pernicious Western interference. Yes, there is a monster coming over the hill, but it's us. So how can we run? We have to face ourselves' (McKay, 2009).

In the same way that oppressive religion does not exclusively affect select countries in the East, but also in the West, women's rights are not an exclusive privilege of Western society, and the efforts of non-Western women organising against Muslim law must be noted.[1] The attempt at organising, as exemplified in the novel by Marguerite's aunt, is obviously condemned by the Islamic governments as defiant of tradition. In the interrogation room of the Orap prison, when Marguerite is chastised and told that she has no understanding of tradition, she boldly states: 'I asked them why when they persecuted men for religion or colour, it was viewed by the world as oppression, and when they persecuted women, it was dismissed as tradition' (Martin, 2007: 19). Women are supposed to conform to patriarchal tradition, and the principle of obedience is inculcated into young girls all along, in real life as well as in metaphors, in Orap as well as in Ireland: 'When I was a young girl, they told me that women are like water: their lives should flow into their family's desires, and a good woman should take on the shape of whatever container she is poured into' (30).

Multiculturalism in Ireland: salad bowl or pickles in a jar?

In Part II of *Baby Zero* we learn, retroactively, about the Middle-Eastern origins of Marguerite's family, the Fatagagas, as well as the prejudices towards ethnic, religious, and class difference among Orapians. Because Orap functions as a mirror of Western society, and Marguerite is an Irishwoman of Middle-Eastern origins with an American passport, it is not difficult to recognise that Martin is highlighting ethnic difference, discrimination, and racism at home as well as abroad. In the novel, Ishmael Fatagagas and his younger brother Mo, two cosmetic surgeons, are routinely stigmatised as foreigners and outsiders in their own country because their parents, goat herders and political refugees, were not native of Orap. Even though their prestige increasingly grows, Farah, Ishmael's wife, who is from an upper-class family in Orap, openly looks down on her husband because of his parents' foreign origins.

East and West have this in common: preconceptions and hatred for the Other. What they also have in common is the perception of the female body and its objectification. In both cultures most women, conforming to a mainly patriarchal model and a narrow definition of beauty, aspire to be one type of woman they are often not: blonde, slim, and with pert noses. Through plastic surgery performed with his brother, Mo is able to forge new faces and identities for women, in California as well as in Orap: 'The young women and their mothers were invariably bleached blondes, and he gave them new pert noses' (Martin, 2007: 35). About the East and the West, Emer Martin states:

> Both cultures have something in common. Namely, the battleground fought over women's bodies. Is it more oppressive to cover the body entirely or to slice it open and put in implants, to inject botulism into women's heads? These are grim choice[s] and we can only hope to steer away from such extremes. Neither furthers the cause of women, and women's equality is vital to changing the world, there is no freedom without it. (McKay, 2009)

Global economic, political, and cultural pressures from the West (plastic surgery among them) translate into local anxieties over the loss of traditional values, the control of power, and the understanding of difference in the Middle East. As signs of political and religious unrest intensify in Orap ('Then they looked over the roof of the house and saw a man hanging from a newly erected barricade, his feet cut off and flies cupping the stumps. Ishmael told [his son] Zolo that he was of a different religion' (Martin, 2007: 57)), Ishmael's brother, Mo, leaves Orap behind to start a new life as an immigrant in the US. Ishmael, who instead delays his departure, is caught with his family in a mass exodus to a refugee camp across the mountains. Refugees' stories describing the tragic loss of human life, especially of young girls, resonate powerfully in the communal tents, while reminding the contemporary reader of the many abuses of children and women in war:

> It was a bad time for girls. The news came over the mountains. The revolutionaries in Orap were using girl soldiers, and their distaste for them was illustrated by

the fact that they were putting them in the most danger. Poor as goats, scrawny, fingers of straw, and inside as alone as caves. The new Orapian regime scooped them up. Trained them to run ahead of the regular forces. … Bad years for girls in the mountains. Folded into each other, limbs entwined, a sleeping carpet of ruin. (134)

This compassionate description provides the reader with a glimpse of the extreme conditions that force people to flee – conditions that are often overlooked in the context of asylum debates. In the refugee camp it is then established that Zolo and Leila (son and daughter of Ishmael and Farah) will join Uncle Mo in the US by falsely claiming that they are his children. They finally leave, while Ishmael and Farah stay behind, trying to find a placement for themselves in host countries until they can reunite with their children at a later date. In the camp, Farah is surprised to find out that she is pregnant at age forty-three with another 'Baby Zero': 'This is the year zero again … My point is … we're going to have another Baby Zero' (Martin, 2007: 137–8). When Farah, still in the camp a few months later, gives birth to her second daughter, whom she names Marguerite, she is concerned about the colour of her skin: '"What colour is she?" Farah asked' (143). Also, when Farah finally learns that they are being assigned to go to Ireland as refugees, she asks: '"Are the people white?" "Yes, of course." Farah seemed somewhat comforted' (146). Of course Farah's concern over both the colour of her daughter's skin and that of the Irish people simultaneously betrays her racial prejudice and her desire to belong in a privileged ethnic group. She assumes that baby Marguerite will eventually be granted Irish nationality, and will therefore blend in more easily with the new Irish ethnicity if the skin colour is going to match. Once in Ireland, Ishmael pins a yarmulke to his head and walks through the Dublin streets in order to go to the North American Embassy to try to get a visa ('"I'll say I'm a Jew", he told his wife. "They love the Jews"'. (155)). Although he refers to US politics, nevertheless the irony of the scene does not escape the Irish reader, who knows that Ireland had refused to take Jewish refugees in the 1930s, and persisted with this attitude after the war (see Keogh, 1998; and Ó Gráda, 2006).

Martin's literary portrayal of Ishmael and Farah's exile to Ireland certainly reflects the existence of the numerous political refugees and asylum-seekers that the country has been accepting ever since the end of the twentieth century. Over the years, individuals from a wide range of countries have made Ireland their home and, as a result, Ireland in the new millennium hosts more than 100 different nationalities (Cullen, 2000: 17). Since the late 1980s, more asylum-seekers came into Ireland from Africa, Asia, and the Middle East. As observed by Clair Wills, the applications rose in the second half of the 1990s up until the passing of the Refugee Act in 1996 and the Dublin Convention in 1997 (Wills, 2002: 1656–7). This legislation in Ireland ironically tightened restrictions on the movement of refugees, while in other European countries 'zero immigration' policies were applied. Wills also notes that, while little public and institutional attention has been given to the ordeals of refugees in Ireland (including racism, xenophobia, and intolerance), the experiences of women refugees have been even harder to access (*ibid.*). For instance, asylum applicants often face problems of isolation – an isolation which is worse for women who are enclosed in the domestic sphere. In Ireland Farah resents her own diminished status as a refugee and is simultaneously a victim and an instrument of racism. She seldom opens the blinds on the window, afraid both to acknowledge her dark neighbours (it is assumed that she lives in a black neighbourhood in Dublin) and to invite hostile looks from the native passers-by:

> The room was a dark hole. She rarely opened the blinds on the window … More refugees. Blacks. Moving about their rooms like olives in a jar. The suspended way refugees were kept alive was very little to do with living, more like pickling. The blacks had told Farah that they didn't like the streets. Too much hostility. (Martin, 2007: 157)

This description offers the reader a new and interesting metaphor for the concept of multiculturalism. Often contrasted with the notion of assimilationism such as the American 'melting pot', where immigrants and various ethnic groups are absorbed into the dominant culture, multiculturalism in Europe has instead been consistently compared to a 'salad bowl' (the equivalent of what in Canada is named as 'cultural mosaic') where immigrant groups have been prevented from fully integrating into host societies (see Thomson-Smith, 2012). Emer Martin adds another layer to the metaphor. In Ireland, the refugees are kept alive, but are not allowed to function within and be an integral part of Irish society. They are therefore seen not so much as salad ingredients in a bowl but as pickles in a jar. Most refugees live in poverty as they wait for government agencies to process their requests of asylum. This indeterminate period of waiting and marginalisation has also been described as 'limbo'. Chinedu Onyejelem, the editor and publisher of Ireland's multicultural weekly *Metro Éireann*, has used this metaphor to make it clear that 'to continuously allow several thousand people to remain in limbo does not augur well for multi-ethnic Ireland. Many of these people are able-bodied and ready to work, but are not allowed to do so. As such, they are being forced to remain on social welfare and be seen as good-for-nothings by many Irish people' (Onyejelem, 2005: 74).

While racism and discrimination generally affect both male and female refugees, minority women may find it even harder than their male counterparts to discover ways of reaffirming their dignity. An Irish 2002 report on maternity-care needs of refugee and asylum-seeking women revealed the fear and loneliness created by language difficulty as well as the absence of the social support which was provided by the communities they left behind (Kennedy and Lawless, 2002). In the novel, after giving birth and after having lost her native community, Farah experiences post-partum depression and resents both the social worker who visits her at home and the doctor who cares for her baby in Tallaght Hospital. While the doctor treats her as an object of curiosity ('May I take your photo?' (Martin, 2007: 158)) or charity ('The doctor had given her a can of powdered formula and had told her she would contact the authorities in charge of them to make sure she could always get some more' (159)), the social worker, whom Farah refers to as a 'nosy bitch' in spite of her genuine effort to be useful (162), has been assigned to frequently check up on Farah, who has no choice but to accept her visits, which she therefore perceives as intrusions in her private life.

In addition to financial deficits, language barriers are also what keep Martin's as well as real asylum-seekers and refugees from education and other services. Even though the novel is written entirely in English, readers are supposed to imagine Farah speaking a Middle Eastern language to communicate with her fellow country people, while using a more or less broken English to communicate with Irish citizens and other refugees. By means of this linguistic difficulty, Martin's novel emphasises the fact that genuine interculturality between the Irish hosts and their 'guests' is a complicated, troubled process, fraught with many difficulties.

Another significant barrier to integration in such a multicultural society is created by the media. In Ireland, as has happened elsewhere, journalists – instead of offering compassion while covering stories of racist violence and human rights abuses in order to build consensus – have for the most part demonised asylum-seekers, immigrants, and refugees, denigrating an entire category of vulnerable people often only for the sake of filling a quiet news-day. This reality is illustrated in *Baby Zero* by the fact that the funeral of a clandestine boy from Orap, victim of a deadly racial attack ('some men spotted him as a foreigner and beat him to death'), is ignorantly used by a reporter to incite hatred and fuel further intolerance (Martin, 2007: 195, 199). Indeed, although not all Irish newspapers have been so prejudiced in their coverage of asylum-seekers and refugees, it is a fact that much of the coverage is trivialising and lacks compassion as well as knowledge of human rights law. Journalists have been able to publish these stories, even supplementing them with pictures, only because, as Cullen claims, 'these nameless, wordless, powerless people are in no position to seek redress. The law of libel is the only rule that modern-day journalists absolutely wish to adhere to, and it simply doesn't apply in the case of subjects who have no money and no access to wealthy lawyers' (2000: 42).

Identity politics: limits of sisterhood and internal minorities

For certain aspects, the emerging struggle of minority groups for equal rights and protection against discrimination in Ireland has its parallels in the feminist movement. In *Repulsing Racism*, which was published in the ground-breaking series of Lip pamphlets issued by the feminist Attic Press in the early 1990s, Gretchen Fitzgerald acknowledged that '[a]fter long and hard battles sexism is now at least recognised as existing, though we have not yet managed to free Irish society of sexist thinking and behaviour. Racism is still struggling to be recognised as an inequity' (1992: 253–4). What needs to be added to this broad parallel is the consideration of how women experience gender differently because of their access to or lack of social privilege, often based on the grounds of race and even degrees of skin colour. In the above-mentioned pamphlet, Fitzgerald tellingly writes of her own abiding memories of being bullied and taunted as the darkest skinned in a class of Anglo-Indian children in a primary school run by an order of Irish nuns in India. Both women and men are capable of racism. Sisterhood is complicated, and acknowledging one's own politics of location is essential in order to work toward achieving feminist goals.

If, on the one hand, in *Baby Zero* Farah perceives the whiteness of Irish people as unhealthy and unappealing ('The people were so pale and unhealthy looking' (Martin, 2007: 160)), she also mirrors white supremacy by being guilty of colourism, as she feels that those with lighter skin like her ('I think I pass for Italian or Spanish' (194)) should be awarded privileges that are denied to their dark-skinned counterparts. In an exchange with the African women who live next door, it becomes clear that they all have a common history as oppressed refugees. The proud Farah, however, rejects this implicit association and accuses the clandestine African women of being 'irresponsible', suggesting that Irish racism toward the likes of them might be justified after all:

> 'I'm a programmed refugee. I'm here on invitation. Legally. I can work. … I certainly would not have put my family at such risk to just arrive uninvited. How did you get past customs?'
> 'We came on a truck, Madame. We pay all our savings and he take us. An agent in Togo arranged it all. We give all our money to come here for our children.'
> 'Hiding on a truck? With your children? You must have known what reception you would get. How could you expect anything else? Are you that naïve? It's just irresponsible to come to a country without proper documentation and expect to live off charity'. (169–70)

Farah's self-identification as a 'programmed refugee' sets her apart from other refugees and aims to assert her feeling of personal entitlement over other women who are less lucky than she is. Despite the prevalence of hierarchies that normally privilege men, it is a fact that in every culture some women (such as elites or legalised citizens) enjoy greater opportunities than many others (workers or immigrants, for instance). Also, some women have higher status than other women or men. One of the feminist lessons in the novel is that if these overlapping hierarchies are ignored, we run the risk of creating a feminism that serves only the interests of women who have more privilege, thus reinforcing other social inequalities that disadvantage both women and men in the name of improving women's opportunities. The intersecting identities of women as members of races, classes, and nations raise questions about the nature of feminism and identity politics. By recognising that there is no single, universal female identity, there comes the understanding that gender has been constructed differently across place and time. Because of historical, social, national, and personal differences, women cannot assume a universal sisterhood, even though there can be common ground on particular issues.

For this very reason, it is important to consider, in close association with multicultural theory, the values of identity politics, the politics of difference, and the politics of recognition, as they share a commitment to revaluing disrespected identities and changing dominant patterns of representation and communication that marginalise certain groups (see Young, 1990; Taylor, 1992; Gutmann, 2003). In so doing, we also need to acknowledge, as many political theorists have done, that there are serious tensions between multicultural group rights and women's equality. An essential question that we need to ask ourselves is the following: 'What should be done when the claims of minority cultures or religions clash with the norm of gender equality that is at least formally endorsed by liberal states (however much they continue to violate it in their practice)?' (Moller Okin *et al.*, 1999: 9).

Because there is a wide range of beliefs and practices within and among cultures about the adequate status and roles of women, it seems almost inevitable that there should be some conflict between aiming to support and protect many cultures and aiming to promote the equal dignity of and respect for women. Ayelet Shachar, who has extensively written on what she calls the 'paradox of multicultural vulnerability', believes that the rights and interests of vulnerable individuals (such as women, children, and dissenters) can be endangered by group rights and other well-intentioned efforts to accommodate groups:

> Multicultural accommodation presents a problem, however, when pro-identity group policies aimed at leveling the playing field between minority communities and the wider society unwittingly allow systematic maltreatment of individuals within the accommodated group – an impact which in certain cases is so severe that it can nullify these individuals' citizenship rights. Under such conditions, well-meaning accommodation by the state may leave members of minority groups vulnerable to severe injustice within the group, and may, in effect, work to reinforce some of the most hierarchical elements of a culture. (Shachar, 2001: 2–3)

In other words, extending protections to minority groups may come at the price of reinforcing oppression of vulnerable members of those groups (especially women and children), which is what some have called the problem of 'internal minorities' or 'minorities within minorities' (see Green, 1994; Eisenberg and Spinner-Halev, 2005).

In the novel, the thirteen-year-old daughter of Farah's former gardener, Sakina, exposes the clash between her own individual rights as a girl living in a non-Muslim country and her cultural and religious group's internal restrictions about purdah, the Muslim practice of gender segregation, which includes the mandatory veiling of women. Sakina pleadingly refuses to wear the headscarf that Islamic tradition imposes on women: 'If we wear it in Orap so no man will look at us, then wearing it here makes everyone stare at us. So it's silly. ... Besides ... I was drinking water from a paper cup, and a man walked by and put money into my water' (Martin, 2007: 173). Even though, unarguably, there is considerable dissent among Muslim women regarding the practice of purdah, the older women's identification with their group that is based in a foreign country is often stronger than their dissension: in Farah's words, '[t]hose girls pretending to be so modest in their veils. My husband spotted them hanging out with boys and with no veils on. Not that I agree with the veil. But still' (199). Especially when they are in a non-Muslim country, many Muslim women end up forgoing their individual rights and conforming to their group right in order to identify with Islam and follow its traditions, whether by personal choice or not. Sakina, in the end, will have to wear the headscarf (175).

The difficulties experienced by these female refugees in the novel are intensified by the clashing of their local ethnic customs with the moral values of their new country of residence. While Sakina is in Virgin Megastore, she befriends a Nigerian seventeen-year-old girl who has come to Ireland alone on a truck and is therefore one of the many unaccompanied minors roaming the streets in Dublin. Her new friend, who is pregnant, had decided to escape from Nigeria because, as prescribed by Sha'ria laws for unwed pregnant mothers, she was going to receive a hundred lashes (Martin, 2007: 179).[2] Not only is it ironic that Sakina meets this pregnant girl in *Virgin* Megastore but it is perhaps even more ironic that she flees to Ireland, where abortion is illegal, and that she would have to travel outside Ireland in order to obtain an abortion.

Amy Gutmann (1993) has carefully analysed the challenge that emerges when different cultures contain different ethical standards that yield conflicting judgments concerning social justice. In particular, women's rights are often rejected by the leaders of countries or group of countries as incompatible with their various cultures. The vast majority of Gutmann's examples concern gender inequalities, and abortion in Ireland is one of them. Not only do Irish female citizens affected by this issue constitute a minority within a patriarchal culture that makes laws, but a Nigerian asylum-seeking pregnant teenaged girl in Ireland is further challenged in the preservation of her personal liberties. As a way out of her desperate situation, she decides to follow a notorious Western entrepreneurial model that is usually employed to exploit minorities in extreme difficulties; she tells Sakina that she is going to sell her baby on the internet.

Conclusion

Emer Martin's book is structured like the *Arabian Nights*, with a story within a story within a story, and the American story of Leila comes at the centre of the novel. A teenaged illegal migrant into the US, Leila (the eldest daughter of Ishmael and Farah) is also an unaccompanied minor, as both her Uncle Mo and her brother Zolo selfishly abandon her to her own devices in order to devote themselves to the pursuit of their respective careers. In the vacuum of her world, which partially mirrors the Irish experiences of her counterparts, she befriends another foreign, desperate girl, a Cambodian teenager named Lan. Lan involuntarily facilitates Leila's rape by the same man who routinely abuses her – a paedophile who bought her from a brothel and then smuggled her into the US. At the centre of the novel, Leila thus emerges as a representative of a vulnerable minority within the minority. She is the moral centre of the book, and all the stories connect to her, symbolically as well as graphically. To fill her lonely days, Leila puts together a scrapbook that illustrates what appears to be her understanding of world history – a history that maps out violent conquest at the expense of the most vulnerable sections of the population, particularly women and children, such as the story of the Wild West, where cowboys are portrayed as misogynistic murderers of Indians (Martin, 2007: 118).

Leila sadly dies of neglect for untreated meningitis. She is secretly buried in the Californian high desert in a shallow, anonymous grave that her brother and uncle dig for her. Like a migrant who is passing through the night, Leila is the key to many stories of ghosts 'rising under all those layers of history' (McKay, 2009) and she is herself a ghost, the ultimate foreigner.

While in the Orap prison, waiting to be executed by the fundamentalist regime as a disobeying woman and a disrespectful foreigner (though born in a refugee camp in Orap, she holds Irish and American passports), Marguerite tells the story of Leila to her baby throughout her pregnancy, until the girl's birth (another 'baby zero') will coincide with her own death (the regime waits for the incarcerated mothers to deliver their babies and then executes them).

With dreaded anticipation, the novel's ending comes, however, to offer sudden, unexpected redemption. Even though throughout its pages we, as its readers, seem to move into an ideological sphere of female negation, at the end we advance towards a new access to the feminine. Following Alice A. Jardine's suggested route, presented at the beginning of this chapter, we are encouraged to reconsider history from the perspective of space, in particular from the perspective of new female spaces. In the last pages of *Baby Zero* we learn that Farah visits her daughter in prison for one last time, on the night before Marguerite's execution. She will have to take her newborn granddaughter with her, and say adieu to her daughter. In sensational fashion, Farah instructs Marguerite to swop her black burka and walk with her baby out of the prison in her place. The ultimate sacrifice. The mother's renewed gift of life. The end of the novel thus signals how '[t]he past has an end. It ends right here in the present. It is always ending' (Martin, 2007: 313). Jardine, quoting Jean-Joseph Goux, proposes that the end of patriarchal history – the most encompassing of master narratives – can only take place with the 'crossing-over into the place of the Other, the *return* to the place of signifying productivity, then its conscious extension' (Jardine, 1986: 86). At the end of history, the gesture of crossing over into the place of the Other, with its stories and its deaths, is a matter of ethics. Only embracing such ethics and *her stories* can we begin history again.

Notes

1   In Martin's view, '[w]omen's rights are not a Western prerogative. It is not something unique and integral to our culture. The West has only made progress very recently on this front. We only had a women's movement in the 1970s. Men still have the political and economic power in the Western world. Feminism cannot be imposed on other cultures for political kudos. Women's rights in the East must come organically from within, from those women's own sense of injustice. Otherwise, it will be fatally resisted as a Western imposition' (McKay, 2009).
2   Martin seems to have been inspired by the BBC-reported story, in January 2001, of Bariya Ibrahim Magazu, who was sentenced under Islamic law after three men forced her into having sex. In real life, the girl did not escape, however.

References

Braidotti, Rosi (1994). *Nomadic Subjects*. New York: Columbia.
Cullen, Paul (2000). *Refugees and Asylum-Seekers in Ireland*. Cork: Cork University Press.
Eisenberg, Avigail and Jeff Spinner-Halev (eds) (2005). *Minorities within Minorities: Equality, Rights, and Diversity*. Cambridge: Cambridge University Press.
Fitzgerald, Gretchen (1994) [1992]. *Repulsing Racism: Reflections on Racism and the Irish. A Dozen Lips*. Dublin: Attic.
Green, Leslie (1994). 'Internal minorities and their rights', in Judith Baker (ed.), *Group Rights*. Toronto: University of Toronto Press, 100–17.

Gutmann, Amy (1993). 'The challenge of multiculturalism in political ethics', *Philosophy and Public Affairs* 22.3: 171–206.

—— (2003). *Identity in Democracy*. Princeton, NJ: Princeton University Press.

Jardine, Alice A. (1986). *Gynesis: Configurations of Woman and Modernity*. Ithaca, NY: Cornell University Press.

Kennedy, Patricia and Jo Murphy Lawless (2002). *The Maternity Care Needs of Refugee and Asylum-seeking Women: A Research Report Conducted for the Women's Health Unit, Northern Area Health Board*. Dublin: Social Science Research Centre, University College Dublin.

Keogh, Dermot (1998). *Jewish in Twentieth-Century Ireland*. Cork: Cork University Press.

Kristeva, Julia (1991). *Strangers to Ourselves*. New York: Columbia University Press.

McKay, Niall (2009). 'Interview with Emer Martin', *The New Review* 19. www.laurahird.com. Accessed on 10 April 2012.

Martin, Emer (2007). *Baby Zero*. Dingle and London: Brandon.

Moller Okin, Susan, Joshua Cohen, Matthew Howard *et al.* (1999). *Is Multiculturalism Bad for Women?* Princeton, NJ: Princeton University Press.

Mullan, Peter (dir.) (2002). *Magdalene Sisters*. Magna Pacific.

Ó Gráda, Cormac (2006). *Jewish Ireland in the Age of Joyce: A Socioeconomic History*. Princeton, NJ: Princeton University Press.

Onyejelem, Chinedu (2005). 'Multiculturalism in Ireland', *Irish Review* 33: 70–7.

Shachar, Ayelet (2001). *Multicultural Jurisdictions: Cultural Differences and Women's Rights*. Cambridge: Cambridge University Press.

Taylor, Charles (1992). *Multiculturalism and 'the Politics of Recognition'*. Princeton, NJ: Princeton University Press.

Thomson-Smith, Lydia D. (2012). *Multiculturalism: The Salad Bowl of Cultures*. Saarbrücken: FastBook.

Wills, Clair (2002). 'Ethnicities', in Angela Bourke, Siobhan Kilfeather, Maria Luddy *et al.* (eds), *The Field Day Anthology of Irish Writing*, vol. V, *Irish Women's Writing and Traditions*. Cork: Cork University Press, 1656–8.

Young, Iris Marion (1990). *Justice and the Politics of Difference*. Princeton, NJ: Princeton University Press.

17

'Goodnight and joy be with you all': tales of contemporary Dublin city life[1]

Loredana Salis

Tales of Dublin city life are a significant feature of Irish literature and drama. From Joyce's *Dubliners* to plays by Seán O'Casey, Brendan Behan, Hugh Leonard, Bernard Farrell, and, more recently, Conor McPherson and Mark O'Rowe, Dublin and its people have definitely been the protagonists of many a story. In the 1990s, Ireland's capital city became the epicentre of a large-scale transformation, which affected both its geographical and cultural landscapes, and which was inevitably reflected in theatre productions. 'Dublin itself' – as Keating put it in the *Irish Times* – 'became a stage again' (2010: 5). This study focuses on plays set in the city of Dublin, which testify to the impact of globalisation both at the personal and at the public levels. More specifically, this reading of Paul Mercier's unpublished *The Dublin Trilogy* (1995–98),[2] Sebastian Barry's *The Pride of Parnell Street* (2007), and Dermot Bolger's *The Parting Glass* (2011) seeks to investigate the cultural implications of Ireland's modernisation in terms of representations of the migrant Other and its location in Irish culture. Questions will be posed as to the kind of images of the city that emerge, the tales we hear, who conveys and who receives them, and the depiction of the 'non-native' Other.

The Dublin Trilogy was written and premiered between 1995 and 1998. A production of Mercier's Passion Machine Theatre Company, the trilogy includes *Buddleia* (1995), *Kitchensink* (1997), and *Native City* (1998), providing an in-depth chronicle of Ireland's capital city and its people (White, 1998: 2). The staging of *Native City* brought Mercier's reflection to its conclusion: the trilogy was like an imaginative journey which took him from the suburbs (depicted in *Buddleia* and *Kitchensink*) to a physical and symbolic core, the centre of Dublin, where *Native City* is set. Significantly, the notion of a trajectory from the margins towards the centre was confirmed in performance as *Native City* played in a double bill with either *Buddleia* or *Kitchensink* (Keating, 2011). By 1998, having explored the impact of globalisation upon the Irish landscape and people in the first two plays, Mercier turned his attention to the impact of cultural globalisation. Urban redevelopment, in fact, had meant more than foreign investments and property boom; it had attracted thousands of immigrants in search of better life and career prospects. A number of them included refugees and asylum-seekers from the former Yugoslavia, who would come to Ireland and make their new home in Dublin. These added to other foreigners who had been there for decades.[3] Before long, the significant increase in the number of immigrants living in the country posed a threat to the traditional notions of 'home' and 'belonging', as being 'native' no longer represented an exclusive right for the Irish-born. The question of belonging to a place by birthright proved crucial to debates going on in Ireland at the time, given that anti-racial feelings and attitudes became frequent among the 'natives', and being born in another country was considered to be synonymous with lesser rights (Lentin and McVeigh, 2002; 2006).

The incidence of intolerant behaviours finds expression in Scene One of *Native City*, in which an Irish man called Parkie addresses a couple of Bosnians to assert his sense of ownership of the place: 'It's a fucking invasion this. I mean if it isn't them it's the fuckin' blacks. Turning *my* bleedin' *home* into a campsite. And as for those mullahs out there' (emphasis added; Mercier, 1998: 5). The scene takes place in a hackney shop in Dublin city centre where a group of people are queuing for a taxi home after a football match.[4] Though he is drunk, Parkie articulates the largely felt perception that in the 1990s, as a consequence of international wars and of the EU enlargement, Ireland was yet again being 'invaded' by foreign people. That the presence of the Bosnians is defined in military terms – it is an 'invasion' in Parkie's words – resonates with the country's colonial history and its legacy: 'We want to watch the queen on the BBC, seeing as we are being *invaded* again', says another character called Happy (emphasis added; Mercier, 1998: 23). Similarly, Traverse, the father of an Irish volunteer in France, feels that the Irish are being dispossessed: 'We don't belong here', and Dublin would be the greatest city on earth '*if* we were let run it' (emphasis added; 55).

The resentment voiced by these characters suggests that modernisation had failed to solve the issue of Ireland's relationship to Britain and thus it remained in the grip of its troubled past. The circular narrative pattern of the play confirms such a notion. *Native City* is divided into fourteen scenes, and it ends at the point where it begins. The play opens in the present – 'Hackney Shop 1998', and similarly closes with the same characters in the same Hackney Shop in 1998. Scenes 2–13 are all set in Dublin at different moments in the past, going backwards to the year 1900. Thus, Scene Two is centred upon a 'Millennium' celebration of Ireland's nineteenth-century history through a 'public street event' in 1988 (Mercier, 1998: 8); Scene Three is set on the day when a bomb dev-astated the city centre in 1974, Scene Four is set in 1969, Scene Five in 1955, followed by scenes respectively set in 1941, 1932, 1922, 1920, 1916, 1915, 1913, and 1900. Such a cyclical pattern is strategically designed to suggest a Joycean nightmarish notion of history, and a form of paralysis which evidently affected Irish life in 1998. The trauma of her colonial past surfaces as Ireland, a land of emigrants, turns into the land of opportunities for thousands of immigrants in the 1990s, and 'the pain of emigration returns to haunt the Irish (King, 2007: 43–4). Eruptions of violence in the play reinforce the notion of fear, which re-sults not simply from anxiety about the Other but is rather rooted in the culture and history of a people (King, 2007: 43–5; Salis, 2010: 30). Violence is ritualistic and pervasive. It can be 'real', as observed in the street riots depicted (Mercier, 1998: 57) or re-enacted; sometimes, it 'becomes real … in theatrical terms', while the 'recreation of history' itself also turns serious (15).

These historical revisitations bring characters and audiences back to crucial points of the past, allowing them to see things differently. Thus, it is significant that Mercier uses a séance in one of the scenes, while in another, he has a group of actors from a Variety Show claim their 'native city' back (Mercier, 1998: 31, 33). In this way, history appears to be constantly in the making, and violence intertwines with revisited episodes of the past to form the basis of narratives uttered by the protagonists. There is a feeling, as we listen to them, that for all its epochal change, Dublin and Dubliners have had no epiphany yet: some people celebrate the Queen or follow her Christmas address on TV while some do not; some want to forget and 'put [their] past behind' (14) while others cannot do it (2); for some, this 'beautiful city' (29) 'was once the pride of Europe' (30) and 'the greatest city on earth' (54), but to be saying that now is to be 'raving' (54). These images may be taken as celebratory of diversity and of mutual recognition, but the opening and the closing scenes are there to remind us that paralysis, like violence, is also self-replicating. Thus, in 1998, Dublin has yet to take a leap into the future, and though foreigners have long been there, they are located on the margins and largely seen as invaders. Significantly, there is a reference to the Huguenots, who 'fled religious persecutions when the Edict of Nantes was no longer worth the piece of paper it was written on … and landed in this city' (11). These were once the invaders; today, it is the Bosnians.

The Huguenots 'set up shop and … transformed [Dublin] into the splendour we are celebrating today', says one of the actors in the Variety Show (11), open-ing to the possibility that new immigrants too may one day integrate. The play offers a second hint of a positive outcome as a local man named Ward gets into a fight with Parkie to defend the two Bosnians, who eventually make it home safely. The passage below is emblematic of the marginal space occupied by the immigrant Other:

Enter driver. MANAGER: (Re. Bosnians) These two.
DRIVER: Ye right?
BOSNIAN 1: (To WARD) Thank you.
WARD: Look after yourself.
BOSNIAN: You okay?
WARD: Yeah
The hackney driver waits impatiently
BOSNIAN 2: (To WARD) You are honourable and brave. And very foolish. Take care.
WARD: What's he saying?
BOSNIAN 1: You are honourable, brave and very foolish. Take care.
WARD: Tell him to watch his language.
MANAGER: Okay, lads, when you're ready. Thank you.
BOSNIAN 1 Gives Ward a big ceremonious handshake.
DRIVER: (Going out) Ah, here, this city's gone to fuck.
BOSNIAN 1: (Going) Goodbye.
Exit Bosnians
MANAGER: (To WARD) Sorry.

(77)

Interestingly, this passage shows that while Ward's intervention may reflect a changed attitude on the part of the Irish, intolerant behaviours are not the exception (for example, the impatience of the driver, and the fact that the shop manager apologises to Ward but not to the Bosnians). Reading between the lines of the exchange above, it is also evident how the representation of alterity replicates stereotypes. Thus, the 'ceremonious handshake' and the use of language by the two Eastern Europeans are clear racial markers, which make their diversity all the more evident in the eyes and ears of the locals.

Sitting 'in a corner of the shop', the two Bosnians are doubly marginalised as they 'talk to each other … They speak Bosnian (underlined text is translated speech)', or a bad English with a strong foreign accent (2, 4). Their Otherness thus exposed is a reminder that difficulties arise in the renegotiation of concepts like 'home' and 'belonging'. This is the case with some local people, like a man identified as 'Drunk':

DRUNK: Open the gates! Money, no object. Fly them in. Give them the keys. Put yous on a bus with no roof. Sure we'll even organise the weather for ye. Fuckin' right. We've been doin' that for centuries, don't see why we should stop now. (Laughs.) But I have a son and he doesn't get a look-in cos he's got the wrong address in his own fuckin' city.

(3)

The politics of identity underlying Parkie's and the drunk man's behaviours need urgent revision in a globalised world where nationality is no longer 'defined in terms of an individual's identification with the physical spaces of geographic territory', and where the entitlement to nationality 'is realised by the exercise of intellectual consent' (Lonergan, 2010: 21). In Ireland, the 1998 amendments to the Constitution formalised new concepts of nation and nationality, while the Peace Process in the North also contributed to ongoing debates about traditionally rigid categories.[5] The implications are voiced by different characters in the trilogy as they lament an alienating sense of uprooting. The hostility and rage of the two men above are symptoms of a generalised malcontent, which is eloquently articulated by Dermot in *Kitchensink*:

> So, where does that leave us, my friend? Destitute in a land of plenty. We have come a long way, haven't we? … We have come from small farms and small towns, small streets and small worlds, small-mindedness and want … [t]o build a new city of hope on the frontier of civilisation as we know it … They have landscaped the playing field. Our existence has been shruberized! Yet there is great pain … There is crying … And there is rage behind the mask. (Mercier, 1997: 69)

The condition lamented by this fifty-year-old Irish man echoes the image of the buddleia in the first trilogy play. *Buddleia* takes its title from a fairly strong plant found on the grounds of the development site where the action takes place, which, in the eyes of the builders, is 'a weed', and 'a scavenger' (Mercier, 1995: 47). Firmly rooted into its native ground, this shrub is a powerful image of resilience and resistance to change, and a metaphor of nostalgia for people like Dermot, who strive to accept the tyranny of cement, and somehow resent the new Ireland. Characters such as this resent 'a world that has been uprooted, where the old contours and social landscape has been bulldozed … and turned into a sanitized depersonalised generic shrubberized suburban landscape' (Salis, 2012). Their frustration is the frustration of Mercier himself, for whom

> the shrubbery of suburban life whether it be the plantation in our gardens or around our shopping centres represents something that is alien and disconnects us from the indigenous natural wild world in which the suburban was created … And there is no lonelier place that the dead shrubberized landscape of modern living. (*Ibid.*)

Sebastian Barry voices analogous preoccupations as he responds to recent transformations of the Irish cultural landscape and dramatises the effects of change at the turn of the century. Set in September 1999, *The Pride of Parnell Square* recounts an eventful decade of Irish life through tales by Dublin born-and-bred couple Janet and Joe. The play was commissioned as part of the 2004 Amnesty International's 'Stop Violence Against Women' campaign by Jim Culleton, artistic director of Fishamble Theatre Company, who also directed the first production. A monologue at first, by 2007 the piece was expanded to alternating monologues – 100 minutes with no interval – spoken by the protagonists in a distinctively north-Dublin accent on a minimalist non-naturalistic stage.

247

Janet, aged about thirty-three, 'sits on a nondescript chair downstage left' (Barry, 2007: 1), and Joe lies on a bed in the shadows to the right (as the play unfolds it becomes clear that he is in hospital and dying of AIDS) (40, 58). The lighting shifts from one character to the other as they start speaking; Janet's voice is the first we hear: 'In them days – in them days, long long ago, it seems like, when we was girls only really ourselves – sounds like some story book, but' (10). The language is typical Barry: affective and evocative, transporting 'the reader to a place which is viscerally familiar, and yet imaginatively uncommon' (Cregan, 2006: 61). Janet is a 'normal inner-city girl', and this is Dublin no doubt, a place that is immediately recognisable but also somehow uncommon. The location is the Parnell Square quarter, a deprived area across O'Connell Bridge, 'a foreign country' for the non-residents, and a world apart, where people 'carry diseases like rats' (Barry, 2007: 25). Like in a children's tale, Barry's prose is simple, and in its simplicity exceptionally evocative; it takes us to a place and time that are distant: 'long long ago … sounds like some story book' – and imaginatively uncommon – 'in them days … when we was girls'. Such a strong incipit locates the story immediately in a past that is not 'once upon a time', but rather 'in them days', and which is evoked nostalgically and in a language that is indeed 'captivating' and especially Irish (Cregan, 2006: 62). 'Them days' are recounted through private memories blended with public narratives, a dramatic strategy which allows Janet's existence to be mapped onto the broad canvas of Irish life, and thus 'be rescued from oblivion' (Roche, 2006: 149). Her tale, retold by Joe from his perspective, runs parallel to the public tale of Irish life: 'In them days the Irish were doing real well at the football and … began to think we could win the World Cup maybe, and that lifted the spirits' (Barry, 2007: 13). Janet's life story also runs parallel to the tale of the new, multiethnic nation: 'In them days – I'm fucking counting on me fingers and it's only nine years ago and it could be ninety, for all the changes … In them days before the Africans came to Parnell Street' (11).

'Changes' is a key-term here, evoked again and again in the play, and used to reflect the impact of intercultural encounters: 'The Africans came to Parnell Street, and got everyone wearing beads in their hair, and got old shops all new again' (14). In Janet's view, Dublin is the centre of an expanding nation; hers is the 'Ireland of the welcomes', an image which starkly contrasts with Parkie's in Mercier's play above. There is no sense of an 'invasion', here, but rather an attempt at representing the new Ireland as a melting pot of diversity and adaptability. Barry reads between the lines of the official 'Ireland of the welcomes' narrative, a profitable self-representation of that country as an irresistible and fascinating Eldorado, inhabited by friendly and funny people, and in this context he seeks to retrieve the untold stories of people living on the margins.[6] The voices we hear are still those of the marginalised natives of Parnell Square; the real foreigners remain silent and are mentioned in passing, at times depicted through popular urban myths (see Chomsky, 2007): 'The Africans, the Chinese, and the Romanians have tooken the best jobs off the Irish and are only sponging off of the state' (Barry, 2007: 25). Spoken by Joe's intolerant mother, these words testify to common perceptions of the migrants since Ireland was at the time the new land of opportunities: 'Jobs galore. Got a job in Geldof's factory, no bother' (Barry, 2007: 55). Janet's utterance adds to Joe's consideration that 'there's all sorts a' lads in Dublin now, very nice lads, Russians, Romanians. I think there must be a college for robbing in them countries, because these lads, they are professionals. It's a crying shame, a Dublin man can't hardly make a living at the robbing anymore' (50). Migrants too find jobs, and if jobs are 'tooken' off the Irish these are not 'the best' jobs, but rather the illegal activities for which Russians and Romanians are known for. There is a good level of irony and a clever use of stereotypes here, both of which contribute to expose, provocatively, a self-pitying attitude of the Irish, in contrast with the self-critical notion that people on the dole, not the foreigners, were really sponging off of the State (Lee, 1989: 552–3).

Barry reflects upon the eruption of indigenous violence, and he does so in the face of the profound transformations of the new cultural landscape of Ireland. The intercultural encounter has done little to alter the fact that 'it is not the past that needs to be rescued or redeemed, but the future' (Cleary, 2000: 126; quoted in Merriman, 2011: 223). Worryingly, the Ireland Barry portrays shows an innate capacity for self-destruction, a 'queer thing', as he calls it, which prompts him to return to the theatre after eight years of silence (Orel, 2009).[7] The alleged reason is the recurrence of disturbing episodes of domestic violence, the reflection of an underlying unease whereby self-confidence gives way to violence, and foregrounds the realisation that Ireland remains, in some respects, an unsettled country in which economic triumph actually signifies the establishment of a subtle, yet pervasive, form of cultural neo-colonialism through independent Ireland's 'negation of Irish nationalism's historical aspiration to decolonisation' (Merriman, 2011: 29).

While decolonisation appears to be an unaccomplished task, there is a strong feeling that 'Irish theatre … has the capacity to imagine a Decolonised Ireland of solidarity in diverse citizenships' (Merriman, 2011: 225). Reading Irish theatre of the 1990s, Victor Merriman advocates an interventionist theatre that acts as 'a witness', a central figure which 'stands among the facts and struggles of history … so that their materiality and their meaning may be available to the lived present, and the desired future' (*ibid.*). In such a view, the plays by Mercier and Barry considered here denounce the fact that marginalised narratives are still largely 'expunged from official histories and formal narratives of citizenship' (222), and that there is no place for those who do not conform or fail to actively participate in the country's economy. The immigrants we see are both foreigners and internal exiles, marginalised people who are not at home in their country of birth, and who represent a valuable resource for drama in the 1990s (Said, 1991: 39; Merriman, 2011: 217).

Interestingly, *Internal Exiles* is the title of a collection of poems by Dermot Bolger from 1986. Bolger returned to the theme of emigration in *In High Germany* (1988), and later on he further contributed to cultural debates on the new Ireland in *The Parting Glass* (premiered in 2010 and published in 2011). A sequel to his celebrated play of 1988, *The Parting Glass* is a stand-alone one-act play featuring Eoin, a returning Irish emigrant, his family, and closest friends. The play is set in 2009 'on the infamous night when Thierry Henry caused Ireland's World Cup exit with two illegal flicks of his wrist' (Bolger, official website; see section 'Plays'), and it looks back at twenty years of profound transformations of Irish life as seen by the protagonist, his old-time friend Shane, an illegal immigrant now living in New York, and Dieter, Eoin's son. *The Parting Glass* is another fascinating tale of Dublin city life. It shares the same cultural background as the plays by Mercier and Barry, but its narrative perspective is that of the new millennium, a decade past the boom, and a vantage viewpoint from which the play can chart the Celtic Tiger years in their aftermath. The transformations of its geographical and cultural landscapes are explicit as characters testify to the 'cranes and earthmovers [and] a pandemic of SUVs' (Bolger, 2011: 14). In Dublin, the 'nurses are foreign' and 'all the waitresses speak Latvian' (11, 14); the city is full of 'Polish shops and Romanian bodybuilders and African mothers outside schools' (14). Bolger's 'foreigners' are the 'new Irish', who have settled in and integrated well. Not only that, but they have also changed the local people to the point that Maire's husband, Eoin's Irish brother-in-law, 'has become an American' himself (12). The multiethnic nation 'is brimming with people', Maire continues (*ibid.*), as she suggests that the presence of immigrants brings life to an otherwise alienating world of 'unexpected estates dropped from space' (15), which Eoin strives to recognise, and where 'some mornings [he feels] an exhilarating sense of belonging. On other mornings I feel more of an immigrant than Frieda', his German wife (14). Once 'a poor … emigrant' (12), Eoin now occupies a liminal space, as do his old-time friends, Mick, a gay man who used to live in New York, and Shane, who is 'glad Ireland is bankrupt' and 'hates the Irish' but besides that he 'hate[s] the Dutch more': 'I've become like them in so many ways. I bore myself as a Dutchman when I'm not boring people as a Paddy in O'Shea's Bar. I keep criticizing Ireland and biting the head off anyone who dares to' (10–11). Shane, Eoin, and his son Dieter are emblematic of a condition of internal exile to which Bolger dedicates his attention, and he does so to an interesting and exceptionally refreshing effect.

The Parting Glass is about (de)parting. The play tells of parting with and departing from that same suffocating Joycean condition to which Mercier and Barry also refer, and in the face of which Bolger attempts at an imaginative escape. The play provocatively poses the question of agency to confront life's unpredictability, where one day you have it all, and the next you do not. When something goes totally and unexpectedly wrong, what do you do? You can either wait (and hope) until it gets better, or you can do something for yourself and make it better. And thus the play calls for commitment to action – neither paralysis, nor a passive going with the flow, but a readiness to take up real change, as it relocates Dublin city at the centre of a somewhat third-millennium rebirth. Shane fails to understand Eoin's resolve to 'go home', back to Ireland (Bolger, 2011: 11); Eoin, on the contrary, finds a way out of his mid-life crisis, and does so thanks to his twenty-year-old son Dieter. Their encounter enables a dialectics that is at once intergenerational and intercultural. Born of a German mother and an Irish father, Dieter is raised in Hamburg, moves to Ireland, and is planning to go to Canada. Unlike Eoin, he lives in the present and belongs both nowhere and anywhere. He simply does not need to: 'You Irish are so desperate to belong and yet desperate to escape. I don't need to belong anywhere' (31). His words '[w]elcome to the twenty-first century' are not just about social networks and online dating agencies (33); rather they reverberate with the necessities of a globalised vision of the world and of one's place in it that is utterly and ultimately liberating. So, by the end of the play, Dieter's hybrid worldview produces Eoin's resolve to part with his older self, to depart from Paris and start afresh. It is highly significant, in fact, that the play opens in an airport – a non-place that is quintessentially liminal – and there it ends as Eoin realises that he has spent his life 'waiting to catch up ... it's only half time in it, with extra-time to come' (42). Life is pictured as a game to be played. Given a new chance and tired of waiting,[8] Eoin behaves like the emigrant in the traditional song that gives the play its title: he bids goodnight and joy to all as he prepares to exit, finally confident and ready to 'let the rest of my life begin' (*ibid.*). The optimism of Bolger's play contrasts with the delusional self-confidence observed in plays from the previous decade; his is of an enabling theatre out of which the project of decolonisation may be realised. Significantly, the key to cultural liberation rests in the hands of liminal characters, who may return to a geographical place they call 'home', but live as internal immigrants. Theatre thus viewed responds to change critically: it enables 'present, possible, creative and generous experiences of being, belonging and becoming' (Merriman, 2011: 224).

Dermot's words come to mind as the present reflection draws to an end: 'We have come a long way, haven't we?' The plays by Mercier, Barry, and Bolger all tell us of Ireland's transformation in the 1990s. Though they meet at the crossroads between the twentieth and the twenty-first centuries, these theatrical endeavours do so from different historical perspectives. Mercier writes at the height of the economic boom, and so he deals with the making up of a new Ireland, a construction site signifying to the unfinished project of modernisation, suspended between its haunting past and the desire for globalisation. In this context, the politics of identity are paralysed by traditional notions of home and belonging, feeding into racism and violence. By the time Mercier completed his trilogy, Ireland's economy showed early signs of arrest, and as the Peace Process in the North reached a crucial phase, the Irish Constitution was amended accordingly. At least officially, the Republic subscribed to conceptual/ non-geographical notions of 'home' (the nation) and 'belonging' (nationality); old unresolved questions dragged into the new millennium with outbreaks of unexplained and unexplainable violence. Barry's shock and need to understand the dynamics of violence, from public frustration to domestic tragedy, shapes the powerful tales of Janet and Joe. Drafted against the *grand récit* of the globalised jobs-for-all Ireland of the Welcomes, theirs are anonymous stories from the cul-de-sacs of North Dublin about the premature death of a child, drugs, jail, AIDS, and pride. *The Pride of Parnell Street* is the pride of its people, and the pride of a nation largely reconciled with itself, which, however, still carries the burden of its turbulent past. Looking back at that moment in Irish history, Bolger chronicles the lives of people who also live on the margins, but whose definitions of belonging and entitlement are clearly different. Here, the fates of Eoin, his family and friends, and the fate of Ireland's national football team, cheated out of the 2010 World Cup, are metaphors of the nation's recent fall from grace. There is a 'collective sense' of being repeatedly, unfairly, and inexplicably robbed, and of being lied to.[9] It feels like being stuck and frustrated, but there is no pride, this time, no unchecked violence. Eoin *parts with* and *departs from* that mindset, and he chooses to start afresh, embracing the truly modernised and globalised vision of a new Ireland as he unburdens himself of historical and geographical ties – now his wife is 'the only country' he belongs to (Bolger, 2011: 18). Ready to 'enter my native city like a foreigner' (42), this returning migrant gives voice to a different Ireland, self critical and willing to move on, whatever was, whatever may come.

Notes

1   For this study I am especially indebted to Patrick Lonergan, who helped me choose the plays here analysed, and to Lucia Angelica, who proofread the first draft.

2   I am very grateful to Paul Mercier, who kindly provided me with working scripts of the three plays in *The Dublin Trilogy*, giving permission to quote from them, and sharing his views about the productions and their reception.

3   As Bradley and Humphreys explain, '[i]n 1956, five hundred and thirty Hungarians ... arrived in Ireland ... Other refugee groups who have been offered protection of the Irish State are the Chileans (1973), Vietnamese 'boat people' (1979), Iranian Baha'i (1985), Bosnians (1992), and more recently the Kosovars (1999) ... Bosnian refugees are ... the largest group of programme refugee in Irish history to date' (Bradley and Humphreys, 1999: 14). This study was published a year after *Native City* premiered. By then, there were 1,089 Bosnian refugees resident in Ireland.

4   A 'hackney shop' is a place where people can hire a cab. The author deliberately uses a terminology that is common in the English spoken in Ireland.

5   As Patrick Lonergan observes (2010: 21), the amendment of the Irish Constitution in 1998 produced a rethinking of Irish nationality 'not on the basis of territories, but in terms of individual consent'. Up until then, the Constitution 'had ... defined nationality in relation to the physical space occupied by the island of Ireland. The amendment revoked this territorial claim and redefined nationality as based on personal entitle-ment'. It marked a transition 'from geographical to conceptual' notions of belonging and entitlement.

6   Promoted by the government and by Bord Fáilte at the time, the 'Ireland of the Welcomes' image was also marketed among the diaspora Irish in Britain, North America, and Australia through a magazine of that title. Founded in Dublin in 1952, *Ireland of the Welcomes* aims to 'showcase the best of Ireland's history, scenery, culture, traditions and lifestyles to the world at large'; targeting a readership of 'global Irish' and 'many people with Irish ancestry who look to Ireland for their roots and cultural heritage' (see its official website, www.irelandofthewelcomes.com).

7   In an interview, Barry refers to the fact that, following the death of a friend, Donal McCann, he distanced himself from theatre as he felt that he had 'lost the ability to write words that would "sit in actors' mouths"'. In 1998, during the Football World Championship, he used to live in the Parnell Square area and noticed that 'there was a sea change between elation and when the fellas watching the games got home ... they would attack their wives. The women's refuge would be full the next day' (Orel, 2009). In the play, Janet is attacked by Joe on the night of the semi-final: 'It was all so sudden like. I couldn't believe it ... Why it didn't stop him beating the shite out of me, I'll never know' (Barry, 2007: 16). The play explores the possibility of Janet 'never knowing', but uses that as a narrative pretext to make sense of the self-replicating nature of violence in Irish life and history.

8   The play runs with no interval, so technically there is no first or second half; yet at one stage, 'a slight pause marks the play's halfway point' (20). The term 'wait' is repeated strategically in the first half to suggest the overwhelming feeling of living a life in stand-by. Interestingly this is not so in the second half, where the term does appear, but less frequently, and where the words 'new', 'bright', 'future', and 'fresh start' recur.

9   In his official website Bolger speaks of 'a collective sense that we have been massively robbed: robbed of jobs, robbed of hope, robbed of our children's future by a self-regulated elite of bankers, developers and politicians. And not only robbed, but herded into a collective hysteria where people were panicked into buying over-priced property in a suburban sprawl that started in Dublin and ended with apartments perched on stilts in Galway Bay'.

References

Barry, Sebastian (2007). *The Pride of Parnell Street*. London: Faber.

Bolger, Dermot (2011). *The Parting Glass*. Dublin: New Ireland.

—— *Official Website*. www.dermotbolger.com/plays_thepartingglass.htm. Accessed on 2 January 2012.

Bradley, Siobhan, and Niamh Humphreys (1999). *From Bosnia to Ireland's Private Rented Sector: A Study of Bosnian Housing Needs in Ireland*. Dublin: Clann Housing Association.

Chomsky, Aviva (2007). *'They Take our Jobs!': And Twenty Other Myths about Immigration*. Boston, MA: Beacon.

Cleary, Joseph (2000). 'Modernisation and aesthetic ideology in contemporary Irish culture', in Ray Ryan (ed.), *Writing in the Irish Republic: Literature, Culture, Politics 1949–1999*. Basingstoke: Macmillan, 106–29.

Cregan, David (2006). 'Everyman's story is the whisper of God': Sacred and secular in Barry's dramaturgy', in Christina Hunt Mahony (ed.), *Out of History. Essays on the Writings of Sebastian Barry*. Dublin: Carysfort, 61–82.

Ireland of the Welcomes Website. www.irelandofthewelcomes.com. Accessed on 8 August 2011.

Keating, Sara (2010). 'Dublin itself has become a stage', *Irish Times*, Special Supplement – *City of words: Dublin and its writers*, 29 September: 5.

—— (2011). 'Ordinary lives, but full of drama: Paul Mercier in conversation with Sara Keating', *Irish Times*, 16 March. www.irishtimes.com/newspaper/features/2011/0316/1224292257575.html. Accessed on 13 January 2012.

King, Jason (2007). 'Black Saint Patrick revisited: Calypso's "Tower of Babel" and culture Ireland as global networks', in Karen Fricker and Ronit Lentin (eds), *Performing Global Networks*. Newcastle Upon Tyne: Cambridge Scholars Publishing, 38–51.

Lee, Joseph (1989). *Ireland: 1912–1985*. Cambridge: Cambridge University Press.

Lentin, Ronit and Robbie McVeigh (2002). *Racism and Anti-Racism in Ireland*. Belfast: Beyond the Pale.

—— (2006). *After Optimism? Ireland, Racism and Globalisation*. Dublin: Metro Éireann.

Lonergan, Patrick (2010). *Theatre and Globalisation: Irish Drama in the Celtic Tiger Era*. Basingstoke: Macmillan Palgrave.

Mercier, Paul (1995–98). *The Dublin Trilogy* (*Buddleia*, 1995; *Kitchensink*, 1997; *Native* City, 1998). Unpublished scripts.

Merriman, Victor (2011). *Because We are Poor: Irish Theatre in the 1990s*. Dublin: Carysfort.

Orel, Gwen (2009). 'Sebastian Barry returns with *The Pride of Parnell Street*', *The Village Voice. Theatre*, 25 August. www.villagevoice.com. Accessed on 31 May 2011.

Roche, Anthony (2006). 'Redressing the Irish theatrical landscape: Sebastian Barry's *The Only True Story of Lizzie Finn*, in *Out of History*', in Christina Hunt Mahony (ed.), *Essays on the Writings of Sebastian Barry*. Dublin: Carysfort, 147–66.

Said, Edward (1991). 'Reflections on exiles', in Russel Ferguson, Martha Gever, Trinh T. Minh-ha, Cornel West (eds), *Out There: Marginalisation and Contemporary Cultures*. Cambridge: MIT Press, 357–66.

Salis, Loredana (2010). *Stage Migrants. Representations of the Migrant Other in Modern Irish Drama*. Newcastle Upon Tyne: Cambridge Scholars Publishing.

—— (2012). Private correspondence with Paul Mercier, 5 March.

White, Victoria (1998). 'Mercer's *Dublin Trilogy* is the best Irish production in theatre awards', *Irish Times*, 21 October: 2.

18

Mean streets, new lives: the representations of non-Irish immigrants in recent Irish crime fiction

David Clark

One of the most interesting phenomena to appear in Irish literature since the late 1990s has been the rise of 'homegrown' crime fiction. Irish crime narrative has been strong, historically, as a sub-genre, but until the 1990s had largely been concerned with the representation of fictional crime in non-Irish settings, usually the US or the UK. Since the period immediately prior to the economic boom commonly known as the Celtic Tiger, however, a number of circumstances have given rise to a situation in which, for the first time, Irish readers are demanding novels and other narratives which portray Irish crime taking place within contemporary Ireland and involving Irish criminals, Irish police, Irish representatives of the law and of the media, and other related social groupings. The not altogether coincidental concurrence of this new crime fiction with a period of fast and all-encompassing economic and social change has meant that of all literary forms, it is crime narrative which has most accurately and most successfully mirrored the profusion of transformations which have taken place in Ireland. Thus the crime novel has provided a codified narrative of contemporary Ireland wherein a number of writers use the crime mode as a means by which they can reveal the contradictions and incongruities apparent in the new Ireland of the Celtic Tiger economy and after. One of the most outstanding contributions of this popular narrative has been the way in which crime writers have been able to represent the impact of immigrants in the process of change which the country has undergone, and the effect that the presence of new non-Irish inhabitants has had on the 'mean streets' of Dublin, Galway, Limerick, and Cork (Chandler, 1944).

David McWilliams states that immigration is 'probably the most accurate and clearest barometer of positive social change in a country' (2005: 21), and this indicator of collective transformation is reflected in the crime writing of the period. While crime fiction by its very nature deals with 'deviant' sectors of society, the excesses of Tiger Ireland and the growth of white-collar crime have helped contribute to the fact that immigrants are usually portrayed in the role of victims of unscrupulous native Irish people in the fields of employment, housing, and legal residence and they are often exploited in criminal activities, usually involving crimes such as prostitution, the trafficking of narcotics or the illegal movement of the migrants themselves. Popular literature in general, and crime fiction in particular, 'often addresses hopes and fears affecting large sections of a nation's population, especially when in the throes of social, political, and economic change and upheaval' (Bertens and D'haen, 2001: 175), and it is tempting to look at Irish crime narrative since the mid-1990s as representing to a large extent the aspirations and dreads of the Irish as they entered into and were subsequently dragged out of the economic boom. The growth of immigration starting in the last decade of the twentieth century can be seen as a serious challenge to the myth that Ireland 'had always been a homogeneous society and that Irish identity is unchanging' (Fanning, 2002: 2), giving way to the reality that Ireland was every bit as racist as other western nations.

Contemporary Irish crime narrative is, of course, part of a historical and transnational literary variety, and as such must inevitably share many of the traditional motifs of the genre. Crime fiction has typically dealt with issues such as racial difference, immigration, colonialism, and other markers of Otherness as signs of potential or actual deviance. In early crime fiction the criminal was normally an outsider (Scaggs, 2005: 10), and although the so-called Golden Age fiction of the inter-war years to some extent changed this norm by using as criminal a deviant member of the dominant social group, the feared stranger, the foreigner, and the unknown are still essential features of the genre. Much recent criticism questions the generally held tenet that crime narrative is grounded solely in rationalism and post-enlightenment ideas of deduction and reason, tracing part of the early history of the genre back to distinctly non-rationalist areas such as the sensational, the Gothic, the supernatural, and the pseudo-sciences including physiognomy and phrenology, the occult and atavism (Ascari, 2007: 146–7; Cassuto, 2009: 236). Thus nineteenth-century views on the physical and biological aspects of race were common in much crime fiction from that period, involving issues such as purportedly scientific theories of atavism which claimed that supposedly degenerate – deviant – individuals were in danger of changing back to their pre-civilised state. This 'paradigm of atavism' was used for 'both those deviant groups marginalized within western society and for those populations who belong to non-European undeveloped territories' (Ascari, 2007: 147), effectively criminalising both the western working classes and the victims of colonialism. The use of 'atavistic aliens' (Cassuto, 2009: 236) was common in crime narrative throughout the twentieth century, from the xenophobia of spy thrillers through the hard-boiled classics such as Dashiell Hammett's *The Maltese Falcon* in which the alien Other was generally perceived as a figure of menace and danger. The dominant consciousness of traditional crime fiction is generally that of a white, heterosexual male (Gregoriou, 2007: 54), despite the 'feminisation' process apparent in many Golden Age works (Horsley, 2005: 38). Even the recent 'appropriation' of the genre by transgressive non-white, non-male or non-heterosexual protagonists has failed to alter the fact that racism, like sexism, is 'a necessary element' of crime fiction and 'it is in fact a cornerstone of that fiction's ideological orientation' (Reddy, 2003: 27).

Racism, therefore, plays an integral part in the ideological connotations of crime fiction but, then again, this is tempered by the liberalism that permeates many of the works that make up the genre. Recent critics have been keen on pointing out that, despite its reputation as a transmitter of intransigent ideological mores, crime fiction in itself is not intrinsically reactionary. Marxist critic Ernest Mandel highlighted the historical tradition of social protest in crime fiction, and although 'the mass of readers will not be led to seek to change the social status quo by reading crime stories' (1984: 10), crime fiction often criticises both implicitly and explicitly the society in which it is rooted. Andrew Pepper notes that although the crime novel may be formally reactionary it can still be subversive on a thematic level. The genre, he states, 'is shot through with an uneasy mixture of contradictory ideological inflections' and 'is coded to both resist and re-inscribe the dominant cultural discourses' (2003: 211). Irish crime fiction from the period since the mid to late 1990s up to 2012 reflects these contradictory impulses well, echoing both the racism and the voices which welcome the benefits of multiculturalism, while approaching both on a mimetic and a figurative plane the changes taking place in Irish society of the epoch. If we examine a number of works published during the period, the significance of the contribution of crime fiction to the debate should become clear.

Hugo Hamilton's *Sad Bastard* (1998) was the author's second (and to date, last) crime novel featuring 'renegade' Garda Pat Coyne, following the character's appearance in *Headbanger* (1997). *Sad Bastard* is interesting in that it represents one of the first works of the genre to pay attention to the question of illegal immigration which was starting to appear with some regularity in the national press. Coyne, who in this novel has left the Garda Síochána na hÉireann, becomes inadvertently involved in a case in which immigrants are being brought into the country in fishing boats. The novel anticipates the generally liberal stance that will be apparent in crime novels published throughout the next decade in that the immigrants are perceived to be innocent victims of adverse circumstances along with the avarice and inhumanity of Irish criminals. In common with later works, the protagonist actively sympathises with the immigrants, as Coyne helps a young Romanian woman accused of shoplifting. Hamilton's East

European characters are favourably compared with their Irish hosts, and the novel makes repeated references to the similarities between the immigrants and the Irish. Thus the Russians who sing 'Danny Boy' in the Anchor Bar are 'as bad as the Irish' because they 'can't go anywhere without starting a party' as they get drunk on plum brandy 'enjoying themselves singing sad songs' (Hamilton, 1998: 15). Inevitably, these similarities are used to compare the situation of these 'new Irish' and the Irish emigrants forced to leave their homes in past times. As Coyne ponders, the new immigrants were 'the Blasket Islanders coming home' (59). Hamilton thus employs two motifs which will be used with some consistency in subsequent novels, with the immigrants as victims and the heirs to the Irish of past periods.

Another recurring motif is that of the 'unsympathetic Garda'. This model takes the figure of the police officer who is openly hostile to the presence of immigrants in the country and who is generally challenged by another officer or person of authority whose views are more often than not supported by the action of the plot. An early example of this can be found in Des Ekin's *Stone Heart* (1999), where Garda Steve McNamara is generally suspicious of foreigners who he believes are 'up to their necks in drug dealing and refugee smuggling' (Ekin, 1999: 75). These characters voice some of the fears and prejudices commonly found, but are inevitably contradicted by the fictional events. In the case of Ekin's novel, for example, the Garda's foil and chief ideological rival, a woman journalist, marries an Estonian at the end of the novel. In Rob Kitchin's *The White Gallows* (2010), one Garda challenges the 'xenophobic assumption and prejudice' of a colleague (Kitchin, 2010: 7).

Perhaps one the most convincing examples of the unsympathetic Garda is that of Jimmy Kilmartin in John Brady's Matt Minogue series of novels. Brady's series began in 1988 with *A Stone of the Heart*, but it would not be until his sixth novel in the series, *Wonderland* (2002), that the Dublin-born Canadian resident would start to deal with the question of immigration. From this novel onwards, Brady's literary production of the decade provides an important contribution to the debate on questions regarding immigration in Celtic Tiger and post-Celtic Tiger Ireland. Kilmartin, Minogue's friend and superior, provides the voice of dissonance which repeatedly criticises the presence of non-native 'aliens' in the country, but Minogue himself is drawn into debate and self-questioning. Kilmartin believes that the immigrants 'must think this is heaven here' and that the 'native' Irish are 'gobshites here, ready and willing to be led down the garden path' (Brady, 2002: 372). As that of Minogue is largely the focusing consciousness throughout the series, the counterpoint he provides to Kilmartin's often openly racist diatribes is generally corroborated by the turn of fictional events in the novels. Like the reference to the Blasket Islanders in *Sad Bastard* as seen above, Kilmartin also refers to Irish history when contemplating the situation of the immigrants, but denies any link or comparison between these:

> 'You don't get it, do you? This isn't some Famine thing all over again. This is about the doors being wide open to seasoned criminals. They're laughing themselves off the boat here. Tell me this: Did you ever expect to be handed money, to be given a place to live when you came up to Dublin? To be taught a new language – and then, for Christ's sake, actually encouraged to go out and have it off so's you could get pregnant in time to have the baby here so, bingo, instant citizen – and the ma gets to stay forever!' (Brady, 2002: 158)

Kilmartin's discourse ironically echoes the official Gardaí line on the case he and Minogue are investigating concerning the death of two Albanians, but this is countered by Minogue who realises the benefits inherent in the construction of a multicultural reality. Thus, on the streets of Dublin, Minogue enjoys what is almost an epiphany:

> But this was his city still. It was a steady gladness he felt when he met with foreign faces in the streets this past while. The accents and the languages – Arabic the other day in Mary Street – and he walked closer to hear them. The olive and brown and coffee skins he wanted to look at closer; how dark a woman's hair was, how white an eye set in that face. All somehow new, all beautiful, every day. Would they always be that exotic? He'd have to watch himself, too. The trouble he could get himself into for staring, asking questions. People took offence easily this day and age. (Brady, 2002: 296)

Novels such as *Islandbridge* (2005) and *The Going Rate* (2008) provide further examples of this dialectic between Minogue and Kilmartin, while the Eastern European population of the country rises. This rise is similarly reflected in a number of the novels published by Arlene Hunt over the period. In her first novel, *Vicious Circle* (2004), the use of immigrant girls for purposes of prostitution is highlighted. Irish gangs are seen to be moving into the trafficking of Eastern European women who are considered to be less troublesome than Irish girls. *Black Sheep* (2006) and *Undertow* (2008) continue with Hunt's concern for the situation of immigrant women used as sex workers by local gangs. A similar theme is to be found in Declan Hughes' *The Colour of Blood* (2007) and in Niamh O'Connor's *Taken* (2011). The former highlights the plight of Polish women who are unable to go to the Garda as they have no passports, while the latter examines the alleged involvement of the Gardaí in the trafficking of drugs and women from Eastern Europe. Brian McGilloway, whose novels have compared both implicitly and explicitly the situation of new immigrants in Ireland with that of Irish Travellers, also touches on the question of the trafficking of women from Eastern Europe. In *Bleed a River Deep* (2009), the trucks which smuggle military software from Ireland into Chechnya are used to bring laundered fuel and people out.

Anti-immigrant feeling, apart from that of members of the security forces, is often expressed by minor characters in the novels. The operator of a taxi company in Arlene Hunt's *Undertow* calls Polish employees 'fucking shovel-heads' (2008: 103), while a taxi driver in Declan Hughes' *The Colour of Blood* complains about the 'cushy fucking number all these fucking immigrants have around here' (2007: 203). The young thug Karl Prowse in Gene Kerrigan's *Dark Times in the City* is philosophical about the situation, believing that 'the one good thing about the waves of immigrants over the past few years was that you didn't get so many stroppy Irish bastards behind the counter. Not that the stroppy Asian bastards were much of an improvement' (Kerrigan, 2009: 120).

These negative attitudes are countered, nevertheless, by a degree of sympathy towards the newly arrived immigrants. Saxon – the American-born, ex-FBI protagonist of the crime novels written by the husband and wife team known as Ingrid Black – is shocked at the hypocrisy she detects in Irish attitudes towards immigrants, and feels sympathy for the night workers in Dublin in *Circle of the Dead* (2008), all of whom seem to be 'foreign women with sad, defeated eyes cleaning for the minimum wage' (Black, 2008: 94). Similarly, in *Islandbridge* another of John Brady's Garda characters, the hard and seemingly unshakeable Dubliner Tommy Malone, is haunted by guilt at the way in which the new arrivals are treated, again, like so many characters within the genre, drawing parallels between the situation of the contemporary immigrants and the Irish of the past:

> 'Are we doing to people what was done to us? … Them people who are cleaning toilets and cleaning offices in the middle of the night. And then, bejases, we turn round and tell them their time is up and they can go home. Home to what?' (Brady, 2005: 260)

Mostly, however, the dominant attitude is one of absolute incomprehension. The process, it would seem, has been so rapid, so complete, that the ordinary 'native' Irish are portrayed as being bewildered by the degree of change. Questions and doubts regarding the immigrants are bountiful, such as, in *The Going Rate*: 'Do they have their own language, these people?' and 'where is Slovenia anyway?' (Brady, 2008: 49, 72).

Rarely are immigrants shown as being involved in any criminal practice, although some recent works do touch on the topic. As noted above, Brian McGilloway's *Bleed a River Deep* shows how a Polish immigrant, Pol Strandmann, is involved in trafficking with immigrants, and has raped the Chechen girl Natalia and forced her into prostitution. In Arlene Hunt's *Blood Money* (2010), a Bosnian ex-convict is responsible for a revenge killing on his arrival in Ireland, while Rob Kitchin's *The White Gallows* discusses the crime figures among the different immigrant populations, commenting that the murder rate amongst Lithuanians living in Ireland 'was twice that of their native country' (Kitchin, 2010: 5). This phenomenon, it would appear, did not occur amongst other Eastern European immigrants such as Poles or Latvians. In Ingrid Black's *The Judas Heart*, Garda Inspector Fitzgerald has arrested people of seven different nationalities within the preceding month (Black, 2007: 13).

The alleged involvement of Eastern European immigrants in criminal activity is further treated in Brian O'Connor's *Bloodline* (2011), which deals to some extent with the fears about the possible participation of Eastern Europeans in the increased circulation of narcotics throughout the country:

> There has been a sharp rise in the number of Eastern Europeans coming to Ireland and being caught with significant amounts of drugs. Our intelligence people now say there is no question but that there are supply routes coming into this country from that part of the world. It's no coincidence that the number of Eastern European nationals at the centre of gun crimes in this country is increasing. (O'Connor, 2011: 95)

Bloodline, a novel pertaining to the sub-genre of crime thrillers based in the world of horse racing, is notable in that it is one of the few Irish crime novels which actually give fictional voice to the immigrant population. As no immigrants have, to date, taken to the writing of crime novels, the 'native' Irish writers are noticeably reticent to portray the 'new Irish' as anything other than victims or perpetrators, and particularly reticent to 'allowing' these characters to speak 'for themselves'. In *Bloodline*, the first novel written by Brian O'Connor, Liam Deed – a young Irish jockey, racing correspondent with the *Irish Times* – is initially accused of the murder of Anatoly, a Ukrainian stable-boy at Bailey McFarlane's horse-racing yard. The stables reflect some of the tension which exists between the local people and the Ukrainians who have arrived to work with the horses. The foreigners 'coming over on the cheap' (O'Connor, 2011: 53) are described as 'quiet stoical workers' who 'laughed among themselves in their own language and smiled shyly when dealing with anyone else' (10), but who were resented for ostensibly taking jobs from local residents. As one stable worker says, '[s]urely you look after your own first. Do you think if we went over to their place, we'd get better treatment? Would we hell!' (53). The jockey Liam enters into a relationship with Lara, a Ukrainian stable-hand who articulates the views of the normally silenced immigrant workers:

> Don't treat me like a child. What better way to look at this. Oh, just more of those foreigners killing each other. It happens all the time. Just let them get on with it, as long as it doesn't affect any of us. We're all the same to you people – Russians, Ukrainians, Lithuanians, Poles, it doesn't matter. We're only the help, doing what you Irish are not prepared to do. We're your cheap servants, or your cleaners, and

if we're not good enough for that, then we are good for being whores or strippers, isn't that right? (98)

Lara further analyses the xenophobia she perceives in the yard. Racism, she claims, is

almost too big a word for it. You say racism to the lads in the yard and they think 'black'. They do not use foul words to us because we are white and look like them. But the fear and resentment is always there. Why don't you go back to where you belong? Why should you get a better job than me? You're not even Irish. Ask any of those who were at Anatoly's remembrance party – they will tell you the same thing. You can see people storing up their prejudices behind stiff manners and not being sure how to behave around us. But when that veneer disappears, it can turn into something sinister. (163)

This 'something sinister' that Lara feels neatly summarises the uncomfortable co-existence between the old and the 'new Irish' found in *Bloodline*. The sensation of being similar to, yet distinct from, the new immigrants is one which is repeatedly echoed in works within the genre. Eastern Europeans are likened to the Irish not only because of their physical similarities, but also due to the historical context of oppression and struggle to which they are perceived to have been submitted. John Brady's Matt Minogue considers the connections in *The Going Rate*, thinking of the similarities between the Irish and the Poles, which 'couldn't just be their Catholicism' but included 'a rough history too, maybe, with their own overbearing neighbours, and their own wide scattering to America' (Brady, 2008: 38). In Declan Hughes' *The Colour of Blood* his private investigator Ed Loy muses on how 'if Ireland had been in the Eastern bloc, we would have been riddled with secret police' (Hughes, 2007: 210).

It may not be surprising, given the statistical analysis of the origins of immigrants to Ireland since the early 2000s, that the central focus in recent Irish crime fiction is on immigrants from the Eastern European countries, but it is no less surprising that immigrants from other parts of the world are given such a low profile in the crime fiction coming from and using as its subject matter the Ireland of the Celtic Tiger and immediate post-Celtic Tiger periods. Asian, African, and South American immigrants appear in the fiction of the time, but their appearance is usually anecdotal and of minimum importance to the development of the plot. One Garda in the Matt Minogue novels has a girlfriend from Macau, but her character, although recurring, is never developed. Although Celtic Tiger Dublin became increasingly cosmopolitan, and according to Gene Kerrigan 'it was like every hotel, pub and café and most of the shops had become a mini-United Nations, staffed by Asians, Africans or Eastern Europeans' (2009: 30), it is the latter grouping which dominates Irish crime fiction.

The only crime novel which deals centrally with immigrants of a non-European background is Andrew Nugent's *Second Burial* (2007), focusing, as it does, on African immigrants in the Dublin of the early twenty-first century. The novel concerns the murder of a young Nigerian man whose mutilated body is found in the Dublin Mountains. The initial belief that the crime was motivated by racism is gradually dispelled as Nugent's Garda protagonist Jim Quilligan investigates the Nigerian community in the city's 'Little Africa', with the immigrants who had 'come to hitch a ride on the Celtic Tiger' (Nugent, 2007: 16). Quilligan, who had first appeared in *The Four Courts Murder* (2006), is of a tinker or Traveller background, and his own recollection of his people's historical mistrust of authority allows him to sympathise with the situation of the African immigrants.

From both a literary and a socio-historical point of view, arguably the most relevant crime writer to emerge from the Celtic Tiger period is Galway-based Ken Bruen. Bruen's early works were, befitting his status as an emigrant, set outside Ireland, and the author achieved something approaching cult status in the UK and the US with his iconoclastic noir thrillers, often parodical, rarely politically correct. Works such as *Rilke on Black* (1996), *The Hackman Blues* (1997), and *Her Last Call to Louis MacNeice* (1998) were excellent black comedies which used London as a backdrop for their often wild and anarchistic plots. The subsequent success of Bruen's Inspector Brand novels, also set in London, came close to achieving mainstream recognition for their author. In 2001, with the economic boom at its height, Bruen relocated, in a literary sense, to Ireland with the first of his Jack Taylor novels, *The Guards*. Jack Taylor is an alcoholic, drug-using, apparently misanthropic 'renegade' ex-Garda who, in his role as a private investigator in a land in which the very concept of a private investigator 'brushes perilously close to the hated "informer"' (Bruen, 2001: 5), provides an excellent filter for a critique of the new Ireland. In this respect, the Jack Taylor novels offer an interesting gallery of immigrant experiences in the Galway of the first decade of the third millennium.

In *The Guards*, a barman predicts the multiracial Ireland of the new decade when he states that 'ten years from now I'll be serving Romanian-Irish, African-Irish' (Bruen, 2001: 233). The successive volumes in the series bear witness to this forecast, and in *The Killing of the Tinkers* Jack Taylor sees two black men cleaning tables as a 'sign of the new Ireland' (2002: 130), while in *The Magdalen Martyrs* all of Galway appears to Taylor to be staffed by non-Irish and the private investigator is 'lucky to hear English, never mind a hint of brogue' (2003: 173). Bruen's novels also depict the growing racism generated in the country at both street and institutional level, so in *Sanctuary*, one character complains that 'niggers' are 'stealing our country right from under us' (2008: 64) while a pre-dawn government sweep on illegal immigrants camped beside the M1 motorway sees them summarily deported. The recession is also well documented in the Taylor novels, and in both *The Devil* (2010) and *Headstone* (2011) the detective character notes how the jobs previously occupied by immigrants are once again being taken on by 'native' Irish: an Irish person is seen working in a hotel in the former and an Irish waitress serves him in the latter.

One of the most interesting topics which Bruen touches on in his Jack Taylor novels is the similarity between the new immigrants and 'native' Irish Travellers. While he is not the only crime writer to draw comparisons between the treatment of people recently arrived in the country and the tinkers who have been the traditional target of prejudice in Ireland, Bruen is unique in that he makes this comparison a continuous theme in his novels. The anti-Traveller sentiment shown by a wide variety of characters, not least by Gardas and other figures of authority, is easily and comfortably transferred to the immigrants. In *The Devil* Taylor morbidly comments that the tinkers were 'once seen as the dregs of our caring society' but had recently 'moved up a notch since we started to resent the non-nationals' (2010: 188).

Bruen also presents what is probably the only recurring immigrant character in Irish crime fiction, in the figure of the young Romanian immigrant Caz who had 'managed to avoid the periodic roundup of nonnationals for deportation' (2011: 134). Caz first appears in *The Killing of the Tinkers,* where his rapid adoption of local customs leads Taylor to note that he had 'gone native' (2002: 24). Caz tells Taylor that in Ireland generally people were 'not fond' of Romanians, but that this state of affairs was different in the city of Galway where 'they hate us' (80). Caz joins Taylor in numerous cases throughout the series until in *Headstone* he demonstrates his ability to adapt to changing circumstances. He learns, as Bruen quotes in the words of Louis MacNeice, 'the dark cunning of our race' and works as an interpreter for the Garda Síochána – an occupation which, like that of private investigator, is forever equated in Irish eyes with that of informer – and is considered to be 'as trustworthy as the eels that swam in the canal' (2011: 134).

Although the Celtic Tiger phenomenon and its temporal coincidence with a series of global factors (including the adhesion of new states to the EU) saw an important rise in the number of immigrants arriving in the Republic of Ireland, the changing situation in the North of the island following the Peace Process of the 1990s and the ensuing Good Friday Agreement created more stable social and economic conditions, conditions which also resulted in an influx of immigrants to Northern Ireland. This phenomenon moreover coincided with a substantial growth in crime fiction from the North which, freed from the dominating criminal nexus of terrorist affairs, began to experiment a period of 'normal' criminal activity. In the words of Stuart Neville in *Collusion* (2011), 'the consolidation of the European Union alongside Northern Ireland's stabilization had drawn prosperity to this part of the world, but the criminals followed close behind' (63).

Writers such as Stuart Neville, Adrian McKinty, and Brian McGilloway deal in their fiction with the problems facing an area in which crime had been dominated by the Troubles and the paramilitary movements, so the new situation of peace-time prosperity provided new opportunities both for criminals and the writers who would use these and their criminal behaviour as the raw material for their fiction. While, as we have seen, crime narrative from the Republic generally portrayed the immigrant population as a real or potential victim of criminal acts, fiction from the North would seem to hint more at the involvement of sectors of foreign arrivals in criminal activity in the Province. The Polish pimp and rapist in Derry-born Brian McGilloway's *Bleed a River Deep* (2009), discussed above, can be seen to be representative of this tendency amongst Northern crime writers. In *Collusion* Stuart Neville comments on how, although organised crime in the Republic had increased greatly, the situation in Northern Ireland was also changing: 'the paramilitaries still kept control of the rackets; ordinary decent criminals didn't have a look in, but competition from Eastern Europeans was starting to bite' (Neville, 2011: 63).

As in crime fiction from the South, Northern writers also document the racism found amongst police officers and other characters, often demonstrating the close relationship between prejudice and ignorance. Thus in Adrian McKinty's *Falling Glass* (2011), a party of Travellers, traditional recipients of xenophobic and racist treatment, is mistaken for a group of foreign immigrants and is told to '[g]o back to Poland, ya gypsy bastards!' (McKinty, 2011: 264). Stuart Neville similarly captures the anti-foreign feeling on the streets of Belfast as one of his characters in *The Twelve* utters this diatribe:

> A bunch of fucking Liths … Dirty bastards. I swear to God, this place is getting so full of foreigners it won't be worth getting the Brits out. Fucking Lithuanians, Polish, niggers, pakis, chinks. You walk through town you hardly hear an Irish accent. All foreigners. And Dublin's worse. (Neville, 2009: 29)

Shane Hegarty wrote that 'no one would have guessed in 1994, a year of net emigration, that a decade later one out of every 10 people living in Ireland would have been born in another country' (2009: 189). Such a demographic shift is of paramount importance to the understanding of a period in which the country shifted from 'the pre-modern to the post-modern without ever fully creating the structures and the habits of a modern democracy' (O'Toole, 2009: 213). The rise of crime over these years was influenced by a variety of factors. The easy availability of arms thanks to the paramilitary activity north of the border, the growth of organised crime based on an expanding narcotics market, and the large amount of white-collar crime resulting from the property boom, all captured the attention of the Irish reading public as crime writing, writing about crime within a distinctively Irish context, moved away from the incidents pages of the national press and, via the increased popularity of 'true crime' narratives, reached the pages of domestic crime novels in a relatively short space of time. Woody Haut wrote that 'to examine a culture one need only examine its crimes' (Haut, 1999: 3). These novels, while demonstrating that Ireland was 'never immune from the racist ideologies that governed relationships between the west and the rest, despite a history of colonial anti-Irish racism' (Fanning, 2002: 1) and that 'those cosily termed the "new Irish" have not always received a hundred thousand welcomes' (Foster, 2007: 34), also reveal a society coming to terms with change. The crimes examined in them reflect this process of change and collectively represent a fascinating literary portrayal of society in Celtic Tiger and post-Celtic Tiger Ireland.

References

Ascari, Maurizio (2007). *A Counter-History of Crime Fiction: Supernatural, Gothic, Sensational*. London: Palgrave Macmillan.

Bertens, Hans and Theo D'haen (2001). *Contemporary American Crime Fiction*. New York: Palgrave.

Black, Ingrid (2007). *The Judas Heart*. London: Penguin.

—— (2008). *Circle of the Dead*. London: Penguin.

Brady, John (2002). *Wonderland*. Toronto: McArthur & Company.

—— (2005). *Islandbridge*. Toronto: McArthur & Company.

—— (2008). *The Going Rate*. Toronto: McArthur & Company.

Bruen, Ken (1996). *Rilke on Black*. London: Serpent's Tail.

—— (1997). *The Hackman Blues*. London: The Do-Not-Press.

—— (1998). *Her Last Call to Louis MacNeice*. London: Serpent's Tail.

—— (2001). *The Guards*. Dingle: Brandon.

—— (2002). *The Killing of the Tinkers*. Dingle: Brandon.

—— (2003). *The Magdalen Martyrs*. Dingle: Brandon.

—— (2008). *Sanctuary*. London: Transworld Ireland.

—— (2010). *The Devil*. London: Transworld Ireland.

—— (2011). *Headstone*. New York: The Mysterious Press.

Cassuto, Leonard (2009). *Hard-Boiled Sentimentality: The Secret History of American Crime Stories*. New York: Columbia University Press.

Chandler, Raymond (1944). 'The simple art of murder', *Atlantic Monthly* 174.6: 53–9.

Ekin, Des (1999). *Stone Heart*. Dublin: O'Brien.

Fanning, Bryan (2002). *Racism and Social Change in the Republic of Ireland*. Manchester: Manchester University Press.

Foster, Robert Fitzroy (2007). *Luck and the Irish: A Brief History of Change, 1970–2000*. London: Penguin.

Gregoriou, Christiana (2007). *Deviance in Contemporary Crime Fiction*. London: Palgrave Macmillan.

Hamilton, Hugo (1997). *Headbanger.* London: Vintage.
—— (1998). *Sad Bastard.* London: Vintage.
Haut, Woody (1999). *Neon Noir: Contemporary American Crime Fiction.* London: Serpent's Tail.
Hegarty, Shane (2009). *The Irish and Other Foreigners: From the First People to the Poles.* Dublin: Gill & Macmillan.
Horsley, Lee (2005). *Twentieth-Century Crime Fiction.* Oxford: Oxford University Press.
Hughes, Declan (2007). *The Colour of Blood.* London: John Murray.
Hunt, Arlene (2004). *Vicious Circle.* Dublin: Hodder Lir.
—— (2006). *Black Sheep.* Dublin: Hodder Headline Ireland.
—— (2008). *Undertow.* Dublin: Hachette Books Ireland.
—— (2010). *Blood Money.* Dublin: Hachette Books Ireland.
Kerrigan, Gene (2009). *Dark Times in the City.* London: Harvill Secker.
Kitchin, Rob (2010). *The White Gallows.* Brighton: Indepen.
Mandel, Ernest (1984). *Delightful Murder: A Social History of the Crime Story.* Minnesota, MN: Minnesota University Press.
McGilloway, Brian (2006). *Borderlands.* London: Macmillan New Writing.
—— (2009). *Bleed a River Deep.* London: Macmillan.
McKinty, Adrian (2011). *Falling Glass.* London: Serpent's Tail.
McWilliams, David (2005). *The Pope's Children: Ireland's New Elite.* Dublin: Gill & Macmillan.
Neville, Stuart (2009). *The Twelve.* London: Harvill Secker.
—— (2011). *Collusion.* London: Harvill Secker.
Nugent, Andrew (2006). *The Four Courts Murder.* London: Headline.
—— (2007). *Second Burial.* London: Headline.
O'Connor, Brian (2011). *Bloodline.* Dublin: Poolbeg.
O'Connor, Niamh (2011). *Taken.* London: Transworld Ireland.
O'Toole, Fintan (2009). *Ship of Fools: How Stupidity and Corruption Sank the Celtic Tiger.* London: Faber & Faber.
Pepper, Andrew (2003). 'Black crime fiction,' in Martin Priestman (ed.), *The Cambridge Companion to Crime Fiction.* Cambridge: Cambridge University Press, 209-26.
Reddy, Maureen T. (2003). *Traces, Codes, and Clues: Reading Race in Crime Fiction.* New Brunswick: Rutgers University Press.
Scaggs, John (2005). *Crime Fiction.* London: Routledge.

Index

Note: literary works can be found under authors' name; 'n.' after a page reference indicates the number of a note on that page.